THE LAND
WITHOUT A NAME

Alain-Fournier and his world

THE LAND WITHOUT A NAME

Alain-Fournier and his world

ROBERT GIBSON

I would not love the Land without a Name so much
— so that I feel faint at the mere thought of it — if I did
not believe that it actually exists somewhere in the universe.

ALAIN-FOURNIER

Paul Elek
LONDON

For Sheila

First published in Great Britain 1975 by
Elek Books Ltd
54–58 Caledonian Road, London N1 9RN

Copyright © 1975 Robert Gibson

ISBN 0 236 31062 3

726898

(c

600 022256 0

Printed in Great Britain by
A. Wheaton & Co., Exeter

Contents

Illustrations

Foreword

I ought to establish from the outset that this is not merely a re-issue of a book which was first published in 1953 under the title, *The Quest of Alain-Fournier*, and I feel I ought briefly to explain why, when it eventually went out of print in the mid-sixties, I declined various offers to reprint and elected, instead, to re-write it from beginning to end.

I first discovered *Le Grand Meaulnes* as a schoolboy, thirty years ago, and, for reasons too complex to enumerate here, I have remained intermittently involved with it ever since. Of the fruits of that involvement, which include to date a doctoral dissertation (1953) and a critical edition of *Le Grand Meaulnes* (1968), *The Quest of Alain-Fournier* was the first in date and, so it has for some time seemed to me, distinctly the last in quality. It did not take long to dispel the mood of euphoria generated by the indulgent reception the *Quest* was accorded by the critics. As the months passed, I grew increasingly irritated by the discovery of various minor errors of fact in my text, working themselves to the surface like so many thorns from under the skin, and by the defects of my adolescent prose-style, as embarrassing to contemplate as an old love-letter. To enumerate what I have long considered to be its manifold faults would doubtless be to lay myself open to the charge of being a masochist in the cause of truth, so let me content myself by declaring that where my dwindling band of admirers still see youthful bloom, I diagnose a severe case of literary acne.

By the time the *Quest* went out of print, I felt impelled to recast the original work completely, for reasons more compelling either than personal pride or than the obligation we all have to review our literary and emotional allegiances once per quinquennium, if not every Old Year's Night. Over the intervening years, a considerable body of fresh information about Fournier has become available, principally through his sister's remarkably candid study, *Vie et Passion d'Alain-Fournier*, which appeared in 1963, and the dramatic disclosures made in 1957 and 1964 by his last mistress, Madame Simone Porché. Further revelations were provided in 1968, in Jean Loize's monumental and all but definitive biography, *Alain-Fournier, sa vie et 'Le Grand Meaulnes'*, and in 1972, with the publication of Fournier's letters to Péguy.

I have made use of all this fresh material about Fournier's life in this brand-new volume and, in my final chapter, I have reviewed the most important of the many books and articles which, over the past two decades, have been published on *Le Grand Meaulnes*. Moreover, since my hope has been to provide not merely a less simplistic account of Fournier's life and work but also a study of his 'world', I have sought also to provide rather fuller portraits than I did in my first book of his relatives and his friends, as well as a much closer analysis of his reading. I have also taken the opportunity to review my quotations from Fournier's writings; these and all the additional quotations I make in the present book are in my own translations throughout.

For assistance in the preparation of this book, I owe a particular debt of gratitude to Alain-Fournier's literary executor, M. Alain Rivière, for permission to make such liberal use of material from the archives he has inherited from his mother, whose great generosity and kindness to me, over a considerable period, I shall remember always.

I am especially grateful to Muriel Waring who had the unenviable task of deciphering the emendations of my emendations but, even more, of transforming the chaos of, what must have seemed, my endless long-hand pages into the immaculate order of her final typescript.

I must express my very real gratitude and sympathy to my wife and children, not only for accepting so patiently, for most of the time, that a writer really *is* working even when he would seem merely to be looking out of the window, but also for allowing the spirit of Fournier to be present at many a family meal and on many a car journey.

There are other spirits I feel bound to invoke in conclusion. I owe an incalculable debt of gratitude to friends who, had they lived to read these words, would doubtless have been amazed to discover that though we never spoke of literature together, it was very largely through them that I learned how to read *Le Grand Meaulnes*: I was introduced to their remote farmstead in the same year as I discovered Alain-Fournier, and, all too soon, it became my own lost domain.

I propose to describe and analyse this at rather greater length on another occasion. For the present, I shall content myself by stating that the writing of this book has been something more than an exercise in revaluation and something more than an act of homage. It has been a service of exorcism, and it will be for Time to establish whether a number of kindly ghosts will henceforth cease to haunt me.

Sandon's, 1944
St Stephen's, 1974

Acknowledgments

For permission to quote from texts still under copyright, I have to thank Editions Alphège of Monaco, the publishing houses of Gallimard and of Hachette, the editors of *Le Figaro* and the Director of Le Centre Charles Péguy.

For their generous permission to reproduce the photographs shown in this book I am indebted to Madame Isabelle and Monsieur Alain Rivière, and for invaluable technical assistance in preparing the material, I am grateful to Mr James Styles, of the Photographic Unit, University of Kent at Canterbury.

Proem

The primary impulse of the artist springs, I fancy, from discontent, and his art is a kind of crying for Elysium. In this single respect, perhaps, there is no difference between good and bad art. For in the most clumsy and bungled work (if it has been born of the desire for beauty) we should doubtless find, could we but pierce through the dead husk of it to the hidden conception, that same divine homesickness, that same longing for an Eden from which each one of us is exiled. Strangely different these paradisian visions. For me it may be the Islands of the Blest 'not shaken by winds nor ever wet with rain . . . where the clear air spreads without a cloud', for you the jewelled splendour of the New Jerusalem. Only in no case, I think, is it our own free creation. It is a country whose image was stamped upon our soul before we opened our eyes on earth, and all our life is little more than a trying to get back there, our art than a mapping of its mountains and streams.

FORREST REID : *Apostate*

1

An Atlas of Nostalgia

> All nations that have a history have a
> paradise, an age of innocence, a golden age.
> Nay, more than this, every man has his
> paradise, his golden age, which he remembers
> with more or less enthusiasm according as he
> is more or less poetical.
>
> Schiller[1]

I

The land men have always longed for most is not to be found on any map. A variety of names have been employed to designate it – Eden, the Earthly Paradise, the Elysian Fields, the Fortunate Isles, the Bower of Bliss, Arcadia, Eldorado, Shangri La or simply The Great Good Place – but all these are merely signposts that point in the same direction, to the land where one's sorrows are no more and where one's every wish is gratified. Even when the exile can give an authentic-sounding name to the place for which he feels most home-sick, it is arguable that he is yearning for a kingdom of his own imagining: Matthew Arnold's Oxford 'spreading her gardens to the moonlight and whispering from her towers the last enchantments of the Middle Ages'[2] is just as much a dream as Yeats'

> land of faery
> Where nobody gets old and goldly and grave,
> Where nobody gets old and crafty and wise,
> Where nobody gets old and bitter of tongue.[3]

The Innisfree Yeats dreamed of, the Tipperary World War I soldiers yearned for, bore about as much relationship to reality as the American hobo's Big Rock Candy Mountains or the 'little grey home in the west' so beloved of music-hall or drawing-room songsters.

What these regions all have in common, apart from their being fashioned out of memories and desires, is that they are all felt to be indescribably remote. There would seem, indeed, to be a direct correlation between the distance separating the exile from his beloved land and the degree of pleasure he anticipates enjoying once he has finally reached it : this lesson was driven home for many of us in schooldays, with the insistence of the reiterated adverb in that childhood hymn

> There is a happy land,
> *Far, far* away . . .

and confirmed in adolescence with the repeated adjectives of the camp-fire song

> There's a *long, long* trail a-winding
> Into the land of my dreams . . .

The nostalgia of which all these diverse localities are the expression is rooted in disenchantment with the present : the grass is seen to be greener on the *other* side of the hedge, the laughter is consistently heard coming from the *next* room, 'there' is always held to be preferable to 'here' and 'then' to 'now'. Sometimes the solution to one's ills is located in the future, in which case one plans for Utopia or the New Jerusalem, but much more commonly, it is situated in the past, in the Good Old Days, the days of 'auld lang syne', far away and long ago.

If the prime requisite of the earthly Paradise is that it should be remote in space, if not lost forever, then the essential quality of its temporal equivalent, the Golden Age, is that it should be far distant in time. Latter-day scholars are wont to locate our cultural Golden Age in the Renaissance; the artists and thinkers of the Renaissance situated it in the days of Greece and Rome; the Greeks and Romans, for their part, placed it further back still in time, before recorded history.

> First of all, the deathless Gods who dwell on Olympus made a golden race of mortal men who lived in the time of Cronus when he was reigning in heaven. And they lived like Gods without sorrow of heart, remote and free from toil and grief; miserable age rested not on them; but with lips and arms never failing they made merry while feasting beyond the reach of all evils. When they died, it was as though they were overcome with sleep, and they all had good times; for the fruitful earth unforced bore them fruit abundantly and without stint.

Even by the time Hesiod was evoking the joys of the Golden Age, they were already felt to be irretrievably lost, and it was believed that

4

mankind had by then descended through the Ages of Silver and Bronze to the Age of Iron, in which harsh era we have ever since remained imprisoned. Intermittently, in Classical and Renaissance history, it was felt that the Golden Age might perhaps return, although the expression of this belief seems so often in the cause of a panegyric addressed to some regal patron, who is expected to usher in a new period of unparalleled prosperity, that it is difficult to distinguish between fulsome flattery and genuine faith.[4]

With the waning of widespread faith in the supernatural, the figures of the Gods, so central to Hesiod's picture of the Golden Age, faded altogether from the scene, and once these had been spirited away, it did not take very long for the bucolic setting to vanish too. It was left to the arch-individualist Rousseau to provide a blueprint for a Golden Age wide and generous enough to accommodate every desire and every dream:

> I created a golden age in my fantasy, and filled those beautiful days with all the scenes of my life that left me pleasant memories, and all those which my heart could still desire.[5]

From Hesiod's times to our own, the features of the Golden Age may have changed, but its location has remained invariable; the Age of Gold is everything that the contemporary age is not, and like all things truly golden, it remains forever beyond the reach of almost all of us.

II

Most versions of the Earthly Paradise and the Golden Age have one further feature in common in addition to their essential remoteness: this is the important role ascribed within them to primal innocence. It has been well observed that 'the earliest age of mankind is associated with the verdure of springtime, with the spontaneity of childhood, and often with the awakening of love,'[6] and this has inevitably meant that upon the palette of the artist of nostalgia, green is a colour no less important than gold. If gold is the colour of splendour, wealth, intensity and rarity, green is no less the colour of freshness, naturalness, young growth and innocence; inevitably, therefore, it features prominently in poems which hymn the praises or, more commonly, lament the passing of childhood and adolescence:

> Such, such were the joys
> When we all, girls and boys
> In our youth-time were seen
> On the Echoing Green . . .[7]

Mais le vert paradis des amours enfantines,
Les courses, les chansons, les baisers, les bouquets,
Les violons vibrant derrière les collines,
Avec les brocs de vin, le soir, dans les bosquets,
– Mais le vert paradis des amours enfantines.

L'innocent paradis, plein de plaisirs furtifs,
Est-il déjà plus loin que l'Inde et que la Chine ?
Peut-on le rappeler avec des cris plaintifs,
Et l'animer encor d'une voix argentine,
L'innocent paradis plein de plaisirs furtifs ?[8]

When all the world is young, lad,
And all the trees are green,
And every goose a swan, lad,
And every lass a queen . . .[9]

. . . And I was green and carefree, famous among the barns
About the happy yard and singing as the farm was home,
   In the sun that is young once only,
   Time let me play and be
   Golden in the mercy of his means,
And green and golden I was huntsman and herdsman, the calves
Sang to my horn, the foxes on the hill barked clear and cold,
   And the sabbath rang slowly
In the pebbles of the holy streams . . .[10]

The high regard for childhood and youth which is so manifest in this sample of extracts is indicative of a comparatively recent phenomenon. The Ancients, who first painted Europe's picture of the Golden Age, had a very low opinion of children insofar as they had any opinion of them at all. Children, it was felt, could evidently experience the sensations of pleasure and pain but were no less evidently incapable of reasoning. The role of the educator, for both Socrates and Plato, was to teach the child to put childish things behind him and transform him without delay into an adult.

This view persisted for centuries. The figure of the Infant Jesus may have become a subject of predilection for the Mediaeval and Renaissance artist but to childhood in itself no special qualities were attributed. It was left to certain seventeenth-century English writers to detect in childhood those distinctive qualities for which it subsequently began to be so cherished. John Earle praised the essential innocence of infancy :

The Child is the best copy of *Adam* before he tasted of *Eve* or the apple; and he is happy whose small practice in the world can only write this Character. He is nature's fresh picture newly drawn in oil, which time, and much handling, dims and defaces. His Soul is yet a white paper unscribbled with observations of the world, wherewith, at length, it becomes a blurred note-book . . .[11]

For Henry Vaughan, childhood innocence was to be equated with proximity to God:

> Happy those early days, when I
> Shin'd in my Angel-infancy!
> Before I understood this place
> Appointed for my second race,
> Or taught my soul to fancy aught
> But a white celestial thought . . .
> Before I taught my tongue to wound
> My Conscience with a sinful sound,
> Or had the black art to dispense
> A several sin to ev'ry sense,
> But felt through all this fleshly dress
> Bright shoots of everlastingness.
>
> O how I long to travel back
> And tread again that ancient track!
> That I might once more reach that plain
> Where first I left my glorious train;
> From whence th'enlightened spirit sees
> That shady City of Palm-trees.[12]

For Thomas Traherne also, childhood meant innocence, and innocence meant not only happiness but special knowledge. In his childhood, he declared 'I knew by intuition those things which since my Apostasy, I collected again by the highest reason . . . I seemed as one brought in the Estate of Innocence. All things were spotless and pure and glorious.'

For Earle, Vaughan and Traherne, the acquisition of physical maturity was accompanied by spiritual regression, just as, for the Ancients, the Age of Gold led inevitably to the Age of Iron. This was the view adopted and persuasively re-expressed by Rousseau more than a century later in *Emile*, in which he laid great stress on the innate innocence of childhood, and castigated the educationists and social institutions of the day for so successfully sullying that pristine purity.

7

For Wordsworth also, childhood was a state to be cherished as the seed-time of the soul, and its unique visionary insights were lost almost irretrievably in the transition from infancy to maturity. In this respect, the title of what is probably the best known of his shorter poems is, in itself, sufficiently explicit and expressive: *Intimations of Immortality from recollections of early Childhood* :

> There was a time when meadow, grove and stream,
> The earth, and every common sight,
>   To me did seem
> Apparelled in celestial light,
> The glory and the freshness of a dream.
> It is not now as it hath been of yore –
>   Turn whereso'er I may,
>   By night or day,
> The things which I have seen I now can see no more.

In the light of these trends, it is not surprising that a significant number of nineteenth- and twentieth-century writers should have sought to exploit the theme of childhood.[13] The Romantic Movement dethroned reason as the supreme human faculty, championed the individual against all Authority, and made a positive cult of the emotions, most particularly those involving wistfulness, yearning and regret. Childhood served all these ends most admirably : it was held to be specially rich in intuitive wisdom, to be particularly sensitive to beauty and to moral values, and it could itself be equated with lost Eden or the vanished Golden Age.

III

For a significant number of twentieth-century writers, however, the Golden Age of the individual human being has been located not in childhood but in adolescence, and Cyril Connolly has splendidly described, and sought to explain, the fascination that this age has exercised over generations of English public schoolboys :

> Were I to deduce any system from my feelings on leaving Eton, it might be called *The Theory of Permanent Adolescence*. It is the theory that the experiences undergone by boys at the great public schools, their glories and disappointments, are so intense as to dominate their lives and to arrest their development. From

these it results that the greater part of the ruling class remains adolescent, school-minded, self-conscious, cowardly, sentimental, and in the last analysis homosexual. Early laurels weigh like lead and of many of the boys whom I knew at Eton, I can say that their lives are over. Those who knew them then knew them at their best and fullest; now, in their early thirties, they are haunted ruins. When we meet we look at each other, there is a pause for recognition, which gives way to a moment of guilt and fear. 'I won't tell on you', our eyes say, 'if you won't tell on me' – and when we do speak, it is to discover peculiar evidence of this obsession . . . Once again romanticism with its death-wish is to blame, for it lays emphasis on childhood, on a fall from grace which is not compensated for by any doctrine of future redemption; we enter the world, trailing clouds of glory, childhood and boyhood follow and we are damned . . .[14]

In France, where the boarding school tradition is neither deeply rooted nor widespread and where Old Boys' Reunions are conspicuous by their paucity, the cult of adolescence has been even more assiduously practised.[15] The phenomenon is comparatively modern. In 1854, George Sand could comment: 'I find that poets and novelists have tended to overlook that prime subject of observation and that source of poetry to be found in the unique and transient period in human life that is adolescence.'[16] In 1909, a French observer was still able to note that 'adolescents rarely feature as characters in novels,'[17] but by 1930, a leading critic of the day was complaining that 'nowadays there are just too many adolescents in our novels.'[18] There was some substance in his complaint because between 1900 and 1930, virtually every French novelist of stature and a whole host of minor novelists besides, wrote at least one novel in which the principal character was an adolescent.

The French novelists' preoccupation with adolescence matched a general concern with this particular age throughout French society. That adolescents were a group quite separate from children and adults began increasingly to be recognised by physiologists, psychologists, sociologists, parents and teachers, and one of the first comprehensive studies of adolescence to be produced anywhere in the world, *L'Ame de l'Adolescent* by Pierre Mendousse, dates from 1909. The Church admitted its negligence and at least one of its officiants proposed a 'culte de Jésus adolescent'. At the turn of the century, in Paris and other major provincial cities, a 'fête de l'adolescence' was instituted at which speakers promised to guide adolescents through what was felt to be the most difficult period of their life, and looking

9

back, just after the end of the First World War, a French scholar observed :

> Critics of the future shouldn't fail to note that at no period in our history was the nation's youth cross-examined, appealed to or analysed with more fervent curiosity or more brotherly sympathy than in the course of the eight or ten years which preceded the 14–18 War. There was a widespread feeling that there was 'something new' about the generation born round about 1900.[19]

Of the various hypotheses, psychological, sociological and metaphysical, which have been advanced to account for this remarkable upsurge of interest in this particular age-group at this particular time in France, one of the most persuasive is the widespread feeling of personal humiliation which pervaded much of the populace after the crushing defeat inflicted by Prussia in 1870. To the up-and-coming generation was going to be entrusted the sacred mission of *la Revanche*, the war which would win back the lost provinces of Alsace and Lorraine and restore lost pride. In this respect, there is no more significant, if not sinister portent than the spectacle presented by Maurice Barrès in his book *Les Amitiés Françaises* which appeared at the turn of the century. Barrès commanded such a wide national following amongst the young at this time that he was hailed as 'The Prince of Youth', but in this book, which reviews the chief sacred shrines in France, he addresses himself directly to his own son as they stand together looking out over the blue hills of the stolen provinces :

> *Barrès* : We declare, we *swear* that we're going to train ourselves and equip ourselves. We're going to choose the right moment and get our revenge.
> *Son* : Are you sure that the French are going to win?
> *Barrès* : Yes, quite sure. Haven't I just told you so?
> *Son* : But you never said *when*.
> *Barrès* : When you're a *man*.

A further hypothesis to account for the modern French cult of adolescence was advanced in the early 1920s by the critic Henri Massis, a friend of Fournier's, who discerned close affinities between the fluid and malleable nature of the adolescent personality and the philosophical climate of the epoch :

> We ought not to be surprised that a world which exalts life and the powerful drives within human nature – the basest of these

10

especially – should have chosen to venerate the most irrational period in human life, should have set up monuments to the greater glory of puberty, the age when we're so much at the mercy of our instincts and of the will of other people. Classical Man is free, has a moral sense, is responsible for his actions, and that's why there are scarcely any children in seventeenth-century literature . . . But if you subscribe to a philosophy which stresses 'becoming' and mobility and which despises the intellect, then the child, or better still, the adolescent – in whom what has been indoctrinated clashes with the spontaneous, and where the 'social self' is in conflict with 'the living self' – is the character to be cossetted both by the philosopher and the artist.[20]

For the literary artist, whatever his own personal compulsions may be, the subject of adolescence is, in itself, extremely rich in dramatic potential. Each of the adolescent's distinctive roles can be exploited by the playwright, short-story teller or novelist – falling in love for the first time, discovering his own identity, rebelling against authority – and any or all of these can be portrayed against a background of artistically fruitful tensions : the tension between extreme egocentricity and universal sympathy, the tension between soaring euphoria and leaden despair, the tension between total cynicism and the urge to devote oneself and all one's passion to some single great cause. Modern French novelists have exploited one or more of these aspects of adolescence in turn[21] but it is youth's capacity for idealism which has inspired the highest of their lyrical flights. Henry de Montherlant, for example, looked back in 1920 to his school days at a Jesuit boarding school and, like Cyril Connolly, was disconsolate over what had been lost :

Ah! College priests, why don't you realise that what really matters is not so much the effect of your religious instruction or the pure poetry of your religious rites, but the fact that by skilfully moulding a pupil's soul you can make it yours for ever.

Never again will you find anyone so vulnerable as those thirteen- to sixteen-year-olds. For many of them, what is going to exist once and once only in their lives, exists now and only now. Hermes, the God of Adolescence, is also God of the Twilight. This is the first and the last time that they will have any sense of beauty, any desire for virtue, any appetite for things divine. This is the first and last time they'll know what it is to suffer. They are at life's zenith . . . How lucky we'll be in the

11

future if, just now and then, through some quite inconsequential act – picking out a tune on the piano, re-arranging the furniture, drawing up a report – we feel once more our soul of yesteryear re-emerging, all tremulous and plaintive . . . Yes, indeed, these thirteen- to seventeen-year-old boys, with their lives all disorganised and dislocated, are God's favourite battlefield.[22]

Mauriac voiced the same view of adolescence, more succinctly but no less lyrically, when he wrote: 'At the end of youth, everything which is going to grow to full fruition has already taken root within us. As we prepare to step across the threshold of our adolescence, *les jeux sont faits, rien ne va plus* – the game's been joined and the die is cast.'[23] The finality of youthful decisions, the high idealism of youth, and youth's haunting conviction that, over the brow of the next hill waits a happiness which will ravish one's very soul – these were to prove constants in Fournier's life and work, and given Montherlant's similarly high regard for the heroic qualities of youth, it remains a mystery why, in 1938, he should have dismissed *Le Grand Meaulnes* with the single laconic comment 'an insignificant book'.[24]

Opinions may vary about the enjoyability of the literary merits of *Le Grand Meaulnes*, and the nature of the critic's response will doubtless be conditioned by the dictates of his own personality and by his own experience of life and love. While any evaluation is legitimate, provided that it is substantiated by argument and illustrative evidence, the use of the epithet 'insignificant' seems especially inappropriate. However much *Le Grand Meaulnes* was shaped by factors peculiar to Fournier himself, it was also the product of its age: it owes something to the modern French cult of adolescence and in its turn contributed powerfully to that cult's continuance.

IV

Nostalgia remained the most constant of all Fournier's emotions, to such a remarkable extent, indeed, that it could be described as his stock-in-trade or even as his *raison d'être*. It coloured his views on life, on love and on literature, determining his responses as a reader and his projects as a writer. 'For me', he once wrote, 'Woman has always been like a landscape, a means to bring back lost hours and country scenes and landscapes.'[25] He announced in 1906, echoing Baudelaire, 'My credo in Art and Literature is childhood. I want to recapture childhood without becoming childish,'[26] and two years later he declared, 'Amongst my works, I should like there to be a book or a chapter entitled: "The End of Youth".'[27]

He remained as inconsolable for the loss of his childhood as Cyril Connolly and his fellow Etonians over the end of their schooldays, and when he was well into his twenties, his greatest friend frankly told him:

> Your childhood was so beautiful, so rich in dreams and so like Paradise, that now you've left it behind, you're quite disillusioned by what seems to be the drabness of later life. It's as though you've lived out your life already, as if there's nothing left for you to do now except relive it in your memory; telling the same story to yourself over and over again.[28]

His dilemma then was precisely that of Cesare Pavese, who wrote to himself in his Journal: 'Your worst enemy is the belief in a happy prehistoric time, in Eden, in the Golden Age, and the belief that everything essential has been said by the first thinkers. The two things are one.'[29]

All his life, he remained passionately attached to the countryside where he grew up and whenever, as often happened, he thought of emigrating, the prospect of unbearable home-sickness always, in the end, dissuaded him from departing:

> From time to time, my heart misses a beat when I see photographs of far distant towns, of a sun-drenched square or perhaps a palm-tree. I think of cutting myself off from everything, of packing my clothes and my papers in my trunk, of leaving behind the many things so dear to me: La Chapelle-d'Angillon, Epineuil, Nançay, the Cours-la-Reine, the boulevard Saint-Germain. I thrill to see a photograph of wild mountains with a cutting being driven through for a new railway – then I think of the little line from Saincaize to Montluçon. I recall the awful homesickness which used to overwhelm me in England if ever I was reminded of a lane or a house or door in the Berry – and I multiply that by a hundred![30]

He was perceptive enough to be able to diagnose his own malady and, at the same time, honest enough to concede that he did not really want to be cured:

Ah! If I wanted to, what couldn't I do. If I were to give up everything, what obstacles could I not overcome, if I could be cured of my wonderful and delectable weakness.[31]

This 'weakness' was, in fact, nostalgia, and for Fournier it was so much more than a mere emotion that it was something like a sacrament, and he cultivated it so assiduously and to such artistic effect that one feels justified in creating a special title to designate his role : he was a *nostalgician*. He was nostalgic for lost childhood, lost youth, lost love and lost enchantment, and he located them all in his own ideal kingdom. This he graced with no traditional title, such as Eden, Elysium, the Land of Heart's Desire or the Golden Age : he called it simply 'The Land Without a Name'.

2

The Land of Lost Content

1886–1898

> The die is cast before we are twelve years
> old. Twenty years, thirty years of strenuous
> labour, a whole lifetime of work cannot make
> or destroy whatever was made or destroyed
> once and for all before our time, without
> our connivance, for us or against us.
>
> Charles Péguy[1]

I

Unlike other authors whose adult personalities and writings were
indelibly marked by childhood events or situations, Henri Fournier's
infancy was remarkably unremarkable. His early years were not, like
Stendhal's, dislocated by the premature loss of a particularly beloved
parent; they were not warped by the excessively demanding love of
mother for son, as were J. M. Barrie's, or of son for mother, as in
the case of Baudelaire or Proust; neither did he, like Dickens or Zola,
have to suffer the humiliation of a sudden and catastrophic diminution
in the family's income. Till he was twelve years old, Henri's life was
comfortable, cloistered and calm and outwardly, at any rate, his
childhood would seem to have been as ordinary as that of Racine
'whose biographers', Valéry once said, 'acquaint us with a great
number of things he had in common with ten thousand other
Frenchmen.'[2]

He spent all his formative years in the very centre of France where
his parents and most of their ancestors had lived and worked before
him. His father, Sylvain Baptiste Augustin Fournier, was born in
what was then the remote village of Nançay, deep in the Sologne
country, a lonely barren region of rolling bracken and heather wastes,
and fir and juniper forests, particularly rich in rabbits and guinea

fowl; it is liberally dotted with lonely pools and with solitary châteaux or hunting-lodges used by wealthy visitors mainly in the autumn and often left empty for the rest of the year. The Fourniers were an industrious family who never, at any time, were confronted with the prospect of either affluence or penury. Henri's grandfather, Jean-Silvain Fournier (1837–1890) was of impeccable plebeian stock, and worked at a variety of jobs from carter to maker of sabots; his paternal grandmother, née Hélène Sophie Charpentier, was born and brought up in the Sologne, and by all accounts,[3] before her marriage to Jean Fournier in 1860, had been a strict, industrious and unimaginative shop-keeper. Two sons and four daughters were born of this marriage, of whom only three played an important role in Henri's upbringing : his father, who was the oldest child, born on 11 February 1861; the second child and oldest daughter, Augustine, who was born on 22 July 1862, subsequently married a Florent Raimbault and, with him, ran the village general store in Nançay; and the third child, Lucien, born on 27 November 1863, Henri's godfather, who became a professional soldier and served in the Sudan.

To live the life of a professional soldier early became, and for long remained, the consuming ambition of Augustin Fournier also, but his mother had different plans. At the age of sixteen, he was despatched to the teachers' training college at Bourges, the county town of the Cher *département*. He was awarded his teacher's certificate on 17 July 1880 and dispensed from compulsory military service as a professional teacher when he drew an exemption slip in the lottery held at Vierzon. It is highly unlikely that he saw cause for celebration in this, indeed, doubtless for this very reason, he was, for the rest of his life, periodically plagued by a chronic wanderlust which set the household in frantic turmoil and which, as will be seen, he was able to assuage in tragic circumstances only after his family had been fragmented.

He began his professional career as an assistant teacher in Herry and became a full teacher, in his own right, on 1 October 1884 when he was posted to the tiny hamlet of Gué-de-la-Pierre. It was while he was teaching there that he met, courted and married Marie Albanie Barthe, in the nearby village of La Chapelle-d'Angillon.

The Barthes' family chronicle had been rather more colourful than that of the Fourniers. The maternal grandfather, Jean Baptiste Mathieu Barthe (1820–1898) was the one member of Henri's close family circle to come from outside the Cher *département*. He hailed from a hamlet near Alban, in the Tarn *département* in the far south, and in his time, he worked as a shepherd, as a soldier under Louis-Philippe, then as a gendarme in La Chapelle-d'Angillon. There he met and married his first wife, and there she died in the autumn of 1861. From La Chapelle, he was posted to Vailly-sur-Sauldre, and there he met and married Flavie-Catherine née Blondeau. She too had been married before, to a cousin, Augustin Pinon, who died of 'fever' on 9 March 1861. She was born on 2 November 1833, brought up on her father's farm of Les Laurents at Sury-en-Vaux, and was, in her youth, generally acclaimed as the great beauty of her district. Always known to her friends as 'Adeline', she was Henri's favourite grandparent, and throughout his life, he took particular pleasure in making her reminisce about the songs she used to sing, or the dances and courtships of the days before her first marriage. She was specially fond of recounting the tale of a wealthy Englishman who brought his son to the neighbourhood to recuperate from some illness : the son readily fell victim not only to her beauty, but also to the anger of local suitors who knocked him senseless one dark night, and prompted him and his father to depart as abruptly as they had arrived.[4]

Marie Albanie, the Barthes' only child, was born on 24 April 1864, at Vailly-sur-Sauldre, in the north of the Berry, a region which contrasts dramatically with the adjacent Sologne to the east. In the Berry, the many hedges, woods and gentle hills deny to the observer those sweeping purple and golden vistas which so characterise the Sologne. Unlike the Sologne which, to many a traveller, seems brooding and somehow resentful of man's presence, the Berry is positively cosy, tamed, quite manifestly lived-in, and it was in the midst of such scenery that Albanie Barthe spent her childhood and youth : she was educated at the pension Quisset, in the little country town of Aubigny-sur-Nère, and she worked in her village post-office and as a pupil-teacher before she married Augustin Fournier in her parents' village of La Chapelle-d'Angillon, on 11 October 1885.

Two children were born to them, both at La Chapelle : a son, Henri Alban, on 3 October 1886, and a daughter, Isabelle, on 11 July 1889. From 1886, M. Fournier taught for five years in the village school at Marçais. Then, on 1 October 1891, he was transferred to the village of Epineuil-le-Fleuriel, in the extreme south of the Cher *département*, and it was here that Henri really began to garner those memories which, like a miser, he was never afterwards to tire of secretly recounting.

II

Epineuil-le-Fleuriel is a smaller village than La Chapelle, is certainly more secluded and, even today, is set apart from the dust and din of the main highways. Situated amidst green fields and gentle hills some seventy miles south of Bourges, between the market-towns of Saint-Amand and Montluçon, it is built around a junction where cross the narrow lanes from the four neighbouring villages : to the north, across the Canal du Berry, flowing straight and sedately between two well-trodden paths, and over the Cher, which snakes its way tortuously beneath the willows and poplars, lies the village of Meaulne; four miles off, to the south, raising its tall spire in the distance like an admonitory finger, is Saint-Vitte; beyond Saint-Vitte, at the top of a hill and visible from miles around, is an old chapel dedicated to Sainte-Agathe; to the west, up the lane which mounts a long, gentle slope, the hamlet of La Bouchatte; to the south-east, along a white lane twisting between thick-set hedges, is the village and station of Vallon, on the railway line to Bourges. The Barthe grandparents arrived once a year at this station on the way to Epineuil for the Christmas holidays; through it, the Fournier parents and children would set out and return for the summer holidays back in La Chapelle. This lane to Vallon, therefore, was for Henri, the one richest in bitter-sweet associations of arrival and departure.

By the cross-roads, strategically placed to tempt the rare traveller who would occasionally pass through, stood the café Daniel, where the villagers would sit out of doors in the summer twilight and raise their wine-glass in salute as donkey-cart or horse and trap clip-clopped past. Opposite stood the house of Monsieur Virot, a retired lawyer who took particular pride in the massive nails which studded his venerable front door and squat round tower at one end of his façade, incongruously conspicuous amidst the modest houses around it, like some Royal personage at a village fête. To any enquirer, he would readily expatiate on the historical significance of his property, and of his house's previous existence as an abbey with grounds extending back to old Martin's farm in front of the village school, some hundred and fifty yards away.

Along the road to Saint-Vitte still stands the tiny village church with two gable-ends and its bulbous black spire, for all the world like a discarded old hat or like a handbell misshapen because someone pressed down on it before its cast had been allowed to set. The inside was always cast in shadow, each wicker chair bore a little slip inscribed with the regular occupant's name, and when the candles were lit, there was an atmosphere of cosiness and intimacy, as though the church were merely the room of some family home. In summer, the air would be heady with the scent of lilies, and when, on Feast days, the children passed out in proud procession, the village streets were strewn with rose petals.

Beyond the Church, to the right, a lane led between a huddle of dilapidated cottages, 'Les Petits Coins', which were inhabited by the poorest workers. The lane ended at La Vieille Planche, a single wooden plank over the stream where the village boys would seek to conjure shadowy fish from the placid waters. This same stream, the Queugne, flowed gently on, under the shadow of overhanging trees, to skirt the far end of the schoolhouse garden along one of the sides of which ran the lane to Vallon. In Henri's childhood, this side of the school garden was flanked with tall trees which stood like tall sentinels guarding the Fourniers' kingdom from the outer world.

In the village schoolhouse at Epineuil, the Fourniers lived in a little world that was very much their own. Now the walls of the school-building are bare, but in the Fourniers' time, they were gay with roses, nasturtiums and jasmine, and virginia creeper trailed over the playground-shed. When they first arrived in 1891, there was a young assistant master, Monsieur Suc, to teach the younger children, but on 1 May 1893, Madame Fournier herself was appointed infants' teacher. It seemed at first that the tenure of her appointment was not wholly secure because on 26 August 1893, it prompted a protest petition from eighty-three misogynistic villagers who wrote, in not very grammatical French, to the Prefect of the *département* :

> We, the undersigned, have the honour of informing you that the post of assistant teacher at Epineuil has just been given to the wife of the schoolmaster. We protest against this change because we prefer teaching to be given to our children by a man.[5]

The affair was finally settled on 23 September 1893 with the following judgment from the Chief Education Inspector of the *département* :

> In my opinion, we should not accede to this request. According to information supplied to me, only two of the signatories to this petition have children in the class taught by Madame Fournier who, in any case, is carrying out her duties most satisfactorily.[6]

Whether or not resentment lingered with either of the parties to this dispute it is not now possible to verify; it is not all that material in any event, because in their special position as teachers to a small and secluded community, and with Monsieur Fournier, like all French village school-teachers, having to take on the additional responsibilities of being secretary to the local mayor, the Fourniers inevitably had to remain somewhat detached from the other villagers.

Madame Fournier had decided views on what was and was not respectable and on where and with whom her children could play. Looking back on her Epineuil childhood, Isabelle Rivière recalls an incident when she and Henri were scolded for playing with some children from the village and she comments:

> I don't know how it came to pass that two or three of the school-children happened to be with us that afternoon, because, curiously enough, I was the only one who was occasionally allowed to have friends in to play although that was later on, and then, only in school holidays.[7]

Inevitably, in these circumstances, Henri and his sister spent a great deal of time not only in each other's company but also with their parents. Rather less inevitably and possibly, indeed, surprisingly, there would seem to have been no sense of constriction experienced at the time or expressed subsequently. In Epineuil, links were forged between the Fournier parents and children and between brother and sister which the passing years did nothing to weaken: in later years, they were temperamentally never far apart and, as will be seen, their attempts to remain in close physical proximity with each other were dramatic if not, on occasions, spectacular.

Though French gossip columnists have occasionally speculated to the contrary,[8] all available evidence establishes incontrovertibly that the Fourniers were a happy as well as a united family. The speculation was inspired by Madame Simone Porché's revelation that her novel, *Le Paradis terrestre* (1939), was largely autobiographical and it was inferred from this that the hero's father must have been largely based on Augustin Fournier. The character in question, one Auguste Surville, is impulsive, erratic, decidedly unbalanced, and a constant source of worry and embarrassment to his long-suffering wife and children. The resultant gossip drew from Madame Rivière the following spirited rebuttal:

> No doubt our father was not always easy to get on with: he would get worked up all too quickly over mere trifles; his head was full of romantic dreams which bothered our mother much more than they ever need have done because while these might have crystallised two or three times around one of the new schoolmistresses, everything took place only in his mind; he was a bit too whimsical for my mother's taste with her inordinate regard for order and decorum. All in all, I'd say his faults were those of a child – but he could charm like a child too. He was

temperate and generous without being a spendthrift. He used to leave mother to run the household and to manage the money. He was hard-working and very intelligent. Like my mother, he hungered for reading and for culture. Also like her, he was entranced by the slightest sign of beauty in the countryside and the garden, which took up all the leisure-time he didn't otherwise devote to his fishing or to the long walks which, at Epineuil as at La Chapelle, often brought all the four of us together (with me always perched on his shoulders when I was small). To sum up, all the time they were teachers in the country – which is to say, until 1908 – he provided for our mother and ourselves a peaceful life, a life filled with many small joys which seemed big to us, and if there were occasional thorns along the way, they never scratched very deeply: I can remember so many moments in our childhood when we had the feeling that we were a happy family.[9]

One such moment for both the Fournier children was when they were permitted to enter the 'Red Room' in their parents' living-quarters at Epineuil. This was the parents' bedroom and also the repository of the Fourniers' prize possessions: the red velvet upholstery which gave the room its name, a tapestry woven by Grandmother Barthe, gilt candlesticks and exotic curios brought home by Lucien Fournier, the soldier uncle who, much to the envy of his schoolmaster brother, had served in Africa and had once voyaged as far as China. Also in the 'Red Room' stood Madame Fournier's piano. She had inherited not only her mother's gentle good looks and blonde hair, but also her attachment to the more carefree past, and this she best expressed by sitting alone singing old romances to her piano accompaniment. Henri and Isabelle would often listen outside, sitting on the stone steps which led down to the vegetable garden behind the house.

They found easier access to the other rooms in the school, to the two classrooms, for instance, where their own formal education began; these stood side by side on the ground floor between the Fourniers' exiguous kitchen and the office of the Mayor's secretary with its maps of the district and its standard weighing-machine. Monsieur Fournier could slip through the little door at the back of his classroom and pounce on trouble-makers as deftly as he landed pike or bream. Madame Fournier would sometimes move quietly in from the junior to the senior classroom bringing with her an infant who was to have the dubious privilege of displaying his reading gifts to his elders. Two sides of Monsieur Fournier's classroom were brightened with windows : to the south, the pupils had a view of his vegetable garden to the line of trees lining the stream at the foot and over the field of old Monsieur Martin, the neighbouring farmer; to the north was the playground with its cherry trees, its well with the creaking handle and, through the railings of the school gate, a glimpse of the village crossroads.

From the tiny kitchen, a narrow wooden stairway led upstairs to the attics and this was the children's special domain. The stairway opened into the first attic where a box of toys and another of books were kept and there, by the light of the small window overlooking the playground, Henri and Isabelle often sat reading. A space cut in the wall – there was never a door – gave access to a much darker attic lit only when sunbeams shone through between the eaves; wisps of straw protruded through the undersides of the birds' nests and just occasionally, birds ventured through to the attic itself and perched on the rafters festooned with spiders' webs. Next to this attic was the spare bedroom where the assistant master once slept, and at the far end of the house, above the 'Red Room', another attic where, in wild weather, the washing was hung to dry and, before the eyes of imaginative children, sometimes take on sinister life as it flapped and billowed in the draughts and the gloom.

This attic world, shadowy and suggestive enough even in the daytime, must often have inspired real awe at night and it was there, in a tiny garret between two of the attics, that Henri had to compose himself for sleep, all alone. There was a little fanlight through which the children, when perched on their father's shoulders, could look out over the garden, across the river and the trees to the far ends of the earth. At night, the bedroom walls might sometimes be brightly patched with moonlight but more often than not, Henri had to make a solitary voyage through the watches of the darkness, either in an almost tangible stillness or with the wind whining to be let in and all manner of nameless rustlings from the attics on either side of him.

The Fournier parents were discerning enough to appreciate that it might well have been an ordeal for Henri to sleep upstairs alone at night : he seemed that much more imaginative that Isabelle who was something of a tomboy in spite of having to limp as the legacy of a hip-joint that had once been dislocated. For a while, when Henri had to cross the playground at night to visit the outside lavatory, Isabelle would be despatched with a lantern to light his way and stand waiting in the dark outside till brother and lantern re-emerged and they could hurry back into the light and the warmth. It was because they knew he was sensitive, therefore, that Henri's parents provided him with a stick to pound on the floor and summon them from the

'Red Room' below if fear got the better of him. Madame Rivière remembered the stick well but had no recollection of its ever being used.

But the attics were something other than a realm of mystery and foreboding, more than an airy domain near the sky, full of sunbeams and glinting dustmotes or winds and darkness: they were the private retreat into which the children used to withdraw when they needed to nurse their pain or to read without let or hindrance. There was a running battle between the children and their mother over the subject of reading because while they could never find enough to read, she was chronically anxious that their sight might be permanently impaired and she took the country person's normal view that excessive reading is a poor substitute for vigorous outdoor activity. In his later years, Henri attributed his preference for 'life' to literature to 'the austere and serious education I received in childhood, when art came a long way after life and when we used to hide ourselves away so as to read the book prizes.'[10]

'Ah, those book prizes', he wrote to Jacques Rivière on another occasion. 'Only God knows the part played in my life and my sister's by those crates of books, bound in gilt or pasteboard, which used to arrive every year in July.'[11] These *livres de prix* were the Fournier children's earliest reading matter, and they used to try to read through the eighty or so in each consignment before they were distributed on Speech Day, the last day of the school year. There were three main types: books for the oldest children, such as *Les deux Gosses* or the celebrated *Sans Famille*, invariably tales of exotic or domestic misadventure with virtue eventually vindicated; smaller books, usually set in some romantic castle or shepherd's hut visited by enchanted royalty in disguise, again with good characters finding happiness in the ever-after; the smallest books of all were simply cautionary tales showing the penalties for bad habits, *Adolphe – ou la gourmandise punie* or *Julie: la petite querelleuse*, and these were read as avidly as the rest. The whole collection, still sharp with the smell of printer's ink and brand new paper, drove home the moral lessons taught and practised by their parents and grandparents: virtue meets with its just reward, the true success is to labour, true love ends in happiness and true love is the reward for a blameless life.

The book beloved of all the family, and generally admired in late nineteenth-century France as much as in Victorian England, was *David Copperfield*, first translated into French in 1851. Madame Rivière recalls that her mother would grow as indignant over Murdstone as though he were a real, live village neighbour whose ways could be mended by a sharp lecture, and that her father's voice would grow strangely gruff when reading aloud to his assembled family of the death of David's mother. So protective were the Fournier parents that they forbade their children to read the second half of the novel. This was a challenge they readily took up, and with one reading frantically while the other kept watch, Henri and Isabelle were able to learn of the misfortunes of Emily, weep over the death of their beloved Steerforth and, as is normal in such circumstances, wonder at the end what the parental fuss was all about.[12]

Another English book which Henri came to love was *Robinson Crusoe* which, like his Uncle Lucien's exotic curios and his own father's plans for a colourful new way of life, transported him in imagination from the land-locked heart of France to the shores of the sounding sea. And yet one more English evocation came to quicken his appetite for travel and hint at worlds more romantic than everyday Epineuil: Monsieur Suc, the young assistant master at Epineuil when the Fourniers first arrived at the village school, once called to pay his respects and, as a present for the Fournier children, handed over a set of one year's issue of an adventure comic, *Le petit Français illustré*, full of riddles, gobbets of extraneous erudition and tales of derring-do. One of these in particular fascinated Henri and Isabelle, *Willie: l'écolier anglais*, and English schoolboy with an Eton jacket, high collar and heavily bandaged forehead. His adventurous career was cut off in full flight because he was still in the midst of some perilous escapade when that particular year's issue came to an end, and his ultimate fate was, for the Fournier children, a matter of much surmise and for long a spur to their powers of invention.[13]

III

But Henri Fournier did not spend all his days and nights secretly reading or sitting meekly under the fretful eyes of his ever-anxious mother. He was a strong and healthy boy and he had every normal boy's love for games, for explorations and discoveries. He wrote in 1912 to a fellow-author Louis Pergaud to thank him for the presentation-copy of *La Guerre des Boutons*, a robust novel about country schoolboys' feuds and fights:

I find it *excellent*. The opening chapters take me back to those happy days when the boys from Vallon [in the Allier *département*] used to do battle with us, boys from Epineuil [in the Cher]. I remember the Magnard boys, sons of the corn-chandler, who used to arrive at breakneck speed in their horse and cart. We would leap up at the horse's bridle and they used to greet us by flicking their whip. I'm rediscovering the joyous, glorious life of those bygone times through [your characters].[14]

There would be violent tournaments, with smaller boys mounted on the larger boys' backs and trying to unseat their rivals, 'Prisoners' Base', and innumerable ball games; in all these, Henri took a leading part. In summer, there would be picnic excursions to the willow-hung banks of the nearby Cher, in a donkey cart, with bottles of fizzy lemonade from the café then owned by the mother of Lucien Painchaud, one of the older pupils. There would be swimming and fishing in the shadows and on some occasions, Monsieur Fournier himself used to organise the activities with an ancient pistol in his belt. On other occasions, Henri and his friends would wander along the lane to the Canal du Berry, stopping now and then to dam a stream, or to clear the grass and weeds from a spring and let the water run free. From the canal bank, or by the more exciting lock-gates, they would watch the barges pass by, wonderful floating houses with weather-beaten inhabitants, coming out of the unknown and to the unknown departing.

In winter, the barges would sometimes be held prisoner in the ice, and the school registers of those days, still meticulously preserved, record in Monsieur Fournier's careful handwriting, the brief passage of the sons of bargees who stayed for a few weeks only, before slipping away into their other world. From another world too came the gipsies: there would be nocturnal scufflings at the Fourniers' back-door, a few shouted insults outside the windows, and the parents would look at each other with ill-concealed anxiety. Theirs was a house right on the village outskirts and on these occasions, it always seemed to be the one house left awake. Next morning, burnt matches would be found on the lane beside the side of the house, and the village folk would congregate in angry groups to count the number of chickens stolen and vegetables uprooted to enrich the marauders' stock-pot.

Other visitors from afar, whose arrival was as welcome as the gipsies' departure, were the wandering players. Arriving in caravans in the fair season of the year, they used to perform on the small square by the village church and children were drawn to their presence as moths to the light. Henri and the others circled and hovered, sometimes being rewarded with a glimpse of the inside of the gaily-painted caravan and the realisation that it was an exciting sort of home that could actually be lived in; and after the last performance, when the performing goat had balanced for the last time with all four feet on its glass tumbler, and the acrobat had turned his final somersault, more than one child's thoughts and dreams must surely have followed the vagabond performers out of the village and beyond the horizon.

What, however, were to prove the most persistently haunting of his Epineuil memories were connected not with his adventurous schoolboy games or excursions, but with sedate and formal occasions, particularly those involving Church ritual. Monsieur Fournier, like all employees of the anti-clerical State, was not a Church-goer, but his wife and children regularly attended Sunday Mass. Writing in April 1905, Henri looked back with a reverence he was never to lose :

> I remember, with so much tender yearning in my heart, those Sunday mornings when my mother used to take me to Mass. I was quite small at the time, wore a white sailor collar, and used to cling on to her dress. Once she had gone through the gate of our vast school playground, she would slowly begin to pull her gloves on over her long fingers and, slightly pursing her lips, she would then fasten the wrist-buttons of her leather gloves from which I caught the mingled scents of her wardrobe, the perfume satchets of the drawing-room, incense and consecrated bread. Slowly, one by one, she would press home each button, and when we reached the mossy wall of the church from inside which, even before we'd entered, we could hear the hymn-singing, the little bell and the sacristan, her hands were all long and soft and perfumed, and the colour of ochre; and with them, she would gently propel me through the Church porch.[15]

In that same month of April 1905, he wrote one of the earliest of his handful of published poems, 'Conte du Soleil et de la Route', which recalls another Epineuil church occasion rather less halcyon : dedicated to 'une petite fille' it tells in rhyming couplets of a very young alter ego – 'un petit garçon qui me ressemble' – who looks forward to taking his place in the cortège at a village wedding, and to the ineffable pleasure of being allowed to walk beside the girl he silently worships :

> On me mettra peut-être – on l'a dit – avec Elle
> qui me fait pleurer dans mon lit, et qui est belle . . .
>
> Si vous saviez – les soirs, quelquefois – ô mamans,
> les pleurs de tristesse et d'amour de vos enfants![16]

26

He rehearses the melting words he will whisper in her ear and imagines her tearful reply, but what happens in reality is rather different: a high wind is blowing on the day of the wedding, his brand-new, beribboned straw hat is whisked away just as the procession moves off, and amid the onlookers' laughter, he runs despairingly and unavailingly to retrieve it, blinded with bright sunlight, dust and tears.

Not all Church festive occasions ended so catastrophically for him. On the feast of Corpus Christi, the village children dressed in their best finery, and singing hymns in slow procession, would pass through the centre of Epineuil along the petal-strewn street to the grottoes decorated with crucifixes made of flowers. And there were lay ceremonies too like the Fourteenth of July when the whole village would return to childhood and indulge in sack-races, contests in which a live frog had to be borne intact to the wining-post in a wheelbarrow, the local fire-brigade would parade, all manner of fireworks would be let off and the grown-ups would dance beyond the dusk in the village square. In 1908, Henri looked back to these festive moments and wrote:

When I was a child and counted over my joys, when I listed, as children do, all my reasons for being happy, I took good care never to leave out our public holidays. For children still retain the marvellous primitive gift of being able to participate spontaneously in any joy or sadness around them. On the eve of Shrove Tuesday, as I came home in the twilight through the village streets, I would be overwhelmed by a sense of great joy mingled with terror: I imagined that all the children and all the grown-ups would, that evening, be playing their part in the same delightful yet distressing game; they would be hiding behind the hedgerows or in doorways, and they were going to come leaping out at me with their fearful masks and their absurdly disguised little voices. Towards the end of May, when, for the first time, people would begin to discuss our local fête, at the start of September when the carpenters used to nail up, at the entrances to the village, the triumphal arches for our agricultural show, I would feel welling up within me a rapture I have never since recaptured. The Fourteenth of July, the Fifteenth of August, School Prize Day – these were so many lovely staging-posts along the road through summer. Whenever I felt sad, I would recite these dates to myself under my breath, like a child with his hand in his pocket silently counting the marbles he has won.

27

I know that childhood was at an end when these joys ceased to affect me, and it filled me with sadness.[17]

However, there were moments in Henri's Epineuil childhood even more treasured than these : the occasions when he was allowed to accompany his mother on social visits to other houses in the village. These visits gave him temporary access to another world grander than the drab school kitchen or the dusty attics. Though the Fourniers were not specially poor nor the village ladies inordinately wealthy, their houses, simply through being large and unfamiliar, seemed, in comparison, to be all that was regal and romantic. Looking back in 1910, he evoked the late afternoons he spent with his mother in the drawing-room of Monsieur Virot, the lawyer who owned the house with the tower by the village cross-roads :

> I remember the time when, in a country drawing-room, Sunday evenings were long silent visits to Paradise. The ladies would play the piano while the children sat on thick carpets and turned the pages of big books filled with adventure tales and carols. In those days, little girls used to wear toques made of otter-skin, and when they dropped crumbs at tea-time, they would carefully pick them up again. While they were looking at the illustrations in the books, they would pensively nestle their warm cheeks against mine.
>
> It was a small drawing-room set below ground level in a corner of the house which stood by the village cross-roads. As night came down, a man would sometimes go past outside, as tall as the window, walking so quietly that we couldn't hear his footsteps. He seemed to be part of another world.[18]

But the most eagerly awaited of all the Epineuil visits were those to a house on the village outskirts, beyond the church and beside the road to Saint-Vitte. This belonged to a Madame Benoist and was the most distinguished residence in the village; it stood back from the road in a very large garden, with a dovecot at the end of it, and was approached through imposing iron gates and along a sanded drive between well-trimmed lawns. Henri sometimes sat in the shaded drawing-room while his mother and Madame Benoist exchanged village gossip but, more often, he and Isabelle would play in the garden with the three Benoist children Albert, Alfred and little Jenny. Memories of these afternoons remained vivid in Henri's mind for ever afterwards and regularly recur in his letters and work; Madame Benoist's house and garden are evoked in his most successful poem,

'A travers les étés', written in the summer of 1905 and partly dedicated 'to a house'; they regularly appear as the ideal setting in any
of his blueprints for his own future happiness; they occur regularly
in his working notes for *Le Grand Meaulnes*, and a month before his
death, he reported in a letter that he had just had a painful dream
about Alfred Benoist.[19]

IV

Every summer, at the end of the school year in July, the Fourniers
would journey ninety miles northwards to spend the holidays with
the Barthes at La Chapelle-d'Angillon. They would set out in the
early morning in the donkey cart belonging to old Monsieur Martin,
their farmer neighbour, and drive along the narrow lane to Vallon
railway station. There was invariably a three-hour wait at Bourges
before the connection on to La Chapelle, and the Fourniers would
regularly go on a hurried tour of the city, through the shopping-
centre for a sight of the great façade of the Cathedral and, if the
weather were kind, a picnic in the stately municipal park nearby.
Eventually, to the relief of the ever-anxious mother and the joy of
the impatient children, their next train would chuff off down the
little branch-line towards La Chapelle, through the dense woods and
rich fields of the Berry, stopping at every little station whose names
Henri was later to tell, over and over, like an incantation:

> On the train-journey from Bourges to La Chapelle, you go
> through little leafy valleys and stop at stations which have been
> in my memory now for twenty years: 'Asnières', 'Arrêt de
> Fussy', 'Menetou-Salon', 'Saint-Martin-Saint-Georges', 'Hen-
> richemont', 'Arrêt d'Ivoy-le-Pré' (formerly 'Arrêt du Moulin
> Girard'), then, to the left, in the valley of the Sauldre, the whole
> expanse of the façade of the château and – La Chapelle.
> Whenever the château came into view, Mother would say,
> 'Look at me, darling' and, with her handkerchief, she'd wipe
> from my face some of the black dust of the train.[20]

La Chapelle-d'Angillon has lost every vestige of the picturesqueness
it had in the days when the Fourniers used to arrive there for the
summer holidays. The little stream which flowed in front of the
Barthes' front garden has long since been filled in, and the creeper
stripped away from the front wall of the little house to let the
telephone wires hang free. Like Epineuil, La Chapelle has lost nearly

29

all the flowers which used to adorn both the public and the private buildings, but, unlike Epineuil, it has also been robbed of its peace and seclusion : today it is bisected by the main highway from Paris to Bourges, and cars, coaches and lorries go thundering through, at times almost incessantly.

In the more leisurely summer days before the turn of the century, one of the Fournier children's favourite pastimes was to play beside the bridge taking the main road over the Petite Sauldre. They would sit dangling their feet or floating paper boats down the stream, wondering if these could possibly be borne by the water along its whole course, on into the Grande Sauldre, thence via the Cher and the Loire and out to the open sea.

Across the bridge, at the junction of the main road and the narrow lane sneaking off to the neighbouring village of Ennordres, was the small cluster of cottages called Les Sablonnières, so called because of a disused sandpit in the close vicinity which provided the children with all manner of secret dens and 'smugglers' caves'. In one of the tiny cottages lived an old lady, Rosine Deschamps, close friend of Grandmother Barthe, and the Fournier children were sometimes invited to gather as a special treat, windfalls from beneath her fruit-trees.

Henri's other main pleasures in La Chapelle were getting to his grandmother to talk of the past, and exploring the vicinity of the deserted château de Béthune, then – as now – the chief tourist attraction of the village and standing on its outskirts. The château is an impressive edifice, a mixture of Gothic and Renaissance styles, and was renovated by the great Sully himself : its grey walls and black-capped towers rise above the waters of the Petite Sauldre, and the Fournier children would sometimes play in the rose-gardens which replaced what was once the moat. Throughout his short life, however, Henri's responsiveness to literature or places was determined by strictly personal rather than conventionally cultural associations, and the château he most preferred in the region of La Chapelle was historically rather less significant than Béthune. This was the old country house of Loroy, five miles or so to the south of La Chapelle-d'Angillon, hidden away in the Forêt de St-Palais, in the commune of Mery-ès-Bois. Loroy is inhabited again today but when Henri was a boy, and the Fournier family used to ride out from La Chapelle in their hired donkey-cart to picnic under the trees which enclosed the clearing in which it still stands, it was derelict and abandoned; the reed-fringed lake in front was tenanted by wild birds only, the shutters tightly closed over the two rows of windows, the whole edifice apparently about to crumble into ruins like the ivy-clad remains of

the Cistercian abbey behind it, with its spire rising above the grey
slate roof of the deserted manor.

But for Henri the high peak of the summer holidays came at the
end when the family moved on from Madame Fournier's native
Berry to the sylvan scenery of the sweeping vistas of her husband's
beloved Sologne and his birthplace in Nançay. Henri described the
journey westward from La Chapelle in a letter of August 1905 when
he felt deprived and exiled in London :

> You eventually get to Nançay after travelling for five leagues
> along remote roads in an ancient trap. It's a region buried deep
> in the Sologne. The roads are dry. For the whole length of the
> journey, there's a carpet of needles from the fir woods on the
> surrounding plains, gadflies in the air, game flying across in front
> of you. I could tell you tales of breakdowns, of sudden rain-
> storms, of the time when the horse got stuck in the mud of the
> ford when they tried to make him drink. And here and there,
> at the edge of a wood, a glimpse of horizons beyond the trees
> and the roads, the like of which you probably can't see even at
> sea.[21]

In Nançay, the family stayed with Monsieur Fournier's brother-
in-law, Florent Raimbault, who kept the general store there and
supplied all manner of provisions to the surrounding district for miles
around – food and drink, powder and shot, clothes, gloves, hats,
umbrellas and paraffin oil – and the children were free to range
through the complicated system of alcoves and counters, each with
its own unique and unforgettable smell. Everything about the Nançay
setting contributed to the holiday atmosphere : there was Uncle
Florent himself, large, moustachioed, noisy and expansive like the
Spirit of Christmas Present in person; there was Aunt Augustine,
always lively, always laughing, not content unless her guests were
fed to bursting-point, for ever producing cups of coffee that had to
be drunk on the spot, or proffering succulent pieces of rabbit which
had to be devoured there and then; there were the ten Raimbault
children, one son and nine daughters; there were all the relatives,
friends and neighbours continually wandering in to participate in
the general gaiety and to look back on or forward to a day's shooting
out on the heath.

To accompany the men and dogs on one of their day-long shooting-
parties was always, for Henri, a joy that was quite ineffable :

> We go shooting in the fir woods, and we spend the whole day
> in the heather. Incessantly, you hear the crack of rifle-shots and

everywhere, there's the smell of gunpowder. You eat your mid-day meal wherever your fancy takes you, sometimes with the private gamekeepers attached to those Sologne manor-houses, nearly all of which are marvellous examples of good taste, elegance and poetry in the midst of that wild landscape.

You return home exhausted. You go through the shop which does a roaring trade before dinner-time, and which, since darkness descends so soon in September, is lit by dazzling oil-lamps. You slump down exhausted in a chair in the kitchen. There you wait for dinner which will resound with children's laughter, when even Mother will join everyone else in wild peals of laughter, when merely our two families will, together, be enough to make up whole tables of diners. Perhaps dinner will be inter-rupted in the middle of the night when my uncle's delivery-carts return, or when other aunts and uncles are fetched from some far-off railway station. They climb down in the light of the lanterns, you exchange kisses without really knowing who they are, while the horses are led off to the stables which you restock with hay, and which are filled with the steam from the horses' coats.

You wait for dinner in the kitchen where the candles are dim and where the dishes are being got ready. You begin to nod and to keep you awake, they take the smoky old photographs from the walls and pass them round. These turn out to be school groups, and you see my father at the age of five, with his teacher Monsieur Jauvy who used to beat him so hard, and who now salutes him with such an extravagant sweep of his skull-cap. You can see all the little boys of that school of long ago; they're grown men now and call my father 'Guste'.[22]

It is not difficult for us to see why the Nançay holidays always retained a place of very particular significance in Henri Fournier's private mythology: the sense of physical well-being fostered by days out in the pure autumn air, the atmosphere of conviviality in which everyone so readily participated, the openness and gregariousness of the Raimbault stores compared with the closed-in world of the Epineuil schoolhouse – everything combined to make of Nançay what was, in effect, another world. The child's world is not circumscribed by the adult's rigid concepts of space and time: for a child, the world might well end on the horizon where the earth touches the sky, and a journey to the next village can be as fraught with excitement as an exploration to the Pole; Time can seem to be frozen motionless, and tomorrow equivalent to never, but it can also seem utterly boundless when he glimpses that mysterious world where his parents were somehow children too. In his Nançay holiday world, with those splendid vistas of heather moorland sweeping into the far distance, where visitors burst in from nowhere, where adults' memories were taken out and dusted and passed from one to the other with ancient photographs, the grown-ups were like children too, for space and time seemed to have neither beginning nor end.

But, inevitably, an end there had to be, and when the Nançay holidays were over, Henri grieved as bitterly as for a death. He wrote in 1905 :

> When in childhood, we used to drive away from Nançay, I would always long for some accident to happen that would cause us to turn back. I left a bit of my heart behind with each milestone we passed – and it was an intense sadness to know that it was goodbye, for a whole year, to Nançay, to my holidays and to the summer.[23]

And he wrote again, five years later :

> When I had to come away from Nançay and my uncles there, I would yearn so despairingly for the lovely land of my vanished holidays that my cousins used to say : 'We just don't know what's wrong with him. He looks quite *glazed*.'[24]

This condition was to remain chronic for the rest of his life.

V

As a young man growing up, Fournier looked back on the whole of his childhood in the same way as, at the end of the holidays, he used to look back to Nançay. In August 1907, just before Jacques Rivière was due to meet the whole Fournier family for the first time, Fournier wrote a letter warning him not to talk too freely in their presence about the past :

> I just haven't been able to bring myself to take you to Epineuil. I don't know if I'll ever go back there myself. When I recite the list of stations on the line from Bourges to Epineuil, it's sweet beyond telling. But I'm quite overcome with anguish when I try to recall the little villages around our old home. For a long time my parents considered my love of Epineuil, like my love

for Nançay (although my feelings were well concealed) as unreasonable and indeed as immoral as love for some woman. The only time it's now mentioned is to rejoice that it's now all over.[25]

It was, in fact, anything but over: Fournier still had to negotiate the passage from childhood to manhood, and this proved more than usually painful in his case for a number of complex reasons. His problem can in part be seen as a struggle between the male and female elements in his nature, a conflict epitomised in those excited family debates which more than once disturbed the normal tranquillity of the Fournier home during his childhood, when his father, with the male's desire for change and movement never adequately satisfied, unveiled plans for moving to Africa or the Far East, while his mother, ever faithful to the past, like her mother before her, resolutely reiterated the female preference for stability and home in long familiar surroundings. Together with that love of physical action encouraged by his father and by the tales of Uncle Lucien and Grandfather Barthe, Fournier inherited from his mother and Grandmother Barthe a deep love of home and their sentimental attachment to their country past. His dilemma was to achieve a compromise between his thirst for adventure and his need for domesticity, between setting out for the unknown and clinging to established order. Nearly all his efforts to take an action decisively affecting his career, his hopes of becoming a naval officer, his plans of travelling to the Far East, his thoughts of becoming a missionary or a monk – each of these is essentially the same conflict in a different guise, a conflict which he almost certainly never quite resolved. And his long and painful struggle to complete his only novel is part of that conflict too, because to write effectively of one's past is, in a very real sense, to exorcise it. For Fournier, this meant to eradicate, or very seriously to dilute, the richest source of his literary inspiration: his powerful sense of nostalgia.

What Fournier came to prize particularly in childhood was not so much like Peter Pan the fun and irresponsibility of boyhood games, nor, like Proust's Marcel, the protective presence of an all-forgiving mother, nor like Baudelaire a sense of innocence before the Fall. What he mourned most, like Wordsworth, was the waning of his sense of wonder, the fading of that visionary gleam with which, in retrospect, even the simplest sights and sounds of his outwardly ordinary childhood semed to him to have been invested. What is particularly striking about all the many reminiscent passages he wrote about his childhood is the absence of references to Heaven or to

34

happier lands, far, far away. Henri Fournier's imagination took wing not at the prospect of clouds of glory trailing from some marvellous world before his birth, but at half-glimpses of other lives around him to which he was normally denied access : the notes of a piano from behind a closed door, a large country house seen from across a lake or through the railings of forbidding gates, a barge on a canal, gliding past oblivious to his presence, a caravan vanished under cover of darkness, with just the ashes of the wandering actors' fire to prove it ever existed, a silent and solitary pedestrian seen dimly through a casement in the gathering dusk – these were the sort of intimations which made up his 'poetry' of childhood and from them he was to make his own potent spells.

Not for the only time, he was particularly lucid and explicit about what he understood by the 'magic' of childhood when writing about his beloved Nançay :

> When, in the old days, I used to stay in Nançay – a place which I wanted to be marvellous, unknown and unique – I didn't like to see people I knew or who came from districts I knew. I can remember waiting for relatives to arrive by trap from far distant villages. I was disappointed and disgusted when one of my aunts would get down from the trap, utter remarks I'd heard a thousand times already and look around her with a self-satisfied expression. You could sense her conviction that, as far as she was concerned, there was nothing more to be learnt about life or about living. You felt that there was nothing new about her, that she'd brought nothing new with her, that in her humdrum way, she'd long since learned the truth about everything.
>
> There are, of course, plenty of women like her whose every attitude and every gesture convey the same wretched com-placency that my aunt expressed. So how much dearer and more desirable do we find the woman who, as night is falling, seems to be part of a dream, as full of mystery as the land she's just come from, her eyes perplexed and dazzled at the prospect of the new world before her.[26]

As he grew up, Fournier felt with increasing insistence that he had been disinherited. What he came to yearn for most was his capacity for wonderment, and his awareness of its loss consistently inspired in him those two complementary emotions which constitute the essence of all nostalgia : the sense of deprivation and the urge for renewal.

3

The Land of Exile

1898–1902

> You can re-create what you love only by
> giving it up.
>
> Marcel Proust[1]

Like his father before him, young Henri could, perfectly properly, have completed his primary and secondary education at village schools in the Cher region and then have proceeded to the teachers' training college at Bourges. His parents, however, impressed by the regularity with which he occupied first place in the Epineuil form-order, and doubtless determined that he should be given all the opportunities for advancement and for travel which they had been denied, had rather more ambitious plans for him.

In a fiercely meritocratic educational system, they realised it was essential for Henri to compete on equal terms with his rivals. In this situation, for all their dedication, the Fourniers' own school at Epineuil was simply inadequate. So it was, that at the beginning of October 1898, Henri was sent away from the close family circle for the first time in his life, to undertake the longest journey in his experience to date, and embark on a new school career at the lycée Voltaire in Paris.

This marks the beginning of a nine-year process in the course of which he was to discover, sometimes painfully and sometimes ecstatically, that his parents' hopes for him and his own ambitions are two quite separate things.

I

Whatever misgivings Madame Fournier had about letting her closely protected son pass far beyond her care were largely overcome by the realisation that he was not being thrust unguarded into some dangerous

Henri Fournier's father in 1886

His mother in 1915

The earliest photograph of Henri and Isabelle Fournier, taken in 1892

Senior class at Epineuil, 1895–6. Henri Fournier is second from right in the middle row, and Isabelle is the only girl in the picture. Alfred Benoist is second from left in the back row. The middle row includes from left to right, first, Louis Delouche; fourth, Lucien Painchaud (the model for Jasmin Delouche in *Le Grand Meaulnes*); and fifth, Moucheboeuf

and loveless world. She arranged for him to stay with a Madame Bijard, formerly Mademoiselle Gabrielle, a mistress at the girls' school in Epineuil. She had married a foreman-printer, moved with him to Paris, and there established a small private school for girls at 196 rue de la Roquette, in the eleventh *arrondissement*, near the vast Père Lachaise cemetery. Henri boarded with the Bijards while, to provide room and reduce expenses all round, the Bijards' son, Théodule, was sent to lodge with the Fourniers in Epineuil.

The Fourniers remembered Mademoiselle Gabrielle as a charming and vivacious young lady, who took particular pride in her flower garden, and who regularly accompanied them to the wandering players' shows in the village square. Madame Bijard was a rather different proposition : continually distraught, harassed by the cares of her teaching establishment and the outbursts of temper from her husband, a man of volatile disposition with the habit of retiring early to bed with a bottle of wine and whatever delicacies he could purloin from the table or the larder. There was also a regular visitor, plump and pomaded, whose solicitude for Madame Bijard did little to preserve the harmony of the household. To heighten the contrast between the new life and the old, Henri found himself confronted not with an adoring and always understanding sister but with a provocative band of little girls, for ever whispering and giggling. His sense of deprivation was further increased when Isabelle herself was brought to a Paris hospital for a complicated operation on her hip, and, because of a particularly strict regulation prohibiting visits from children under fourteen, he was never allowed to visit her. He was turned back at the hospital gates when he arrived for his first visit with a parcel of books and cakes, and pointedly told not to come back again.

The sights and sounds of the district around the Bijards' home offered very little for his comfort : in addition to the vast array of graves in the Père Lachaise cemetery, there was a stonemason's yard where tombstones were cut and inscribed, and two prisons of particularly sinister aspect. Henri was only twelve, and was not yet old enough to be allowed to wander freely along the banks of the Seine, down the boulevards or through the parks. He had still to discover the many consolations which were later so to endear Paris to him, and during the first three years he spent there he destested city life as only a countryman can.

None of this, however, was expressed in his letters at the time. He was naturally resilient in any event, and he was considerably consoled and encouraged by initial academic success. He at once established himself as the leading pupil in his form and at the end of each of the three academic years he spent at Voltaire, he emerged with the *prix d'excellence* for the most outstanding all-round performance. His prizes included Nodier's *Contes*, and Scott's *Quentin Durward*, and it was in this period that he discovered Daudet's *Lettres de mon moulin* and *Don Quixote*.

Henri ended his second year at Voltaire with no less than fifteen prizes but, in spite of these successes and the plaudits they earned him, he was neither unpopular with his class-mates nor lickspittle before the masters. René Bizet, perhaps his closest friend at Voltaire, has recalled[2] the care he regularly bestowed, even in his early teens, on his physical appearance, his ready repartee and his fondness for practical jokes; he remembers Henri as an extremely studious pupil but one who was never afraid to speak up to the masters on behalf of his cause and to cling obstinately to his point if he was convinced he was in the right. He remembers also that when the whole class – like the whole country – was split into two bitterly opposed factions because of the Dreyfus case, Henri Fournier remained calmly aloof. This is the more surprising not only because of his penchant for playground battles but also because local and national political conflict was a subject in which he evinced a lifelong interest.

Among the treasures he brought home after his second year at Voltaire were a copy of Rostand's play *L'Aiglon*, in which, not for the only time, Sarah Bernhardt scored a spectacular triumph playing a male role. He also acquired a camera. Photography appeals not only to the gadget-minded or to the would-be portraitist and landscape-artist but, at the deepest level, to those of nostalgic disposition who seek to be readily reminded of the past. This, undoubtedly, is why it became rather more than a hobby for Henri from the turn of the century onwards.[3] In the summer holidays particularly, it became a very particular enthusiasm, and the large number of photographs he took of his parents and of scenes in and around his grandparents' house in La Chapelle are eloquent evidence of his growing, but still unvoiced, concern to seize and retain something of his precious past from the unreturning years.

The preciousness of that past was brought home to him because he was now beginning to be separated from it not only in time but in space as well. The end of the summer holidays had been poignant enough for him when he had had to leave his beloved Nançay for Epineuil: how much more so now, when he now had to travel directly from the purple and golden heathlands of Sologne to the cheerless household of the Bijards in Paris. Always, when the moment for departure came, he was able to conceal his sadness from those around him, but once he was alone at 196 rue de la Roquette, he could indulge his yearning to the full by measuring just how far he was from his land of heart's desire.

His letters to his parents at this time continued to bring encouraging news of his successes in the class-room; only years later, in a letter to Jacques Rivière, did he fully reveal what his dominant emotions at Voltaire had been :

> From the age of ten or twelve onwards, this is the picture I have of my sadness. Sitting in front of my open trunk, in the empty room where I used to be deposited on my return to Paris after the holidays – every article I lifted out was a part of my bruised and abandoned heart. The hand which had packed it, the mind which had neatly arranged it, how I pitied its gentleness and its poverty. In the train, what a terrible torture it was to try to read the comics they'd bought to keep me amused. The targets for humour in those comics were poor, pitiful, simple and sad. And I thought of the people I'd left behind me, I recalled all the words I ought to have listened to, all the kisses I ought to have responded to, all the complaints I ought to have left unspoken. And, more than anything else, all the things I hadn't looked at enough or touched enough, or taken out of their stable, their box or their field, and *which were now grieving because of it*, now that it was too late.
>
> How I've suffered from my irreparable words of spite, from pity I've expressed too late and from the awfulness of that word 'Nevermore'.[4]

From the autumn of 1900 on, 'nevermore' was a word he could apply, with melancholy relish, to the regime of Madame Bijard because, in the course of that summer, she moved out to a more prosperous Paris suburb to provide a boarding-school for richer young ladies. Uncongenial though 196 rue de la Roquette often seemed, it had nevertheless been run by a kindly – and, even more important, by an Epineuil – personality. She was replaced by a total stranger, the austere, cold and morose Madame 'Pauline' whose only interest in Henri Fournier was the rent she could collect for his keep. He found occasional consolation in the intermittent visits he was able to make to the comfortable home of M. Léopold Bernard, a prosperous Jewish businessman who acted as his *locum parentis* throughout his Voltaire career, and whose younger son Jean remained one of Henri's most loyal friends. He remained popular with his fellow-pupils at school, continued to achieve good results and once again crowned the academic year with the award of the *prix d'excellence*, but when he left the lycée Voltaire in July 1901, it was never to return. With a change of direction as sudden as it was dramatic, it was decided that he should resume his studies after the summer vacation in the lycée of Brest in far distant Brittany.

II

The ostensible reasons for Henri's transfer from Paris to Brest were uncomplicated enough : he had decided to embark on a career in the French navy and to take the entrance examination to the training ship *Borda*, the naval equivalent of the rather more famous Army academy of Saint Cyr; the *Borda* was anchored at Brest and the lycée of Brest was reckoned to provide the best training available for the specialist entrance-examinations; and so, in October 1901, from the land-locked centre of France, to the Atlantic coast he went.

The deeper motives for the transfer, which seems to have been prompted exclusively by Henri himself, were doubtless more complex. It was certainly a running-away from conditions which had become insufferable since he had had to return from school each day to a room without curtains, to an uncomfortable bed without a pillow, and to a morose landlady with never a kindly word or a smile. But more positive ambition also counted in his decision to move in the direction of the sea, and his friend René Bizet recalls Henri's anticipating the transfer with very real enthusiasm and of his intention to complete two years' work in one so as to make quite sure of fulfilling the examination age-regulations.

He had a deep-seated longing for adventure, action and exploration, fed by his boyhood reading and intensified by his never once having seen the sea in the first fifteen years of his life. His imagination was further fired by his father's often voiced, but permanently thwarted, wanderlust so that, in a very particular sense, when Henri set his sights on a career of exotic journeys, he was accepting the challenge of fulfilling high embitions that were not wholly his own.

The period Henri spent in Brest marked a crucial stage in his development in more than one respect : it was his first experience of boarding-school, his first real taste of exile and of academic disappointment, and it was the first really major conflict between those irreconcilable factions within his own nature – the siren voices eagerly calling him into the maritime future opposed by other voices, no less insistent and rather more insidious, singing soft praises of his country past.

Living full-time in a boarding-school would have posed Henri

40

problems of adjustment in any event, however congenial the surroundings, because hitherto, even in Paris, he had always stayed
within a family. The atmosphere of the Brest lycée was, however,
anything but congenial : the school was remarkable at this time for
the paucity of its creature comforts and for the astringent military
flavour of its general atmosphere. The boys were summoned from
bed at half-past five each morning to the insistent sound of drum-
beats, and had to parade outside in the school yard – 'barrack square'
seems somehow more appropriate here than 'playground' – whatever
the season or the weather. In spite of the military ethos, however –
indeed, directly because of it – the pupils were notoriously undisci-
plined in the classroom. Lessons sometimes got completely out of
hand, a favourite trick being for every boy gently to rest his head
flat on the desk-top when the master was writing on the blackboard,
so that when he turned back to address the class, he was confronted
with forty or so closely cropped heads, arrayed before him like so
many boulders : this form of ragging was known as 'Playing Stones'.
The most favourite technique for expressing public displeasure of
any particular supervisor was for all the pupils in turn to hiss out his
name in a sepulchral stage whisper in the course of 'prep', everybody
ostensibly working away the while, with head bent over his books.
Nobody was ever caught, doubtless because the teacher rightly realised
that to detect and punish the culprits would have proved a cure
rather worse than the complaint.

These occasional tilts against authority, together with infrequent
excursions into the Breton countryside, were the only distractions
from an institution where the grimness of the buildings was matched
only by the toughness of the syllabus. Henri, who enjoyed both the
ragging and the outings, was subsequently to look back and say that
he never had to work harder in his school life. His letters to his parents
at this stage were devoted almost exclusively to the marks he had
received for his various school exercises, to details of essay subjects
he had been set ('Compose an imaginary letter from Roger Bacon
to Pope Clement V on his scientific discoveries'),[5] to incidents like
his being reprimanded for having a dirty comb, or to descriptions
of occasional outings to the home of Madame Elegoët, a widow
acting *in loco parentis* or into the Breton countryside which he found
cheerless and outlandish. Re-reading his Breton letters ten years later,
he commented :

> I look back on Brest as Hell, yet I find the letters I wrote home
> from there full of good temper and very dutiful – so dutiful, in
> fact, that they wring the heart, because you can feel all the fever

and fret beneath. Outwardly, though, they're merely the letters of a little schoolboy listing his good results in class.[6]

In the letters he wrote at the time to his parents back in Epineuil, his wistfulness and distress are revealed through chance hints only: in his request for some photographs of the Epineuil schoolhouse, garden and stream, preferably with his parents included, in his letter-endings – 'From your son who loves you', 'from your son far away from you', in his entreaty that they write back without delay ('a week is such a long time to be without news! The day when your letter is due is a veritable Feast Day for me').[7] Once again, it was only years afterwards that his sense of deprivation could be fully orchestrated :

> One morning at Brest, as I came down from the dormitory, in front of the caretaker's lodge I caught the smell of damp wood being lit. It was in November. How imprisoned I felt then, how excited, how full of longing. And I haven't changed a bit.[8]

Two years later still, he again looked back and recalled that he was not even allowed out of the lycée for Christmas or for New Year's Day :

> December again, the time when, at the lycée of Brest, when there was no Thursday afternoon walk, the boys, all shut-in and sad, would squabble over *L'Almanach Vermot*. Some would be eating oranges. I would walk up and down all alone, with my hands in my pockets, over the paved stones of the narrow courtyard. I reflected that that year there was going to be no Christmas Day for me, no New Year's Day, no oranges in tissue paper, no long, aimless rambles into the countryside, through the ice and snow.
>
> How I longed to be free then, and how full of regret I was! The school caretaker would light his fire and the smell of faggots and burning paper would bring back early country mornings when I was small, and I had to stand on a chair to be dressed for catechism.
>
> All hunched-up, with my head bare as I paced the yard, and my long dishevelled hair being blown across my eyes by the wind, I would savour each of my memories in turn with the same bitterness. I should like to have had someone to love. I went over in my mind all the girls I'd known. I was fifteen years old. So were you, and you really ought to have been there, on

the other side of the school-gates, one of those rare passers-by whose heads were all that we could see of them and whom we envied so much because they were free.[9]

There were few consolations for Henri while he was a prisoner at Brest, but to what there were, he devoted himself with more than ordinary enthusiasm. At this period in his life, he still counted himself a Christian, went regularly and fervently to Communion, and became known to his much less devout companions as 'Pious Fournier'. He began to appreciate the consoling powers of literature and it was while at Brest that he first discovered what was to remain one of his lifelong favourites, Fromentin's *Dominique*, that most delicate story of unrequited love in which hero and heroine, out of respect for their marriage vows, choose to preserve their honour and their dignity, and spend the rest of their lives apart, ever-mindful of what might have been. Fournier never forgot *Dominique* and that when he read it for the first time at Brest, he felt as though 'a long fine needle had been driven into his adolescent heart'.[10]

But his most consistently effective source of consolation in the barren Brest period was the store of memories from his own past, not only his happier childhood days in Epineuil, La Chapelle and Nançay, but even the more recent years, at the time so thankfully left behind, in Paris. 'During my first three years in Paris, I hated it as only a country boy could', he wrote in 1905, 'but how I dreamed of it and longed for it in the course of those sixteen months I spent at Brest in the midst of a dirty province and a lot of brutal souls.'[11]

What is particularly revealing about all those letters he wrote at the time from Brest is the lack of enthusiasm, and even of discussion about the future. There are occasional references to his steady academic progress and to his examination prospects, but no excited anticipation about the end to which the passing of examinations was merely the means – that exciting career as a naval officer. Fournier's attachment to his past was so profound that it would almost certainly have remained unbroken even had a more congenial setting than Brest put a greater strain upon his loyalties. Because, in the event, it proved so traumatically unpleasant – and of all the periods in his life, it is the only one which was never sentimentalised by recollection – he had no difficulty and no compunction in putting an abrupt end to his naval ambitions. In December 1902, with two terms of his second academic year at Brest still to run, he abandoned his plans to prepare for the entrance examination to the *Borda* and went back to his native Cher countryside.

He did not, however, return to the beloved schoolhouse of his childhood in Epineuil-le-Fleuriel. In October 1902, when he returned to begin the new year at Brest, his parents were transferred by ministerial decree to the village of Menetou-Ratel, thirty-two miles northeast of Bourges. It is somehow appropriate that the sixteen months spent at Brest which ended with a decisive victory for the forces tugging him back towards childhood, should include his enforced and final separation from the village he most dearly loved. In fact, the surest way to bind him to the past was, as he was not to take long to discover, to cut him off from it.

III

Henri's career prospects did not lie for long in disarray after the humiliation of Brest; he merely retrieved his parents' plans which had first sent him away in 1898, and he turned his attention once more to the State's *grandes écoles*. By the beginning of 1903 there was no longer any doubt which of the various entrance examinations he should prepare for : it was to be, what was then and what still remains, the toughest examination in an inordinately tough national system, the entrance competition to the Ecole Normale Supérieure. Situated in the rue d'Ulm in Paris, close to the Panthéon, the Ecole Normale Supérieure is one of the most prestigious of all the French *grandes écoles*. It was founded by Napoleon with the view of training the intellectual élite of the nation's youth for the best lycées and University departments throughout France. The annual entrance examination has always been ferociously competitive, not only because a place in the Ecole is most desirable in itself and, almost unique in France, provides the scholar with the individual tuition and creature comforts which used to be the prime prerogative of the Oxbridge undergraduate, but because merely to have gained a pass virtually guarantees security and unfailing esteem in later life. Of the thirty or so *lycéens* who are admitted to the Arts section each year, a fair proportion eventually emerge to achieve distinction, though not necessarily wide renown, as lycée or University teachers. Even more impressive, however, is the number of *normaliens* who may well indeed serve as teachers at the outset of their careers but who go on to achieve national or international recognition as writers, philosophers or statesmen : Henri Bergson, Charles Péguy, Jules Romains, Jean Giraudoux, Jean-Paul Sartre and Georges Pompidou are just a few of the better-known *normaliens* in this latter category – from all of which, it should have emerged that in aiming at the ENS scholarship competition instead of the entrance examination to the *Borda*, Henri

Fournier was not meekly acquiescent in defeat : he was bidding for something like a junior equivalent of All Souls!

In January 1903, in the middle of an academic year, it was not considered feasible to undertake full-scale preparation for the Ecole Normale Supérieure which necessitated enrolling once more in a Paris lycée. He set himself the more modest and, in any event, essential task, of passing the second part of the *baccalauréat* examination, having already qualified in the first part while still at Brest. To achieve this end, he spent two terms as a boarder at the lycée of Bourges.

Inevitably, Bourges was to Fournier a much more congenial environment than Brest : it was close enough to his parents' new home for him to make fortnightly visits; it was full of associations with his own childhood when the family, en route from Epineuil to La Chapelle, would visit the great Cathedral and picnic in the municipal gardens; the lycée itself, with its grey-bonneted towers, looked from the outside like one of those gracious country châteaux in which he always found so much poetry. It is somewhat surprising, therefore, that the few months he spent there seem to have made little impression on him. Life inside the lycée did not match its picturesque exterior, and when Fournier looked back in later years, he could remember only that the dormitory bed-linen had a foul smell, that the headmaster was an out-and-out snob, and that he spent much of his leisure-time walking alone in the parks wishing he was in love. It was only recently revealed[12] that on Shrove Tuesday 1903, together with two other schoolmasters' sons, he went on a trip into the nearby Sancerrois region, returned two days late, and was severely reprimanded by the headmaster as a consequence.

Apart from this, his rebellious streak seems to have been kept well under control, and he remained a quietly studious and inconspicuous pupil. He played Rugby for the school fifteen in a period when physical education did not feature prominently in the official curriculum, and in July 1903 he duly passed the second part of his *bachot*, thereby leaving himself free to set off over the academic assault-course leading to the Ecole Normale Supérieure.

More important, however, for his future development than the passing of the second *baccalauréat* were two other incidents in 1903 : at Eastertime that year, came his first experience of family bereavement with the death of Grandfather Barthe who was buried in the churchyard by the Petite Sauldre, where he had so often come to watch his grandchildren at play. And in the summer, before the annual family holidays at La Chapelle and Nançay, Henri returned to Epineuil, to visit the house and garden of Madame Benoist and to look once more at the school : he found that the new master had uprooted all his father's flowers and put nothing in their place. Never again, for the rest of his life, did he return.

Somewhat light-heartedly, in one of the very first of the dutiful letters he wrote from Brest to his parents, he commented, 'You come to realise how much something means to you only when you've lost it.'[13] He spoke more truly than he knew, and it did not take him long to realise that the only way dead people and flowers and places could be restored to him was through the sorcery of Art. These lessons he was shortly to learn in what was to prove the richest intellectual and emotional period in his life, the years he spent in Paris as a member of the scholarship form at the lycée de Lakanal.

4

The Land of Promise

October 1903–September 1907

> Youth is not made for pleasure, it is made
> for heroism.
>
>   Paul Claudel[1]

I

At the mere sight of the outward appearance and physical setting of Lakanal, Fournier must have recognised that it promised him more consolation and inspiration than any of the three other lycées he had previously attended. It is situated in the leafy outer suburbs to the south of Paris and adjoins the splendid park and château of Sceaux, formerly the country retreat of the Duchesse du Maine, daughter-in-law of Louis XIV and Madame de Montespan. The lycée's own wooded grounds, in which a tame goat could be seen grazing, the tree-lined avenue down to the neat and rural station of Bourg-la-Reine, the Grand Canal in the château gardens, for years now once more trim and orderly, but at the beginning of the century all overgrown with grass and bushes, like some stretch of desolate Sologne marshland – all this compensated Fournier for his absence from the Cher countryside : in November 1903, he wrote to his sister, herself now a boarder in the girl's school in Moulins, reporting delightedly that his bedroom looked out over a vista of green fields, that he could regularly hear the calls of nearby market-gardeners, and that he was writing to the accompaniment of the chattering of a shrike.

In other important respects, Lakanal was a distinct improvement on anything he had previously experienced after leaving his country home : instead of the more characteristic communal dormitories, regularly a trial for someone like Fournier who was jealous of his privacy and was nauseated by offensive smells, each pupil had a little cubicle of his own into which he could retreat in peace; the

47

boys were allowed out of school on Thursdays and Sundays, and though officially Fournier was supposed to spend much of this time with his Parisian moral guardian, Monsieur Bernard, he devoted more and more time to enjoying the manifold pleasures of Paris which he was by now old enough to savour and which he was to love for the rest of his life.

The Lakanal régime reflected another progressive trend in contemporary French education by paying increased attention to modern foreign languages and literature at the expense of classical studies. Because of this, Fournier was reintroduced to English literature which had made its initial appeal to him through *David Copperfield* and *Robinson Crusoe*: he had not been long at Lakanal before he was being confronted with Shakespeare, the English Romantic poets and by such contemporary figures as Wells, Kipling and Hardy, all of whom, for different reasons, were profoundly to stir him.

The over-riding aim, however, of the Lakanal teachers was to train as many young academic showjumpers as possible to clear the towering hurdle of the Ecole Normale Supérieure competition. To achieve this end, their prize charges in the Arts scholarship stable had to be drilled not only in literary appreciation in French and English, but in translating from and into French, English and Latin, in French History, in Philosophy, all at what still seems a remarkably sophisticated level. The pressures were rigorous and continual, the crucial importance of the examination the subject of regular sermonising, the masters' critical attention to detail constant, personal and often perspicacious. 'Don't be *too* flashy or you won't pass', was the advice given by the French Literature teacher, Monsieur Vial, to Jean Giraudoux, a near contemporary of Fournier's at Lakanal: Giraudoux heeded the advice, saved his verbal pyrotechnics for later, and passed brilliantly.

Fournier did not find it quite so easy to conform. The longer he stayed at Lakanal, the more difficult he found it to concentrate on those aspects of the syllabus, Philosophy, History and Prose Composition, which totally failed to engage his deeper being. The Ecole Normale entrance examination called for a high all-round level of performance, and Fournier was essentially interested only in literature and in the contemporary arts so readily available for his delectation in the Parisian world, a short train-ride away. At Voltaire, undistracted by Parisian temptations, and needing to forget the gulf between the uncongenial present and an ever-more attractive past, he had devoted himself single-mindedly to his place in the form-order and carried off all the prizes that mattered. At Lakanal he worked consistently only at those few subjects which aroused his interest, tried frantically to get up to standard in the others on the eve of the examinations, and performed catastrophically. The only school prizes of consequence he ever won at Lakanal were for gymnastics, and though he was occasionally to produce a really superlative piece of work, praise of which encouraged him to dream momentarily of ultimate success, he was never more perspicacious or prescient about his examination prospects than when he wrote to his sister in November 1903, soon after embarking on his Lakanal career:

> I've got to get down to work because, inevitably, I'm in the lower reaches of the form-order. Now it's up to you to retrieve our family honour.[2]

In other respects too, Fournier was a non-conformist at Lakanal, and his spirit of independence and sense of fair play, which had been asserted more than once at Voltaire and Bourges, were soon prominently in evidence again. The scholarship forms at Lakanal were known as the 'Cagne' (or 'Khagne') and to these attached a well-established special vocabulary and code of conventions: the first-year pupils (or *bizuths*) were regularly ragged by, and expected to remain meekly subservient to, the second years (*carrés*) and third years (*cubes*). Against this system and its attendant rituals, Fournier's pride and innate country common sense readily rebelled, and he quietly became one of the leaders of a revolutionary movement which, through subversive pamphlets and active demonstrations, protested against all that seemed pointless and outmoded.

On occasions Fournier could be boisterous, and he delighted both in verbal humour and in practical jokes, and for all these reasons had quickly established close ties with a number of friends. There was René Bichet, from a poor country home near Orleans, cautious in his behaviour and his judgments, and quite the most brilliant examinee of his year; there was Jean Chesneau, from a well-connected family in Bordeaux, a friend of Giraudoux's, amiable, witty, genuinely interested in poetry and consistently whimsical; there was Alexandre Guinle from Tarbes in the Pyrenees, an inveterate punster with a beautiful singing voice; and there was Jacques Rivière.

Jacques Rivière was born on July 15 1886 in Bordeaux into a prosperous conservative Catholic family. They lived in a well-to-do old quarter of Bordeaux, damp and enclosed, very close to the sounds and the smells of the river. Their home was on the second floor of a big seventeenth-century house with carved female faces above the windows of the façade.[3] There was also an old, turreted country house up on a hill at Cenon, a small village to the south-west of Bordeaux, and this came to mean as much to Rivière as Nançay did to Fournier.

Jacques' father, Maurice, was a self-made man and a triumphant vindication of the French educationalists' claim that anyone can get to the top of the system provided he has talent and application. He came from a small Bordelais village where his father was a telegraphist, and he moved straight up the academic ladder to become Professor of Obstetrics in the University of Bordeaux and finally Head of Maternity Services for the region. He was eager for his son to emulate his own success, albeit in another field, and had mapped out well in advance the route he was to follow : early schooling in Bordeaux, a crack training lycée in Paris, the Ecole Normale Supérieure, thence another of the top specialist institutions, l'Ecole d'Athènes, and finally on to a University Chair of Greek.

High hopes of this order did not seem misplaced as Jacques moved on through childhood and was hailed at school as an exceptional performer. At school he was immensely studious, shy, sensitive and easily hurt; with the other Rivière children at home, however, he revealed another side of his character. His only sister later recalled that he liked to organise violent games for herself and their two younger brothers and to recount lurid blood-and-thunder stories :

> He would sometimes sit reading for five or six hours on end.
> Then suddenly he would leap down from the window sill or
> fling himself on us with fierce cries, threatening and jostling us.[4]

He also adored to travel at speed, either in a home-made wooden go-kart or on a bicycle, and both he and Fournier were always to remain passionate devotees of bicycle-sprinting and car-racing.

But the great love of Rivière's childhood was his mother, Reine Fermaud, a gentle, pious woman, who was devoted to her children. She died when Jacques was ten years old and the event left a profound scar which never healed. In August 1907, just before his first visit to Fournier's home, he wrote from Cenon to his friend :

> I ought now to let you know how moved I am to think that you
> have a mother, that I am going to meet her and that I shall love
> her. Last night I dreamed that my mother was still there. I
> saw again her exhausted face, the lower half emaciated, with
> just a tint of that horrible colour it took on the moment she
> died, which I can still clearly see. But in my dream she was
> alive, I took her hands in mine and she placed a hand on the
> back of my leaning neck. And I spoke to her about extremely

simple things, as though we had never been separated. It was in this very room, in front of the dining-room windows. She was wearing a blue dress.[5]

Years later still, in a book about his religious experiences, he was no less haunted :

Death of my mother, summoning up her last reserves to stay alive till I'd got home from school to kiss me. May she be with me in my final hour and may she appear before God with thoughts of me in her mind and in her eyes.[6]

The death of Madame Rivière left Jacques with an ineradicable sense of despair and desolation and the conviction that the Universe was essentially at the mercy of chaos and unreason. His pessimism was greatly intensified at the age of fifteen when his father remarried and his step-mother, in order to make a clean start, disposed of all the furniture, the children's toys and the established family servants. After his mother's death, Rivière identified his true home as the maternal grandparents' country house out at Cenon, and his excursions there became all the more desirable when his step-mother made it clear that she strongly disapproved.

When he arrived, still bruised and intense, at Lakanal, at the same time as Fournier, Rivière had already decided that he had no desire to become a Professor of Greek; the supreme consolation of his life was music and he had set his heart on becoming a music critic. When he came to Lakanal, he was confidently expected to achieve the most glittering examination successes, but he quickly found, like Fournier, that to dedicate himself single-mindedly to the syllabus called for personal sacrifices he was not prepared to make. His attitude was summed up in a letter he wrote to an old school friend in Bordeaux :

Here there is nothing but dictionaries and boredom. If your flesh and spirit can survive such a regime, then you're unbreakable for evermore . . . I weep for the poor stupid souls here, obstinately, ferociously and pitifully mutilating their lives.[7]

When, in the autumn of 1903, Fournier began his campaign against the Lakanal 'System', Rivière was quick to recognise a fellowspirit, though his own innate diffidence in public, together with his well-bred respect for convention, inhibited him from openly declaring himself.

51

THE LAND OF PROMISE

For a long time I maintained the strictest neutrality in this campaign which divided my class-mates into two groups. From early on, Fournier's personality particularly intrigued me. Out of all those boys, several of whom were schoolmasters' sons just as he was, and who were already showing slight signs of a staid and conformist University outlook, he really stood out as a free and playful spirit, his youthfulness overflowing. Whenever the all-enveloping school atmosphere got just a little too pedantic and artificial, he would find some comic formula for melting it and for giving us back that sense of fun we needed in order to breathe.

I watched him hatching his plots against the Establishment. I would read the little revolutionary petitions he used to circulate during 'prep'. I felt a bit scandalised, a bit intimidated, yet strongly attracted by his personality.[8]

Scarcely surprisingly, Rivière left it to Fournier to make the initial approaches, and these took the form of mocking banter or more exuberant horse-play such as the regular ransacking of Rivière's desk:

Time and again, I'd come in from 'break' to find my desk turned over and my books in disarray: Fournier had left his mark. I was absolutely livid with him. But he evidently liked me, and as I came to realise that he was sincere about it, I allowed myself to be convinced and finally won over. It was only then, I gradually discovered, that as well as having a militant streak, he had quite another side to his character which I could not fail to love. Beneath that rebellious exterior, I found he was tender, innocent, filled with the stuff dreams are made of, infinitely less equipped than I was to confront life – which is saying a very great deal.[9]

It fairly soon emerged that they had rather more in common than youthful innocence, distaste for the 'System' and emotional vulnerability: they also had similar tastes in the arts. This seems first to have been established – at any rate, publicly – in December 1903, when their French Literature teacher, Monsieur Vial, wished to thank his class for the traditional end-of-term compliments they had just paid him:

I gave ordinary schoolwork a holiday and started to talk to the boys about contemporary poetry; I spoke to them about Sym-

illage school at Epineuil-le-Fleuriel in the 1890s

au de Béthune at La Chapelle-d'Angillon

Photograph taken by Fournier of his family at his grandparents' house at La Chapelle in 1899. His mother and father are at the gate, his grandparents and Isabelle in front

Paris studio portrait of Henri Fournier, Spring 1900

bolism, read them some Symbolist poetry which was still very much a novelty and, in particular, some poems from *Tel qu'en songe* by Henri de Régnier. The pupils were all attentive but the way they divided themselves into two groups surprised me.

The 'high-fliers' displayed sheer astonishment : this was not at all like Boileau. But amongst the rest, I can still see two or three who had in no way distinguished themselves in academic battle who sat staring fixedly at me with passionate intensity. Alain-Fournier and Rivière were among them. I was struck by their attitude . . . This hour's reward was for them the great revelation. They plunged into poetry like divers into the sea.[10]

Once Fournier and Rivière had established effective contact with each other, they became almost inseparable. They would walk and talk interminably in the school grounds, visit plays, concerts and art exhibitions together whenever they could escape into Paris, passionately dissecting what they had just read, seen or heard, living the Arts to the full as only young people can. Their tastes were not identical, indeed the abiding interest of the voluminous letters they were later to exchange derives from their basic differences, but at the outset of their friendship, they were both equally enthralled by their explorations in the world of Symbolism. Rivière wrote later :

As soon as we got back from the Christmas holidays in January 1904, we abandoned so-called 'serious' work and revision for the Ecole Normale examinations, we bought the works of Henri de Régnier, Maeterlinck and Viélé-Griffin and we devoured them. I don't know if it is possible to get across what Symbolism meant to those of us who actually *lived* it. It was a climate for the spirit, a ravishing place of exile – or, rather, of repatriation, a Paradise.[11]

Though Fournier and Rivière were entranced by Régnier's romantic allegorical figures – Love sitting by a crystal fountain, sweetly plucking sad notes from his lyre, or Forgetfulness strewing dead petals from the faded flowers of yesteryear – what really transported themselves and their friends was Debussy's opera *Pelléas et Mélisande*. Based on Maeterlinck's play of 1892, the opera had its *première* in Paris at the end of April 1902 and, like Monsieur Vial's readings from *Tel qu'en songe*, it at once divided its audience into two hostile camps. The old guard were derisive, jeeringly called on Debussy to get back to music school and learn his trade, and quickly produced satirical parodies of the famous scene where Mélisande, from her tower, lets down her golden hair for her lover to kiss in the moonlight. For the young, of whom Rivière was an outstanding example, *Pelléas* was always much more than a theatrical occasion : the drama of the ill-starred lovers, the setting of the gloomy castle in the heart of a dark forest, above all, the haunting wistfulness of the music, combined to make each performance something like a ritual act of worship, demanding frequent attendance and total acceptance. Rivière, particularly, returned again and again in 1904 and 1905, and writing to him the following year, Fournier reported that he had just unearthed an old blotting-pad of Rivière's, with the names of the cast inscribed across it and the one word *Pelléas* written out fifty times.[12]

Both Fournier and Rivière responded enthusiastically to the appeal of Symbolism because since it was, in essence, a protest against a spiritually stultifying age, it served as a substitute for their lost religious faith. By the time he had made friends with Rivière at Lakanal, Fournier had ceased to be the pious communicant of Brest; Rivière, for his part, had not forgiven God for the death of his mother. Like many adolescents, they had come to look upon Church ritual as a hollow charade, they had scant sympathy for priests, and their own Bibles had for some considerable time remained unopened. Yet neither of them was temperamentally equipped to become a thorough-going atheist : each was firmly attached, as though by some powerful taproot, to his childhood, and in the private pantheon of each, a prominent position was occupied by a gentle and pious mother. If they could no longer accept the rites of the Catholic Church, neither could they subscribe to the faith of scientific materialism. The world of the minor Symbolists provided them with a richly satisfying temporary solution : it was musical and mysterious, it demonstrated that there was a world beyond the senses, it was vibrant with pleasurable emotions – emotions all the more pleasurable, poignant and powerful for being essentially vague. In a world which was still predominantly mechanistic and in a school which was rigorously utilitarian, Symbolism became for both Fournier and Rivière the inspiration of their hopes and the justification of their dreams.

For the young person fascinated by words, it is but a short step from enriching his imagination through the words of others to seeking to express it through words of his own, and in this respect, Fournier was no exception. In a letter he wrote to Rivière in the summer of 1905, he claimed that he had thoughts of becoming a writer from as far back as he could remember :

As long ago as my faraway childhood days in the country and my nights in school dormitories, plans began to be drawn in my mind which I didn't dare openly admit even to myself – plans to become a writer.[13]

In fact, the first recorded unveiling of those plans took place in a letter he wrote to Rivière in September 1904, after the usual family holidays in the Berry and the Sologne, and shortly before returning to Lakanal to begin his second year. He speculated on the secret lives lived by the country folk he had been observing around him :

> I would like so much to know why they're there and what they're doing there. There those countryman are, under their old rafters, in the darkness of their rooms which are scrubbed clean by their fertile wives, or bent low beneath the sun. They know nothing – except the mystery veiled behind the curtains of their vast beds in the dark corner of their rooms, hatred for the stranger passing by and love, quite inadequately expressed, for those members of the family who have gone away and whose much admired portraits still hang there on the walls.
>
> They're dreamers all, and the songs they sing are sad. They respect things we don't know and the language they speak is a song which is rough and chaste above all others . . . When I was a child, I used to roll in their heaps of hay. Now they get me to drink their sweet cider. My admiration for them goes on growing and I wish so much I could get to know them better.
>
> Drawing my inspiration from the nooks and crannies I've merely glimpsed, from a few furtive words here and a few faint and sudden blushes there, I've dreamed up so many lovely stories that I'll doubtless have to wait for ages now before I can sketch them in.[14]

A similar preoccupation with the rural scene is even more strongly evident in a letter he wrote to his parents on 20 March 1905, on the eve of the official start of spring. He was no longer quite as guarded with them about his nostalgia as he had been while at Brest, and he had already engaged in a bout of overt reminiscing about the past when he wrote to them from Lakanal in December 1904, gratefully recalling the presents they used to give him long ago on New Year's Day, and thanking them for surrounding him with so much goodness, security and mysteriousness.[15] In March 1905, he looked forward eagerly to the Fournier family reunion at Easter in La Chapelle, to where his parents had been transferred in October 1903; he gave himself up to the tide of nostalgia and allowed it to bear him and them far into the past, back to Epineuil:

Here [at Lakanal], the large blind of the big window looking out over the vast, depressing suburb, flaps to and fro; from time to time, either across my eyes or on to the corner of this letter, falls a bright beam of sunshine which is almost gay . . .

And yet I'm just a little sad at heart because all that this sunshine can light up around me here, are the dust-motes stirred up by the dirty, ugly boy beside me, and the dusty set books, always the same.

Because all that the great and glorious sunshine can now light upon is that dry, grey little playground where your pupils are shouting – pupils who aren't the brothers or the children of those who used to stay behind after school to play with me *in the other place*;

– because beneath this same sun, you have only a paltry garden, practically public property, where Mother with her sunshade and Father with his spade can no longer linger for as long as they please, for as long as they used to along the paths of long ago between our strawberry beds, near Old Martin's field, all big and still and silent, beside the stream which used to hide itself away in that field, covered with branches, full of shadows and mystery;

– because nowhere now can this sunshine light on the *things* I love and which belong to me – belong to me to such an extent that they're almost part of me – such as the hawthorn hedges in the garden, full of nettles, garden mint, chervil and sweet-smelling herbs; like the wistaria on the playground shed; like that little wooden door with the squeaking bolt which you'd pull back to find three eggs nestling in the straw.

I don't suppose that any of those things are part of *your* hearts because you'll scarcely even have seen them, because you were already grown-up and caught up in the business of living. But that is where we were just emerging into the world, and all that we've learnt to feel and know about our hearts, about happiness, about sweetness or sorrow, we learnt in the school playground where, on our melancholy Thursdays, all that could be heard was the crowing of cocks from the village, and in my bedroom where, through the fanlight, the sun would shine down on my two statuettes of the Holy Virgin and on the red cushion, and in the classroom where, as Father supervised 'prep', through the open windows would come with the branches of the apple-trees, all the gentle warm sunshine of five o'clock and the full, fine fragrance of freshly dug earth.

You simply have to realise that for me, all those things are all the world, and I feel that my heart consists of nothing else . . . I want to write books and books for you about everything *one* saw and felt in that little corner of the earth which was our whole World – and about the corner in my heart where it goes on living still.[16]

This exquisite exercise in nostalgia recalls, on more than one count, Proust's Combray: the nostalgia is deeply felt but finely analysed, and it is kept rigorously under control because of Fournier's care to record the specific causes of his emotion rather than the emotion itself; within its limits, it is a most effective piece of writing because he knows perfectly well both what he wants to say and how best to say it. In content and in form, it is quite different from the writing of the Symbolists whom Fournier so admired during the early years of his literary apprenticeship: while their abiding preoccupation was to evoke, by allusion and suggestion, the inner recesses of their own psyche or some ideal realm of Platonic essences, Fournier's concern here is, pre-eminently and directly, with remembered sights and sounds of an everyday country world. It was to take him some considerable time, and cost him no little anguish, before he re-discovered his own authentic technique and it is not markedly dissimilar from the technique deployed here in this moving letter, written while he was still a schoolboy. The letter clearly establishes that he was not mistaken in thinking he had a literary vocation, and incontrovertible supporting evidence was provided by his reactions to the experience of falling in love.

II

It was in the winter of 1903, during his first term at Lakanal, that Fournier first fell in love. In the course of his regular train-journeys from Bourg-la-Reine to the Luxembourg station in Paris, his attention was more than once caught by a girl of about his own age, who usually travelled with another girl as companion, and who seemed to look in his direction as often as he looked in hers. One afternoon, when Fournier was on his way to visit his friend Jean Bernard, he plucked up his courage and decided to follow the pair when they all alighted from the train at the Paris terminus. When the girls got to the Panthéon, Fournier took note of the route they were following, turned left round the building when they turned right, sprinted right round the block, and slowed down to advance on them with calculated insouciance, just as they were looking back to see if he was still following. He introduced himself with a bow and an extravagant sweep of his school cap, and when the mirth had subsided, all three went back into the Panthéon,[17] that monument to the nation's most illustrious dead where Fournier's own name is now inscribed.

The following week, the original girl of the train journeys met Fournier unaccompanied, and they spent a considerable amount of their free time alone together from then on. Her surname has never been divulged but her Christian name was Yvonne: she was slightly older than Fournier, a student, and, like him, came from the Cher region. So conscious was Fournier of his outward appearance that on four successive Sundays in the winter of 1904, he rented a bedroom in a small hotel near the Panthéon where he could change out of his Lakanal uniform into his most elegant town clothes.[18] He and Yvonne went for frequent walks together, went regularly to plays, to concerts and, inevitably, to *Pelléas,* and they exchanged books and letters; the letters were to provoke high drama in the Fournier household.

The separation enforced by the summer vacation could be endured only if letters were regularly exchanged, but Fournier was anxious to conceal the fact that not all of his time at Lanakal had been spent in study; accordingly, he arranged with Rivière and Yvonne that she should always use and be referred to by the male equivalent of her name – 'Yves'. In July, 1904, when Fournier was in hospital at Bourges for a minor operation, two letters arrived for him at the family home in La Chapelle. They were opened by Madame Fournier who was horrified to discover that they were highly scented and full of amorous protestations. Her fretful mind, always quick to anticipate the worst, quickly sized up the situation: her own Henri, the pride, joy and high hope of the family, and a mere eighteen years old, had taken leave of his moral senses; here was the *true* explanation why the boy who regularly came home from Voltaire, bent low under the weight of prizes, was now always floundering in the lower depths of his form at Lakanal: *cherchez la femme*!

Fournier, for his part, would offer neither apology nor explanation, and in August 1904, he wrote from his home to Rivière:

> For a fortnight now life has been intolerable in this house; I'm refusing to give any sort of explanation to those around me – or to unmask myself or Yves.[19]

He was sensitive enough to his mother's distress to undertake to mend his ways, and he promised solemnly that he would immure himself in Lakanal, even at weekends, in order to fulfil his promise of qualifying for the Ecole Normale Supérieure. He wrote secretly to 'Yves' to tell her of his situation and of his vows, assuring her that while he would certainly try to study more diligently, he would no less certainly continue to see her. Yvonne promptly replied, tearfully insisting that she had no wish to wreck his career, that he must carry out his mother's wishes to the letter, and as earnest of her honourable intentions, she left the envelope unsealed. Madame Fournier was again the first to read the contents, and the consequences were a violent attack of the stomach cramp which always occurred at the height of a family crisis, and a further solemn promise from Fournier to break the relationship and get down to some serious work.

The promise was not kept: he continued to see Yvonne and they were still very much in contact in April 1905 when he wrote the one letter to her which has survived, or so far been published.[20] It is a long, lyrical letter and not the least interesting aspect of it is what it reveals about Fournier's deeper feelings and his expectations of the relationship: this was unmistakably less frivolous and less trivial an affair than either he or his sister were later to consider.

The letter begins with fairly conventional protestations of gratitude and affection:

My Yvonne,
I almost knew you'd send me something yesterday evening. It's as though you guessed how much I needed late in the evening to have a sight of you, distant, happy, beautiful, in your room, surrounded by your chiffon creations and your white dresses – and so you wrote to me, all perfumed and tired after the dance, to tell me that I'm the one you love, that I'm the one you danced with all evening, and that you've stored up all the fragrance of your hair and the gaiety of your heart to send me yesterday evening.
Thank you, my darling.
Yesterday evening, I needed your joyful kiss on my lips. I was physically exhausted by that lecture which I began to prepare on Tuesday . . . and which I delivered this morning with your happiness in my heart, in a room full of life and sunshine, in front of sixty people who look, listen and understand.
It was a triumph, but I won't go on about that. I want instead to let you know that I'm tired, that I haven't really a minute to write to you and that in spite of that, Yvonne, I'm

59

going to write you a long letter, as you've asked me to, on the white and light blue paper which the prep-supervisor and Guinle have noticed, and which is there in my pocket with my poems to you, your letters to me, my dreams of love, and all that there is between us, my darling . . .

Then a decidedly more sombre note is sounded :

On Tuesday, as I walked along the cold and windswept paths of the school grounds, right through the grey and desolate afternoon, there was only one thing I wanted, just as there was only one thing I wanted to do the next day when I was close to you, and throughout the dreadful days which followed after : to nestle my head on your knees, bury my head in the folds of your skirt, and stay there for hours and let you soothe and console me – to know only you, to feel only you and your gentleness, the fragrance of you and the warmth of you. But, oh my darling, even your voice, your dear little voice, was hard put to it to drive away my despairing thoughts which caused me so much pain throughout all those days and which I went on suffering in silence even when I was close to you.

Oh ! how well and truly have those thoughts now returned, violent and profound, very much my sisters, which have no name, which I alone know, which take refuge in the very core of my heart when strangers are present and which flee away when you come to me . . .

But that evening, my darling, they wouldn't leave me. Back they came, bringing me such pain when you walked back with me, leaning on my arm and full of sadness too. I can't tell you how, the following morning, before going back to school, how I woke up thinking of life's last moments, or what I said in the course of the days that followed to my anxious friends like poor Rivière, or how, with all the frantic amount of work confronting me, I was able to do anything at all.

I won't tell you that I couldn't even think of you any longer, of what more I wanted, of the pain I found in everything.

But now I'm more or less completely cured. I love you. It's noon. In a couple of minutes, I think I'll go out, with my hair blowing in the wind, and my heart quite empty, and play football with all the enthusiasm I can muster . . .

It would be insane, cruel, impossible if you weren't to come on Sunday. Come. You're kind, you've given me a lovely surprise. I love you. Can I expect anything on Thursday?

For want of further reliable evidence, the cause of Fournier's despair at this period can only be guessed at. One ingredient may conceivably have been unspoken guilt over betraying his parents' trust or transgressing his own moral code, but the anguish seems more deeply rooted than simple remorse, to stem from some inner darkness which was born with him and to which he never really found an antidote.

The letter provides fascinating evidence not only of Fournier's emotional state in the spring of 1905, but also of his literary pre-occupations : like anyone who has ever been in love, he reiterates his regret, throughout the letter, that he should be separated from his beloved, but he also repeatedly expresses of concern that is the peculiar prerogative of the professional writer : the need to communi-cate the minutest details of his thoughts and the finest nuances of his feelings :

> Clearly what I must do is speak to you very slowly, and almost in a whisper, while I try to find the words to express what I felt, in order to make you feel it too . . . This is why I'm writing such a long letter to you, as I try to tell it as it was, to make you feel it as it was.
>
> It's absolutely heart-breaking when I've recalled some sweet memories of the past or been mulling over some deeply sad thoughts for some time, and I then try to convey these to you as we walk along the street. Everything vanishes away, every-thing is ruined by a smile, by words spoken too soon or phrases that are simply clichés.

As an example, he described in detail how his memories of going to Mass in Epineuil with his mother were suddenly and vividly brought back to him by the sight of Yvonne's button-up gloves,[21] and how distressed he felt because instead of relating the memories to her there and then, he diverted their conversation into triviality. His anguish here is not so much of the lover unfulfilled as of the author frustrated because he has not done justice to his story.

On other occasions, he was moved to convey the feelings she inspired in him through the more formal medium of poetry. The titles of some of these poems are now known[22] – 'A toi qui trembles à mon bras dans la rue', 'A celle qui n'est plus', 'Sur ce grand chemin' – but only two have to date been published in their entirety. Each is clearly derivative : 'Tristesse d'été',[23] evoking the melancholy aroused in him by the notes of distant piano music on summer Sunday afternoons, exploits a favourite *motif* of Jules Laforgue; 'A l'heure où vos doigts musiciens' is reminiscent in its languorous manner of Berlaine, although the subject – the young lover listening to his beloved quietly playing the piano in the dusk, and picturing her as his wife and the mother of his children – is quite distinctively Fournier's own :

> A l'heure où vos doigts musiciens
> Avec de calmes airs anciens
> M'apaisent,
> Au crépuscule des soirées
> Quand nos deux âmes rassurées
> Se taisent,
> Je songe à celles qui seront,
> Frêles et brunes au salon
> – A l'heure grise . . .
> Avant les lampes allumées –
> Petites robes, soies froissées
> Nos filles . . .[24]

In common with most lovers, both young and old, Fournier was only too ready to make light of his feelings for Yvonne when he fell in love with someone else, and just how much Madame Rivière shared Fournier's desire to play down the affair can be gauged merely from the dismissive title of the relevant chapter of her memoirs of her brother : *Rien de sérieux.* It surely ought not to detract from the great love which immediately followed to concede that the affair with Yvonne was, while it lasted, as serious as both partners were able to make it, and that it brought them both its due measure of pleasure and pain.

What Yvonne was really like, and how she viewed the end of the affair, must await further revelations that may never now be forthcoming, but that the affair was fated, sooner rather than later, to end, is not difficult to understand. Whatever her physical or intellectual or emotional qualities, she possessed one attribute which prevented Fournier from loving her on his own highly imaginative terms : she was *readily accessible.* It was difficult, therefore, for him to enact the rôle of his favourite literary heroes, Fromentin's Dominique, Rostand's Cyrano de Bergerac or Maeterlinck's Pelléas, each of whom worshipped from afar and was denied the great love of his life. Neither was it possible for him to live out in practice the theories expounded in Maeterlinck's *Sagesse et Destinée* which both he and Rivière discovered and profoundly admired in the course of 1904. It abounded in precepts such as 'It is with the so-called disillusionment caused by

little love-affairs that, most simply and surely, you feed the flame of
the great love which perhaps will light up the rest of your life', or
'Don't be afraid to have an ideal too lofty ever to be put into practice
in real life.'

Fournier's opportunity to love on terms closer to these ideals was
not long in coming, and it did so less than two months after protesting
his adoration for Yvonne – on 1 June 1905.

On 1 June 1905, Ascension Thursday, Fournier went into Paris to see
an art exhibition, the Fifteenth Salon de la Société Nationale des
Beaux-Arts, in the Grand Palais, which is situated between the
Champs-Elysées and the Seine. It was between four and five o'clock
in the afternoon as he came out to the head of the twin stone stairways
going down to the Seine and the Cours-la-Reine. He saw descending
the steps in front of him an elderly lady accompanied by a tall, slim,
fair-headed girl, so lovely and elegant that he at once took her to be
an actress. As she drew level with him, she glanced momentarily in
his direction. Her eyes were so intensely blue that for a moment he
stopped in his tracks. Then, as the couple moved slowly off along the
Cours-la-Reine, with the elderly lady doing most of the talking and
frequently laughing aloud, and the young one's head by now out of
sight beneath a white parasol, Fournier was drawn tremulously after.
He followed them on to a Seine river bus, and while it chugged its
way across the water, as often as he could dare to, he surreptitiously
observed them.

As soon as he got back to Lakanal, yielding to his chronic and
compulsive urge to transform all his experiences into words, he
scribbled down his impressions at high speed. The pages, wrenched
from a school exercise book, survive to this day, and the handwriting,
often quite unpunctuated, in contrast to his normally immaculate
script, is in places such a fevered scrawl as to be hardly decipherable :

> There's silence on the river banks almost solitude. The boat glides
> along to the quiet sounds of engine and water, through the white
> sunshine of the afternoon too calm. It seems to me we're going to
> land somewhere, she's going to get out, disappear, with the old
> lady, and that the house where they're going to spend the rest of
> this afternoon is in an excessively quiet quarter – perhaps in the
> outer suburbs, perhaps in the country, a house like one I know,
> with a space in front shaded by chestnuts, surrounded by walls
> where roses with four petals yellow and bright red shed their
> leaves and give out perfume too strong, too sultry and sad. I
> think of the dove-cot in the darkest corner of this garden court-

yard. All evening the doves and pigeons coo. She must come to read beside the dove-cot because of the shade but not for long because the cooing of pigeons filling each minute of long hot afternoon is too sad. I think of the corridor where the ladies who come to call leave their sunshades and of their talk which will go on till four or five o'clock when the gardens are cool while the children play and the ladies go past on the way out to dinner . . .[25]

Whether he thought all these thoughts on the deck of the river-bus or whether they flooded in on him when he sat writing shortly after, what is highly characteristic and immensely significant is that from the very outset, he is overwhelmed not by the immediate present but by the distant past : the beautiful blonde girl is not even mentioned; instead, there is a fond re-creation of one of the most treasured scenes of his childhood : Madame Benoist's house and garden at Epineuil.

Meanwhile, back in June 1905, after the river-bus reached the left bank of the Seine, Fournier followed the two ladies as discreetly as he was able. They eventually arrived, not at some rose-covered villa in the outer suburbs, but at an imposing house in the boulevard Saint-Germain, one of the most fashionable districts in the Paris of *la belle époque*. Fournier waited outside for a while, just in case a fair head might appear at one of the windows, then he hurried back to his room at Lakanal to write. He returned to the house to resume his vigil on every possible occasion thereafter : two days later on the Saturday evening, the next day, the following Thursday, and on the wet evening of Saturday 10 June, when the young lady parted the curtains to look out at the pouring rain. She was wearing black, she was holding a book and she smiled faintly.

The day after was Whit Sunday and Fournier returned early to his watch, convinced that she would be bound to emerge sooner or later to attend morning Mass at nearby Saint-Germain-des-Prés. He wanted to see and not be seen, so he chose a vantage point across the boulevard and some little distance from the front door. He waited. After some time, just for a moment, he turned his imploring stare away from the closed front-door, and there she was, on his side of the boulevard, walking slowly towards him. He moved forward; she noticed . . .

Later that day, he once again tried to ensnare in words his impressions of what happened. The writing, over the criss-cross lines of the pages of a school graph-book, is particularly feverish and disjointed :

A second's hesitation – a detour – she disappears behind a group, a bus, some conductors, then suddenly there she is on my pavement, on the pavement where I'm walking, fairly slowly, straight towards her as now she quickens her step. Three, four people pass by us – and then I'm in the cloud of her lace of her boa, of her dress, and I say as she passes, very close, in a voice I can't recapture, so close she hears, so quickly she's gone by, without reflecting, 'You are beautiful.' She's gone past – I think she's at her door, is going in, has disappeared, and without fully knowing what I'm doing, I move across to the left hand pavement, over there, the end of the pavement where the flower-seller is, where I turn slowly round, where I wait for the window – now I shall know, this is the minute . . . the window doesn't open – I take ten steps then turn round – window doesn't open – and then suddenly there She is, coming out again, *there* in front of me, walking quickly, looking straight in front of her (I say to myself half-aloud : My destiny, my whole destiny, my whole destiny – you exaggerate when you speak aloud to yourself) – goes into bus office – where is she going? This Sunday morning filled with the cries of flower-sellers, of sunshine, light coloured costumes coming from Mass, light coloured costumes going to Mass, light coloured costumes going to lunch somewhere. Is she going to lunch somewhere? I wait back on my pavement because on her account I'm afraid of the window.

The tram car. She gets on. Me too. Going up the three steps, our glances meet, her eyes turn away, stare elsewhere, slightly amused but very dignified terribly dignified. Now I'm on the platform. I don't think of anything in particular. I'd like to catch sight of her skirt. When is she going to get off? I think I glimpse her hand. Can't think of anything any more – long, long – where will she get off? – question . . .

Now she gets off – so gently, and the brown train of her dress is in front of my eyes, the whole long brown train – I've got to be very careful not to step on it. Ten steps along the pavement and I'm up with her by her right side and not too moved at first, without knowing what I'm doing, without knowing, I say to her : 'Say you forgive me for saying you were beautiful – for having followed you for so long.'

But, Sir . . . do you *mind* . . .'

Oh! with such finality! in a little voice so firm and disdainful, which leaves me shattered and crestfallen, classes her as one of those lovely young ladies who can go out walking by themselves, and puts me in my place in the gutter, shattered and crestfallen.

She goes on her way . . . crosses the square.

She went on into the great church of Saint-Germain-des-Prés. After a moment's hesitation, Fournier followed, to find she was already lost to view amidst the vast congregation of Whit Sunday worshippers. Mass was being celebrated not only in the main body of the church but also at other altars in various side-chapels. He edged his way through the ranks of celebrants who were crowding the very aisles until eventually, in the Chapel of the Sacred Heart, he saw her again, her back to him, kneeling in prayer, her impossibly fair hair flowing from beneath her rose-trimmed hat. He watched from beside a pillar till Mass was taken and he followed her out into the sunlit street outside.

Once again, this time on notepaper, headed 'Sceaux, 17 June 1905, "Continuation",' he set down what happened :

> After ten steps I'm beside her again. She doesn't look at me. She looks straight ahead, head held high, neck inclined slightly forward. And I say to her : 'Now you've said what you were bound to say, it's all over, you're not going to say anything else, it's really over, isn't it?'
>
> 'But – what's the point of this? (a very gentle but very firm little voice, which lingers a little over each syllable, less – but still very inaccessible) I'm leaving tomorrow . . . I don't live in Paris.' A glance all blue and despairing – and I say, 'Well, at least I'd like you to forgive me, Mademoiselle, forgive me for having embarrassed you and annoyed you.'
>
> Oh! and then, very sure of herself and of what she's saying, stressing each word as though she were defending someone,
>
> 'You haven't annoyed me. You did it very respectfully. I have no reproaches to make. I forgive you.'

Again she moved away from him; again he followed. She stationed herself by a bus-stop and Fournier suddenly realised he had no money to pay his fare. Again he spoke to her, again she reminded him that she was leaving Paris, again she asked the unanswerable question, *A quoi bon?* What's the point of going on? Buses came and went while they stood at the stop and then, finally, she agreed to walk with him back to the banks of the Seine.

Between the long periods of silence, Fournier did most of the talking. He revealed that he was still at school, that he was aiming for the Ecole Normale Supérieure, that his real ambition was to become a writer. She told him that her father worked for the Admiralty, that her home was in Toulon, and that her name was Yvonne de Quiévrecourt. At this point, Fournier later told his sister, he told her that the name he had already bestowed on her was rather more beautiful but he could not pluck up the courage to reveal that this name was Mélisande. His very first words to her – *Vous êtes belle!* – had been a doubtless unconscious echo of Golaud's opening words to Mélisande when he comes across her in the heart of the forest, *'N'ayez pas peur . . . Je ne vous ferai pas . . .Oh! vous êtes belle!'* And almost the last words Yvonne spoke to Fournier when, after their long conversation together, she prepared to walk away, are yet another, again no doubt accidental, echo of *Pelléas*. When Golaud sees his young brother Pelléas kissing Mélisande's golden hair as it cascades down from her casement, his first pitying and wondering comment is *'Vous êtes des enfants – Vous êtes des enfants.'* Yvonne de Quiévrecourt took her leave of Fournier with the words *'Nous sommes des enfants. Nous avons fait une folie.* We're children. We've behaved foolishly.'

She did not elaborate, and more than two years were to elapse, before Fournier was to learn that she meant him to understand she was already engaged to be married. At the end of that Whit Sunday morning in June 1905, he stood where she had asked him to remain, on the right bank of the Invalides bridge, while she walked back over the Seine towards the boulevard Saint Germain. More than three years afterwards he recalled :

> I leaned against a pilaster of the bridge and watched her depart. For the first time since I'd known her, she turned round and looked back at me. I took a few steps forward to the next pilaster, dying to rejoin her. Then, when she was much further away, she turned right round a second time, stood perfectly still, and looked back at me, before she disappeared forever. Was this because, silently, from the distance, she wanted to reinforce her order that I shouldn't follow her? Or was it to let me see her face to face for one more time? I've never discovered the answer.[26]

Over the months and years after she had walked out of his life, he was to brood luxuriously over that answer and, as he realised she was lost to him, to make each subsequent Ascension Thursday and Whit Sunday occasions for ritual mourning; nourished by that brooding, and enriched with the discoveries he made through his explorations of the worlds of Literature and Art, visions of Yvonne de Quiévrecourt were to haunt his dreams of human happiness and his plans for literary fame.

In the days which immediately followed, however, the scribbled notes on their brief encounter were, for Fournier, consolation enough. In any event, in the second half of June 1905, there was a powerful disincentive to brooding : the longest and most exciting voyage of his life to date lay immediately ahead of him : his journey to London.

III

The object of Fournier's visit to London was to improve his English and thereby enhance his chances in the University first degree (*licence*) examination in English he planned to take later. To further this aim, and to help pay his keep while in London, he was to work as a clerk for the well-known firm of wallpaper and fabric manufacturers, Sanderson and Co., of Heathfield Terrace, Turnham Green, and for his opportunity to do this, he had, once again, to express his gratitude to his influential friends, the Bernards. Léon Bernard, the elder brother of his friend Jean, was the firm's Paris representative, and he arranged for Fournier to be interviewed by no less a personage than Mr Sanderson himself. The interview took place in June 1905, Fournier made a favourable impression, and he crossed the Channel from Dieppe to Newhaven for his two-month engagement on 2 July.

Up till that date, Fournier had learned to look on England as a land of quaint characters and high romance; the quaintness was supplied almost wholly by Dickens, the romance by Defoe, by the anonymous creator of that adventure story read and loved at Epineuil, *Willie: l'écolier anglais*, and by his own Grandmother Barthe who had been loved – not very wisely and not at all well – by that fleeting English visitor in her youth.

On 3 July, in the first of his many frequent and perceptive newsletters to his parents, he reported back that he was finding it easy to make England and the English match his literary preconceptions:

> From the gare Saint-Lazare in Paris to Dieppe, I'm content to re-read the letters of recommendation with which I'm positively loaded. It's dark. I begin to get my own particular feel of England, and this consists of seeing it in the persons of an English farmer, his wife and a *little darling* [sic] through what I've read of England, especially *David Copperfield*. As a sample, it was thoroughly sweet and quaint. The illusion was made complete by two London workmen at the other end of the carriage, grotesque in their wretchedness, intermittently giving vent to their feelings with violent outbursts.[27]

In his much longer first newsletter to Rivière, he tried to recapture his impressions of the Channel crossing:

> I begin to want to see England through the eyes of Dickens. I invent a whole little novel about the English farming couple opposite me. I feel as though I'm going to spend my holidays in

the English countryside and that I'm a *schoolboy* [sic] from some provincial town. Of course, I realise this is merely literature.[28]

And in that same opening newsletter, he made his first (oblique) reference to Yvonne de Quiévrecourt and, at the same time, to the wreckage of his hopes at Brest :

> On the emigrants' deck. English ship. Sinister departure-orders shouted out which I don't understand. People start to walk about the deck. We depart. Once beyond the fairway, the darkness over the sea mingles in the mist with the lightness in the sky faintly dotted with stars. A ship like ours passes : that's to say, a shape in the mist perforated with lights. I'm irresistibly reminded of Whistler and his twilight seascapes . . . The crossing lasts six hours. One hour sitting drowsing, half an hour walking round the deck, and so it goes on.
>
> As each hour passes, the look of the sea changes. In the dawn, it's like milk, and a destroyer passes in the distance in the morning mist. I'm a little cold in my overcoat, I'm sorry that I'm not an ensign on that boat, that I don't wear a black uniform, live the tough, disciplined life of a sailor, so that I may one day go to Toulon to ask for the hand of a proud blonde girl whose father has five times sailed round the world.

But there was to be scant opportunity for vain regrets when he reached his destination and was confronted with the challenge of coming to terms with a wholly new world. For the duration of his stay, he lived in the west London suburb of Gunnersbury, at 5 Brandenburg Road, a name which, because of anti-German sentiment in the First World War, was subsequently changed to Burlington Road. He lodged with the chief secretary of the firm, a Lancastrian in his late thirties, with a wife and two small daughters, Clara and Florence : it was somehow appropriate, given Fournier's appetite for the quaint and charming, that his hosts' name should be 'Nightingale'. He was provided with a small room of his own, with lace-curtains, a gas wall-light and a selection of framed Biblical texts; the cost of full *pension* was twelve shillings per week. There were two other lodgers, the Misses Martin, of uncertain age, both teachers of French.

Each working-day, Fournier got up at seven o'clock in order to get to the office in nearby Turnham Green at eight. His hours of work were from eight till noon and from one thirty till six. His duties were to sort all the incoming mail, to keep the post-book and to translate business correspondence from and into French. He was paid ten shillings a week, no niggardly wage for a schoolboy in an age when an experienced British agricultural labourer was expected to raise his often large family on just two shillings per week more. His income was further supplemented by his father to whom he took considerable pride in sending the envelope which had contained the first money he had ever earned.

Life with the Nightingales was unpretentious and, for the most part, cosy. He particularly admired Mr Nightingale, fair-headed, a pipe-smoker, with an athletic physique and a sly sense of fun. Of Mrs Nightingale he was rather less enamoured, principally because she never gave him enough to eat. 'I'm more and more in danger of dying of hunger here', he wrote home to his parents after three weeks at Brandenburg Road.

> Mrs Nightingale has a way of saying '*Do you wish* another cake more?,' and stressing the *do you wish* to make it clear that what she really means is 'You *must not* wish, you have enough.'[29]

He complained that meals were always served without bread, that the bread was tasteless anyway, that he had to drink lemonade while he wanted wine, that there was nothing to eat between high tea at six p.m. and breakfast at seven next morning, and that he was apparently expected to eat marmalade morning, noon and night; the Nightingales, he felt, were like a pair of children, simply playing at cooks, serving up toy meals to be eaten with toy utensils. To assuage his hunger, he urgently begged his parents to send him some French breadrolls, but to enclose his English-French dictionary in the package as well, to enable him to avoid offending his hosts: his parents promptly complied, and he sent back a postcard of Grove Park, Chiswick, to thank them:

> The breadrolls, which tasted of dictionary, which weren't cooked and which were no longer fresh, were delicious.[30]

However, he found a great deal to admire in what he was able to observe of the London scene in that summer of 1905. He was lyrical over the high standard of English laundering and the glistening whiteness of his collars and cuffs was a source of constant delight to him. He never ceased to marvel at what struck him first of all on arriving in England and his particular corner of London: the cleanness and the greenness everywhere and not only in such obvious show-places as Kew Gardens, Richmond Park or Hampton Court, each of which in turn entranced him, but the sylvan calm of suburbia, which, to him, seemed continuously haunted by the sound of distant music.

'London is huge', he wrote in his first newsletter to Rivière,

There are innumerable villas *in London itself*. Without going on
about the greenery or the lawns, I would like, during those first
days here, to have stopped in front of every villa and to have
admired it in my own good time. Each one is like a miniature
château, so different from the villas of the Paris outer suburbs!
– with their solid little polished doors, exquisitely tinted windows
and stonework, lace curtains everywhere and the sound of piano
and flute music everywhere, absolutely everywhere.[31]

A fortnight later, he was writing to his parents about the London
Sunday:

On Sunday mornings, you get up late. For those who want to go,
there's the one Service at eleven o'clock. When you wake up,
you're struck by the silence of the vast city. Up till now, Sunday
mornings have all been cool and cloudy. You got the feeling of
any immense peace. All the trees and greenness everywhere made
you feel as if the enormous city had got up early and gone for
a Sunday nap out in the country.[32]

His favourite Sunday diversion was to visit London's major public
art-galleries: at the National Gallery, he was especially impressed by
Constable's *Valley Farm* but, most of all, by Turner's *Approach to
Venice*; at the Tate, the Pre-Raphaelites were what most engaged
his attention, in particular, Ford Madox Brown's *Christ washing the
feet of the apostles*, but most of all the canvases of Watts, whose
blonde and soulful female figures were always to remind him of
Yvonne de Quiévrecourt.
'I'd like to tell you about Her,' he wrote to Riviére soon after
arriving and while still taking stock in London.

Suddenly (after a period of near-forgetfulness and calm – because
I felt that a completely fashioned new presence was just about
ready to emerge and join my memories) I saw her face again the
other evening, so terribly clearly that I was moved to the heart,
moved to tears. I'm quite sure that this is something more than
a little romantic episode.[33]

From the beginning of his London stay till the end, he was quite
untempted by English girls. At the very outset, he reported his
impressions to Rivière:

71

Women. I can't get used to them. There they are, available, and you scarcely bother about them. The current practice is that a young man has his *girl* with whom he walks out quite unaccompanied, and on the very first evening here, my young English friend asked me if I had my own special girl back in Paris. Stupefaction! And then the way they dress in clothes that are too homely, too short and too light. It took me some time to work out what put me off the most : then I noticed that they don't wear corsets and the result is that everything they wear doesn't seem properly joined together. To add to that, they go round on bicycles, in masculine fashion with their noses in the air.[34]

Right to the end of his stay, after working beside three talkative girl clerks each day at Sanderson's and meeting other girls on such occasions as the annual works' party or the local Baptist Church Fête, he remained immune. At the beginning of September 1905, on the eve of his return to France, he met his English pen-friend, a Miss Lilian Weber from Bristol :

I've met my English girl who anyone other than me would possibly consider pretty. Very different physically from how I'd pictured her. Charming in manner, just as I'd imagined she would be. There must be some exquisite girls in England but they get too chummy too soon . . . She must have been surprised to find me so cold and reserved, so different from how she must have imagined me and from what everyone here imagines Frenchmen to be.[35]

To have melted his reserve and made a really durable impression on him, she would have had to approximate rather more closely to the ideal evoked in that letter to Rivière written at the very beginning of his visit :

As far as [English] women are concerned, I've nothing to fear. They're so very different from Frenchwomen, whose face is unknown behind their veil, who remain distant and silent in their distant, silent *salons* – so feminine, enveloped in their dark dresses.[36]

Fournier evaluated femininity as he judged landscape and all intimate personal experiences : their power to enchant him was always a direct function of their distance from him.

72

It was while he was working in London, that Fournier first began to consider his writing aspirations really seriously and to make his first real bid for public recognition : significantly, these plans for his future were closely bound up with both his immediate and his far more distant past.

On 13 August 1905, in the course of the longest letter he ever wrote to Rivière – in the original edition of their correspondence it runs to twenty-three pages – Fournier discussed his literary ambitions and how he hoped to achieve them. Although, at this stage, he felt best able to express himself in verse, like his two current literary idols Jules Laforgue and Francis Jammes, he already recognised that his true *métier* was going to be to write fiction. Three modes of novel seemed to him possible : the picaresque form, modelled on his beloved *David Copperfield*, consisting of a long series of loosely linked episodes, the unity of the work being ensured by the presiding consciousness of the central character; documentary Realism in the style of the Goncourt brothers, necessitating minute observation of the subject in the cause of photographic accuracy; and the so-called 'poetic' novel after the fashion of Laforgue's short stories, in which plot is minimal, and the emphasis throughout is on the wealth and richness of the author's own subjective impressions.

In August 1905, Fournier had no doubts that the Laforgue formula was what suited him best of all. What interested him especially, he claimed, was the inner world of the characters, what he called their 'dream-life' and this 'dream-life' he proceeded to define :

> What I mean by 'dream' is this : a vision of the past, hopes, a rèverie of long ago which comes back to mind while a new vision begins to fade, the memory of an afternoon set beside the white-ness of a sunshade and the freshness of another consciousness . . . The rest of characterisation is more or less mechanical – social or animal – and isn't of interest.[37]

What is offered here as an abstract formula is, in fact, the synopsis, in general terms, of a poem he wrote a month earlier and dispatched to Rivière on 23 July. Given the title 'A travers les étés', and firmly based on the scribbled notes he made on his brief encounter earlier that June on Ascension Thursday and Whit Sunday, the poem reveals how much more positively Yvonne de Quiévrecourt has now become linked with his lost childhood. He is not now content simply to imagine that they will walk together from the banks of the Seine into a quiet country house, complete with its shady garden and leafy dove-cot, and there be man and wife with children of their own; now he pictures her being drawn towards him through all the lonely summers of his childhood past, all the summers he has ever known, and that as soon as they meet in the calm, warm sunshine, they recognise one another at once.

Fournier's poem bears a triple dedication, 'To a girl, to a house, to Francis Jammes,' no thoughtless tribute but a carefully calculated acknowledgment of his chief sources of inspiration : Yvonne de Quiévrecourt is the female figure whose gracious presence rules the poem, while Madame Benoist's house at Epineuil provides the setting which is made to seem her natural and pre-destined home. Francis Jammes would appear to have provided Fournier with some of the poem's content and most of its form : the loose and irregular rhyme-scheme was very much a Jammesian trait, as was the simple and direct vocabulary, and typically Jammesian also, seem to be a number of specific details – the girl with the parasol, the old lady on her arm, the quiet country house with wistaria on the walls and cooing doves in the petal-strewn gardens, the book-prizes read in childhood. One of Jammes' novels is specifically mentioned in the poem, for long one of Fournier's favourites, *Clara d'Ellébeuse*, in which the seventeen-year-old heroine, woefully ignorant of the facts of life, exchanges a single kiss with a young man in *la maison fermée*, an abandoned cottage overgrown with wild flowers, and, believing herself to be pregnant, finally commits suicide.

Anyone knowing Fournier really intimately would at once have recognised that all the picturesque visual details of 'A travers les étés' were authentic reminiscences of his own past; to complete strangers, however, and, in particular, to literary critics well-versed in contemporary French poetry, it must have seemed almost wholly derivative. Not surprisingly, therefore, when he offered it to the editors of *L'Ermitage* for publication shortly after it was completed, they promptly but politely turned it down. *L'Ermitage* had been founded in 1896, was the leading Symbolist review of the day, and numbered Gide, Valéry and Jammes himself amongst its leading contributors. It was one of the several literary magazines to which Fournier, Rivière and their friends jointly subscribed at Lakanal, eagerly passing the quickly worn copies from hand to hand. To have been the first of the group actually to get into print would have been a formidable *succès d'estime*, but Fournier declared, when announcing news of his rejection to Rivière, that there was another reader whom he was even more eager to impress :

It is hard, I assure you, to reflect that at this very moment, there is perhaps someone very blonde, and possibly very determined, who has got herself a regular subscription to *L'Ermitage* and to the *Mercure* (*de France*).[38]

His rejection by *L'Ermitage* acted more as a spur than as a deterrent and in that same London summer of 1905, his thoughts began to turn towards something more like a novel, to what he was subsequently to entitle, *Les Gens du Domaine* (*The People of the Farm* or *The People of the Manor*). One of the very few fragments of the work which have survived and, almost certainly, were ever even written, was composed in London in August 1905, and was directly inspired by the spectacle of Mrs Nightingale and her infant daughter. It depicts a young mother, sitting in the summer sunshine, and patiently encouraging a little child to climb the few steps leading up to the front door of their quiet suburban villa. The chief interest of the passage is the evidence it provides of Fournier's abiding interest in the survival into the present of evocative relics from one's private past :

> Later, the mother found in a white box two bride's slippers, two slippers of white satin which she wore once, for one morning only, and which will remain there for the rest of her life to turn yellow with age in a drawer, two tiny slippers with high heels which aren't worn any more.
>
> The fair-headed baby is there too, its head very close to that of the kneeling mother. It stares unsmiling because its mother isn't smiling. And in that baby's fair hair, there will now always be a hint of the faded colours of those things from one's youth which you turn out under the hot roof, in an upstairs room.[39]

The same gently elegiac note is sounded in another poem Fournier wrote in London, 'Sous ce tiède restant', 'Beneath these warm vestiges' (of sunshine), which is addressed to Rosine Deschamps, the old countrywoman of 'Les Sablonnières', the tiny hamlet just outside La Chapelle-d'Angillon, whose little garden and orchard he always loved to visit : Rosine still bustles about her daily tasks, filling her apron with windfall pears from her orchard, spreading her laundry out to dry over her raspberry canes, but now she is old, the September gales are coming, the leaves and fruit will come tumbling down and her candle will soon be snuffed out; he alone, in the whole village, will remember her hard-working ways, and how, under the calm skies of early autumn, she would tell him 'old stories of her young time.'

Sunt lacrimae rerum et mentem mortalia tangunt, was Fournier's most fertile theme, even at the height of his youth.

There were particular reasons why Fournier should have become nostalgic in London's high summer of 1905 : the Nightingale family went off on a fortnight's vacation in the second half of August, leaving him alone in the house to fend for himself, and August was always a special month, reserved from his earliest childhood for his holidays in the Cher countryside. He continued to derive satisfaction from doing an efficient job at Sanderson's, and from coming across evidence of English quaintness – whether it was the little flags which bedecked the London omnibuses, or a hell-fire open-air preacher, shouting to the world and his wife that the Day of Judgment was upon them – but his heart was elsewhere.

In that massive letter he wrote to Rivière on 13 August, he went on from analysing his literary projects to evoking his country past :

> And now a section on the way in which I'm here beset by all my memories of past holidays which I'm now deprived of – all my memories of the countryside, now that the countryside is denied to me. From my present vantage point, I'm no longer quite sure whether I miss the countryside of some specific region, or the past times I spent there. This fills me with a very sweet and very profound emotion which we can call 'nostalgia for the past'.
>
> In this way La Chapelle-d'Angillon, where I've spent my holidays for the past eighteen years, seems to me the land of my dreams, the land from which I'm banished – but I see my grandparents' house as it used to be when my grandfather was alive : smell of the cupboard, squeak of the door, little wall with pots of flowers on it, peasants' voices, it stands out in such detail I'd need pages yet even to begin to evoke it. I even have to admit – and here my excuse is the deprivation I'm suffering because of all this English ham and jam – that I think longingly, so longingly, of the smell of bread which used to arrive at noon, the odour of the cottage cheese at four o'clock, Grandmother's cherry brandy, all the healthy scents of her cupboards, her wardrobes and her garden.[40]

As the end of his exile drew nearer, he wrote exultantly to his sister that he was determined to extract every last drop of enjoyment from the French holidays that would still be left to him :

> I want to cram into a fortnight the two months of holidays I haven't had, for which I've been sniffing for two long months like a tiger in a cage. I want to gulp down cubic kilometres of

76

country air after having had to swallow so many brackish, nauseating fumes in the factory; and I want to exercise my muscles, my biceps and calves, after being bent two and a half months over a desk, after being imprisoned two and a half months in a little second-floor room where my great (second prize for gymnastics) body could scarcely find room to move between the bed and the writing table. I want to get hungrier even than I am here where, to cure my craving for food, I'm given a sardine and two spoonfuls of jam. I want to get really hungry and then gulp down whole slices of vegetable garden and whole pails of cows' milk. I want it to go on and on – for two months. I don't want a single hour to go to waste as they so often are wasted hanging around the dining-room, or yawning because we don't know what to do. If I can possibly arrange it, I want every single hour of this coming fortnight's holiday to be planned in advance.[41]

In spite of his complaints of malnutrition which run like a refrain through his letters home, he was fortunate to have had the friendly Nightingale family as his hosts. For the rest of his life, he was to look up to Mr Nightingale as a representative of all that was best in the English character: reserved but warm, dignified but playful, firm but kindly. Conversely, he returned to France with a thorough detestation of the Francophobe's stereotype Frenchman, 'little men with goatee beards and moustaches, unable to control their tongue or their affairs.'[42]

He was fortunate too in having been sent to work not, as he might have been, to one of the less salubrious London regions to the east or immediately south of the river, but out in the west, to what was, in effect, virtually a garden suburb. In this way, the England he discovered was able to confirm all his poetic preconceptions of it and, for this reason, even before his characteristic nostalgia had had time to transfigure it, it very soon became a hallowed place to which he longed to return. Even before he left, in fact, he was planning to come back. Just before his departure in September 1905 he wrote to his sister:

Would you believe that before I leave, I must buy a present for the baby? I'd like to do this for my own satisfaction, to show Mr N. how grateful, how infinitely grateful I am, and also to leave behind me a corner of London which will be well disposed towards me later when I come back a year before the *agrégation* exam, with my expenses paid by the Ecole Normale.[43]

He returned to France on September 16, passing through Paris on his way to rejoin his parents in the Cher. Before catching his train to Bourges, he made a particular point of revisiting the banks of the Seine :

> I spent just one hour in Paris. For me, this was the crucial test. Without thinking of anything, I drove in an open cab to transport my trunk from gare Saint-Lazare to the quai d'Orsay. Once I got there, the Seine, the river banks, the bridges – all inspired delicious thoughts.[44]

Those thoughts doubtless lingered on when, a few days later, in the front garden of his grandmother's house in La Chapelle, he posed for the three most famous photographs which were ever taken of him. The background to each of them is the dense screen of vine-leaves which used to adorn the façade of the house : in the first, he is seated, chin cupped on his clenched left fist; in the other two, he is standing, wearing, in one, his Lakanal peaked cap and cape, in the other, his trilby, town suit and exaggeratedly high stiff white collar. It was his intention at the time to send a copy of one or all the poses to Yvonne de Quiévrecourt but, for reasons over which one can only conjecture, he never seems to have done so.

He enjoyed what remained to him of the summer holidays in La Chapelle where, he found, he much preferred listening to the drumming of the threshing-machine to coining aphorisms, and where he always readily gave up reading his Laforgue and his Jammes for a ramble to Neuvy-deux-Clochers or to Presly-le-Chétif. Inevitably, he derived great pleasure from the annual fortnight he was still in time to spend in his beloved Nançay but, possibly because the expectations built up in London were too great, or because the advancing years were bringing him more self-knowledge, he found the Sologne somewhat changed :

> My fortnight's holiday was quite unforgettable, though I'd be very hard put to it to explain why . . . I begin to feel less and less of a mediocrity when I'm confronted with men and with fields. Just as in England, it is from out of myself and myself alone that I draw the wealth of poetry with which I invest the most ordinary scenes.
>
> At Nançay, I found absolutely none of my impressions of bygone times, not even – or scarcely at all – on the road back. It's all changed now, and I'll probably now have to look elsewhere for my Nançay of yesteryear.

In the same way, all sorts of other long past impressions gradually go on getting enriched here, there and everywhere, and when you can carry them about no further, then, one day, you write about them.[45]

Fournier found time to write one more short poem before the end of the holidays, 'Premières brumes de Septembre'. It is a repository of his own private images of approaching autumn : early morning mist over the heather and the ferns, fires crackling in the household hearth for the first time in the new season, the breath visible from the nostrils of the delivery-man's horse, the villagers' conversations about the return of night frosts, chestnuts on the roads, and children being wrapped in shawls just before, in silent misery, they are driven away along lonely lanes. It is a rather more thinly orchestrated version of Laforgue's haunting ode to autumn, 'L'Hiver qui vient', and a line from Laforgue is, in fact, inserted at the head of Fournier's poem by way of epigraph, 'Believe me, it really is over until next year.'

However, in September 1905, life was too full for Fournier to brood for long : the Berry and Sologne landscapes lay all around, demanding to be explored on bicycle or on foot, and immediately ahead lay the long, heavy haul up to the entrance examinations for the Ecole Normale. He wrote to his parents on his return to Lakanal :

This year I'm going to force myself to think nothing, to feel nothing and *to be nothing* but a candidate for the Ecole Normale. Practice makes perfect.[46]

IV

No sooner had Fournier got back to Lakanal than he was submerged beneath a tide of black despair.

'Here I am back at school,' he wrote to Rivière on 4 October. 'As soon as I've got back, it's as though I'm being stifled. I'm making desperate efforts to regain all that courage and confidence which have drained away. It's a severe attack, dark and inexplicable. So sorry, old friend, to have to tell you this, but I have to tell somebody. I've so much need of courage . . . I miss you enormously. I'm so alone! so alone!'[47]

But this was one of the very few occasions in their lives when Rivière could provide no solace. In October 1905, he was even more in need of consolation than Fournier was. Because he wanted to acquire his qualifications with the minimum possible delay, and because he was reckoned to be a good examinee, Rivière elected to try for the Ecole Normale entrance examination a year earlier than Fournier. He failed, but narrowly enough nonetheless to be awarded a University scholarship of 1200 francs. Throughout August and September, there was still hope that he might be able to use it to study in Paris, but at the start of the new academic year, it was finally confirmed that it was tenable only in the University of Bordeaux.

At first, Rivière was quite inconsolable. To his friend André Waltz, to whom, back in Bordeaux, he would recite the names of the Paris *métro* stations as though they were a litany, he declared that he was ready to give up his scholarship and work as a bus-conductor or museum attendant or indeed as *anything*, just as long as he could go to a Paris theatre or concert hall each evening.[48] To Fournier he announced :

> I wept like a child when I learned the news yesterday evening. I never suspected the ties binding me to Paris were so strong. The thought of not coming back has made me suffer as I've rarely suffered before . . . At the present moment, while realising it would be the death of me, I long violently for the prison of Lakanal which, at least, I'd share with you and which opens up once per week. Here, the only hope left to me is a fortnight's escape to Paris about the middle of the year.
>
> You can't imagine how much I needed to see you again. I'd promised myself so much joy in the Sundays we were going to spend together. I felt so stifled at not being able to describe – and in that way *to define* – the multitude of impressions with which my heart is full. To calm myself down, I got into the habit of saying : 'In a fortnight now, I'll have someone to talk to.' Now it's impossible. We'll have to go on communicating by letter only, which means an end to direct contact, to the immediate exchange of thoughts and feelings. Now, almost reluctantly, I must think out what my ideas are, compose them for you instead of discharging them at you all alive and quivering. What a painful prospect – the worst I can contemplate ![49]

Because each went through his period of compulsory Army service at a different time, and under different dispensations, Fournier and Rivière were, in fact, to remain separated for the greater part of the following four years. The consequences were irksome and sometimes painful for them both but, for all other readers, immensely rewarding. What resulted, in fact, was an exchange of letters as full of artistic and human interest as any in French literature.

Each was intensely interested in himself and in the other; they felt not only free, but indeed *obliged*, to describe and dissect their emotional, spiritual and artistic development, and they did so with consummate sense and sensibility. At the same time, they were passionately preoccupied by the cultural world around them, at one of the most richly creative periods in French literary history, and without benefit of pundits or weekend colour supplements, they excitedly made their own discoveries, bravely backed their own winners and, no less fearlessly, burned their own idols. That the correspondence, like the friendship, should have been so exemplary was due, in no small measure, to the fact that neither was prepared to allow his deep devotion to the other to weaken the sense of his own individuality. They were drawn and held together, in fact, as much by their differences as by their similarities: they were both extremely sensitive, intuitive, and empathetic, both were inclined to make the most of their pain, but both were capable also of experiencing acute pleasure. However, while Fournier was content to *feel* and then, with all the verbal skills at his disposal, to express, Rivière's prime concern was always, meticulously, to *analyse*, the better to understand. For Fournier, the end of emotional experience was a story or a poetic image: for Rivière, it was a philosophical axiom.

The most striking – and the most fruitful – difference between them was in their approach and response to the work of others. Perhaps because his beloved mother died too young and he never accepted the authority of his father, Rivière was always looking for a Master who would assume control of his life and thoughts and whom he could serve as a disciple. To 'serve' the Master meant to explain and justify his writings to others, and in order to be able to do this, he was only too ready to allow his whole personality to be invaded and occupied. He wrote to Fournier, soon after the start of the new school year at Lakanal:

> I can't help laughing at myself when I consider my frightful plasticity. As soon as I find a thought which resembles mine, I abandon myself to it. I adopt the shape it imposes on me. I go deliciously inert. And then, when I examine myself, I wonder in some anguish whether I have any originality at all, so readily am I transformed. I think that my mind will assume every form that a mind can possibly adopt. But will it ever set?[50]

He need not have felt such concern: though he gave himself up so readily to the writings – and music – of others, he always retained his rare gifts both to analyse and to synthesize, to translate his always passionate responses into lucid words of his own. These powers of surrender and control were to establish him as one of the most brilliant of all twentieth-century French literary critics, and he learned most of the rudiments of his craft through his letters to Fournier.

When, however, he began to exercise his still developing skills on Fournier, the response was not always favourable. Fournier was quite prepared to reveal aspects of his personality in his own time, and on his own terms, but efforts to wrest them from him, or to explain them by some formula, were violently repulsed, as though they were attempts upon his virginity. After one more move to label him he wrote to Rivière :

> I, sir, don't go in for theories, and I'd be extremely hard put to it to classify myself. I'm revolted when you find any sort of classification for me, no matter how brilliant or beautiful it may be. Firstly, because if I let myself be seduced by the terms of your formula, that always cramps my thoughts and feelings for at least a week. And then because it makes me long to shout out : What a nerve ! Just because I've performed a host of little gestures in front of you, and said thousands of insignificant little words – the majority of which were made or said automatically because I already knew the false image you had of me and, in spite of myself, I didn't want to disillusion you – the sheer nerve of it ! You tell *me* that you know what makes *me* tick, you who don't even know how many little girls I once loved or the colour of their dresses, how each of those loves was different, each one unique, each one new beneath the sun, you who will never, never know a single one of the landscapes where I grew up . . .[51]

And some months later,

> Most of all, you must flee from those who claim to be your friends, that's to say those who claim to know you and who brutally explore you . . . All those who have concerned them-selves with my life have bruised me.[52]

For all these vehement strictures, Fournier was subsequently to recognise that as a friend and critic, Rivière was someone quite exceptional, and he never expressed his sense of indebtedness more eloquently than in a letter to his mother, written from the depths of despair while he was on Army service :

> At this time when I've been shorn of all superfluous thoughts and all pretentiousness, when out of all my impoverished desires

only the most vital one remains – a desire which doesn't even have a name, I clearly see that the only person who has been able to help me get close to the unknown and very special world of my yearning is Jacques Rivière, with his limpid theories, and his great, so-called abstract writings.[53]

No less a personage than the great Paul Claudel was to make much the same point with similar eloquence when he gratefully wrote to Rivière in 1911 :

You are that ideal reader of whom every author can't help thinking whenever he writes.[54]

Both Fournier and Rivière were voracious readers throughout their lives, but at no period were they able to read more voraciously than the years 1905–1907 when they were free to follow their literary fancies down every inviting byway. In that period alone, their letters mention the names of over one hundred different authors, almost invariably accompanied by an evaluative comment, and often with long paragraphs of polemic, as each seeks to infuse the other with the delights of his latest discovery. Here again the letters are enriched because of the differences between the correspondents who find themselves challenged continuously to explain, to justify, to persuade and convince.

One of the crucial differences between them as readers was in their approach to the text before them, a difference which Rivière identified for Fournier with characteristic precision :

When *you* read, you quickly extract from those authors you admire what you consider essential or novel because you have your masterpiece to write, and this so preoccupies you that you look on everything in the world around you as so much raw material. In one sense, you *comprehend* nothing. But I, for my part, have nothing to do but comprehend, so I leave myself empty for the next invasion, and it's essential for me to be passive, and, in the first instance, to become the body and soul of whoever I yield to, so that I can understand him and possess *him* in my turn . . . But you are a creator, which means that other people are there simply to teach you about what your own resources are, and how to tap them. Your chief reason for liking them is because of the services they render you.[55]

In fact, as schoolboys, both Rivière and Fournier read literature ın a highly idiosyncratic manner, but what is even more interesting than the different ways in which they came to their texts were the different things they took from them. In the years 1905 and 1906, each strove, with considerable energy and ingenuity, to convert the other to his own particular cult. Because of temperamental differences which owed much to their different past experiences, their efforts were largely in vain : Fournier could never subscribe, as passionately as Rivière did, to the doctrines of Maurice Barrès, for some years the self-styled 'Prince de la Jeunesse', who, in the novels of his 'Culte du Moi' series, demonstrated how the idealistic young should disdain their uncomprehending elders and boldly and elegantly develop their own distinctive style; for his part, Rivière was never able to share Fournier's enthusiasm for the studied rural simplicities of Francis Jammes, or the whimsicality of Jules Laforgue whose irony, as Fournier was very quick to point out, only thinly disguised his need to be loved and his fear of being hurt; and unlike Fournier, Rivière remained wholly unmoved by the gently languorous verses of the Belgian Symbolist Charles Van Lerberghe who in 'La Chanson d'Eve' (1904), expressed Eve's regret at being banished from the Garden of Eden :

> Comment ce qui, dans le matin,
> Etait si proche de ma main,
> Que tout, il semble, s'inclinait vers elle,
> Ce soir est-il devenu si lointain?
> O paradis de mon âme ingénue,
> O beau jardin de mes rêves d'enfant,
> Sans même que l'ombre d'une nue
> Légère ait éteint un instant,
> Sur la terre, ton éternel printemps,
> Sans qu'une fleur se soit flétrie,
> Mon paradis t'ai-je perdu?
> Sans le savoir, de toi suis-je bannie?

Fournier's heart could not fail to be touched by this poem because, as his childhoood receded into the past, the theme of lost paradise was more and more becoming a particular preoccupation of his own. Similarly, in 1905 and 1906, he responded much more excitedly than Rivière to Wells, Kipling and Hardy because each of these in turn struck an answering chord deep within his nature : with *The Time Machine* and *The First Men in the Moon,* it was the exultation he always felt at the prospect of departure, and, significantly, his chief criticism of Wells was of what he considered to be the unexciting worlds created for the characters when they reached their journeys' end; *Kim* appealed to his love of play and to his appetite for the exotic, and *Tess of the D'Urbervilles*, not only to his love of the countryside, but to his haunting sense of a happiness so near at hand as to be almost tangible, yet for ever tantalisingly just beyond the reach. For this reason, he had no hesitation in passing on to Rivière the brisk command of their Lakanal Philosophy teacher, Camille Melinand, an idealist and himself the author of a study on childhood psychology :

> Don't live a month longer, not a single month, without reading *Jude the Obscure* and *Tess of the D'Urbervilles*. They're greater than the greatest of d'Annunzio and the best of Tolstoy . . . I can't, unfortunately, think of a French writer to touch him.[56]

Throughout the school year 1905–6, Fournier's dreams of earthly happiness were confirmed and fortified by his discoveries both in the world of books and in the world of painting. On 1 November 1905, he attended the Salon d'Automne exhibition and was suddenly stopped in his progress round the gallery by the sight of a small canvas by Georges Decote, a pupil of Gustave Moreau's. He described the experience to Rivière :

> It was a lady at the piano, her back towards me, with blonde hair and a large chestnut brown cloak . . . I simply couldn't tear myself away. I hadn't had such a precise reminder for two months. I would have given my dying oath that it was Her, tall like her, with her head inclined slightly forward, sitting there in the dusk.[57]

A few weeks later, still haunted by piano music, he wrote to his sister at her boarding-school in Moulins :

> I'm writing this on a Thursday afternoon. The school grounds and the landscape are lost in fog. These are always the most morose and misty hours in the whole week. They generally make me think of the afternoons children spend in drawing-rooms, where someone is playing the piano, where the little girls wear muffs and toques made of otter-skin, where they browse through books of illustrations, where they play at lotto, near at hand to me here in Paris or far away in the country, in some village château.[58]

These images of November, his own memories of children peacefully at play indoors, together with his impression of Decote's picture, were stored away for his own future use beside his recollections of that real ride over the Seine in June and the imaginary walk to the house with the dove-cot. To these were added in January 1906 a few lines copied from another letter he wrote to Rivière about Yvonne de Quiévrecourt:

I'd like to have conveyed to you just how sad it is when you lose a lovely image. When shall I find it again?

O, the efforts I've made to recall her each evening! The eyes of one of Botticelli's Madonnas helped in London. Elsewhere, I've been able partly to recall her smile, partly her mouth, partly her hair. How, *how* can I remember?

Then there's that marvellous, melancholy dream which is almost real: young and lovely ladies going past all in a line. One has a hat like hers, one is leaning forward as she did, one has a light brown dress like hers, another has the blue of her eyes, but not one, not a single one – however many go past, however long I stare – not one is *her*.

That's what I dreamed. And every evening that procession moves through my memory – sometimes, indeed, down our splendid streets.[59]

In January 1906, in the Christmas vacation at La Chapelle, he wrote the last but one of his adolescent poems, 'Et maintenant que c'est la pluie', which is full of cross-references to 'A travers les étés', and, in fact, acts as a pendant to it. The January rains and high winds have come to destroy every last vestige of the previous June; the wistaria has been ripped down from what would have been their arbour, the birds' nests are scattered and rotting, umbrellas have replaced parasols, and pools of water stand on the gravel paths down which she might have walked with him. He wonders where she now may be, and whether she might be standing pensive somewhere beside a casement window:

Elle est très loin . . où est-elle . . son front pensif appuyé à quelle croisée?

He resolves to close the window-shutters flapping noisily in the wind, and to bring in the one last relic of the summer, the neglected croquet set all wet with rain.

It was also in January 1906, during the Christmas vacation, that his thoughts turned once more to *Les Gens du Domaine*, the novel he had vaguely begun to consider during his London summer of 1905. His plans over the intervening months had grown no clearer, but they centred very definitely on a past which was just beyond his own reach, yet near enough to be personally recalled by others. If the reminiscences were vivid enough, he could almost believe that they were actually his own:

> I've been making my grandmother talk a great deal about what it was like round about 1850. I listen for the fifteenth time to 'The Social Evening at the Laurents Farm' or 'The Meeting at the General Market'. It gets more beautiful each time it's told. Each time I'm on the look-out for the word or the tone which evokes something different, because she is someone who was actually there.[60]

Essential though it was for Fournier's own fulfilment to write copious letters to Rivière, to dream his dreams of Yvonne, to read so indiscriminately and to polish away so doggedly at his own literary plans, as far as his Lakanal teachers were concerned, this was all time and energy wasted. He had begun the school year in promising style by coming fourth in class of thirty-eight for translation into French, and he was even top, from time to time, for a Latin translation exercise, but, almost invariably, he finished very well down in the form-order. He remained totally uninterested in History and Geography, and consistently sub-standard in translating from French into Latin or English. Living and working in England had brought inevitably some improvement in his command of English, though that there was a certain need of improvement might be judged from one of the few English sentences he proudly wrote back from London to his parents:

> I was very astonished by hearing of 14 July. I had quite forgotten. Good 14 July![61]

From the point of view of the impending Ecole Normale examinations, Fournier's trouble was that he was far too easily distracted, and that he reserved for his distractions the wholehearted commitment he should have given to school work. He described his mediocre results in a letter to his sister in November 1905, when he also revealed that he was still very much the active rebel at Lakanal that he had been from the outset:

> I grow more and more stultified with each passing hour. My

87

school marks are adequate but no more than that. I translate elegantly into French and execrably out of it. I can't help taking more interest in the English Pre-Raphaelite poets than in Spenser Edmund [sic], and in Jammes than Montaigne. I struggle on and the lamentable result is neither one thing nor the other, something between mediocrity and torpor. What I mean by this, is that I've given up my own writing and my own thinking, yet I'm not really a better student for it. I've vague expectations of making progress but no real hope.

My great aesthetic pleasures at present are to rag junior masters nobody else has the nerve to rag. This is sad. All the same, one of the least stupid of this year's bunch has just sent a short article to *La Libre Parole* [a leading Right-Wing newspaper], in which he denounces the so-called revolutionary, internationalist spirit of the lycée Lakanal, which he depicts as full of Jews and foreigners and where the few patriots who sing the *Marseillaise* in the games' room are howled down by almost everyone, and persecuted by the headmaster.

In point of fact, even though the incident reported did indeed take place, the lycée is a den of Jesuits and the headmaster a hundred times worse than any Jesuit.

What we needed to do was write a piece attacking him, and publish it in the paper of any party who'd take it, to hurt him in any way possible, bring the maximum possible discredit on this individual, who has built up the lycée's reputation and his personal fortune on downright lies and false claims, this creature whose talk is always filthy, who holds on to you and sneers as he speaks to you, and spits in your face while prating about family life.[62]

Fournier dedicated himself as energetically to his friendships as he did to this rare example of his hatred, and a keenly awaited opportunity to practise the arts of friendship presented itself in December, when Rivière was finally able to escape to Paris from desolate Bordeaux. It was just before Christmas and Fournier elected to spend with his friend some of the time he could have spent with his family back in La Chapelle. Between the time when Fournier met the train, at half-past-five on the Saturday evening, and saw Rivière off, at seven o'clock on the following Tuesday morning, they had been to the Paris Opéra and to the Théâtre-Français, attended a Wagner concert, visited the Louvre, especially to study the English Pre-Raphaelites, listened to a Palestrina recital in the chapel of the

Sorbonne, and talked long hours down the nights and down the days about themselves and about everyone and everything. Fournier described a typical bout of conversation to his sister :

> I take Rivière along the Champs Elysées. Night has fallen. He has to dine with friends of his parents. It's Christmas Eve. All along the Champs Elysées and behind the Palais de l'Automobile, there's a background of red glowing. Motor-car headlights flash their beams all over the sky. We have a long delightful conversation about philosophy, Schopenhauer, Leibniz, Hegel and Pascal. Then Renan. Then Barrès, on whom Rivière is shortly going to publish a long study in a review. Quickly we walk, so quickly, and all we see is our thoughts. We touch everything with the tips of our fingers.[63]

Three months later, Fournier threw himself almost as enthusiastically into the role of companion and guide to Mr Nightingale when he came to Paris on a ten-day visit and when, once again, Fournier was lost in admiration :

> Like many Englishmen, he's a poet and doesn't know it, a poet of the home and the country. He has this air of putting his soul into everything he says. All Frenchmen seem tiny little flibberti-gibbets beside this blond giant with a head like an eagle who, in those areas where he doesn't operate like a machine, is a mere child.[64]

Fournier's consistent lack of conviction in his 'official' studies was matched – and in large measure caused – by his chronic uncertainty about his future career. The Ecole Normale Supérieure was – and still is – one of the greatest teacher-training colleges in the world, but as his schooldays dragged on, Fournier found the prospects of teaching less and less attractive. He wrote to Rivière near the start of the spring term, 1906 :

> I keep telling myself that I'm quite incapable of passing this examination.
> And supposing I did succeed, a fine situation I'd be in then! A University scholarship or even – *even!* a teacher with a ten year contract!
> Anything rather than having to go on being shut up like this, physically and mentally.
> The thought of living with other junior masters, living with

people whose job it is to take the heart and soul of the past and serve it up as so many formulae – and I'm supposed to torture myself wearing my brain out for the privilege of doing the same thing![65]

A week later he wrote to his sister :

My life shouldn't have to be swotting for the *agrégation* till I'm mentally exhausted. I'm searching for what my life should be.

The only remorse I feel is on account of my parents. For a long time now I've ceased to see things through their eyes. I shan't realise their ambitions for which they've sacrificed a great deal of money. Yet all the same, I did try to give them the happiness they wanted by renouncing my true life, that's to say, working for the Ecole Normale exam and forgetting my poetry and the Berry. I now find this quite beyond human capability.[66]

Fournier thought long and hard about the French Colonial Service, an idea which first came to him while he was in London. To Rivière, he listed other possible alternatives :

I could be an English clergyman, a priest like [the poet] Le Cardonnel, a justice of the peace like Sébastien-Charles Lecomte whose verses I've been browsing through this morning, I could be an accountant in Fou-Tchow. *Anything*, as long as I can call my brain my own![67]

About one thing alone did he remain adamant in the midst of all his other wavering : the only sure way he could find fulfilment was through writing, writing at his own pace and on his own terms. In February 1906, he wrote to Rivière :

The main thing is my horror, my dread of being given a label. I'd rather be nothing at all than scribble away after the fashion of the Symbolists – rather a long way after.[68]

A month later, he declared to his sister :

I want my own personality to burst forth. I know there's *something* there inside me, something very fresh and new. I'm not going to take my little poems which are partly me and partly – through no fault of my own – other people's, and go cap in hand to the poetasters now in vogue asking to let me join their group and write verses just like theirs.

I'll give up writing altogether for a little while if that's possible. I'll find something that pays 6,000 francs a year and then I'll really be *myself* – that's to say, perhaps a peasant in Marçais with the gift of the gab.[69]

Fournier found another powerful disincentive to study with his realisation that the Ecole Normale entry competition was going to coincide, more or less, with the first anniversary of his meeting with Yvonne de Quiévrecourt and as early as February 1900, he was complaining to Rivière :

Imagine what it's going to be like doing Prose Compositions and History in June, on Ascension Day, instead of standing looking up at a window, under the trees all leafy and buzzing with life, at the fall of the summer's night. After my pilgrimage between the shrubs and along the well-watered wooden walk of the Cours-la-Reine, backwards and forward, waiting . . . Just imagine it.[70]

And in that same letter, he demonstrated how the far-distant Yvonne and his lost childhood had now merged with his favourite Pre-Raphaelites in a vision of all that he most desired and all he could never be :

Profile of Beata Beatrix. Glance intensely blue like Botticelli's Madonnas, extremely distant and haughty like the women of Dante Gabriel Rossetti, extremely confident and frail and blue like *Life* by Watts – you're buried in the flowers of the Summer as those tall bodies of Watts are enveloped in drapery. You're the whole of art and literature, and the whole of life too! O, your fragile soul of old satin and yet, behind it, all that ardent life along the gravel drive and across the lawn in front of some château, or my grandmother's front garden, with her pots of heliotrope on the little front wall, or sitting round the blackened table of country folk who feed themselves on potatoes, hard work and tales of old – because your soul is simple, old-fashioned and true, as mine is. Your soul bestows on the Rossettis and the Watts all the delightful atmosphere that make up the little happiness I can enjoy on my closed-in Thursday afternoons, staring at them in my little cell. O my slim-waisted girl! Never again will I see your big brown cloak. And never will I be able to bury my head or my heart in one of its folds, my heart so full of all the horizons, of the sounds of distant trains and cock-crows. Never will I be able to shed soft tears there after we've got home from some afternoon visit.[71]

In his more realistic moments, Fournier knew that he had no more hope of seeing Yvonne again in June than of satisfying the Ecole Normale examiners, but over the weeks and months that followed, he prepared for his encounter with each.

The atmosphere at Lakanal was not exactly conducive either to melancholy meditation or to concentrated revision because at the beginning of April, the troubles of the previous November once again flared up, and Fournier and three other schoolboys were given two and a half days' detention. He wrote to Rivière :

We weren't actually caught, merely picked on as the ringleaders. The whole lycée is up in arms . . . I'm not a revolutionary : I'm merely revolted, just as I used to be, that's the long and short of it.[72]

A fortnight later, he was writing :

Till the Ecole exams are over, go on writing to me whether I reply or not . . . These are hard times. I'm desperately in need of help. In every sector, I'm in critical condition.[73]

On the anniversary of the day of his first sight of Yvonne, he returned to the steps of Grand Palais at the precise time of the original meeting. He wrote afterwards to his sister :

Last Thursday, on Ascension Day, I went to the Société Nationale des Beaux-Arts. I was as beautiful as an angel in my dark suit, with my long hair and my black hat. But I didn't really expect anything, anything at all, and the result was that nothing happened, that nothing could have happened.[74]

To Rivière, he commented :

She didn't come.
For a long time, I'd told myself simply this : one Thursday, on Ascension Day, we lived that beautiful episode which I've described to you. We have no acceptable way of re-establishing contact, and all that we had in common between us, as the

saying goes, is that we knew the day and the time and the place of our extraordinary adventure. So I kept telling myself : she *might* come.

But for a long time now, I've known that she *couldn't* possibly come, and now, more than at any other time, I know how right I was.

In any case, even if she had come, she would not have been the same.

And if she ever does come, she will not be the same . . .

Later that evening, I think – though I can't be sure – that I went with Chesneau to the Folies-Bergère, or something even worse.[75]

He never elaborated, at least in print, on that final comment, and one is tempted, therefore, to interpret it as mere bravado, or as an aesthetic rather than a remorseful moral judgment.

In the first week of June, he sat the written papers of the Ecole Normale entrance competition in a state of nervous and physical exhaustion, running a high temperature and stuffed with caffeine and with glycero-phosphate to keep him awake : he felt he had made a reasonable showing with his Literature answers (English : 'the simplicity of Wordsworth' and French : 'the Romanticism of Molière's *Don Juan*), but performed appallingly in History ('the struggle between Parliament and Monarchy in the 18th Century), and in Philosophy ('the logical and psychological conditions of certainty').[76] He now had to wait to see whether he had performed well enough to be allowed to proceed to the second – and even more formidable – oral stage of the examination, and he wrote to Rivière for consolation. Rivière did his best to help, though he had just been called up and was himself despairingly trying to come to terms with the filth and brutality of Army service.

While preparing as best he could for the oral examination, Fournier found some consolation in once again playing a leading role in yet another campaign of protest against the Lakanal authorities. He wrote to Rivière at the end of June :

I am happy to announce that the stupid rabble here have now been smashed : I heckle Loule from my desk, asking him to have the goodness not to look at me. There's been such a revolt in the school this time, so many cat-calls, so much chanting, then so many sudden and protracted pre-arranged silences, that when Bazin finally came into the refectory, they surrendered. The day before yesterday, there was a session (which I didn't take part in) when Bazin tried to brazen things out. He sat on a chair behind a second year suspect, and he coughed and went white and red by turns in a terrifying silence, under the gaze of 120 pupils. He summoned two Philosophy suspects whose parents are well-connected, and in a fit of frankness, they let him know all we think and say about him. 'And how long are you going to go on in this vein?' he said. 'We've no intention of stopping. The best thing you can do is not come back.' As a result, he's now ill in bed, and all the punishments have been annulled.[77]

A week later, Fournier was in bed too, in the school sanatorium in a state of complete nervous exhaustion. It was almost with relief, therefore, that he received the news that he had performed so catastrophically in the written examinations that he was ineligible for the orals, and that he had permission to leave, before the official end of term, to recuperate with his family back in La Chapelle.

V

On the last day of July 1906, Fournier wrote from the schoolhouse at La Chapelle to congratulate his Lakanal school-friend Bichet on his achieving a brilliant pass in those same Ecole Normale examinations; he went on to report that he himself still had not recovered from his harrowing ordeal and described his attempts to find a cure :

At the present moment, I can neither read nor study nor even take part in a long conversation. I was several times afraid that I was going down with cerebral fever or cerebral anaemia.

Each evening I go for a bathe in the meadows : there's a bend of the river there, where I swim for a quarter of an hour at a time . . . I've been to visit a mill in Le Gué de la Pierre, the district where I was more or less born, where the hamlet is so tiny it's enclosed with its public square within a hawthorn hedge. It's all on such a miniature scale that when you go through the hedge it's like entering someone's garden. Then you see it's a little village because there's a school in what was once a blacksmith's shop, a letter-box on the wall beneath a vine plant, and three old biddies making shirts under the shade of three lime-trees.

The day before yesterday, I went to the fête at Presly-le-Chétif in a light cart, with a friend's little girl on my lap who was

94

holding a sunshade no bigger than a mushroom. There were characters selling caramel, fun-fair booths, lemonade, girls dressed in white and in red, with the black imprints of their dancing partners' hands on the backs of their blouses, a clarinet and a violin – and then, in the inns, the farmers, who have come from a long way off riding on their mares, shy in manner, rough in speech, all freshly starched, who are offered a drink and who, in their thick country brogue, ask for the hens to be put in a loft up above the stable.

I'm going to take some photographs – but nothing picturesque. The only photographs I'll take will be of bunches of onions and beetroot and sheaves of corn for my father. The captions will read : 'Without sodium nitrate', 'With nitrate'.[78]

Further distraction was provided by an exotic temporary lodger, a rich young Panamanian student whom Fournier had brought from Lakanal. His name was Don Pedro Antonio d'Aguilera, and although he was only twenty-three years old, he claimed to have already served as a judge and as a lieutenant colonel in a civil war, when he had been regularly fired on by boys of eight and ten. While staying at La Chapelle, he was supposed to improve his French while giving Fournier Spanish lessons in return, and in one language or the other, he would describe the fauna and flora of his colourful country, the high clear waterfalls, forests of dreadful night and the vast estates of his enormously wealthy mother. Inevitably, the wanderlust of the Fournier menfolk was once again rekindled : Fournier *père* was to go as a teacher and, because Aguilera was an intimate friend of the Minister of Education, he could almost be guaranteed the headship of a college; Fournier *fils* would perfect his Spanish and push ahead with his plans to enter the Colonial Service. When Aguilera went so far as to write off to his friend, the Minister, and the Fournier parents themselves set to work to learn Spanish, Fournier was suddenly filled with misgivings :

> I'm at sixes and sevens over these plans. I was getting used to the idea of submerging myself in the French countryside, denying that there was a world outside it, losing myself entirely in the life of these little French villages which are my very flesh and blood.
>
> And now I'm being uprooted – violently. No longer will I know that bitter-sweet taste of surrendering to the banality of this village where my parents are the teachers.
>
> My horizons are suddenly enlarged and, before I leave my old life behind, I have to pause . . .[79]

95

Fournier need not have worried on this occasion. No summons ever came to La Chapelle from Panama, and for just a little longer, life could follow its quiet country course as it had done for generations. With the threat of departure receding, Fournier could again speak boldly of the rich future that awaited him across the seas. That he continued to do so for some considerable time to come, can be attributed, in part, to the heady example consistently set by his own restless father but also, in no small measure, to the power and influence of his current literary idol, Paul Claudel.

For both Fournier and Rivière, Claudel was the great discovery of 1906, and for once their taste and their enthusiasm absolutely coincided : there was no doubt in the mind of either that Claudel was not merely France's greatest living author but that he was fit to rank with any of the giants of the past, Racine, Shakespeare and Aeschylus included. The early plays collected in the volume *L'Arbre* were what quite enraptured them and, in particular, *Tête d'or*, with its dynamic young hero whose hair is the colour of the sun, who almost conquers the world and whose dying gesture is to rescue and bless the daughter of the Emperor he earlier slew. It was the powerful rhythm of Claudel's verse and the boldness of his imagery which first attracted each of them, though they were, at first, somewhat baffled by what it all actually *meant*. Fournier described his initial reactions to Rivière in January 1906 :

> I've read only a quarter of *Tête d'or* and so far, I have to say that for me Claudel is magnificently, quite magnificently incomprehensible.
>
> Makes me think of Shakespeare.
>
> He's got his brutality, his studied 'naturalism', those immense tirades for no apparent reason, very precise images, always brutal, often beautiful, which come in – again for no apparent reason.
>
> Tremendous stuff. *L'Arbre* is three or four hundred pages long. I've reached the third part of *Tête d'or* and I'm just beginning to get a glimmer or two. Of course, from time to time, I've *felt* the beauty of it, but only felt it. We must wait and talk about it at greater length.[80]

Fournier and Rivière did not wait long before engaging in a discussion about Claudel which was as protracted as it was animated. Claudel's name dominates their literary exchanges throughout 1906, though it took them a long time to discover the essential truth about him, namely that he was a militant Catholic, vigorously embattled against the iniquities of the modern age, and that he was by far the most determined proselytiser of the day. In 1906, however, he himself was as little known to the general public as his works were little understood and that this was so was due, as much as anything, to the fact that he was not a fashionable *côterie* figure but a professional diplomat who wrote in his spare time only and who lived most of his life far overseas.

As they read on, both Rivière and Fournier found in Claudel's work ample confirmation of their highly idealistic views on Love and on Woman. In Claudel's plays, Love strikes suddenly and irresistibly, it regularly over-rides considerations of social convention and marital fidelity, it is more often than not unrequited and, for that reason, is inseparable from much suffering. The lover, like a courtly swain, must strive to attain perfection; the beloved is always beautiful, remote and imperious, and she herself is more or less aware that she is both the agent and victim of a power beyond her control or comprehension. Given Fournier's abiding regard for *Dominique* and *Pelléas et Mélisande*, one may readily imagine how warmly he responded to the words of Léchy Elbernon in the first version of *L'Echange* :

> – Aime-moi, car je suis belle! Aime-moi, car je suis l'amour, et je suis sans règle et sans loi!
> Et je m'en vais de lieu en lieu, et je ne suis pas une seule femme, mais plusieurs, prestige, vivante dans une histoire inventée!
> Vis! sens en toi.
> La puissante jeunesse qu'il ne sera pas aisé de contraindre.
> Sois libre! le désir hardi
> Vit en toi au-dessus de la loi comme un lion!
> Aime-moi, car je suis belle! et où s'ouvre la bouche, c'est là que j'appliquerai la mienne.

Or to the even more moving final speech of Lâla at the end of *La Ville* :

> Il est vrai que mes cheveux sont gris et que bientôt la nuit et l'or seront remplacés par la mystérieuse couleur de la neige.
> Mais ma beauté reste la même.
> Et la vieillesse qui m'atteint dissipe entre qui me suit et moi le malentendu.
> Crois-tu que je n'ai point de place parmi vous?
> Je suis la promesse qui ne peut être tenue, et ma grâce consiste en cela même.

Je suis la douceur de ce qui est, avec le regret de ce qui n'est pas.

Je suis la vérité avec le visage de l'erreur, et qui m'aime n'a point le souci de démêler l'une de l'autre.

Qui m'entend est guéri du repos pour toujours et de la pensée qu'il a trouvé.

Qui voit mes yeux ne chérira plus un autre visage, et que fera-t-il si je souris?

Qui a commencé de me suivre ne saurait plus s'arrêter . . .

This is an expression of the Eternal Feminine worthy to place beside the famous encomium of Enobarbus on Cleopatra's infinite variety, and its effect on Fournier's personal conception of love was undoubtedly most marked.

In that summer of 1906, Fournier found much solace in Claudel's writings. To Bichet, he wrote in July:

> Read Claudel and talk to me about him. The more I bury myself here in the fields and the countryside, the further I go on, the greater I feel him to be.[81]

And a week later, he declared to Rivière:

> Don't think that it's merely Claudel's *poetry* that I appreciate. At the present moment, I really think I'm in the very heart of him. I live with him. Although I can scarcely read at all, his book is the only comfort I have for this feverish emptiness which causes me so much despair.[82]

In fact, Fournier was encouraged by rather more than Claudel's writings at this time: he was heartened by what little he knew of his life-style and, with his reiterated resolve to serve in the Colonial Service himself, he has to be seen as a disciple paying tribute to the Master by seeking to emulate him.

It is piquant to note, in the light of subsequent events, that in that same letter in which Fournier sang the praises of Claudel to Bichet, he should also have had occasion to thank him for *Les Nourritures terrestres*, Bichet's parting gift before going on to a new career – and even more brilliant success – at the Ecole Normale. The piquancy lies, of course, in the fact that while Claudel and Gide were, at this period, close friends, they were later to become the bitterest of enemies, and to compete with each other to secure the allegiance of the young. True to form, Rivière was to serve as the acolyte of each in turn, and to become warmly befriended by both simultaneously. Fournier never really warmed to Gide – an indifference which was tepidly returned – but in the summer of 1906, he found much to admire in *Les Nourritures terrestres*, that breviary of revolt in which Gide hymns the praises of the life of the senses, lately discovered after an excessively repressed and sickly youth, and lyrically incites his young readers to cast off all restraints and to enjoy all the fruits of the earth. In fact, Fournier needed little incitement to get out into the fields and woods of Berry and the Sologne, and he was very quick to denounce *Les Nourritures* as a form of sensuality rather too artificial and too unsubtle for his particular taste. Nonetheless, in the acutely depressed state in which he had been left after his examination *débâcle*, he found something of an antidote in Gide's lush rhetoric, and something of a challenge too, because in his rich evocations of the North African desert, Gide, like Claudel and the ineffable Aguilera, conjured up tempting vistas of lands far from France.

But, when all is said, it was the sights and sounds of his own native countryside which contributed the most towards his convalescence, and he was the first to acknowledge it :

If I have suffered rather less than other young people from the difficulties of adolescence, from anguished doubts about the Self and the trauma of being transplanted, it's because I've always been sure that I could find myself and my youth again here against the gate, in the corner of a field where they're harnessing two horses to a harrow . . . And it's never been more friendly and compassionate than this year of pain and aridity. It cools down my fever, it seeks out the sources of my pain like lavender soothing a wound, and we each seem earthily accustomed to the other's company . . . There's nothing to touch the joy of being alive which fills you as you sweep downhill on a bicycle, over a carpet of fir needles, or when you go to the fair, and for a moment, feel all forlorn amidst the bustling peasants and the girls in their red dresses, and then your pretty girl cousin comes across you and invites you to the ball. And there's that sudden joy of living (at the fair where you've met your male cousins in their smocks and a humble old carpenter uncle in his black jacket), living again for minutes on end, that unknown fair of long ago to which they used to come in their sober costumes riding on 'the white mare'. When I take my leave of them, I just have time to look back and see that the wall opposite and the crowds of coaches parked in the yard are all

99

bathed in the dim light of that vanished gaiety – a gaiety which I experienced there, once and for all, and now the sound of the shouting and the cracking of whips have been muffled by time, just as my footsteps are muffled by the grass in the cemetery I visit in September. That's what life's all about and 'your books are merely paper'.[83]

Before the summer was over, Fournier wrote the last of his poems, 'Dans le chemin qui s'enfonce' (Along the hollow lane). Like all the others, it is in free-verse form, and one may search through it in vain for either a memorable line or a really striking image. Like most of his published poems, it is inspired by and addressed directly to Yvonne de Quiévrecourt, and it is full of unexplained allusions to the world of his private dreams. It records what seems to have been an authentic vision of her in August 1906 which he promptly described to Rivière.

Coming down through the cornfields towards a farm I didn't know, along a hollow lane between the hazelnut trees, I saw her, as vividly as in a hallucination, coming from out of the corn, in a light dress, just as she was on another morning in England. She was letting her white dress and her furled sunshade trail behind her. Her head appeared against the sun and the red poppies, and she laughed because she had arrived, just like that, like a daughter of the harvest. And she was solemn too, because the whole thing was impossible.[84]

After she makes her appearance in this same magical fashion in the poem, Fournier goes on to imagine how they spend their day together, riding through the lanes in a rustic cart, calling at his grandparents' to pay their respects, weaving a garland of wild flowers for her hair, nestling his head against her dress as they listen to the hum of the distant threshing-machine. Over the years ahead, variations on this basic situation were to haunt Fournier's attempts at imaginative writing: the blonde girl suddenly and miraculously reappearing, always grave and stately in his company, but never willing or able to stay.

However, in the summer and autumn of 1906, Fournier was not prepared to admit final defeat either in love or in academic life. He could still cherish the hope that he would somehow meet Yvonne again and, in spite of his humiliation by—and his lack of conviction over – the Ecole Normale, he resolved to attempt its entrance examination again. His family was prepared to make even greater sacrifices to back him. To relieve him of the strains of boarding-school life at Lakanal, his parents arranged for him to attend the crack lycée Louis-le-Grand as a day-boy, and to provide him with a temporary home of his own in the heart of Paris; to supply his home-comforts, Grandmother Barthe was persuaded to act as housekeeper, and so it was that she left her native countryside in the centre of France for the first time in her life, and travelled to Paris in September 1906, one month before her seventieth birthday.

VI

Fournier began the new academic year in an atmosphere of calm contentment. In place of the seething world of school intrigues, he now had a peaceful private home, and instead of fulminating at meal-times against the iniquitous Lakanal authorities, he could now relax in the company not only of his beloved grandmother, but also of his equally beloved sister, who was also now in Paris, as a day-pupil at the lycée Fénelon.

It did note take him long, however, to discover grounds for fretting: the flat, on the mezzanine floor at 60, rue Mazarine, was too small for comfort, and the view of the neighbouring paper merchant's factory a paltry substitute for the splendid park of Lakanal; he promptly forgot how often, and how profoundly, he had been miserable there, and he lingered over the vanished consolations of what he had lost :

> I miss Lakanal, its superb autumnal lamentation, the sadness of its trees, my brothers, on those wet evenings when I used to come back into school . . . Here, my autumn, my countryside, my muddy lanes in the dusk are so far away that I can't recall them, can't even long for them. Where is that Lakanal window against which the leaves would brush, and the rain would lash, to find an echo in my heart? And where is the desire it used to inspire in me to run away?[85]

If his grandmother's solicitous presence was a source of comfort to him, it was also cause for self-reproach : it was solely to enhance his own career prospects that she had been uprooted from the country, and the spectacle of her favourite pieces of furniture in an entirely unfamiliar setting filled him with remorse :

> I'm sorry to have embroiled the people and things I love in the

mechanical life I live here . . . What a crime it is to have transplanted my grandmother in this way. Her clock and her chest of drawers strike such a jarring note here, they affront the sight – and back *there*, they were so beautifully in place.[86]

And even his grandmother and his sister could not altogether console him over the continued absence of Rivière, still away on Army service, and even more miserable than he was:

Like you, my brother, I suffer from loneliness. When I returned to Lakanal last year, and once more now, the one inseparable companion always in my mind is you, still you and only you. I know that there's someone who sympathises, who can talk and know, and that someone simply isn't here. I look for him, trying not to be sad, but my sorrow walks at my side.[87]

The one sure compensation for both of them was to go on writing their voluminous letters to each other, in which pride of place was invariably given to capturing their impressions of the books they were currently reading, but in which they also registered their moments of both pleasure and pain in the passing day.

It was after an unaccountable silence of nearly three weeks, rather summarily attributed to pressure of school-work, that Fournier wrote on 9 November to Rivière to announce that he had at last made contact with some real, living writers whose work had actually been published. The writers in question were the minor poets Paul Fort, Jean Moréas and Adolphe Retté, all involved in the review *Vers et Prose*, and Fournier was taken by a Lakanal friend, Jean Chesneau, to the Café Vachette where they regularly held court. He was profoundly unimpressed: he found Paul Fort, the author of innumerable graceful but facile *Ballades*, to be an indefatigable but incomprehensible lecturer, like so many French café-talkers, forever building up unstable card-castles of abstract words and theories, and he came away with what was to remain an ineradicable impression of a lisping little man, wearing a large high hat, amiably absorbing the adulation of his acolytes. He was positively repelled by the émigré Greek poet Jean Moréas (né Iannis Papadiamantopolous), leader of the so-called Romanist School, the stock-in-trade of which was verse severely classical in content and form: for Fournier, Moréas was an obvious *poseur*, ostentatiously parading his melancholy, totally incapable of a remark that was either intelligent or witty, forever stroking his moustache with the black-edged nail of his forefinger. He felt slightly more sympathetic towards Adolphe Retté who was maudlin drunk

102

on that particular evening, and who divided his time between singing snatches of Wagner and Bizet, giving a minutely detailed account of the anatomical examination of his mistress recently carried out on his sofa, and his repeated offer to repeat the operation with one of the café waitresses : the one feature which redeemed him in Fournier's eyes was the incontrovertible evidence which, according to Fournier, just occasionally came through, of the finer and nobler personality which pre-dated the ruin.

However, Fournier came away from his evening with the *Vers et Prose* clique with something much more valuable to him than a set of disagreeable impressions. As is inevitable when men of letters meet together, much of the time had been given over to gossip about other literary personalities, and it was from Paul Fort that Fournier first received the news that Claudel was a practising Catholic.

This news at first served only to increase Fournier's already ardent admiration. To Rivière, he announced :

> I'd like to clear all the books from off my shelves and leave only Claudel. Claudel is a whole world and you can enter in without fear.[88]

Rivière, for his part, was thoroughly disconcerted and promptly replied :

> I'm thoroughly put out to learn that he's a Catholic. I was very much afraid he might be, but I couldn't be sure.[89]

Rivière's discomfiture had little to do with the fact that he would have to make major alterations to the major essay on Claudel which he was now nearing completion. Ever since he had renounced religion after his mother's death, the prospect of re-conversion to Catholicism had occasionally taunted and tempted him, in a poignant fashion quite unknown to Fournier, and his chronic confusion on this issue was very much confounded with the news that their adored Master was not only a practising Catholic, but a militant one at that. This news was confirmed for Rivière in December 1906 when he made friends with a wealthy Bordeaux art-dealer and bibliophile Gabriel Frizeau, who added the intriguing news that Claudel had married suddenly and brusquely departed the morning after his wedding.

Although there is no evidence that he *consciously* strove to do so, Rivière regularly went one better than Fournier in nearly every field of endeavour : he consistently achieved very much better examination results, he began to publish long before Fournier (with his critical

103

notices in the *Mercure Musical* from May 1906 on) and he was to become a husband and father while Fournier remained a wistful bachelor. It was wholly characteristic, therefore, that, towards the end of 1906, after Fournier's disappointing encounter with a group of irredeemably minor writers, Rivière should have been befriended by Frizeau who was on intimate terms with such prestigious figures as Jammes, Gide and the great Claudel himself.

Claudel had been instrumental in converting Frizeau to Catholicism, had remained in close touch with him, exchanged long letters with him[90] and always sent him advance copies of his newest works. In the autumn of 1906, he sent him a copy of his very latest play, *Partage de Midi*; Frizeau lent this to Rivière, who sent it on to Fournier, and they were amongst the very first in France to read it, months before it became available to the public. They were not only flattered by the gesture: they were deeply moved by the work.

To an extent which neither Fournier nor Rivière were in a position to appreciate at the time, *Partage de Midi* is a profoundly autobiographical work. It is based on Claudel's own experiences at the turn of the century when he believed he had a religious vocation, sough to give up writing to become a Benedictine monk and, after his period of probation at the monastery of Ligugé, was rejected as unsuitable. Believing himself quite cast out from the sight of God, he sailed for China to take up a diplomatic post. On the voyage out, on board the *Ernest Simons*, he met a Polish woman who was travelling to China with her husband and four children. She fell in love with Claudel, abandoned her husband and children, lived with Claudel for four years and bore him a child. She would not, however, marry him and she finally left him, even though her husband had in the meantime died, her grounds being that she saw herself as a threat to his religious vocation. This relationship provided the basic elements for the plot of *Partage de Midi*, with the young Claudel reincarnated as Mesa, and the Rose of real-life renamed Ysé, perhaps the most regal of all Claudel's remote yet passionate heroines. Only the dénouement is different, dramatically – even melodramatically – so: in real life, Claudel married another woman (on 15 March 1906); in the play, Mesa and Ysé are reunited in a beleaguered villa in the midst of a Boxer uprising; the villa is mined with an explosive charge, and the lovers prepare to meet their death and their God, exulting that never more will they be separated.

Fournier was quite overwhelmed by this ending: to Bichet, he described it as 'divine, pure, terrifying in its beauty, asceticism and its ecstasy',[91] while to Rivière, he declared without equivocation, 'I tell you this in all sincerity: at the present moment, I know nothing more beautiful'.[92] More important, however, is the fact that his reading of this particular Claudel play contributed powerfully to the first of the two religious 'crises' he had to live through in his life, the one he underwent at La Chapelle in January 1907.

There are clear indications in his correspondence over the weeks preceding that he was more than usually moody as the end of 1906 approached : he periodically adopted a flagrantly tetchy manner when writing to Bichet, and this is particularly apparent in his letter of 30 November 1906, when he took him to task for not really understanding him, and not, therefore, being a fit person to receive his most intimate confidences. Throughout that same month, he replied relatively summarily to Rivière's letters and, then, after unwonted delay, and on 19 November, he went so far as to propose that they should stop writing to each other altogether until the following April, a proposal he rather unconvincingly dismissed as a joke when a lonely and anguished Rivière painfully protested.

There can be little doubt that his temporary disenchantment with letter-writing had much to do with his troubled conscience. He was all too painfully aware of the sacrifices which had been and were being made to give him his second chance at the Ecole Normale examination; and to cut down his letter-writing was a tactic in his campaign for greater academic efficiency. The campaign was short-lived and quite abortive, and this he readily recognised when he wrote to Bichet at the end of November :

I'm sad at no longer being able to see the leaves falling.

I'd been keeping pretty clear-headed as a result of my regular working habits, but I'm now running a temperature again.

To start with, Louis-le-Grand hailed me as a star translator, an ace at Prose Composition, and a brilliant writer of English essays—but I botched my very first prose and now I'm back in the position I normally occupied at Lakanal. I'm never going to be a *Normalien*.[93]

Nevertheless, to try to justify the high hopes placed in him and satisfy his own self-esteem, he was still resolved to improve on his first performance. Physical exhaustion had been his undoing then, and being particularly concerned not to over-tax himself a second time, he decided to take a whole month's Christmas holiday at La Chapelle instead of the statutory few days : having arrived there, it was not long before he was engulfed by a great wave of homesickness for the lost childhood world of Epineuil. On Boxing Day, he wrote to Rivière :

This evening – which is full of snow and hoar-frost and dedicated here to (military) conscription – I was coming back after a celebration drink of white wine with the conscripts of this district where I was born, but which I don't count as home, when I began to be filled with yearning.

This district isn't *home* to me because no district is home to me – except perhaps the little village where I attended primary school and went to catechism. That's where I'd like to bedeck myself in ribbons with the boys who went to school with me. I know the names of them all. They can give a name to all my memories. I'd like to recite the school-register with them.

I can remember how, after school, on those afternoons in May, they used to stay behind to finish their prep. The windows with the three shutters would be wide open, the scent of freshly dug earth would come through along with the branches, and you'd hear wonderful little girls calling as they went up the lane with their mothers. Those afternoons, flooded with light there in the school and out in the garden, more pure and mysterious than I can ever tell, will these poor words of mine perhaps bring you back to me?[94]

Fournier's religious 'crisis' came on 5 January, on the very eve of his return to school in Paris, after a month largely devoted to reading contemporary (non-examinable) literature, and interspersed with bouts of yearning. The 'crisis', described by Fournier in rhetorical terms, and full of echoes from the books he had recently been reading, has a markedly literary flavour, and Fournier was the first to concede this when he wrote, rather self-consciously, to recount it to Rivière a full three weeks later. He began by compiling a grandiloquent list of the consolations he expected Catholicism to provide :

– Desire for ascetism and for mortification. Old unspoken desires. Desire for purity. Need for purity. Violent, searing jealousy. You would all have been soothed and satisfied in Catholicism.

– Our great soul eternally unsatisfied (Gide-Laforgue). Unrequited love for everything that exists. One-sided sympathy for everything that suffers. Eternal emptiness in our heart, Catholicism would have filled you.

Ever-restless ambitions, ambitions to conquer this life and whatever is beyond.

Your pain would have eased, and your glory exalted, with the promise that would have been held out to you of the Paradise and the landscapes your heart desires.[95]

Fournier then went on to list reasons why he had been able to overcome his 'very old fears of conversion'. The 'crisis' had been finally precipitated by the rhetoric of *Partage de Midi* and to overcome this, Fournier summoned to his aid the rhetoric of *Les Nourritures terrestres*: to become a Catholic on Claudel's terms meant to give up everything which was not Catholicism, and to do this was to give up much of God Himself because God was everything and everywhere. At this stage, Fournier much preferred to Claudel's triumphant and definitive certainties, the articles of faith advocated by Gide: *disponibilité*, being ready to welcome any fresh experience, and *ferveur*, prolonging desire rather than fulfilling it.

It must also be remembered that Claudel spoke for the *minority* in France because religion was now banned in all State schools, the religious orders had been proscribed, philosophy was still dominated by positivistic thinking, and in literature, the great pontiff of the day was the arch-sceptic, Anatole France. Even Charles Péguy, as doughty and individualistic as any writer in the France of his day, was for a time inhibited from professing his return to Catholicism by the thought of Anatole France's smile, and that same smile, or one very like it, was another reason Fournier provided for his remaining unconverted :

> There would always be a smile in our soul which Catholicism wouldn't wipe off (and that same smile stops me from telling you the whole story of the evening of 5 January 1907).[96]

In resisting what seems to have been a not overstrong temptation to become a Catholic in 1907, Fournier was once again asserting his independence. He was by now fully aware of Claudel's formidable reputation as a converter, and he had no more wish to be added to the growing list of his conquests, than he had had to pay homage in public to Fort and Moréas when he attended their court at the café Vachette. Rivière, on the other hand, had no such inhibitions, and Fournier's account of his dim night of the soul seems to have been the final incentive he needed to write to Claudel, who was serving a turn of diplomatic duty in China. Rivière, at any rate, was not smiling, for his long, anguished letter to Claudel was full of sentences like :

> For a whole year now, I have lived with you and through you. You are my support, my faith, my permanent preoccupation . . . The answer, oh my young elder, oh you who know my secrets, the answer, *certitude*, that is what I want from you . . . I know

107

that God is at your side, and that you live in God. Show Him now to *me*. Let me taste Him, let me feel His weight upon my heart . . .[97]

Rivière was to have to wait several months for a reply from China, and then the consequence was to be a protracted exchange of long and ardent letters which ended on Christmas Day 1913, when Rivière ceased to waver, finally capitulated to the not over-sensitive Claudel, and took Communion.

Though Fournier's 'crisis' in January 1907 seems bookish in comparison, it was not wholly superficial and it too had consequences. His description of the episode is full of echoes from Gide and Claudel, but merely because they happened to be fresh in his mind at that particular moment. In fact, the yearnings expressed by both these authors – for purity, for mortification and for a love greater than life can offer – were deep-rooted in Fournier before he really came to grips with their works: these merely expressed and confirmed what he felt already. That is not to say, however, that they could not suggest fresh outlets for those feelings, and Claudel in particular provided Fournier with at least one picture that was periodically to haunt his imagination over the months and years to come: the picture was of himself in some tropical setting as a missionary, as a 'shepherd of souls', dressed in the garb of a monk.

Although he often felt deeply wistful as a schoolboy, Fournier was not the victim of acute world-weariness as Rivière was and in that same letter in which he described his religious 'crisis', he went on to report that he had much enjoyed a recent visit to the French Assembly, when Clemenceau was in full and redoubtable flow, and that he was about to begin a course of riding-lessons to keep in trim for the coming examinations. He also revealed that he had just met the first Yvonne again, an encounter which he awaited with some trepidation after reading *Jude the Obscure*.

In Fournier's published correspondence, the name of the first Yvonne disappears after August 1905, when he told Rivière that he had written to her from London, asking her to return all his letters and suggesting that he would have to get her father to intercede if she would not comply. His motives at that time, he had explained in a note to Rivière,[98] were simply fear that if the letters fell into the wrong hands they would create a scandal with the Lakanal school-authorities. Hardy's novel, which he read for the first time in December 1906, provided him with a new cause for anxiety: the thought that the vows one makes in first love are quite indelible, and that they have power to colour all the rest of one's emotional life.

He did not have long to wait to establish whether Hardy's severe moral laws applied to him, because a month after reading *Jude*, and a year and a half after his last sight of the first Yvonne, he met her again. He described the encounter to Rivière :

> I've very recently met the first Yvonne again. I had nothing prepared in advance. I behaved admirably, all the more so because I was dreading this meeting. I treated her like some indifferent school chum whose health you politely ask after, and whom you ask if they've had a nice time in England. Then 'Good evening'. This was much better, much more than contempt.
>
> I've looked deep within myself but I can't find a glimmer of regret. Just for a moment, Hardy made me afraid. But, honestly, all it ever amounted to was a few kisses, and the whole agonising adventure and the complete idyll took place in my mind, and in my mind alone.[99]

In that same letter, he evoked once again for Rivière, his familiar ideal of happiness, the same quiet scenes of domesticity of which he had dreamed with the first Yvonne, but now with the elusive second Yvonne as his companion :

> We would spend our evenings like the young Bernard family : a married couple just like children, with other children on an immense sofa, talking late into the night. The evenings would be like a permanent intimate friendship – jokes, expressions of affection, familiarity – and would end with our departing into the night, alone or separately, as the mood took us . . .
>
> And now let me speak of my love.
>
> At this moment, I have almost forgotten her face. All that's left is a sense of her expression and her beauty.
>
> You will simply have to believe me when I tell you that she was so beautiful that she just cannot have an equal anywhere in the world.
>
> I was looking for a great love, impossible and distant, and such love came my way. And now I'm in pain.
>
> To me who believed in the spoken word, that lovely face actually spoke.
>
> My friend, if only I could capture for you in words her distant and elusive beauty. Every day, I find some fresh explanation for her beauty, each time I find some new idea to express, and all of them are true. My friend, to what heights had I attained when I found her?

And yet she is a real live person and she doesn't need me to give her advice . . .

I can't help comparing the first Yvonne with the one who has replaced her, whom I still sometimes hope to win and whom I haven't won yet because I'm not *lofty enough* and because she's still *not lovely enough*.

If I've been childish, if I've been feeble, if I've been uninspired, if I've been stupid, if I've been mawkish, then may I be forgiven for having had the strength on occasions, and in the midst of the dreadful city, to make my life something like a wonderful story.[100]

That Fournier was specially susceptible to the charms of the inaccessible is apparent not only in these comments on Yvonne de Quiévrecourt, but also in the literary aspirations he was expressing at this same period. What is also very evident is that his plans for writing, together with his dreams of love, were alike bound up with his particular cult of childhood.

He had first declared his specific interest in childhood in August 1906 when he described to Rivière what it was that he was most concerned to express :

My credo in art and literature is Childhood. I want to be able to express Childhood without being childish, with its depths plunging down into mystery. Perhaps my future book will be a permanent – and imperceptible – shuttling back and forth between reality and dream, 'dream' being understood as the vast, vague world of childhood which hovers above the world of adults and is forever reverberating with the echoes from it.[101]

And in his earlier letters, he had already provided some striking examples from his own experience of these two worlds in juxtaposition : the adults coming and going in his uncle's shop at Nançay, his grandmother's reminiscences about her youth, the young wife and mother musing over her wedding-day shoes – on each of these occasions, his concern is to register the child's dawning awareness that the true dimensions of space and time are vaster than it can really comprehend. There is also his fascination with attics and old lumber-rooms, and with the costumes and customs of not-so-long-ago, when the mood and motives of his inquiry are that of an eager young spectator who arrives at his vantage point only to find that the great procession has just passed by.[102]

In December 1906, when he next provided Rivière with a detailed

THE LAND OF PROMISE

account of his writing plans, he at once made it clear that he was now interested in something more mysterious even than memory:

> I would like – and here I am trying out my formulae on you – I would like somehow to express the mysteriousness of the unknown world I desire. Since this world is made up of old memories and old unconscious impressions, I would like to express the mysterious effect that these particular impressions of the world have on me . . . I want to bring to life this world of mine, the mysterious world and the new and distant landscape of my heart's desire . . . I am not so much concerned with the world of the past, mysteriously felt and transformed in the present . . . as with a world at once past and longed for, mysteriously mingled with the world of my own life, which somehow or other evokes it. Mystery permeates everything, but I don't think that what I have in mind is merely the mystery of the Will or of some Divinity. It's more like an aspect of life which is evoked for me when I recall my own past, another landscape which the landscape actually before me makes me desire. I shall not, like Gide, hunt for the words to suggest the mystery in the real landscape, I shall describe that mysterious *other landscape* . . . Perhaps this sounds like pure mysticism to you, but I'm convinced that this other landscape *exists* and that I could describe it if only I could get through to it.[103]

It is clear from this that, for Fournier, the Other World was not far distant in space or time. It was not some remote Isle of the Blessed, nor an enchanted garden on some misty mountain top, nor deep beneath the sea nor within the hollow hill: it was tantalisingly close, and he was to remain for long convinced that it needed only heightened perception to pierce the thin veil which concealed it from him.

By December 1906, Fournier had come across only one other author who, in his view, had succeeded in recording his transitory glimpses of the Other Landscape, and this was Rimbaud. Fournier first discovered Rimbaud's work while working in London in the summer of 1905. In Rimbaud's early poems and also in *Une Saison en enfer*, Fournier detected signs of softness beneath the aggressive teen-age obscenities and, for this reason, labelled him 'a perverted Coppée', after a particularly sentimental populist poet of the late nineteenth century; but he more than once experienced an authentic poetic *frisson* when reading *Les Illuminations*, and particularly those sections like 'Enfance', or 'Aube' or 'Matinée d'Ivresse' in which

111

Rimbaud registers a boy's vivid impressions of the colours and shapes of the countryside around him and the child's vertiginous feeling that somewhere just ahead in the wood, beyond the next screen of foliage, lies the very edge of the world. Fournier commented :

> We've all had feelings like this, on a summer's morning, on the evening of a party, memories of far distant childhood – but this formidable individual is the first to have written about it and to have understood what he was up to.[104]

Over the months ahead, Fournier sought ways and means of vying with Rimbaud's achievement, and in the process he transformed what he had begun by calling 'the Other Landscape' into *Le Pays sans nom* (*The Land without a Name*). He could, however, work only intermittently throughout 1907, because he still had a score to settle with the Ecole Normale examiners.

When he contemplated his second encounter with the examiners, Fournier's moods fluctuated between lofty euphoria and black despair. At the end of November 1906, he glumly announced to Bichet that he knew he would never get to the Ecole Normale, yet a fortnight later he was enthusiastically declaring to Rivière :

> I so much want to get through. Once I've passed, thanks to the freedom I'll then be able to enjoy, I'll be able to do such great things. A year at Oxford will set me up marvellously, and besides, I'm in such a hurry to live, really to live ! *Je sens que des oiseaux sont ivres!*[105]

In the course of his school career, he might also with some apposite-ness, have quoted the hemistich from Mallarmé which immediately precedes that final quotation, 'j'ai lu tous les livres', but unfortunately for his academic prospects, very few indeed of these books had the slightest relevance to the examination syllabus. Just as he had done at Lakanal, he continued while at Louis-le-Grand to read primarily for his own pleasure and edification, and assiduously to attend art galleries and concerts. He was determined not to suffer the agonies of the previous year, so he followed his extra long Christmas holiday with a further four weeks in La Chapelle at Easter. As the examination drew nearer, his physical reserves were undoubtedly very much stronger than they had been a year before, but his examination preparations still lacked conviction and credibility.

Rivière was demobilised in the last week of April and travelled at once to Paris, lodging in the little hotel in Cluny Square in which, three years earlier, Fournier used to go to change into town-clothes for his rendezvous with the first Yvonne. He stayed for a month, met Grandmother Barthe and Isabelle Fournier for the first time, and was constantly in Fournier's company. As in December 1905, they talked interminably about every conceivable subject outside the examination curriculum, saw their beloved *Pelléas* again, and visited every art-gallery in Paris. At the end of May, they managed to secure an invitation to visit the home of their favourite living French painter, the sentimental Maurice Denis, who was best able to evoke for Fournier the languorous world of his heart's desire. Recording his impressions for his friend Bichet immediately after the visit, he wrote :

> We know all too well that only one thing matters, one thing alone can satisfy us and make life worth living and without it, there can be no contentment . . . Those great upsurges of infinite desire which carry us over into the Other Land, the land of our desires – and perhaps of our memories too – which we must aspire to, and which we must make ourselves worthy of.[106]

At the end of May, Rivière departed, in desolation and in love with Isabelle Fournier, back to Bordeaux, and almost immediately afterwards, at the beginning of June, Fournier left to get down to the serious business of examination revision in the peace of La Chapelle. Even at this late stage, with the examination only a week away, his letters reveal that his thoughts were still on Claudel and Gide, and he wrote asking his sister to go to see *Pelléas* in memory of Rivière.

He returned to La Chapelle to prepare for the orals as soon as the written examinations were over. He was all too aware that he had provided some short-weight answers, but the Literature questions – French (Diderot on dramatic poetry) and English (the imagination of Dickens) – had been well within his compass, and he was not too despairing about the outcome. His preparation for the crucial second stage of the examination, however, was sketchy to a degree, and his letters to Rivière at this period are again full not only of his latest reflections on Gide and Claudel, but of his own religious state. He congratulated Rivière on having seemingly resisted Claudel's blandishments, and then went on :

> When you first got to know me, I was in the middle of an adolescent crisis. I had just been set free and was still rejoicing, still intoxicated with the pleasure that was quite new to me : I get the feeling that you imagine that to be the *essential* me. Well,

> I think you ought to know that two years before that, at Brest, the junior masters used to call me 'Pious Fournier', that I won the prize for religious knowledge, and that I used to take communion in a state of inexpressible fervour.
>
> I can remember that so well. But I can also remember what a marvellous convalescence it was when I got over it.[107]

On July 16, back once more in Paris, Fournier learned that he had cleared the first hurdle of the written examination, and that his presence would be required a few days later before the oral examiners; Rivière wrote at once to congratulate him, to describe the quirks of the individual examiners, and to advise him on examination tactics:

> 'You're going to pass', he added, *'It's absolutely certain.* All you have to do is *want* to pass. There's nothing to it, you'll see. I swear you can do it . . . I'm waiting now for a telegram to come from you on the 30 or 31 July saying simply "Made it. Coming to see you." '[108]

On 24 July, Fournier sent a postcard instead with rather a different message:

> I haven't even got a University scholarship. I'm trampled in the dust. I'd even come to hope I'd got to the Ecole. What can I do? Please reply. I'm quite lost, utterly shattered.[109]

Worse was to follow. On the afternoon of 25 July, Fournier called at the French Foreign Office, where he discussed with a Monsieur Kahn his chances of entering the Customs Service in China. He was advised to aim for a University degree (*licence*) in English, to keep up his riding lessons, and to further his acquaintance with Claudel; if, after his two years of military service, he was accepted by the Selection Board, he would receive a starting salary of seven or eight thousand francs per month. Fournier wrote at once to his parents to inform them of his new plans. That same evening, in the flat at 60 rue Mazarine, a small group of his school-friends came together to commiserate; they included an old Lakanal classmate, Alexandre Guinle, who had succeeded in passing the Ecole Normale examination, and who had always been the star singer of the circle. That evening, he chose to sing Debussy's setting of Verlaine's poem 'Mandoline' which evokes the dancers and the music of some bygone *fête galante*:

> Les donneurs de sérénades
> Et les belles écouteuses
> Echangent des propos fades
> Sous les ramures chanteuses . . .

At this point, as he himself related later,[110] Fournier broke down completely and was racked with a fit of sobbing which went on for some minutes. After Guinle had departed, Fournier left the flat too, and went straight from the rue Mazarine to the house in the boulevard Saint-Germain which he had once seen Yvonne de Quiévrecourt enter and leave. He rang the bell and promptly learned from the *concierge* that she was at that moment in Versailles and that she had been married since that winter.[111] He wrote to Rivière two days later :

> That same evening I went to find out – to be sure of what I already knew! And now my pain over that news mingles with the other. Now I'm on my own and I'm quite free to go.
>
> There really is a remarkable coincidence between this latest piece of news and my decision to emigrate. How easy it was to extract that information once the moment had come for it! This isn't the first time I've noticed that all events have their allotted time.[112]

Fournier's violent reaction at the news from the boulevard Saint-Germain would almost certainly seem to dispose of the theory of Henri Gillet who, alone of all Fournier's biographers, claims that Yvonne told him she was shortly to be married when they spoke together on Whit Sunday 1905, but it leaves one intriguing question still unanswered. Why didn't he call at the boulevard Saint-Germain much earlier, particularly when from June 1905 on, he regularly went out of his way to walk past the front door? Timidity seems to be ruled out since this was never one of his characteristics. Fear of probable disappointment is a rather more likely part-explanation, because she had more than once rebuffed him, and had *seemed* to make it clear that their parting was to be final : as long as he could not quite be sure, he was free to hope, and it is always more pleasant to dream of what-still-could-be than to brood over what-might-have-been. The likeliest explanation is that it very much suited him at this stage of his development for his love to be, as he put it himself, 'impossible and distant' : there were practical advantages in such a situation in that it avoided any possibility of yet another explosive confrontation with his mother, but by far the greatest advantages of all were *aesthetic* : his rich literary imagination was very much better served by a *princesse lointaine* than by a girl he could meet whenever he wanted. What he most needed in the years 1905 to 1907 was a Muse, and few indeed must be the poets who make a Muse from the girl next door.

This is not to say that Fournier's sense of deprivation over this period was not occasionally overwhelming, nor that he was anything

115

other than genuinely overcome when he heard of her marriage. The tears he shed at the news were real tears, and the pain he felt in the succeeding days was real too. When he poured out his feelings to Rivière, it was not simple literary posturing:

> You can't know what she was to me. She was like another soul forever with mine. I'd almost completely forgotten her face. But I knew who she was and I knew she was there. I took her everywhere I went, and with her beside me, nothing could hurt me any more . . . Now I'm left alone with the harshness and crudeness of life. Everything is turning back into the pain it used to be. Only yesterday did I realise how much my thoughts of her had become a part of me, even when I wasn't consciously thinking of her. Yesterday, I had the feeling that without her, I wouldn't be able even to walk across our arid front garden without feeling pain. She's gone away. I'm all alone.[113]

It was not to take him long to discover that he was mistaken, and that he was no more alone than he had been before. The fact of her marriage had left intact her essential qualities, indeed, had enhanced them: she was still 'impossible and distant', she could still remain both his Muse and his voice of conscience, while he could go on dreaming that, in spite of everything, she would one day be his wife and the mother of his children.

At the end of July 1907, however, Fournier's defeat on all fronts seemed as final as it was crushing, and it was, therefore, with real relief that he directed his attention to the practicalities of travelling from La Chapelle to Bordeaux where he was to spend his first-ever holiday with Rivière.

VI

The fortnight Fournier spent with Rivière and his relatives in August 1907 proved the ideal holiday for him in the circumstances: the place he stayed at, the people he stayed with and the activities they engaged in together, all combined to dissuade him from indulging in undue self-pity. He stayed with Rivière's mother's family, the Fermauds, in their large, turreted villa on the hill in Cenon, with a fine prospect over vineyards to Bordeaux and the sea. In his first newsletter to his parents, Fournier reported that his holiday home reminded him of Madame Benoist's house at Epineuil; he made no comment, on this occasion, about Madame Benoist's son Alfred who had died earlier in the year of a sudden fever, the first of the remarkable number of Fournier's friends to die while still in their youth.

116

While at the Cenon villa, much of his time was spent in boisterous activities with Rivière and his two brothers, billiards, pelota, diabolo, long bicycle rides, and a wild game of their own invention which consisted of racing down the sloping garden paths in home-made wooden go-karts. At his host's request, he also attended Mass in the local church, because Rivière had never been able to bring himself to tell his pious aunts that he had long since lost his faith. The high spot of the holiday was Fournier's first ride in a motor car, a brand-new eight-seater belonging to Rivière's Uncle Jean : they drove at the high speed of twenty-five miles per hour to within sight of the Pyrenees and succeeded in running over a dog.

At the end of a fortnight, he wrote to announce his impending return home to his parents :

> I'm coming back with my eyes full of sunshine, with whole kilometres of exercise in my legs, quite dazzled by the shining seascapes of France and Spain. I'll tell you all about it when I get back, but I'll whisper to you now that I'm homesick for my own fields and meadows.[114]

As soon as he returned to La Chapelle, he announced in his letter of thanks to Rivière that he was already anticipating how nostalgic he was going to be for Cenon :

> I sense that I'm going to feel regret not only for you but for your whole entourage. When the time for my leave-taking came, it was a bitter-sweet pleasure to be able to say that I didn't expect ever to return . . . I shall remember most of all your Aunt Emilie and Aunt Marie, saying good-bye and asking for precise instructions about what they should pray for on my behalf at Lourdes, the poor dears . . .[115]

He complained once more in mid-August of his acute sense of loneliness and that his writer's touch had deserted him but, as at the beginning of the month, the working-out of holiday travel-plans did much to distract him. In return for the fortnight Fournier spent at Cenon in August, Rivière was invited to spend a fortnight at La Chapelle, and Fournier's letters for this period, although interspersed with brief expressions of pain, are largely devoted to working out how Rivière could best enjoy his first sight of the Berry countryside through an involved combination of train-journeys and bicycle-rides. Fournier devoted no little effort also to preparing both Rivière and himself for the forthcoming visit :

I won't tell you anything about my family. As in moments of danger, it's the *instinctive* reactions of the new arrival which are going to make or mar everything. Any early warnings or advance advice would be counter-productive. All I can do is repeat what I've told you already. You are still what you've always been, even though it's never been brought into the open : you are the Enemy. But you'll only need twenty-four hours to have them all eating out of your hand.

All the same, I must tell you this. I've never really noticed the way you walk, but you'll be quite lost as far as my mother's concerned if you walk with your toes turned inward – and when I say 'lost', I don't exaggerate . . . Another annoying thing is that here at home, unlike at Grandmother Barthe's flat (in Paris), Isabelle is treated like a little girl. By Mother, naturally. Naturally, I concoct a whole host of ploys to ridicule this way of carrying on. In general, I should add, I don't take my mother's frantic nagging seriously; I fall about laughing. But this year I'm most disconcerted by the level it's now reached. And yet, in the old days, she really was Somebody![116]

Fournier took particular pains to ensure that Rivière's visit should pass off well because, for him – and, as events turned out, for Rivière too – it was a truly momentous occasion :

I just never dreamed that I'd even have the nerve to attempt an enterprise as vast as this : actually to bring you *here*. I wouldn't like to say who in this is getting the greater share of my trust – you or my native district! To be honest, I've never really *loved* this region : I've treated it more as a friend to whom I can talk about the things I actually love, but it's a friendship so deep and of such long standing that it's more vital to me even than love . . . I think you also ought to know that I just haven't been able to bring myself to take you to Epineuil. I don't know if I'll even go back there myself . . . I love my Nançay past as much as I love my Epineuil past, so when they suggest I take you with me to Nançay, I shall refuse.

Forgive me for all these subtleties. I mention them to reassure myself that I'm doing the right thing in bringing you to La Chapelle. These stories of my loves can't interest you, because God knows you can never share in them. But the moment has almost come for me to reveal to you this friendship which is the whole of my existence, and to me, this is as terrible and decisive as if I were introducing you to a mistress.[117]

In the event, Fournier's nervous misgivings do not seem to have been in any way justified : Rivière made a wholly favourable impression on Fournier's father and mother, and the two friends seem to have spent a thoroughly invigorating fortnight exploring the countryside around La Chapelle on their bicycles. Fournier carried out his resolution not to take Rivière either to Nançay or to Epineuil, but he did show him one of his own special show-pieces of the district, the still derelict château of Loroy beside its lake in the Forêt de Saint-Palais. One of the more piquant legacies of that September holiday is that, when, the following year, each of them was planning his first novel, they both proceeded to allot an important place in it to their memories of Loroy and its grounds. In September 1907, however, their writing plans were rather less ambitious : Rivière was concluding what was to prove the first major study ever to appear on Claudel,[118] and Fournier completed the first of his works ever to be published, the essay *Le Corps de la femme*, which was later to appear in *La Grande Revue*.

Le Corps de la femme was conceived as an attack on the ideal of womanhood propounded by Gide's friend Pierre Loüys who, in *Aphrodite* (1890), a novel which achieved a certain *succès de scandale* in its day, had painted a series of sensuous verbal pictures of female nudes. This caused Fournier considerable offence, though on what purport to be aesthetic rather than moral grounds, and there are various references in his letters to Rivière, from March 1907 on, to the arguments he is in process of marshalling for his case against Loüys. This case, briefly stated, is that the glorification of the naked female body is an ideal best suited to a pagan people and a warm climate; the Frenchman's ideal of womanhood is, in spite of himself, fashioned as he grows to maturity in a country which is both cool and Christian, and if he were true to his nature and his past, he would admit that he prefers the female body clothed. Fournier does not argue quite so straightforwardly, however, and uses the occasion for a display of his distinctive elegiac manner :

We will not get to know the sweet body of woman any better by undressing it. For centuries now, because of the climate of our native land, it has gone clothed; since our childhood, we have associated it with clothes. And those clothes are more than mere adornment, they are the very essence, grace and significance of the female body; all the delicate, feminine, maternal atmosphere of our yesterdays, subtly permeates the clothes of the woman who is our life and our family to be : and that is why when we see again those maternal clothes, the children we still remain, in the most profound and passionate part of ourselves, are filled with desires as vast and mysterious as the world of childhood itself, and as bitter as our regret for a past beyond recall . . .[119]

Fournier's argument is punctuated with a set of verbal illustrations of his feminine ideal, and they can all be directly linked with his own experiences, both recent and remote : a young woman with her back towards him, kneeling at prayer in church, in coloured light diffused from stained-glass windows; a young mother stealing down a country lane to Mass in the early morning, with her small son clinging fast to her gloved hand; the same small boy perched on his mother's lap, snuggling his head against her dress for comfort; a lovely young lady gliding down an avenue of plane-trees; a fair-headed young mother sitting beside her children on the deck of a Seine water-bus on a sunny afternoon in June;[120] children engaged in feverish conversations long into the night on the evening of some mysterious marriage. Unlike Gérard de Nerval, Fournier never lost the sense of his own identity but just as, in Nerval's poems and stories, all the women he ever loved and lost merge into the one hauntingly elusive character, so, in *Le Corps de la femme*, does the woman he most loved in the past become the woman he most loves in the present. In a central passage of Fournier's essay, over the image of the fond mother leading her little boy to Mass, is superimposed the image of the young lady walking towards him down the tree-lined avenue, and one is reminded that the epithets he most favours to characterise both his childhood and his love are the same : '*impossible et lointain.*' One is also reminded that when Yvonne failed to appear on the first anniversary of the brief encounter, Fournier wrote to Rivière to describe his vain attempts to recall her and concluded :

I no longer know anything definite about her, except that she is 'blonde like Madame Fournier'.[121]

It is doubtful if many of the admirers of Pierre Loüys were won over by Fournier's argument because this, it must be conceded, is quite naïvely deterministic : he attributes far too much power to heredity and environment, disregarding the obvious fact that an adult's ideals might well be diametrically opposed to those offered as models in infancy, and – surprisingly so on the part of such a voracious reader – he allows far too little influence to writers and writing. The chief interest of *Le Corps de la femme* is, in fact, not dialectic but autobiographical : dedicated, as it is, to his favourite

120

artist, Maurice Denis, who enshrined Fournier's ideals of womanhood in his paintings *Jardin des vierges sages* and *Plages*, it is, in effect, an anthology of his own youthful set-pieces on the Eternal Feminine. It is a revealing piece of stock-taking and, as events turned out, an act of leave-taking too.

On 30 September 1907, he wrote to inform Rivière that he had just finished making a neat and definitive copy of *Le Corps de la femme*. Two days later he sent the following brief card :

> Henri Fournier, 23 Regiment of Dragoons, 3rd Squadron, 4th Troop, much regrets that he will not be able to attend the Salon d'Automne.[122]

On the same day, he sent an even shorter message to his grandmother :

> Just 741 days to go.[123]

5

The Land of Lost Illusions

October 1907–September 1909

> Perhaps the great problem is not Happiness
> but Purity. Purity is the burning question
> and the supreme torment for those who aren't
> pure in heart.
>
> Alain-Fournier[1]

I

On more than one occasion during his schooldays, Fournier wrote to his friends envying them their full and active life on military service while he had more leisure than was good for his peace of mind to brood on the past, the present and the future. 'I'm waiting longingly for my two years of Army service,' he told Rivière in December 1906. 'I want them to be as tough as possible, and I want them to teach me everything it's possible to learn about that way of life.'[2] To Bichet, he declared in May 1907, 'I envy you; I'd like to be forced to live an intensely physical existence for months on end, so that, like you, I can be relieved for a while of all worries about the future.'[3] And less than a week before being called up, he announced: 'The great relief and the brutal physical life I'm going to enjoy for the next two years will sweep away every trace of my emotional difficulties.'[4]

His initiation into French cavalry life was as brutal as he could ever have desired, so brutal indeed that his almost immediate reaction was to look for the quickest possible escape-route back to civilian life. His fastidious imagination had simply not anticipated the filth of his physical surroundings, the ignorance and insensitivity of his non-commissioned officers or the futility of having each day to clean and polish everything, even the soles of his boots. Fournier briefly considered asking his old Paris friends, the Bernards, to use their influence and get him discharged from the Army on medical grounds. In the event, he seems to have thought better of this, but his friends did exploit their contacts, the chief of whom was a French junior Minister, Albert Thomas, to have him transferred from the cavalry to the infantry. After just one month in the barracks at Vincennes, he joined the 104th Regiment of Infantry stationed at Les Invalides, close to the Ecole Militaire.

Almost at once, he demonstrated his by now quasi-instinctive reaction of preferring the recently almost unbearable past to the incomparably more intolerable present, and it was almost with relish, that he explained to his parents how very much filthier his new surroundings were compared to those from which he had just escaped: the Berrichons he had left behind were clean in their personal habits and, in his view, not unintelligent; now he found himself in the company of drunken Normans with the mange, the stench of sweat and excrement was all-pervading, petty pilfering was taking place on a vast scale, and the soldier in the next bed was a syphilitic who insisted on borrowing his drinking mug.

It was not very long, however, before he found consolations. He was soon singled out as a recruit with a superior educational background and given the task of teaching illiterates to read and write. This job not only provided him with a deal of personal satisfaction, it also provided small additional sums of money to spend on extra cups of coffee, on his laundry, and even enabled him to pay another soldier twenty sous per week to polish his leather equipment for him. As a further extra privilege, he was allowed to spend every evening with his grandmother and his sister in the flat at 60 rue Mazarine where Rivière too was now a regular visitor. Unable any longer to endure his lonely existence in Bordeaux, Rivière had given up his University scholarship, and was now studying privately for his Philosophy degree at the Sorbonne, lodging in a hotel room in the rue de Tournon and paying his way with the fees he was earning as a private tutor.

Once he had got through the first traumatic weeks of Army service, Fournier discovered that an infantryman's life could provide positive consolations of its own. At the beginning of December 1907, his regiment went out on a series of lengthy route-marches through the southern suburbs of Paris, and he found that while his body was being vigorously exercised in the present, his mind was free to wander back into the past – indeed, on occasions, it was positively impelled to do so: preparing his equipment for the march made him think of getting ready to set out from Epineuil to start the summer holiday;[5] the howling of the wind made him think of the sunken lanes winding their way round La Chapelle and Epineuil,[6] and after sleeping out for

123

the first time ever, in a vast barn with a hundred other troops, he discovered in the first light of morning that they were encamped within sight of the park and trees of Lakanal.[7] For all that, he reported that he felt unmistakably uplifted when the regiment marched briskly through the streets back into the centre of Paris, singing songs which were so bawdy that the officers had to issue an order for silence.

More consolation of a particularly encouraging sort came on Christmas Day 1907 when *Le Corps de la femme* was published. Fournier did not, however, savour quite to the full the debutant writer's pleasure at seeing his own name in print for the very first time because he had felt obliged to adopt a pseudonym. In 1907, there was already more than one Fournier in the public eye : Admiral Ernest Fournier and the even more conspicuous Henri Fournier who first found fame as a racing cyclist, and later, as a car-driver, winning both the Paris–Bordeaux and the Paris–Berlin races in 1901. After consideration, Fournier decided to write under the name of Alain-Fournier, doubtless after the fifteenth century Norman poet Alain Chartier whose best known poem, 'La belle dame sans mercy' (1424), is a graceful variation on the courtly theme of the lover who dies of his lady's cruelty. Appropriately, he arranged for a copy of *La Grande Revue* to be sent to Yvonne de Quiévrecourt.

In December 1907, Fournier was encouraged to dream not only of his own future literary fame but also of the quick fortune he might win abroad. After a few weeks of infantry service, he was singled out for training as a possible officer, and although he was dismayed at the prospect of having to attend special courses far from Paris, he was consoled by the thought of the benefits that would follow after. He explained to his parents :

For my last six months of Army service, I'd be a lieutenant in the Reserve, and the training would make the two years pass much more quickly. And I'd end up with an extra qualification for my career in the Colonies. My mind is still fixed on that. I don't want, after four years of study, to end up as a miserable little school-teacher. I think that these years in the Army, sad though they are, will toughen me up for that final departure. At this moment in time, the very thought of it breaks my heart. But the prospects are great, promotion should be quick, and it'll always be possible to get back again. At the end of my Army service, I thought of taking things easy at home with you for a month or two, then asking if you might finance me for a year in England. Once there, I could really perfect my English conversation, and this would serve me well either if I decided to leave for Indochina or else if I go peacefully on studying for the *agrégation* exam in English and Literature. In the course of that year, I'd be able to make up my mind absolutely clearly and calmly. Wouldn't you like that?[8]

He followed this up with an enthusiastic letter to Rivière seeking to incorporate him in his plans :

When next I see that high-powered protector of the Bernards, how would you like me to ask him to find for *two* people he can have confidence in, what he can provide at the moment for *one*. I think he could fix it. The two of us could spend a year in England working at the language and at banking. After that, we could leave together for India, and perhaps even work in partnership.[9]

To this, Rivière's reply was somewhat guarded, and well it might have been, because three weeks earlier, on 2 December 1907, he and Isabelle Fournier were secretly engaged. The engagement was officially announced in February 1908, and shortly afterwards, Rivière wrote to Fournier to explain, as delicately as he could, that their friendship could never be quite the same again :

There are lots of questions I no longer see the point of, lots of worries which I now find simply laughable, lots of desires which have left me now forever. Everything is simpler, in place, elucidated. Even the pain I still sometimes suffer has a delightful feeling about it. My poor friend, if only you knew how thoroughly I've now purged myself of all that literature.[10]

Precisely when Fournier himself had been let into the secret is not clear, but his sister distinctly remembers his first reaction to the news. In her memoirs, she reports him as saying :

When Jacques told me about it (by the fountain in the boulevard Saint-Michel), my first instinctive thought was : Is *that* the way a young man and a girl must always love each other? It would have been so beautiful if the pair of you could have lived a love that was absolutely pure ! It seems as though it must always end in *that* way.[11]

It would, of course, be only too easy to read something sinister into the expression of such an attitude, but there is no evidence in the letters he subsequently wrote either to his sister or his future brother-in-law to suggest that it was anything more than pique. The pique is not difficult to understand : he had enjoyed a particularly close relationship both with Rivière and with his sister, and for years he had been the most intimate confidant of each; now, in each relationship, he was to be demoted from first to second position, and for all the good will on everyone's part, the new situation was bound to seem less attractive than the old. Fournier did, in fact, adjust to this new situation, as he did, in time, to all circumstances, and, by all accounts, he remained on excellent terms with the Rivières throughout their courtship and the early years of their marriage : the price that had to be paid was an increase in his sense of loneliness that was both profound and bitter.

Whether or not there is any coincidence between the two events one can only speculate, but shortly after Rivière's secret engagement, one finds Fournier, for the first significant time in his correspondence, beginning to become preoccupied with thoughts of death. On 1 January 1908, he told Rivière that he had just read Kipling's short story, *The Other Man*. He briefly described the setting of the story, a town in India at the time of the Raj, and he outlined the plot – how the demure Miss Gaurey spurns the man who truly loves her, how she marries an older and wealthier brute of a colonel, and how, one day, a cart arrives from a remote frontier outpost bearing the corpse of her first love, tethered upright to the driving seat because of the uneven roads. Fournier quoted the epigraph from an old ballad :

> When the Earth was sick and the skies were gray
>   And the woods were rotted with rain,
> The Dead Man rode through the autumn day
>   To visit his love again.

He added approvingly :

> This evening I've turned that sadness into mine . . . I ask myself, as Chesneau used to, why we don't love and desire Death more than we do.[12]

Whatever first turned Fournier's thoughts in this particular direction, his increasing sense of isolation thereafter did little to divert them and, from this point onwards, there is a striking increase in his letters and, even more so, in his imaginative writings, in images of death, corruption and decay.

In the early months of 1908, however, life, both on and off duty, was simply too full to allow Fournier to brood for long. At the beginning of January 1908, he almost came top in the regimental examinations for promotion to non-commissioned status; on 24 January, he was on all-night manœuvres near Saint-Cloud; on the following day, he was on sentry duty outside the Chamber of Deputies, while on 30 January there was a reunion in the Paris suburbs with the Nightingale family, over on a brief visit from London. Of rather more significance, however, was what took place shortly afterwards, when in order to live closer to their children, the Fournier parents moved from La Chapelle to Paris. The father's bookcase and the mother's piano were auctioned off before they left the Berry, and they proceeded to settle in at 24 rue Dauphine, between a jeweller's shop and a *rôtisserie*. The parents took up teaching engagements in different suburban schools, Monsieur Fournier in Vincennes, and Madame Fournier in Bagnolet; Grandmother Barthe returned to her little country house at La Chapelle which once again became the family base for all their holidays.

On 15 April, Fournier was made a corporal and posted to the Fort de Vanves. In the second fortnight in May, the whole regiment was out on manœuvres in and around the forest of St Germain whence the famous Paris boulevard derives its name. The troops marched with full packs from the barracks at Les Invalides to their reception camp at Mailly where there were tents for 15,000 men. The distance of over 120 miles was undertaken in seven vigorous stages, and Fournier was on the march when the second anniversary of his first meeting with Yvonne de Quiévrecourt came and went. He wrote to his parents about the villages they had marched through on Ascension Day:

> Round about eight o'clock in the morning, one began to notice the tell-tale signs of a Feast Day. In front of the banks of little houses, an expanse of well rolled earth, swept quite clean and all white in the lovely sunshine. One could sense that behind the windows, in front of a mirror, here somebody was combing her hair and there someone was making up her face. Little front gardens, past which we went marching all the time, at the column's steady pace. At the cross-roads, little girls in their Sunday best waiting for Mass.
>
> In the afternoon, in the farmyard where we had fallen out, I discovered over the top of an outhouse, a sort of little open attic, all heaped up with straw, and I went up there for my siesta between noon and three o'clock. I scarcely slept. The

Church bells were ringing for vespers; bright sunshine played over the straw, and the great wind which shook the roof-timbers, blowing out of the heart of the endless plain, told me how lonely and lost and tired and miserable I was, in that barn in Champagne, on that lovely Ascension Thursday, my anniversary day.[13]

After their arrival at Mailly camp, the troops spent their whole day endlessly drilling or on the rifle range, and for the first and only time throughout his period of military service, Fournier had to report sick. While the rest of the regiment were out on a particularly severe route-march which it hurt Fournier's pride to have missed, he was left alone to meditate on another engagement he was unable to keep, his ritual visit to the boulevard Saint-Germain and the banks of the Seine on Whit Sunday. He wrote a letter addressed jointly to Rivière and his sister, reminding them that it was he who had brought them together, and announcing that he was still 'so terribly alone and haunted' :

Remember, if you will, that next Sunday is Whit Sunday. Ah, it was through storm-laden heat just like this, yet already slightly cooled by heavy rain, that a tall girl came to me. Closed doors, honeysuckle trailing over the walls, long stem of thirsty white lilac, amidst the shrubs of the 'old park'.

Across the low wall, beyond the horizon, the large gardens are still there with their sanded paths which are watered in the dusk. And she is gone.

Yet it was a great shared love and words were spoken.

Whit Sunday morning, more mysterious than Whitsun itself. And now I don't want to talk even about her face, or her voice, or that great and gracious sadness which made her so sweetly inaccessible, but about her purity, that purity which turned this love – without words, without letters, without even the presence together of the two despairing lovers – into an act of contemplation, face cupped in the hands, sitting quite still.[14]

And he concluded by hoping that the happy love of Rivière and his sister would remain a refuge for him, and the children of their coming marriage would one day look, 'with gentle wondering eyes' at the countryside their uncle had loved so much.

At the beginning of August, Fournier took his Officer-cadet qualifying examinations at Chanzy barracks in Le Mans, then went off on ten days' leave to La Chapelle. Rivière was also spending a brief holiday there and they devoted much time and energy to trying to establish a new high-speed record for propelling their home-made soap-box racing cart down the main street of the village : Rivière eventually won, but at the cost of overturning the vehicle at top speed, and needing to be revived with a vinegar compress. In between their long cycle rides, Fournier found the time to write one of his comparatively rare letters to René Bichet in which, not for the only time, he expressed regret that his correspondent lacked the qualities he most urgently required from the one, true friend :

Perhaps my earlier letters to you were written too carelessly and perhaps I didn't put enough devotion or enough of myself into them. But whose fault is that? I want someone who can believe and who can will, someone to whom *anything* is possible, with whom anything is possible, someone for whom nothing in the world exists but his desire. I'd like you to be like me and that when you're out in your countryside as when I'm out in mine, you might sometimes feel so full of desire, and so lofty, that you round the next bend in the road – and there you meet your love ! What's the point in having a friend, if he too is riddled with doubts and is overwhelmed by the impossibility of everything.[15]

He went on to express the doubt that his richest source of literary inspiration was in danger of drying up, giving the lie to his fears in the very act of voicing them :

At the present moment, I feel utterly drained. I feel that I'm just a bird of passage here without even the time to lean and reflect on the little white gate. For the first time in my life, here I am back from Paris, and for the first two days I've been listless and morose, no longer able to get the 'feel' of my countryside, incapable of imagining the beloved characters with which I populate it, and the marvellous plots being enacted in it, on the far side of the lane, at the far end of those avenues overhung with chestnut trees. At two o'clock, as the afternoon begins, everything is at rest in the fields, down the lanes shimmering in the sun or deep in shade, I pass through like the King of the realm I have myself created, and for young secret souls, I've discovered by the bend in a lane, a notice saying 'Private Estate Road. No Motor Cars.'

He added that this sunlit afternoon had been preceded by a dark night of despair and this too he tried to describe for Bichet in what he entitled *Essai de Transposition*. It is yet another variation on the theme which dominated most of his early poems, the second coming of his lost Yvonne : this time, the wedding is just over, and the pair of them are now alone surrounded by mist and darkness; he cannot believe she is his at last and he very soon finds she isn't – because she is dead :

> Too sweet! Too sweet! Fear now overcomes me. It's a dreadful dead thing, a woman dead for ages, which stands up now on the other side of the hedge. Her gaze so pure as to melt the heart is fixed and staring, like that of the great Beast which goes prowling through the evening . . .

His artistic or emotional nerve fails him at this point and what could have been a macabre Baudelairean vignette ends as comfortingly as a Christmas card :

> Or else it's just a star, trapped in the branches of the yew trees, on this misty summer's evening when I too am dead.

Fournier's brief literary flourish to Bichet is of little consequence in itself, though it provides clear evidence of the morbid strain that is henceforth so often to appear in his work; its chief significance is that it marks the revival of his interest in creative writing which had been stifled by the first strenuous months of Army service. In that same letter to Bichet of 10 August he reported that both he and Rivière had spent a deal of time discussing the novels they were planning to write. Rivière had for some time been working intermittently on a novel he now planned to call *Le Bel eté*,[16] the subject of which was going to be the totality of his own inner world. Fournier's literary designs had now reverted from prose-poetry back to the novel, and on 26 August, he wrote from Paris to Rivière to announce what he took to be an important break-through :

> This time, I think I've got it. There's to be no theme. The main thing is that it will all take place in a country estate. There I'll put all my non-existent human characters, and I'm leaping with delight here now as the thousand and one different episodes begin to fit themselves together into the still evolving plot.[17]

A week later, he was slightly more specific in a letter to his sister and his parents :

> It's terribly hard to keep up your writing in the Army. You need

so much peace to write properly. When you come off duty in the evening, you've got to be able to switch off from whatever is going on around you and whatever is due to happen to you next.

The one thing that's now more or less definite is that one of the characters has a park. It's the one I'd like to have if I were rich.[18]

Doubtless as a result of their close conversations three weeks previously, Rivière's thoughts about his own novel were moving in the same direction, and in a letter to Fournier on 5 September, he not only laid claim to a park for his characters but identified the real-life model:

Everything is now being transmuted into Le Bel eté . . . The dream park will possibly come into it. I don't yet know where. This is how it might be: all around it, the depths of the forest which, you sense, you couldn't traverse even in a whole day's hard riding. It would be a vast clearing. In front of the château, veiled by some trees, there would be a vast meadow, bounded on each side by the two curves of the edges of the forest, sweeping round to link up in the distance. The meadow to have rushes growing in it. And birch trees blown down by the wind. I readily admit it's a magnified version of Lauroy [sic]. I went back there the other day to find a fearsome gale bringing its own brand of universal disorder to the romanticism that was already there.[19]

Rivière subsequently abandoned Le Bel eté,[20] and Fournier was to need several more years to digest the bitter experiences life still had in store for him, before his first novel was finally completed. By September 1908, however, he already had in his possession what was to prove one of the most memorable parts of it: he had found the Lost Domain.

On 1 September 1908, Fournier was posted back to Les Invalides and given a few days' more leave. He was all alone in his parents' flat at 24 rue Dauphine: his mother and sister were at his grandmother's in La Chapelle, his father away supervising at a colonie de vacances in the Vosges, while Rivière was on holiday with his aunts in Cenon. It was a propitious time for more melancholy rêverie: autumn was in the air, and letters arrived in quick succession from two of his faithful Lakanal contemporaries who both directed his thoughts towards the past. He never spoke to Rivière of these other school friends without coupling with their names an adjective that was part-affectionate and part-patronising: it was always 'poor' Chesneau and 'little' Bichet. On this occasion, 'poor' Chesneau wrote:

> Sometimes you come into my mind and for a while it is filled with exquisite memories. How happy we were at Lakanal for all our wretchedness.[21]

'Little' Bichet wrote asking why Fournier had been neglecting him for so long and to compensate him, and also to console himself at a time of real loneliness, he promptly wrote back a long letter devoted almost exclusively to memories of his lost Yvonne and to Verlaine's wistful lyric about unrequited love which had provoked such a fit of sobbing in July 1907:

> Last year, at this time, someone was singing *Les donneurs de sérénades*. It was the same sort of weather, with hints of winter, leaves turning to russet, the lanes soon to be deserted, made impassable by deep ruts, cut off by the fog. They sang of *leurs molles embres bleues . . . leurs longues robes à queue . . .*: it was in the drawing-room at La Chapelle; and in my mouth, I had the same acrid taste of things that are dead. When you feel that everything is dead, how everything has that dead taste. How lost and gone everything seems. 'The young lady is at Versailles at this very moment,' and that was all I knew; merely that and her name and little else. By then our meeting was several years behind me, and now all that's left are the faint shadows of the dead. I am all that survives, I am eternal Clitandre, in love with the fading visions of those dead ladies, with that sickly taste in my mouth, disconsolately walking down paths covered with rotting leaves.
>
> *A quoi bon?* that's what she said, and she said it with a firm and steady voice, slightly stressing each word in her mannered way, lifting her head slightly when she came to the 'b' sound and somehow isolating it. Then her expression became quite still again, and she bit her lip slightly, and her eyes looked into the distance, unblinking, unwavering and so blue.
>
> There was a time when, if I repeated those words and thought of the way she stood there, I could bring back a complete picture of her . . . She was haughty and aristocratic. At first, she showed me the same disdain that she doubtless reserves for people who try to accost her. She was not the sort of person to be accosted. She was a real lady beneath her white sunshade, the sort who

comes out through the iron gates of some château on a sultry afternoon in the country . . . Our meeting was extraordinarily mysterious. 'Ah!' we said, 'we know so much about each other, and we don't even know the other's name.' And strange to tell, that's how it was. 'We're like children, we've behaved foolishly,' she said. So artless was she, and so great our happiness, that one didn't know what folly she was talking about. Up to that moment, no words of love had passed between us.

That love, which came so strangely into being, and was so strangely admitted, was so passionate in its purity that it became almost unbearable. Now when I think that these were days when I was close to her and that she actually spoke to me, my imagination strives in vain to credit it : you'd have to be mad to believe it.[22]

He recalled in detail Yvonne's departure across the Pont des Invalides[23] and then, with a remarkable *volte-face*, suddenly declared that in spite of the news of Yvonne's marriage, he had not lost hope :

How bitter all this would be were I not certain that one day, by dint of striving towards her, I shall reach such a height that we'll be reunited, in the drawing-room of our own home, at the end of the afternoon when she's finished her round of visits. And while I watch her take off her big cloak and toss her gloves on to the table, we'll hear our children in their room upstairs tipping out their big box of toys.

Possibly taken aback himself at the awesomeness of this piece of wish-fulfilment, Fournier promptly resorted to his usual tactic of putting Bichet rather firmly in his place :

But why am I telling you all this, anyway? We don't feel and we certainly don't imagine things in the same way. To guess what my 'Slim-waisted One' has meant to me and really to be able to picture what 'The Young Lady of the Manor' was like, you would have to have been a country child yourself, to have waited interminably on those June afternoons, behind the iron gates of some courtyard, close to the great white gates which close off the driveways, on the outskirts of the woods of the château.

Nothing demonstrates more conclusively than these last remarks the degree of Bichet's diffidence, and of the reserve that always existed between himself and Fournier. In fact, Bichet came from a rather poorer home than Fournier's, and his childhood also was spent in the countryside of the Cher. Fournier did not, however, learn these details until after Bichet's death, and the effect was greatly to intensify both his sense of loss and his sense of guilt.

Fournier spent the greater part of September 1908 with his regiment on manœuvres when two vast armies, with all their equipment, simulated a full-scale war. Whole days and nights were spent marching, and on pitching or breaking camp. At the outset, Fournier did not view the activities with very much enthusiasm, and he wrote to his mother:

> I'm not too unhappy. I live very obscurely, scarcely thinking of anything, resigned in advance to the hardships of the next stage of the march, and not even looking forward to arriving at our next base. When we arrive, it's always as though we were lost and sodden travellers and as if, after finally coming across a home, we're allowed to enter only as far as the wash-house to share the cold and clutter with the beggars. When we pile our arms in front of some hamlet, even those who are limping and who've been looking forward so much to journey's end, express the hope that '*this* can't be the place' and want to press on. The middle of a little village, with a post-office, a grocer's and an inn – how many men have longed for that over these past days, just that and nothing more! But even this longing is snuffed out after your hopes have been dashed a second time, and you trudge on down the road, muffled up, your head bent low, like some tired horse which just occasionally arches its neck to see where it's going.[24]

However, the Army's theatre of operations for these autumn manœuvres was Touraine, which borders both the Berry and the Sologne, and Fournier's enthusiasm mounted with his discovery that he was operating in the midst of his favourite scenery. A few days later, he wrote from a farmhouse in the Indre-et-Loire region to his father in not very distant La Chapelle:

> This must be Berry country we're in now. I recognise this great countryside about which strangers can find nothing to say because, if truth be told, its immediate appearance seems to have little to offer. You have to have been on familiar terms with it

from childhood on. Here, between two arms of the river, is the little meadow with its tall grass, where, beneath the shade of the poplar trees, the cut hay is drying. Here is the farm hidden round the bend of the track which leads off from the main road. And here on the side of the hill, where the ground is whiter and grows more undulating, is a lime-kiln . . . I should like to be with you for the end of the holidays. We could go to Nançay together. The other Sunday, in the woods on the far side of Lecueillé, I think it was, we met some carts being driven by peasants who were all dressed up in their best finery. At the roadside, between two slopes, a chapel in a clearing made me long once more for the part of the world you come from.[25]

By the time the autumn manœuvres of 1908 were finally over, Fournier was positively enthusiastic : conditions had been as physically demanding as he could ever have wished, but he had been provided with the inestimable consolation of having been transported back into the landscape he treasured above all others :

As it approaches the Loire, the Cher broadens out and the perspective opened out over the woods and islands is infinitely vague and distant. No map, and not even the Loire itself, can give you any idea of what it's like. You descend to it along sunken tracks which run down like the streams which separate the clumps of acacia trees where the châteaux are built : the green lawns, with boats and their oars trailing beside them, come right down to the level of the water; clusters of white reeds bow their feathery plumed heads in the flower beds; swans arch their necks above the banks of the rivulets where they go gliding along. Just as I found it on the banks of the Thames, but here, lost in the very heart of the countryside, right up beside these expanses of water stretching away into the far distance, here – spread out, and at peace, and luxuriant – is the countryside of my yesterdays, the countryside I'm afraid to speak about because it's so special and so precious to me. Here, once more, are the reeds, the willows, the mud and the sand where the bow-nets sink in, the houses from where you can go by twisting paths right down to the water's edge. Those were the waters in which I swam for the very first time, and for days on end, I was longing to dive back into them without being able to believe it would really be possible. I managed to plunge in on the very last night, hidden away in a backwater screened by the willows. Night came down and in the distance, the lights from

THE LAND WITHOUT A NAME

the houses were reflected in the Cher. I paused on the bridge and found in the scene more than a picturesque spectacle : in it was a touching piece of sheer magic as if, suddenly, some lovely evening of my childhood were being reflected in festive waters.[26]

Another memory of childhood carnival days was revived for Fournier almost immediately after his return to regular Army duty at the Tour-Mabourg barracks in Paris: this was when he went to a Paris music hall with some soldier friends and saw the memorable Falling Man. The performer, an emaciated and toothless clown, kept trying to climb to the pinnacle of a miniature mountain of tables and chairs to which his assistants were continuously adding; what happened next, he described soon afterwards to his mother :

> He kept on falling, forever falling. He got tangled up in fifty chairs each time he fell. Once he brought down an enormous table with him. Another time, he fell right into the audience and two of them got hold of his feet and dragged him back on to the stage again. And each time he fell, he uttered a unique little cry with an infinite range of variations to it, which expressed, as his whole mime did, his indescribable air of satisfaction, a demonic satisfaction as if he'd suddenly been liberated from everything that had to do with weight and gravity. The high comedy of the act was when this satisfaction turned imperceptibly into a cry for help . . . At the climax of his performance, when he came tumbling down in slow-motion from the top of a great tower of chairs, his shout went on the whole time he was falling, and ought to have caused all the ladies in the stalls to go into hysterics.[27]

Fournier kept rough copies of most of the letters he sent, and it was doubtless the novelist's instinctive feeling for scene and character that impelled him to file away his impressions of the 'Falling Man', beside his notes on his encounter with Yvonne de Quiévrecourt, to await transmutation into the work of art. This was always to be his mode of procedure; nothing that ever happened to him ever seemed wholly real until he had trapped it and tamed it with words, and he could well have said, with Tennyson's Ulysses :

> I am a part of all that I have met;
> Yet all experience is an arch wherethro'
> Gleams that untravell'd world, whose margin fades
> For ever and for ever when I move.[28]

136

At the end of September, he wrote to Rivière to say that genuinely though he now loved Paris, he longed to spend the autumn elsewhere :

> My yearning grows stronger, banked up as it is with all the yearning I've always felt at this time for the past ten years. For ten years now, I've had to look at the autumn through a window pane or from under a lamp-post. Ah, if only at last, I could live my October and November away from here, going along paths hollowed out by the rain, all choked up with dead leaves . . .[29]

Half of his wish was promptly granted. At the beginning of October he was posted away from Paris, but not back to the Cher countryside he had in mind : he was sent instead for a six-month course of officer-training to the Corbineau Barracks in Laval.

II

Laval is an important cotton-spinning centre and the chief town of the Mayenne *département*. Fournier came to admire its major scenic attractions, the bridges over the river Mayenne, which is eighty feet wide at this point; the two castles, one dating from the eleventh century, the other from the Renaissance; the cathedral, with its mixture of Romanesque, fourteenth- and sixteenth-century styles; the splendid public park. There were also occasionally other diversions not far away such as the flying display by Wilbur Wright at Le Mans, in October 1908, but, for almost the whole of his six-month course in Laval, he assiduously took the train, at every conceivable opportunity, to rejoin his family and friends in Paris, nearly two hundred miles away.

Living in the Corbineau Barracks was very much like being back at boarding-school again : there was a full time-table of classes on such subjects as military history, tactics, administration and drill, compulsory games, which enabled Fournier to demonstrate his prowess at Rugby football, and even that time-hallowed French academic sport of ragging the junior instructors, an activity to which Fournier seems very readily to have contributed in spite of his having been promoted sergeant on 15 October. A few weeks later he reported to Bichet that he had been confined to barracks as a punishment, adding that on *this* occasion he had done nothing to deserve it.

It did not take him long to experience his usual longing to be *elsewhere*. In a communal family letter, written only three weeks after his arrival in Laval, he declared :

> How I wish I was free and out of school at long last! Spending last Sunday here brought back the distress we used to feel as schoolboys when we went out for our routine walk. I won't deny that the avenues and the squares and the public parks here are as beautiful as they're innumerable. The big Botanical Garden, which must once have been a private park, stretches along above the town, following the line of the Mayenne. When you sit up there on a park-seat, you can glimpse, between the trees, the slate roof of the whole of the city. Last Saturday afternoon, life in the city below was encapsulated for me in just a few melancholy sounds : the rumbling of a coach, the chiming bell of a factory or a convent, possibly the Trappistines, or the Ecole Libre or the cotton factory . . . My tears a year ago at the Vincennes barracks were 'tears of frustration rather than grief', like a bird which thinks it's free and then finds it's been caught again and is going to have its wings clipped. But nobody has seen a bird's tears or mine either. Nobody but Isabelle.[30]

And it was to his sister alone that he wrote a month later :

> My picture of ideal happiness right now is a young man in civilian clothes, strolling down the boulevard Saint-Michel on a Thursday morning, on his way to his English lecture.[31]

As well as studying for his officer qualifying examinations, Fournier was preparing to take his *licence* in English. He claimed to be translating three hundred lines of English poetry each day,[32] and he regularly submitted his translation exercises to his sister for vetting. His intention was still to qualify for an executive post overseas, undeterred by Rivière's graphic warning, an echo of Claudel, that 'exile would follow him everywhere.'[33]

Rivière, for his part, was now some considerable distance ahead of Fournier along the academic race-course : in 1907, he had secured his University degree in Philosophy, had followed this in 1908 with a *diplôme d'études supérieures* for a dissertation on Fénelon's *Théodicée*, a dissertation judged outstanding enough to be published,[34] and he was now pressing on for his final objective, obtainable only after these first two hurdles had been cleared, of the extremely tough *agrégation* examination. He was also making significant advances in the world of literature too, because at the beginning of December 1908, he wrote to Fournier to report that he had had his first meeting with André Gide, together with his colleague and fellow-writer Jean Schlumberger, and that they had expressed an eager interest in enlisting his active support for a literary review they were about to launch to be called *La Nouvelle Revue Française*.[35]

The effect of all this on Fournier was profoundly depressing. He promptly wrote to Bichet:

> I feel so out of everything, so incapable of talking. Jacques' brief account of Gide's visit made me grieve for a whole morning. I feel so far away from all that grace.[36]

And he went on to tell his correspondent that after a recent visit to the Trappist monastery near Entrammes, some seven miles from Laval, he could well understand the attractions of shutting oneself away from the world:

> To renounce forever all thoughts of love and fame. A peace more delightful than Paradise, more terrible and more irrevocable than Hell, that's the greatest of all temptations.

A much more acute form of this *tædium vitae* was voiced in the latest of Fournier's pieces of imaginative writing, *La Femme empoisonée* (*The Tainted Woman*), which he wrote at Laval in November 1908.[37] It opens with images of frustrated amorous yearning: the writer imagines his best beloved desperately searching for him throughout some far-distant countryside while he, meanwhile, is imprisoned with his fellow soldier-students in a dreary little garrison town which he knows she will never visit; the soldiers recall their loneliness, earlier in their lives, in boarding-school, when the unique consolation, yet powerful stimulant, for their longing, was their supervisor's daughter, twinkling past with her skipping-rope. With this central image as pivot, the theme of the poem switches to corruption, both moral and physical: the little girl with her skipping-rope is now the garrison whore, her features alluring from the distance, under the shadow of her broad-brimmed hat, but, from close range, seen to bear unmistakable marks of the pox; at long last, the writer finds his only beloved, but she lies dead in the snow, her features also now ravaged with decay:

> He kneels down beside her and he says: 'So, this is the way you came to look for me, my lost love, down lost paths and amongst lost men, wearing that pauper's cloak. And I couldn't find you in time. All that's left for me to kiss is putrescence, here on the

fine skin in the hollow around your eyes, there under your neck, and there, on your lips, which Death has stiffened and opened into something like a smile.'

Bichet was the first of Fournier's friends to be allowed a sight of this and in the brief covering letter he sent with it, on 5 December, he announced :

I thought at first of filing this away with other notes which are going into the book I'm going to write when my Army days are over . . . But this is as good a way as any of safeguarding it, till the time when I can build it into the main body of my book.[38]

On 19 December he sent Bichet the only copy of another short piece he had just written entitled, appropriately enough, *Dialogue aux approches de Noël (Dialogue close to Christmas)*. It is an interesting amalgam of memory and of wish-fulfilment. Two speakers are conversing in the gathering dusk, Alain – a name which, in the original manuscript, replaces 'Henri' – is the voice of wish-fulfilment, and with mounting urgency, urges his companion, Grande, to leave her château and come home, because now she is married to him, and their children will be growing anxious. Grande is the voice of memory : she recalls watching him approach her château when they were still children themselves, and showing him her Christmas dolls and 'a magic lantern in the dark corridor which led to the drawing room', and she recalls the night in their childhood 'when the gipsies came, about eleven o'clock, begging and shouting insults beneath our windows, and we were filled with burning terror because we knew that for miles around, ours was the one house left awake.' Grande's is also the voice of reality, because when Alain's entreaties to depart with him grow more and more insistent, she is finally obliged to bring him back to earth :

I'm putting my hand on your brow, Alain, to calm your fever. As you well know, we're sitting on a frozen park bench here in the avenue. The land you want to take me to doesn't exist. Alas, our coach will never set out, and we will not ride off to that sweet family gathering in the winter's evening. And the children, far from here, will have to spend their night in the lost house all alone . . .

When Bichet returned this piece, he somewhat disconcerted its

140

author by praising him for his use of assonance and for successfully assimilating the influence of old German romances. Fournier commented wryly to Rivière : 'I rather like this way of getting me wrong and of thinking I'm writing fantasy when I'm trying to be moving,'[39] and at the end of the manuscript of his *Dialogue*, he wrote in pencil :

> And so the miserable human family is broken up again. Once again, you've tried in vain to set out for that country where you belong – and which doesn't exist.

La Femme empoisonnée may seem, in its morbid conclusion, to echo some of the blacker work of Baudelaire, and the anxious and querulous Alain in *Dialogue* may perhaps recall the doomed child in *Der Erlkönig*, but both these short pieces are, in fact, something other than exercises in pastiche. Had Fournier's friends been rather more intimately within his confidence, they would have recognised them for what they surely are, distress signals. Emotional tension was now steadily building up, and the many demands of Fournier's very full Army time-table served only to postpone the inevitable crisis.

It is symptomatic of Fournier's very real sense of alienation that in the early weeks of 1909, he should have expressed considerable enthusiasm for Dostoevsky's novel *The Idiot*, which he was subsequently to hail as 'possibly the bridge I have for so long been seeking between the Christian world and mine.'[40] He readily admired the most striking qualities of the novel's hero, Prince Myshkin – being essentially a solitary even in the gayest company, attracting the attentions of women in spite of himself, being intuitively perceptive about the characters of others, and being able to move undefiled through a corrupt and fallen society – and in the months which followed, Fournier was to lay claim to all of Prince Myshkin's attributes except his epilepsy.

More eloquent evidence of his growing world-weariness is provided in a letter he wrote to Rivière on 3 March 1909, in which he recounted his impressions of a visit he had made a few days previously to see an acquaintance from his far-off days at the lycée of Brest. He spent the night at a baker's in the small village of Brulon, some thirty miles east of Laval, and while there, it suddenly came home to him that he had lost his capacity for wonderment :

> No matter how hard I tried to see things very simply, like a little child, I realised all too well that the wonder I used to find in such adventures has now all gone.
> I knew that because of all our travels and our knowledge

and our maps . . . we could no longer feel we were setting out into the unknown, and that never again for us would anything seem new.

I knew that it was no longer going to be possible to enter a village or a shop with the wonderful sense of not knowing what I was going to find there. I knew that to go up into the upstairs rooms to sleep in that big strange house could no longer have for me all the sweetness and mystery that it used to in the old days. I realised all too well that now we know everything, that everything is predictable, and the delightfulness of the house I was staying in made my lack of response all the harder to bear . . . I felt so desolate and so cold that the only remedy was to go for a long bicycle ride through the countryside buried deep beneath the snow. What pity I felt that day, in the heart of that forlorn and featureless landscape, and how well we understood each other.[41]

He may well have believed on the occasion of his visit to Brulon that his sense of mystery had deserted him, but by the time he came to recall his impressions for Rivière a few days later, it had powerfully returned :

The room where the family comes together is quite surrounded with other rooms and dark nooks closed off behind ill-fitting doors. Behind which one shall I see the baskets all lined up and the grey baking racks of the oven?

Village of which everyone's talking and which I still haven't got to know, nocturnal and frozen out there all around us, where do those roads of yours lead to which cut across each other so strangely? What are these men and these celebrations everyone's talking about? Do the children go to school at night here, because there must be a region *somewhere* where lessons take place at night. The children are very afraid of attending, but they come all the same, just for the pleasure of being together in the lighted room with darkness all round. If the children coming in from the most distant parts of the countryside couldn't find their teacher when they got to school, what would they do with everybody else asleep, if they saw the glimmer of the lights through the windows from the field close by?

A narrow staircase leads up to some vast rooms. In mine, over the mantelpiece and in the angles of the room, brides' head-dresses are hanging. Long curtains are drawn across the very narrow little windows which have been let into the enormous wall. They're like the windows of some château; early tomorrow morning, through those windows will come back strange and familiar sounds, the sunlight will leave its square imprint on the red curtain, and when I draw it back, I'll see through the narrow aperture a whole vast landscape.

These impressions also were added to Fournier's growing dossier: the young lady with her parasol in the June sunshine, the dove-cot in the quiet garden, the marauding gipsies in the night, the derelict château with its reed-fringed pool, the magic lantern in the dark corridor, the clown tumbling down from his leaning tower of chairs and the dead face of a girl who was sought in vain and found too late. All of these images were stored away in the hope that with demobilisation would come not only the leisure, but the characters and plot which were still required before they could be organised into a meaningful novel.

A week after writing that letter to Rivière, Fournier was back in his parents' home in the rue Dauphine, on three weeks' leave after successfully completing his officer's training course, and awaiting posting to his new garrison. His chief activity during this period, apart from the usual round of long conversations and visits to concerts and art galleries, was to write another short prose-poem, *La Partie de plaisir* (The Picnic) which he dedicated to Debussy. The picnic takes place on a lake, in a canoe lined with silk, and it is at once established that the shadowy characters involved are not in the world of everyday. They are, in fact, in the world of their heart's desire: the bewigged lady of great wealth is, in reality, a schoolgirl poring over her books; other ladies who are engaged in witty and animated conversations are, back in the real world, forever tongue-tied. Only one voice is heard to question the point of it all and suggest that it is all foolishness, and that belongs to a tall serious blonde girl with a sunshade.

It was unfortunate that Fournier should have chosen this particular sample of his latest mode of writing for courting the approval of the literary pundits of the day: it is a much more mannered and much less effective piece of writing either than *La Femme empoisonnée* or *Dialogue aux approches de Noël* and it falls far short of what Fournier conceivably meant it to be, the equivalent in verbal images of Debussy's beguiling *En bateau.* His cause was not furthered by the grandiose terms with which Rivière tried to explain and endorse the work when he sent it to Gide on 29 March 1909, expressing the hope that a place might be found for it in *La Nouvelle Revue Française*:

143

This is a fragment from the future book of my friend Fournier.
This book is going to be a sort of transfiguration and study in
depth of the real world and what goes on in it. The humblest
creatures and the most poverty-stricken lives will be presented
with something like a halo, their marvellous second reality in
the land without a name: there, childish and impossible events
would become prodigious adventures and everything would go
lingering mysteriously on. One might say that the effect would
be as if scenes from the everyday world around us were
gradually to reveal their ideal reality . . . My friend would like
to be able to capture the repercussions of sensory experience and
express its metaphysical mystery. He would like to suggest that
behind every landscape there is always a second landscape.[42]

Fournier provided a more succinct and rather more accurate
account of his literary intentions in a letter he sent on 16 March
1909 to one of his new-found friends, the Bordelais painter André
Lhote :

I'm probably going to enclose with this letter a page I composed
the other day – even although people say it's very obscure. It's
an abstract from my future *Land without a Name*. To help
you understand it, I'll simply say that in *The Picnic*, as elsewhere throughout the book, the subject is mental escapism : the
characters are unreal or, more exactly, they're somewhere else,
unhappy, flighty and imprisoned . . .[43]

Fournier's *Land without a Name* is no longer the untravelled world
just beyond the gates of perception; it is no longer the 'Other Landscape' he aspired to gain late in 1906 and in 1907; it has now become
that much less mystical entity, the Land-of-Dreams-Come-True.

In the spring of 1909, another more terrestrial land became his
to explore : he was posted as a second lieutenant to join the 88th
Infantry Regiment in a part of France that was entirely new to him.
On thinking over the news, he decided not to ask his friends to exert
their influence to get the posting changed to somewhere nearer Paris,
and on 30th March he wrote to Jean Bernard :

I'm being sent to Mirande, 438 miles and 15 hours' journey
away from Paris . . . For the time being don't bother to pull any
strings. Perhaps it won't be too unpleasant to spend the summer
in that admirable region right up against the Pyrenees.[44]

III

Fournier arrived in the quiet little town of Mirande on 5 April 1909, and the change in life-style that commissioned status brought with it became at once apparent : he was no longer to live with the crowd in a barracks, but on his own in a set of private rooms. He rented a flat from Monsieur Hidalgo, a Spanish refugee, whose other sources of income were money-lending, smuggling and making sausages. From the very outset, Fournier felt so downcast and lonely, that he promptly arranged to share the flat and expenses with another young second lieutenant who promised to give him boxing-lessons. Another diversion was shooting, and he became the proud owner of two pistols, one provided by his friends the Bernards, the other by an uncle of Rivière's. Apart from that the only recreational opportunities available to him in Mirande itself were drinking and talking in the officers' mess, playing tennis with fellow officers and their wives and daughters, or admiring the views of the distant mountain peaks. His working day was long but far from arduous, consisting as it did of daily drilling and inspections or discussing the next round of manœuvres, and time soon began to hang heavily on his hands. It did not take long for him to begin to manifest those signs of emotional distress which the much more demanding activities of Laval had so effectively muffled throughout the months preceding.

A fortnight after arriving in Mirande, he wrote to Rivière expressing his great longing to be a civilian again :

> I'm so impatient to be free. I have a horror of this job. I can't wait to be done with it all. The 159 days still left to go seem to me interminable.
>
> I suffered a great deal, that first week. Waking up each day, with the whole day to be got through, all my chores to be done and my responsibilities to be undertaken, made me feel indescribably wretched. I wished I was back with the 104th Regiment . . . I would never have believed that Army life, unencumbered as it now is with everything that makes it so disgusting for a humble private, could make me suffer so much. I can't explain why. There's no positive cause of grievance I can identify . . . I'm not afraid of physical exertion, I do my job reasonably well, I get on well with the other lieutenants – yet I'd rather desert than have to live their life for two years.[45]

A fortnight later, he wrote to his parents to express how little he felt he had in common with the other men around him :

145

It would be impossible for anyone to be more friendly towards me than the other lieutenants and captains are being, yet I feel for most of them a secret hatred. To see the way they act in front of the men, so rigid, so implacable, so arrogant and so insensitive, seems to me all the more monstrous when they've just been joking with you like a crowd of schoolboys. There are things I'll never do to the men, tortures I'll never submit them to, humiliations it's customary to inflict on them which they'll never have to endure under my command.[46]

A few days later, in a letter to Bichet, he claimed that he also had a 'special' attitude towards women :

I look at them in the same way as *The Idiot* with a stare that penetrates at once to their soul. It's in women that I've found the soul in its most naked state, as though the skin has been stripped away from it, something which is not of this world and which, when you see it so close, almost makes you tremble with delight and disgust at one and the same time. I know how their neck creases when they turn their face towards me with their mouth contorted; the way the haughtiest of them slowly reveals her secrets; the way the most dignified of them painfully surrenders herself. They've all come to me, as they did to the innocent prince, with a love that was no longer innocent.[47]

There is a bookish flavour about this whole letter to Bichet which makes it difficult, without other corroborative evidence, to take wholly seriously Fournier's allusions to such a richly variegated amorous career, at least at this stage in his experience : in addition to his overt self-identification with Prince Myshkin, he has placed at the head of the letter one of his favourite quotations from Henri de Régnier ('Donnez-moi votre main, prince Hamlet, je connais Cette fièvre . . .')[48] and, after alluding to a night spent in the bed of the 'fallen woman' listening to a nightingale, he concludes with a four-line quotation from Claudel's poem 'Hymne du Saint-Sacrament'; en passant, he also devotes a paragraph to *La Porte etroite* by Gide in which he states how well he understands the world-weariness of the novel's heroine, Alissa. The curiously strident tone of the letter is, in fact, sustained to the very end :

I beg you not to be afraid of me.
I have loved those who were so powerful and so inspired that

they gave the impression of creating something like a new world around them.

Why should I not love you?

The fact that Fournier adopted such a literary – and, on occasions, mawkish – mode of expression in writing this letter to Bichet should not lead one to infer that his distress at this time was somehow not 'real': it was acutely real to him and, when due allowance is made for a prose-style in which recourse to hyperbole is a regular feature, it would still be no exaggeration to say that May and June 1909 were, unquestionably, the blackest two months of Fournier's emotional life.

His distress largely took the form of an extremely painful religious crisis, fomented not only by the particular books he was reading at this time but also by a visit he made in May 1909 to Lourdes, just over forty miles to the south-west of Mirande. Fournier did not approach Lourdes in a particularly mystical frame of mind: he travelled there with his athletic room-mate, and they raced each other on bicycles over the last stage of the trip, covering eleven miles of hilly road in three-quarters of an hour.[49] In a letter to his sister, he said that his first impressions on arriving were of the ugliness and commercialism of the décor, and the lack of poetry about the whole proceedings, the waters from the holy spring coming out of ordinary metal taps and being drunk out of painted metal goblets by the queues of invalids. And yet, in spite of himself, he was moved to tears:

> First of all we went up by the Basilica, and we looked down from a balcony over the invalids and the crowd praying before the grotto and the Baths. And then suddenly I was overcome with some tremendous emotion to which I can't give a name. I don't quite know why I needed so much to weep. Perhaps it was the desperate confidence of them all. She said: *Here I will work miracles.* And in trains from all over the world, they come, quietly telling each other of their hopes. And there they all are in a vast crowd, waiting, supplicating . . .

He felt as much revulsion as compassion for the cripples themselves, with their often grotesque malformations, but he was deeply moved by the spectacle of a small invalid child, repeatedly sipping from its metal goblet and looking longingly at the water from the sacred spring 'like some fever patient dying of thirst':

> In the midst of that crowd of sick people giving off the stench of fetid herrings, that child's look said: 'I am the path of ivory.

Everyone who has come to me has been purified. I am the promise which has been fulfilled, for I promise you the happiness not in this world but in the next. I am simplicity itself: "go and eat of the grass there about you." Most of all, I am here. Let that suffice. Gently I place my hand upon your shoulder. The terrible young queen is with you. But I say unto you: Penitence! Penitence! Penitence!'

We too drank from the goblets of the fountain because She said: '*go drink at the fountain and there wash yourselves clean.*' The water was cold and good; but where was the taste I'd like to have found there and which I haven't yet tasted?[50]

Back in his rooms at Mirande, he sipped a rather headier brew, the bitter waters of desolation compounded of lost childhood, lost religious certainty and lost love. Three days after describing his Lourdes trip to his sister, it was once again Ascension Day, the fourth anniversary of his first sight of Yvonne, and he poured out his despair to Rivière:

I'm spending the whole day shut up here in the house to suffer in comfort. For weeks now those who've touched my hand know I have fever. The secret joy of recent times is over and now I must struggle against infernal pain. How, when I'm all alone, can I get through the party to which I've not been invited? In the very early morning, the sun came pouring into the flat through every window and woke me up. During the night, the servant got everything ready for some great and mysterious anniversary – the hedges full of roses, the road burning hot – and at the very moment when he's about to reveal to everybody the secret reason for this joy, he finds his master alone, in tears, abandoned.

Meanwhile the bells are ringing for Mass. From time to time, a peasant cart comes galloping up. I've a hundred trivial reasons for not going; the most serious of which is that I haven't a decent enough pair of shoes. I recall from the depths of the past, the first Communion mass I should ever have attended. After all the strange sweet rites of preparation, the slow procession of tall girls, swaying like so many white censers, moved off without me. My new shoes were too small. Each time the bell rang out during the ceremony which followed, in the low chapel, redoubled my despair. Someone made the sacrifice of staying behind beside me to dry my tears with the promise of Vespers. – But today, there's no woman beside me to sweeten my bitterness, and there will be no Vespers this time for the man who's missed Mass.

I've picked up my sadness again where I left it in the summer holidays, two years ago. Tiredness, hunger, imprisonment have been speaking in a louder voice, but haven't succeeded in stifling it . . . Once again, my wretchedness is wearing her face. Yesterday, out on manœuvres amongst the red trefoil, I suddenly switched off from everything that wasn't her, and for the first time in ages, I stared so hard into her face that, for a moment, I felt I couldn't walk a single step further.[51]

With that, he turned again to the problem which much preoccupied himself and Rivière during their conversations in 1909 – the question of religious conversion :

Yet it isn't this love of mine which is holding me back. I'm no Protestant. In the past, I used to think : if I were to turn Christian, I'd at once become a priest or, if it was too late for that, then a monk. When I visited La Trappe and we had to kneel down in the chapel, since I knew that the first prayers you make in any church are always granted, I was tempted by the monstrous life monks lead, and I had the strength to say : 'If that's how it's to be, then let it be.' But it wasn't to be, and after a great deal of hesitation, ah! how I regret not having asked the Virgin of Lourdes to perform the miracle of giving me back my love! To see her again, just once more, to look upon that pure, pure face of hers and, just for a moment, to rest my sad head against her blonde hair.

I promise you happiness not in this world but the next.

So much purity cannot belong to this world. 'Go and eat of the grass there about you.' I'm going to read *Dominique*[52] again; I conceive as very beautiful the conclusion of the book when, back on his estate again, he tries to live on without his love. But I, for my part, am going to renounce nothing. There is no grief and no pain which isn't essential to me . . . If I can enter Catholicism with the whole of myself intact, then I'm a Catholic from this moment on. And only the other day I convinced myself that the culmination of my whole book would be some great triumph for the Virgin.

The children I have will be brought up in the most Christian way possible. How I'm suffering, my friend, how I'm suffering.

He left the letter for five hours, then added :

Nothing's happened to take my mind off my anguish. If things went on like this, I couldn't for long bear this weight of the whole world in my heart. Something is desperately calling out for me and I'm cut off from it by all the roads of the earth.

At this very hour, four years ago on this same Ascension Day, she slowly began to go down the stone staircase and she fixed me with a glance so pure that I turned around.

I can't write any more. I've a profound horror of this pain that's torturing me. Above all, don't think I'm taking pleasure in it. Perhaps if I were purer and if I attached less importance to the world and reality, I'd be cured. I alone am to blame. I'm going to try to work – or to sleep.

Whit Sunday 1909 was the fourth anniversary of Fournier's only conversation with Yvonne and he chose to spend it in Bordeaux with the painter André Lhote. For his own peace of mind, this turned out to be an unwise choice because Lhote had very recently married, and he spoke freely to his guest about the special pleasures of being a husband; Fournier, always emotionally most vulnerable on this particular day, returned to Mirande in deep distress :

> In spite of being an inflexible optimist, Lhote has sensed, from time to time, what a monstrous thing it is to have one's happiness there within one's hand. He told me how stupefying it was the first time he found her beside him when he woke up, with the sunshine in their eyes, and she said, just like a child, 'My eyes are smarting'. Ever since my childhood, I've tried to imagine that shattering moment and each time I'm filled with the same terror.
>
> The return journey was intensely sad, across the Landes through the oppressive heat of the afternoon. I used to be filled with the same sense of desolation as we drove back across the Sologne, leaving behind us those lovely lands of my childhood. And I felt the same unbearable grief when I went on the first pointless journey after I lost my love. Over and over, I kept on saying : 'What about *me*? What about *me*?'

Once again, he expressed his sense of profound world-weariness. He was now resolved to turn his back on life and only two escape-routes seemed open to him, the monastery or death :

> I'm tired out and haunted by the fear of seeing my youth come to an end. I stand looking at the world before me like a person who has to make his choice before taking his leave. What direc-

tion shall I choose, where is that final harmony I'm looking for, what's to be the meaning of the symbolic presents I take with me on my journey? . . . Should my hour of departure come, everything will be ready. How lovingly have I contemplated death – 'death, our dearest heritage'. You who know me, I beg you to take seriously what I'm now about to tell you, even if I'm fated never to become a Christian. I've been arguing this over in my own mind for years, but this time my mind is made up : on the day I take that final step, if I have to take it, then I'll become a monk and be a missionary.[53]

This letter had immediate and dramatic repercussions in the Fournier household back in Paris : Rivière, still involved in agonising theological disputation with Claudel, was acutely distressed by his friend's 'terrible resolution', and found it impossible to conceal it from Fournier's mother. She was appalled and, with more prescience than the incredulous Rivière was ready to allow, claimed it all sprang from the desire to imitate Claudel. Fournier was at once obliged to explain and justify himself to his mother but the words he chose to do so, in more than one instance echoes or direct quotations from Claudel, could not have wholly mollified her. Having described the peace and loneliness of his rooms in Mirande, he went on :

This solitude is propitious for deep contemplation. Lhote used to say to me : the great religious people are creatures of leisure. How often, as at present, have I tried to make myself believe by imposing on myself the austere life-style of a monk. I used to do this when I was bored with the holidays or in the long winter. When you're turned in on yourself, you have to chew over all the old problems. But when the summer comes, or some departure, or some arduous task, then everything's forgotten and all you hear then is 'the inexorable call of the marvellous voice.'[54] . . . For a true Christian, the only words that count are those of his terrible order : 'If you want to pray, get down on your knees!' And the call of the Virgin : 'Penitence! Penitence!' – In truth, when we were children, then merely to be alive was an endless effusion, the sweetest of conversations with the purest of creatures; and if we prayed at the side of the bed, his face was there, leaning down towards ours, and it was up to him, smilingly, to bring his ear closer. But now that we're no longer children, now that we're more impure than the earth, how can we make God hear our earthly voice? Can our soul utter a cry painful enough or despairing enough to reach him? The time for the Passion has come. It's no longer enough to look with wonder at the carpenter's wood-shavings. 'Man is virtually being crucified and he is being stretched to his very extremities in every direction.'[55] It's only when one finally sweats blood that the voice of the soul can be heard and that Christ receives his answer.

Fournier was to remain preoccupied with religion throughout the summer of 1909, and his reading throughout these weeks was almost exclusively religious in nature : Claudel's poetry and plays, *The Idiot*, Gide's latest novel *La Porte etroite* which, understandably but quite erroneously, created the impression that he had renounced his exuberant hedonism for austere quietism, and the New Testament, which he seems to have discovered for the first time in July 1909, and which he began to read regularly in Mirande in the company of two priests, the almoner of the local old people's hostel and the *curé* of the nearby village of Miramont. The question inevitably poses itself, therefore : why, in the very trough of despondency, with every-thing he read, heard, saw and felt impelling him towards confession and the sacraments, did he resist conversion?

His reasons for doing so were emphatically not, as they were in the case of many of his contemporaries, social or political : insofar as he had any political views of his own, they were vaguely left of centre, but in none of his letters does he ever express any sense of distaste at the prospect of allying himself with what have always been seen in France as the forces of conservative reaction. Neither were his objections philosophical or intellectual : he accepted without question belief in the Holy Virgin, in her capacity to work miracles, in the efficacity of Catholic sacraments, and writing in May 1909 to his sister, about the fellow officer who accompanied him to Lourdes, he declared, 'he was more Catholic than me – but less of a believer'.[56] His resistance was almost wholly emotional and in this, personal pride played no small part : conversion was still seen in terms of victory, for some proselytising power like Claudel, and of defeat for himself. In his religious life as in his school life, he could be stubbornly independent on matters of principle, and he was simply not prepared to surrender.

The one quality most conspicuously lacking in all his pronounce-ments about religion is genuine *humility*: like Claudel, he wanted to be a monk on his own absolutist terms or not at all; he expected religion to restore not only his feeling of purity, but his lost love and his fading sense of wonder as well; he insisted throughout on re-entering the Church strictly on *his* conditions, not on those imposed from without or above, however lofty the authority. His thinking and feeling throughout his crises remained resolutely Fournier-centred, never God-centred, and it would not, therefore, be unreasonable to conclude that he rejected Catholicism not because of the superior counter-claims of some other religious creed, or of Science, or of left-wing politics, or even of Art, but because of his allegiance to a cause more important to him than any of these – himself.

It was inevitable for Fournier, whose 'creative' writing was invariably a transmutation of his own experiences, that these religious pre-occupations should readily have affected his literary plans. Up till the beginning of June 1909, he worked intermittently at *Le Pays sans nom*, and he produced four more pieces to add to *Dialogue aux approches de Noël* and *La partie de plaisir*. In *Dans le tout petit jardin (In the tiny garden)*,[57] the only one of the four he actually completed, he again imagines that his lost beloved has come back to him and that they are man and wife walking in the dusk to their house in the woods; *La Maison verte (The Green House)* or *Le Voyage entre le aulnes (Journey between the alders)*, expresses the narrator's sense of high expectancy as he explores the bird-haunted woods in search of 'the pathway you read about in books, the concealed pathway to which the tired prince cannot rediscover the entrance'; *Ce fut une soirée d'avril (All on an April evening)* describes how the anonymous narrator and his companion, Madeleine, enter a derelict house and find a nest full of dying chicks, and how they vainly try to revive them; and in the few paragraphs only which survive of *Le Dîner de printemps (Spring Dinner)*, a group of children are pretending to prepare for a make-believe lunch while up above them in an attic, someone is practising on the flute.

It is difficult to detect in these pieces any of that metaphysical mystery to which Rivière referred in his explanatory letter to Gide. If *Le Pays sans nom* has dominant characteristics they are not so much other-worldliness, or mysteriousness, as high feverishness and profound melancholy. *Dans le tout petit jardin*, for example, ends with the narrator preparing to spend the night with the wife for whom he has so long been yearning :

> May the unbearable summer night now come ! On to the balcony, which extends out over the shadowy garden, opens the drawing-room door concealed by thick foliage. But this evening, like a beacon at the prow of a doomed ship, full of fragrance and fever, someone has lit the household lamp.

As the girls speak together in their dream world of *La Partie de plaisir*, 'all the voices blend into one, so that all you hear is a vague and confused murmur which fills you with fever and despair, like bells chiming for summer vespers in distant villages'; while in *Ce fut une soirée d'avril*, Madeleine and the narrator feel

> frozen and tormented in the strange house! Every so often, she went to look into the feverish nest and removed another chick that had just died in an effort to save the life of the others. And each time, it seemed to us that through the shattered windows of the attic, something like a great wind, or like the mysterious heart-ache of unknown children came silently lamenting. And we didn't know how to console whatever it was that was weeping. 'We'll have to keep watch all through the night,' she said. And so all through the night, without a sound and without a light, the pair of us kept our vigil, the only creatures left alive in that doomed house.

Neither the fever nor the fretfulness which dominates these passages is difficult to account for: when one tries in vain to make a dream come true through sheer force of longing, one's heart sinks and one's temperature rises. Fournier was just too clear-sighted ever to allow his characters to stay for long in the Land without a Name: sooner or later the words *A quoi bon? A quoi bon?* would break the spell and toll them back to reality. He sought to console himself with one or other of two melancholy conclusions: either human happiness, when achieved, was too terrible to be borne, or else it was quite unattainable in this world beneath the moon.

The effect of Fournier's religious preoccupations upon his literary plans was a marked increase in his use of biblical terminology and much greater insistence on the theme that true happiness is not of this world. He wrote to Rivière on 18 June:

> At the present moment, I'm striving to produce what is really the essential passage. From all the moments, I'm choosing only those which are touched with grace. I'm looking for the key to the escape road to the lands of heart's desire – and perhaps it's death, after all.[58]

By the end of July he was able to report to Rivière that he was hard at work on his writing and, at that particular moment, concentrating on an episode he was planning to situate at the end of the book. The character involved was to be 'the adolescent of the night,

154

the guardian of the doves, the ancient soul most pure',[59] the setting was going to be a tower rising up from a land which is being progressively submerged beneath a rising tide :

> Every day, like a man condemned, he notes down on a piece of paper the rising of the fatal floodwaters. And each time, into the great simplicity of his life, something comes gliding, monstrous because it is so pure and so desirable, like an incomprehensible word in the talk of someone on the verge of madness. At last, one night, from the very top of his tower, whilst below him and as far as the eye can see gleams the world of Joy unknown, he realises that true joy is not of this world and yet, for all that, it is there just outside, about to open the door and come to rest against his heart. And as he dies, he writes something down, a name perhaps (I haven't yet decided) – and on every gate in the fields all around, which are once again terrestrial, a child is sitting, in a white robe, his feet dangling, blowing notes at regular intervals on a flute of gold.

Then, as an after-thought, he added :

> This is all a general outline. I think I'll probably dispense with the tower. Perhaps the name he writes will be 'Mary'. If that should be so, then I wouldn't write my book.
> *O Lord, let me drink of those waters, so that I may thirst no longer and come to the well no more.*

Fournier wrote no more in this particular vein and, for the sake of his posthumous literary reputation, this is just as well. It provides useful additional insight into the state of his feelings at this particular time, but the only comment on its artistic quality would seem to be a sentence from the preface Keats supplied to *Endymion* :

> The imagination of a boy is healthy, and the mature imagination of a man is healthy; but there is a space of life in between, in which the soul of life is in a ferment, the character undecided, the way of life uncertain, the ambition thick-sighted : thence proceeds mawkishness.

To judge from what Fournier actually managed to produce in the summer of 1909, another product of – and doubtless, in its turn a contributory factor to – his religious conflict was artistically more efficacious : this was his sense of personal contamination. This almost

155

certainly arose out of his continued contact with the person who, in his letters to his friends, he described as 'la fille perdue' (the fallen woman) and with whom, he claimed in his letter to Bichet of 7 May 1909, he spent, at the very least, one night. He wrote to Rivière on 18 June :

> I'm going to write some more about the fallen woman or, if you wish, *Le Femme empoisonnée*. It will be one of the most beautiful passages in my book. At present I'm brooding over a passage about her cats which I should like to make as moving as it's to be terrifying.[60]

A short passage describing 'Josépha', the most notorious 'fallen woman' of a little town, and her cat, was found after Fournier's death among the work-notes for his unfinished novel *Colombe Blanchet*, but it is in such skeletal form as to be neither 'moving' nor 'terrifying'. Rather more interesting is the 'fille perdue' who appears as one of the two central characters in *Madeleine*, a short story he wrote in July and August 1909.[61] The discarded first title of the story was *Le Miracle du Dernier Soir* (The Miracle of the Last Evening) and this indicates the time when the action takes place. The story is set on the eve of the Day of Judgment and shows Tristan and Madeleine, neither of whom has found happiness in this world, preparing to find ever-lasting joy in the next. Each of them has had many lovers : Madeleine has been a prostitute; Tristan, a peasant with close-cropped head, lists the women who have given themselves to him in the hope of curing his sadness, but always in vain. They flee together into the darkness 'like a newly married couple made demented by their happiness', and in the middle of a deep forest, within a moonlit clearing, they come across a farm where they find 'the yard swept clean as though it was the eve of a fête.' In the farm, they find a group of children, some old men and 'a farmer's wife who must once have been beautiful', and they all look forward to setting out together for the Promised Land :

> The children know that this time they'll be forgiven for not sleeping right through the night. Since everyone is going on the journey, they'll have to be dressed in their best clothes. They'll be taken to play in a land of abandoned tile-works and deserted convents where they'll discover, as they chase each other in the dusk, down corridors and underground passages, the entrance to a vast city gleaming in another summer.[62]

The story is an intriguing amalgam of echoes from Rimbaud – in

particular the childhood sections of *Les Illuminations* and the last
section of *Une Saison en Enfer* – and of a number of Fournier's
newest and oldest memories: Tristan's catalogue of the women who
have offered him their love to no effect is almost a replica of Fournier's
own list in his letters to Bichet and the newly-married Rivières,[63]
while Madeleine, introduced from the outset as 'la fille perdue', seems
firmly based on his fallen woman in Mirande; the impressions of
moonlit buildings and nocturnal forests almost certainly derive from
his experiences of night manœuvres with the 104th Infantry Regiment;
more interesting still, however, are Madeleine's memories of a coach
journey she was taken on when she was a very young child:

> I'd like once more to go on the first journey I made into the
> town, one summer's night, when I was a very pious little girl.
> The big peasant cart with the white canvas cover went swaying
> along between the willows and the wells in the gardens. We
> crossed over bridges and I could hear the unseen waters murmur-
> ing down there beneath the trailing mist. And my imagination
> began to paint me a picture of the town we were going to as
> something strange and distant, out of this world altogether, I
> sank into a half-sleep. I lay there, wrapped in blankets, and
> when we went round a bend in the road, I felt the nocturnal
> branches brush across my eyes. And close by me, two voices
> which never slept talked aloud about the horse, the scenery and
> the stars. And then on my eyelids, I felt the coolness of the new
> day, like cold water: The cart has stopped at the gates of the
> mysterious city we're due to enter, and there's a man on the road
> talking to us . . . His first words, as I recall, came into my dream
> before I woke up. At first they were like unknown flowers which
> have been silent for ages and then blossom out, one after the
> other, into something like a sentence. And then, I found that the
> sentence was coming from the parched lips of someone enormous,
> standing close beside me, overcome with fatigue. And with the
> words he sent into my dreams, he held out the prospect of a
> kingdom where springs of fresh water quench every thirst and
> gratify every desire.[64]

Given Fournier's characteristic methods of composition, it would
not be unreasonable to assume that Madeleine's memories of childhood
are closely based on those of her creator. More interesting still, however, and certainly of greater import, is that Fournier's 'Other Landscape' has, on the evidence of this passage, once more shifted ground.
The Land Without a Name, dimly glimpsed in the innocence of

childhood, is doubtless as inaccessible as ever to the errant adult, but, at least for the moment, it is nameless no longer: it is now the Kingdom of Heaven and, as such, it will feature in Fournier's literary plans for some time to come.

After the violent emotional storms generated by his visit to Lourdes, by his reading and by the fourth anniversaries of his encounters with Yvonne, a succession of other events in the summer of 1909 combined to intensify his profound *taedium vitae*. On 30 June, 'poor' Chesneau, his friend from Lakanal days, whose own whimsical affectations of world-weariness made Fournier feel more irritation than compassion, died suddenly of acute albumin deficiency. While Fournier was considering the question of his own ultimate salvation and his ever-lasting soul, his more immediate earthly future was very much at stake on two important counts, and in each, what he had to offer was weighed in the balance and found sadly wanting. The artistic breakthrough he hoped to achieve with *La Partie de plaisir* was thwarted when, after unconscionable delay, Gide rejected it for publication in *La Nouvelle Revue Française*. And the hopes he still entertained of a glittering career in the Colonial Service, largely conditional on his obtaining at least the minimal linguistic qualifications, were dealt a shattering blow on 11 July 1909 with the news that he had failed the English *licence* examination which he had taken a fortnight previously: in the vital French into English translation paper, he scored an abysmal 25 per cent.

This further examination failure does not seem to have altogether surprised him, and it was doubtless his conscience-stricken anticipation of having once more to disappoint his parents' expectations that led him to say to Rivière, four days before the result was announced:

> I'm rather annoyed with my parents. I don't want any longer to be judged like everybody else. There is no common ground between the rest of the world and me.[65]

This line was peddled rather more truculently when he wrote to his father and mother after the results came out:

> Before I send my kisses and end this letter, I want to make a point of saying something which has to do with various unspoken reproaches and certain tears that have been shed: if anyone suspects me, then it's because he himself has something to reproach himself for; if anyone censures me for my conduct, then it's because he's already been carrying evil within himself; any-

one who treats me like Tom, Dick or Harry, and seeks to judge me by the common standard, is guilty of a grave injustice; if, in order to understand me and my actions, anyone refers back to his own past experience or to the common standards of the day, then he just doesn't understand me and he's merely widening the gulf between him and me.[66]

It would seem unlikely that this over-reaction on Fournier's part can be attributed wholly to examination-failure (which had, by now, almost become a way of life for him), or merely to adulation of the Testament according to St John which he was closely studying in the first week of July.[67] It owed a great deal also to his relationship with 'Josépha-Amanda', 'the fallen woman' of Mirande : how far and how often she had fallen, and the precise nature of her relationship with Fournier must be largely matters for speculation, though Madame Rivière conceded that it was a brief carnal affair. It must surely be to this fact that must be attributed the corrosive feeling of contamination that pervades his writings at this period, and his aggressive need to justify himself. One feels from this point on that having, in his view, been unjustly deprived of Yvonne when he felt he was truly worthy of her, he was now perversely resolved to have the worst of all possible worlds. Symptomatically, Yvonne, whom he had formerly cast in the rôle of his Muse, was now allotted the rôle of his Conscience. He wrote to Rivière on 2 July to describe his latest 'vision' of her which he had been vouchsafed while on summer manœuvres with his regiment on the plains of Toulouse :

Sometimes, all the ardour of the day seems to have been concentrated in my tent, as though my youth were calling to me. Yesterday evening, after celebrating the anniversary of Wagram, I retired to my tent and there, my love was waiting for me, more tenacious than remorse, her face quite still as it rested on her closed fist, crueller than the guardian angel of purity.[68]

At the end of July, he had occasion to commiserate with Rivière who, in the Philosophy *agrégation* examinations of that year did not win a place high enough in the strictly competitive order to be awarded a pass. After speculating on Rivière's now precarious future, he spoke with penetrating self-knowledge about his own :

Ah ! if I wanted to, what could I not achieve; if I renounced everything, what obstacles could I not surmount; if I were cured of my wonderful and delectable weakness. If I could be sure of making my fortune there, I'd leave for China. At any rate, I'm still looking around and before October, I'll find something.[69]

Rivière's examination failure removed the prospect of a secure academic post in the immediate future but, after urgent family discussions, he and Isabelle Fournier decided not to alter the date of their wedding which, for some time, had been fixed for 24 August 1909. The religious ceremony was performed in the Church of St Germain des Prés and, by ironic mischance, in the side-chapel of the Sacred Heart where Fournier had watched Yvonne de Quiévrecourt kneeling in prayer on Whit Sunday four years previously. The Church was very much less crowded on this occasion : Rivière's father and step-mother, together with their friends, showed their disapproval of what, in their view, was a disastrous misalliance, by staying away.

Not surprisingly, Fournier, who was best man at the wedding, was profoundly affected both at the time and, even more so, when he had returned to his lonely flat in Mirande and had the opportunity to reflect. He wrote to his mother, marvelling at Rivière's great calmness throughout the ceremony, reflecting that the married couple would now have to come to terms with 'that monstrous thing called happiness.' He went on :

> For my part, I'll probably never know the stupor and the peace of sleeping in the house of happiness. There's too much pride inside me, too much dissatisfaction that nothing can mollify and doubtless my soul takes up too much room ever to endure the company of another's beside it.[70]

On the same day, he wrote to the Rivières while they were still on honeymoon at Cenon, recalling that two years previously he had stood on the beach where they were doubtless now walking, and had looked out over the sea beside which they were now so happy :

> In my mind's eye, I see again that despairing August afternoon of two years ago, when I watched, rolling in endlessly from the grey horizon, the foam-topped waves. How forlorn I was then. And how sad I felt beside that infinitely forlorn desolation. Yet how I loved it ! Because I knew that that was something else I should never be able to clutch to my heart.[71]

He then proceeded to list all the nameless women who had tried in vain to console him, including one who danced for him on a dark lawn to the strains of piano music coming from a party in the house nearby, and one who visited him in the small hours, quite naked, 'offering her poor body with the voice of someone who has lost her way and is ready to pay any price to find it again.'

The catalogue is almost identical in details and terminology to that provided by the melancholy Tristan in *Madeleine* and Madame Rivière was insistent that every one of the incidents, in each list, actually took place exactly as he described them. She also added that during the last few weeks of his stay in Mirande, Fournier sought consolation in a 'chaste idyll' with a girl called 'Laurence'.[72] As will be seen, his own transcription of the closing stage of the 'idyll' would seem to indicate that the adjective 'chaste' was here being applied in some abstruse technical sense.

After his amorous confessions, Fournier once more sought to defend himself with a series of quick, oblique references to his favourite books of 1909, *The Idiot* and the Bible :

> Certainly I've known girls and women. And if anyone reproaches me, that will prove that he's failed to recognise the shepherd of souls, the sick prince. Whoever reproaches me for it will be judging according to the flesh.

And he apologised for disturbing their honeymoon happiness with the plea that he needed to assure himself that the marriage had not vitally altered the relationship between them and him :

> I've told you all this to prove to myself that I could tell you everything, just as I could before the marriage, and so that you'd understand that one of us is unhappy and lost and searching still . . . Write to me. I expect a great deal from you. There are no two ways about it, it's from you that I have to seek comfort when I'm sad. Don't abandon me.[73]

Rivière's prompt and lengthy reply to this plea was full of patience and compassion, and did much to reassure Fournier while he was away on a fortnight's manœuvres in Gascony. However, on his return to Mirande, he was immediately plunged once more into despair. Determined not to give up hope, however faint it might be, that he would one day be reunited with Yvonne, he had, some time previously, enlisted the help of a private enquiry agency to find out how she was faring. The agency's report arrived in Mirande while he was away on manœuvres and he read it immediately he returned on 21 September : Madame Yvonne Brochet (née Toussaint de Quiévrecourt) was faring all too well, still happily married and now the mother of a son. Fournier wrote at once to Rivière :

This morning, all the joy in my returning collapsed when I got the news I was half expecting. She's more lost to me now than if She were dead. I'll never find her again in this world . . .

On the wall of a humble room, in a farm somewhere, I once saw a religious text which read : *I seek a pure heart and there will I dwell* (*The Imitation of Christ*).

There's no point in my searching any more . . .

Forgive me for coming to stand outside your happiness every other minute like some beggar displaying his sores.[74]

He was demobilised on 25 September, and his period of Army service therefore ended as it had begun, in a mood of black despair. If a truly comprehensive balance-sheet were drawn up to cover his two years as a soldier, it ought not, however, to consist wholly of debit entries. Physically, he had stood up extremely well to the traumas of the first few weeks, and to the periods of extremely strenuous activity to which he was subjected at regular intervals. From the literary point of view, his close contact with a diverse collection of other human beings and with a variety of French regions had greatly extended the range of his emotional experience. In spite of often severe psychological pressures which built up in the summer of 1909, partly because of difficulties that were already deep-rooted, and partly because of new events and situations quite outside his control, he did not suffer a nervous breakdown, neither did he surrender himself to the Church; and for all his professed love of death, he was at no point in danger of committing suicide. Physically, emotionally and spiritually, he was more resilient than he affected to be or than his friends were prepared to concede.

Fournier's more considered summing-up on his Army experiences might well, therefore, have been the relieved yet triumphant words with which D. H. Lawrence celebrated the end of one of his most intense periods of emotional strain : 'Look! we have come through!' Or what he actually did say to his mother in August 1909 at the end of a letter, full of self-pity and vituperation, about the alleged privations of a soldier's life :

In point of fact, I'm neither sad nor in a state of collapse. There are days when I go around the house like a young colt, saying to myself over and over till I'm out of breath : 'I'm young! I'm young! And a whole long life lies before me.'[75]

6

Sweet Land of Liberty

October 1909–April 1912

> Knowing how to become free is nothing; it's
> knowing how to *be* free that's so hard.
> Gide[1]

Since the autumn of 1898, when he started his senior school career at the lycée Voltaire, Fournier had had to adapt himself to an institutional régime of one sort or another, so his release from Army service in September 1909 was, for him, a particularly momentous occasion: not only was he now to become a civilian and an adult, but, after what he more than once described as his 'eleven-year sentence', he was now going to be *free*.

At first, he seems to have been quite content to rediscover the joys of being young and living in Paris, visiting art exhibitions, attending plays and concerts, browsing through bookshops or along the boulevards and the banks of the Seine.

The aeroplane was still very much a novelty in those days and his letters contain regular references to his high excitement at having seen another plane, or to diners, hearing the rasping sound of engines, and rushing out from their restaurant tables to look up into the sky. Another regular source of pleasure for him was the more sedate sound of plain-chant in the Benedictine chapel in the rue Monsieur, and he often attended Mass there, not in order to participate, but merely to listen.

He lived in his parents' flat in the rue Dauphine together with the Rivières, and these he used to lunch with every day while Monsieur and Madame Fournier were away teaching at their schools in the remoter suburbs. Madame Rivière recalls that during his first weeks of being a civilian again, he tended to get up last of all:

> Light of step, like a child, humming some tune or other, he
> would turn the act of getting dressed into something like a ballet,

163

filling all the rooms in the house with a sense of fantasy, leaving little touches of whimsy in all sorts of places which we'd find later and which would make us smile and would touch our hearts at the same time : my blue scarf draped round the ridiculous Art Nouveau water-sprite in the drawing-room, turning it into a Tanagra statuette : the names Jacques and Isabelle inscribed inside a flaming heart scrawled in tooth-paste over every mirror in the house, for Mother to discover with consternation in the evening. He breaks off from shaving to pick out a tune from *Pelléas* on the piano or he comes into my room with a face-flannel round his head and, with water still dripping from strands of his hair, holding a volume of Claudel in one hand to see what it would be like to act out together the opening scene between Marthe and Thomas Pollock . . .²

For Fournier and the Rivières, Claudel was still the contemporary writer they admired more than any other, and all three of them were flabbergasted when on 1 October 1909, on a day of torrential rain, he arrived at the front door of 22 rue Dauphine to continue in person the impassioned dialogue he had been conducting with Rivière from the Far East since March 1907. Looking back on the occasion a quarter of a century later, in *Le Bouquet de roses rouges* (1935), a 'novel' in which fiction is not far removed from fact, Isabelle Rivière was to recall that the visit left them 'shaken, disconcerted, totally nonplussed, like three schoolchildren.'³ Rivière seems to have found Claudel himself as disturbing as his books, but he continued to correspond with him. Fournier's reactions to the visit are not on record, although it is possibly significant that from about this period on, he found other literary shrines at which to worship.

Rivière, with a wife to support, was working temporarily as a schoolteacher in Catholic institutions outside the State system, first at the Ecole St Joseph and then at the Collège Stanislas. For Fournier, there was now no longer any talk about emigrating to the Far East, though over a period of some months, he engaged in somewhat desultory correspondence about the possibilities of a teaching-post in a school in Margate. In fact, however, he was very little clearer about his choice of future career than he had been at Lakanal in 1904, when his classmates had predicted that Rivière would end up as a full-time music critic, and Fournier as a lecturer to exclusively female audiences. And so, when he was not out enjoying the sights and sounds of Paris, or engaging his relatives and friends in conversation, he devoted his time to what he had always anticipated he would do, to his writing.

In the early days of October, his most immediate concern was to polish three short pieces he had written during his last month at Mirande, and when he was satisfied with them, they were sent to Gide under the title *Trois Proses*, with the hope that they might be published in *La Nouvelle Revue Française*; Rivière made his own literary début in this review in November 1909 with his essay, *Introduction à une métaphysique du rêve*, and to Fournier this must have seemed something of a challenge and a favourable augury. The first two, *La Chambre d'amis du tailleur* (*The Tailor's Guest Room*) and *Marche avant le jour* (*On the March before Daybreak*) both record impressions of that autumn's Army manœuvres and, in each case, the words *Grandes Manœuvres* in fact precedes the main title; the third piece, *L'Amour cherche les lieux abandonnés* (*Love looks for lonely places*), records his feelings while out on his final walk with 'Laurence', and is an interesting variation on that well-worn theme of *The Last Ride Together*. Each of the pieces contains variations on familiar Fournierian themes. In *La Chambre d'amis*, he apostrophises the little room which, he imagines, has been waiting for him all his life :

> From the depths of other summer nights, I brought you all my yearning from the other houses I've lived in, houses where the summer holidays are dying, where children weep for frustration when they see the bright gleams of the night shining on their windowpane, houses in which we used to imagine you, so beautiful, moving out there somewhere in the shadows, a room we didn't know, all filled with people, the guest room to which nobody invited us.[4]

In *Marche avant le jour*, the sight of a deserted road-mender's hut, glimpsed in the darkness as he and his soldiers march down a road, is enough to make him think of two lovers, alone at last with their happiness in their own 'marvellous and precarious kingdom'. This is also the major theme of *L'Amour cherche les lieux abandonnés* in which the two lovers, knowing that they will never meet again, hunt for some lonely refuge in which they can briefly cause time to stand still :

> No earthly domain seemed lonely enough for you, my love! Not the hunters' lodge in the forest, standing like a milestone at the junction where eight paths all seem to have lost their way, and not even, beyond the very furthest bend in the road, that mildewed chapel beneath funereal boughs . . . The place we found for our love on that evening in autumn, when we had to take leave of each other, was beneath the rain, by a deserted

courtyard from which she secretly opened the door for me. When she softly called to me from the threshold, I could scarcely make out the shape of her body and I shall never know the real appearance of the overgrown gardens through which we groped our way. 'Touch my hair,' she said, bringing it close to my eyes, 'see how damp it is.' All around us we heard the vast rustlings of the deep forests of the night. And when I kissed her unseen face that I was fated never again to look upon, I tasted the night itself. For a moment, she pushed her delicate cold hands up inside my sleeves to warm them from my arms – that sad caress she loved. Lost to other men, lost to ourselves, we were like two drowned bodies locked together, floating down the night. We had found the desert where we could at last unfold, like a tent, our kingdom without a name. On the edge of that surrender from where there is no turning back, you said to me, my love, with your head still lolling on my shoulder, in a voice lower even than despair : 'Never! Let this never end!' For ever and ever, we shall go on whispering to each other like this, mouth close to mouth, like two children who've been put into the same bed in an unknown house on the night before some great happiness – and the forest, which comes sweeping right up to their lighted window, mingles its voice with theirs . . .⁵

After brief consideration of the *Trois proses*, Gide declined all three as he had earlier rejected *La Partie de plaisir*. Fournier managed to place *L'Amour cherche les lieux abandonnés* with another review, *L'Occident*, in which it was published in January 1910. In the same month he was issued with an official yellow pass-card to indicate that he was now a professional journalist, though his journalistic activities at this stage seem to have consisted in feeding snippets of gossip to Charles Morice, editor of the paper *Paris-Journal*, for other writers to work up into stories. He finally made his entry into the hallowed pages of *La Nouvelle Revue Française* with a brief book-review in each of the numbers March, April and May 1910.

For a period of at least six months after being demobilised, Fournier was effectively unemployed, living off – as well as with – his parents. He was sufficiently loyal and sufficiently sensitive a son to feel intense remorse about this continuing situation and, at the end of 1909, in a number of letters to André Lhote, so far still unpublished, he described how black his mood had once again become. Characteristically, his sense of personal inadequacy was translated into terms of scholastic challenge and failure, and, not for the first time, his thoughts readily turned to the prospect of death.

166

On 19 December he wrote :

For some time now, I've been haunted by the thought that there is something I have to learn before I die. For the first time in my experience, being ignorant fills me with fear, almost, indeed, with terror. I feel that I'm going to be cast into the darkness, that there I'll be asked what I've learnt, that I'll know nothing at all, and that my torture will be the monstrous remorse over failing to learn what I was supposed to learn. This notion was so vivid in my mind that my first reaction was to force myself to learn something, anything at all. But is it going to be enough just to be able to say, 'Well, now at any rate, there's *something* I know'? Now I'm beginning to wonder if there isn't some special road to knowledge.

If you haven't already dedicated yourself to death, how can you really despise the body and the face you've been given? There's no doubt if I were a woman, I would use make-up. I like dandies. I like their taste for the artificial. I want to rule over this imaginary kingdom which I'm creating day by day . . . In this book I'm writing I want to introduce into my kingdom an ever more penetrating odour of death . . .

At the end of the next letter he wrote to Lhote ten days later, he commented : 'I feel so terribly low here in Paris, both physically and mentally. I don't know whether I'll be able to go on living here for another month.'

In fact, before a month had fully elapsed, Fournier's spirits were restored by the antidote which never ceased to be effective : literary composition. In this case, the subject was the sight of central Paris spectacularly submerged beneath the waters of the Seine which, in January 1910, rose to the highest level in the city's history, and Fournier provided a long and graphic description in an unpublished letter dispatched to Lhote at the end of the month. However gloomy was the prospect of Fournier's innermost thoughts, rare indeed were the occasions when he failed to respond to the beautiful or the bizarre sights afforded by the world around him : in yet another unpublished letter to Lhote written in August 1911, he succinctly described his readiness to counter the constantly renewed challenge of experience with a controlled literary response : 'My only rôle in life is to tell stories and to live them out.'

Throughout the months which followed his demobilisation, Fournier's parents seem neither to have complained nor to have brought undue pressure to bear on him to take a regular job. With the salaries of three teachers contributing to the family income, the household was not uncomfortably off, and indeed, on 26 March 1910, they were all able to move from rue Dauphine to a larger flat at 2 rue Cassini, in a much more attractive district of Paris near the Observatory, with wide and peaceful tree-lined avenues and park lawns in close proximity.

Everyone in the family circle was understanding about Fournier in the months following his return to civilian life, because everyone knew he had a novel to write. Ever since the summer of 1905, when he announced to Rivière that he was going to proceed 'in the manner of Laforgue', his primary concern in his 'creative' writing had been the evocation of *mood*, in particular the mood of entrancement with which, so often as a child and decreasingly as an adult, he viewed people, places and incidents in the world around him. As long as his primary literary objective remained the evocation of emotion, all that he could be expected to produce was a succession of short, isolated pieces of poetry or prose which might eventually be loosely grouped together in a single collection. It seems fair to assume, therefore, that had he persisted with his original plans for *Le Pays sans nom*, he would have produced a book similar in form and, in some respects, similar in content, to Rimbaud's *Illuminations*. To create something more coherent and more extended, like a novel, he needed such unifying elements as characters, setting, theme and plot, and in the autumn of 1909 and spring of 1910, these were what he sought and finally found.

An early note found amongst his posthumous papers shows him fairly near the beginning of his quest and taking the first vital step of establishing distance between his hero and himself :

> The story of a man in process of writing a novel. The two characters are : the woman he loves and a man who resembles him – only he makes this hero more admirable than he is himself. Yet very life-like. He pictures him with extraordinary precision.

A further note, also undated, but clearly somewhat later, shows how further distancing was achieved by splitting the original single hero into two distinct characters :

> Two brothers or two friends, one of whom talks each evening about a woman he has known. I imagine that Suc used to talk to me each evening about the woman he dies for. Put them into a very precise setting – at Madame Benoist's for example – Alfred.

For a long time they imagine, amongst episodes of real life, what life would be like with her in the land of heart's desire. She – The Pages about her – the fine red partition (between her nostrils) – but based on winter evenings really lived.

This second note conclusively demonstrates that while, on the one hand, Fournier was trying to 'distance' himself from his principal characters, he was consciously and consistently building up his fiction by rearranging facts from his own experience : Suc, the assistant master who had charge of the infants' class at Epineuil immediately before Madame Fournier, Madame Benoist's house and garden and her son Alfred, his former playmate now dead, were all memories of boyhood, while the 'Pages about her' – the tell-tale capital letter occurs in his own papers – clearly refer to his hastily scribbled and jealously hoarded notes about the encounters with Yvonne de Quiévrecourt on Ascension Thursday and Whit Sunday 1905. Yet another note shows this process being pursued a fascinating stage further :

A lovely summer's evening in a country drawing-room. Crumbs on the table, fruits, a carafe. A stranger arrives, crosses the garden, comes up the steps and raises his head. It is Julien Meaulnes, the wandering player. He says: 'I am Julien Meaulnes.'
One of the characters has a bandaged head : it is Willie, the English wanderer.
The schoolmistresses in summer – father out fishing – the wandering players.

Here again, he is ransacking his memories of Epineuil in search of character and scene : the schoolmistresses, the father away fishing, the itinerant actors all derive from his schooldays, as does 'Willie, the English schoolboy', the hero of one of the more colourful adventure stories in *Le Petit Français illustré*, a year's issues of which was Monsieur Suc's parting gift to the Fournier children when he left the school; the name Meaulnes too has Epineuil associations, because Meaulne is the name of the next village just a few miles away to the north.
Though there is a regular insistence in these early work-notes on the need to represent reality as convincingly as possible – the need to be 'very life-like', to visualise with 'extraordinary precision', to put the characters 'in a very precise setting', to base scenes on 'winter evenings really lived' – none of this meant that Fournier had turned his back on his other-worldly Land without a Name. Quite the

contrary was the case; on 16 January 1910, he wrote to André Lhote :

> Everybody creates for himself the reality he deserves. Christopher
> Columbus found the shores of America because he'd had the
> audacity to conjure them up. Reality has never disappointed
> anybody who's had the nerve and the imagination to believe in
> it. There isn't a single one of the scenes I carry within my head
> which couldn't be made true, or indeed isn't true and 'real'
> already. The marvellous thing about my mind is that it can
> create. I know that the supreme quality of the landscapes that
> my imagination creates is that they're *real*. I wouldn't love as
> much as I do my Land without a Name, my Soul Kingdom –
> love it so that I turn faint through thinking about it – if I weren't
> sure that it existed somewhere in the Universe . . If the shepherds
> had not believed that something was going to come to earth, they
> would have been content to fall asleep and merely dream of
> Paradise. But they arranged to keep watch and took it in turn to
> mount guard, and it actually came to pass, and now they're rich
> for all time, in their own land, and throughout the world. Why
> won't you believe more in *this* earth?[6]

Fournier's artistic problem was to make his world of everyday seem
mysterious, to make his Land without a Name seem real, and to devise
a plausible way of transporting his characters from one realm to the
other. He did not solve it immediately. At a relatively early stage in
his planning, he decided that the 'real' world of the characters was to
centre around a schoolhouse in a village based on Epineuil, but he
seems, for a brief period at any rate, to have discarded the notion of
localising the world of heart's desire in the château and park he once
would have liked to own had he been rich. One fragment, subsequently discarded, indicates that his imagination was temporarily
attracted by the idea of something other than a large country house.
Two schoolboys look out through the fanlight in their attic bedroom
across the moonlit fields and make out in the silvery distance the
outlines of a chapel :

> 'Ah, if some traveller arrived there at night,' said François, 'who
> can tell what people he'd meet there? Millie used to say,
> "Probably some old friends of Saint Agathe, girls from the
> surrounding district with names like hers who go walking that
> way through the night, so proud of their lovely names that they
> can't sleep." '
> – 'Who's Millie?'

'Millie's my mother. She used to say that just to please me, but I don't believe it any more . . . When we used to get there, it was summer. It'd be in the evenings, and there'd be so much soft shade under the trees you wouldn't be aware that night was falling. It's kept locked.'

Then the moon went in and the sad February night descended again like a deep sleep, and darkness was spread over everything like a great compassion.

By early in 1910, Fournier had evolved a plot and a title, *Le Jour des noces* (*The Wedding Day*) and this, in turn, indicates that by this stage he had also evolved his theme. This derived from his much more recent past, his weeks of religious torment at Mirande, in which he had succeeded in convincing himself that true happiness is not to be found in this world. To convey this in terms of plot, he had first to hold out the prospect of early happiness to his hero by letting him meet the elusive heroine in the Land without a Name, by causing him to lose her and experience the agonies of deprivation, by reuniting them again when to continue hoping seemed futile, and then by making him desert her on or immediately after the wedding day. The motive he for some time seriously considered for this dramatic act of renunciation – which, in his plans, was going to kill the heroine – was cryptically noted in an early schema for the plot:

Third Part. They are married very young. 1st Chapter: Afternoon of the wedding. 2nd Chapter: Night of the wedding. 3rd Chapter: Math. Meaulnes the missionary.

Fournier's apprehensiveness about the very first night of married life, expressed in so much of his writing in the years 1908 and 1909 in terms of the 'monstrousness' of so much happiness, or the 'feverish' atmosphere of the marriage home, doubtless had deep-seated roots in his personality, but it was also nurtured through his reading. In Laforgue's *Pierrot fumiste*, Pierrot is too afraid to begin to make love to his young wife Colombinette, while in one of the tales in his *Moralités légendaires*, Lohengrin turns aside from Elsa on their wedding night, embraces his pillow and begs it to carry him away. The explanation in each of these situations is the immature hero's fear of his own inadequacy rather than any puritanical loathing of the joys of the flesh. In *La Porte etroite*, on the other hand, the motives of the two central characters are somewhat more complex, and sexual timidity masquerades both as altruism and as love of God: Jerome loves and wants to marry Alissa but accepts just a little too readily the lets and hindrances she puts in his way; Alissa loves Jerome but believes that both he and she have a superior duty to love God and that they will each be nobler for it if they love God unreservedly. In this belief, she wastes away and dies, suspecting shortly before the end that her self-sacrifice has been futile. In *Le Jour des noces*, it was to be Meaulnes who was to subordinate his human partner to God, and Anne-Marie who was to die, but there is undoubtedly some similarity between the strategic plans of Fournier and Gide at this period. There is also similarity in some of the tactics devised to execute that strategy, in particular the device of the secret journal, discovered after the main events are over, which provides the explanation for the chief character's enigmatic behaviour. The case for filiation would seem at least to be made out, if one considers that Fournier read and admired *La Porte etroite* a few months before formulating his plans for *Le Jour des noces*.

Gide, however, was by no means the only author likely to have affected Fournier's planning. From childhood on, he had much admired what can be loosely described as the 'English adventure novel', with a sharply drawn story-line and a wealth of exciting incident. While at Epineuil, he had discovered *Robinson Crusoe*, at Lakanal he derived considerable pleasure from Kipling's tales of the Far East and the scientific romances of H. G. Wells, and later in 1910, he was to wax even more enthusiastic over nearly all the works of Stevenson. It would not be unduly fanciful to postulate that the considerable enjoyment he continued to enjoy from works of this nature was largely due to the fact that they enabled him to participate vicariously in exciting and exotic modes of life which were denied to him in reality. He was, therefore, simply being true to his own nature when, while outlining his plans for *Le Jour des noces* to Rivière in April 1910, he broke off to say :

> I'm not altogether sure whether le grand Meaulnes will be the hero of the book – or Seurel? or Anne des Champs? or me, the narrator.
> And I'm not sure either now whether the ideas I've just been describing are really those of the book, because the book is an adventure novel. Jacques wants me to express myself through *ideas*. But why does Jacques want me to conform to *him*?[7]

The uncertainty Fournier displayed at this point was not really due to artistic immaturity. When he first drew up his plans for *Le Jour des noces* late in 1909 and at the beginning of 1910, he was still firmly convinced, as he had come to believe at Mirande, that happiness

172

through human love was either unattainable or, if attainable, then too terrible to be borne, and he established a direct link between adult disillusionment and the inordinate joys of childhood. When he began to outline his latest literary plans to Rivière, the motivation for the flight of Meaulnes was what it had been from the outset:

> Meaulnes, *le grand Meaulnes*, the hero of my book, is a man whose childhood was too beautiful. Throughout his entire adolescence, he trails it after him. From time to time, it seems that the whole of that imaginary paradise, conceived in his world of childhood, is going to rise up at the end of his adventures or be conjured up by one of his gestures. And this is why, on a winter's morning, after three days of unexplained absence from school, he comes back into class like an insolent and mysterious young god. – But he already knows that this paradise can no longer be. He has renounced happiness. His attitude to the world is like someone about to take his leave of it. That's the secret of his cruelty. He sees right through all the mini-paradises that are offered to him and recognises them for the fraud they are. – And on the day when authentic happiness, from which there's no escape, rises up before him and rests its human cheek against his, *le grand Meaulnes* runs away, not at all because of heroism, but in terror, because he knows that true happiness is not of this world!

However, once he had gone on to describe, for Rivière's benefit, the progress he had at that point made towards implementing his plans, he returned to the question of human happiness and declared that his own views on this subject should not now be taken to coincide with those of Meaulnes:

> To the question you ask me: have we an *obligation* to be happy? I reply that we do, that once more, I'm beginning to believe that we've an obligation to be happy, that while Meaulnes may be a great cruel angel, he's not a man. And, whatever you might think, I believe that I have within me a great ability for being happy, and I also have the capacity, hitherto unused, for giving happiness. All that's required of me now is the courage to put this to the test.

In the same letter, he conceded that the chief symptoms of his emotional and spiritual malady continued to be chronic world-weariness, and the abiding conviction that at the ripe age of

173

twenty-four, the best of his life was already over; then he added 'I'm certainly not completely cured, but a great effort I've just been making has considerably relieved things.'

To Rivière, who had been, for some time, chiding Fournier about his apparent apathy and who was, at that moment, away in Cenon, these remarks must have seemed tantalisingly gnomic. They were not, in fact, explained for some weeks, by which time Fournier was once again in despair and ready to concede defeat. When he wrote to Rivière in April, however, he was already committed to a relationship which, he might well have hoped, would exorcise the spell cast by Yvonne de Quiévrecourt and enable him to shed the heavy burden of the past. The result was to be catastrophic failure, much pain for himself and, even more, for his unfortunate partner, and drastic alterations to his plans for the dénouement of *Le Jour des noces*.

Fournier's two principal biographers are in disagreement over the precise date when he met Jeanne Bruneau; Isabelle Rivière always insisted that it was in May 1910 while Jean Loize, deploying a wealth of circumstantial evidence which includes, *inter alia*, Fournier's remarks to Rivière in his letter of 4 April 1910 and an interview with Jeanne's sister, Françoise, has argued not only that they first met in February 1910, but that they went together to see Sarah Bernhardt in *La Dame aux camélias* on 13 February. Loize's argument seems to me conclusive, and the earlier date is, accordingly, the one I accept. In any event, what is more important than the precise date of the meeting is the personality of Jeanne herself and the course the relationship followed, and on these points, the two biographers are not in dispute.

Jeanne was a milliner who lived with her sister in a flat in rue Chanoinesse near Notre Dame, and, very enterprisingly, in an age when French social and legal attitudes still discriminated strongly against women, the pair of them were striving alone together to establish their own independent little business. How she came to meet Fournier is not known, but it is evident that he was readily attracted by her looks and by the fact that she came from Bourges. It did not, apparently, take long for Jeanne to become his mistress or for Fournier to pick a violent quarrel with her. As a sign of her confidence in their relationship, she would seem, rather too soon, to have provided him with details of her previous love-affairs and by so doing, with what was always to remain his major cause of grievance with her : her lack of 'purity'.

In the autumn of 1910, after yet another sequence in the now established pattern of acrimonious separation, passionate reconciliation and a further bitter quarrel, Fournier confessed to his sister :

> As soon as we'd loved one another, she gave up everything for me. On some days, when her business was slack, she would have just twelve sous to live off. She'd always do without dessert to make the money go further.
>
> She had other lovers some years ago. A man committed suicide on her account. In the past, she'd been flighty, spiteful and wilful : for me, she'd go down on her knees in the kitchen and scrub the floor.
>
> There was something childlike yet tragic about her which excited me. I don't think I ever felt deep love for her, it was more a violent attraction.
>
> She was very beautiful and remarkably intelligent. She had nearly all the best qualities.
>
> Except purity. And that's why I hurt her so much. When I think back, I wonder how she stood for so long all that I inflicted on her. She never seemed to tire of my cruel reproaches, my cruel failure to be satisfied, my cruel longing for purity.
>
> I've left her five or six times already, for a day, five days, a week. I'd walk out because of something she'd said or something she'd be reminded of. Then she'd beg me to go back and back I'd go . . .[8]

Near the beginning of the affair, Fournier himself predicted the course events would follow in a note to Jeanne :

> I beg your forgiveness for having wanted us to love one another. I knew, near the start, when you told me everything, that if once we fell in love with each other, the consequences would be dreadful. And I wanted to go ahead all the same. The fault is wholly mine.[9]

For all that, the affair with Jeanne was neither wholly stormy nor wholly carnal, and it was certainly not furtive. Fournier readily introduced her to his friends and in an enthusiastic letter to André Lhote, memorable for a description of Rivière, he described a visit he and Jeanne made in the Rivières' company to watch their great 'discovery' of 1910, the Russian Ballet, which was then enjoying the most spectacularly successful of its pre-war Paris seasons :

> Jeanne and I went to see the Russian Ballet with Jacques. I can't

help feeling just a mite annoyed with him. How can a theatrical representation, a mere artistic manifestation be *the most important* event in a man's life? Right now, Jacques is as wild about Nijinsky, about Ida Rubinstein and about the lady who sells tickets for the Russian Ballet, as he used to be over Mary Garden, Jean Périer[10] and the bookseller who used to sell the score of *Pelléas.* The other evening, throughout *Prince Igor*, he was clinging on to me for dear life, trembling and panting. I love him all the same, much as that sort of thing offends me. This is all due, no doubt, to the severe and 'serious' way I was brought up in childhood, when Art came a long way after Life, and we had to hide ourselves away in order to read the book-prizes. And what condemns his way of carrying on, is that he sacrifices for some performance all sorts of precious things in life itself. Ah! when we were on our way to the Opéra, I'd gladly have made myself late just to have my fill of the sight of a blacksmith in the street *holding hands* with his lady love.

All the same, these ballets at the Opéra are something unique. They're simply not to be faulted. *Prince Igor* is the unchained fury of *terrestrial* dancing – while Isadora Duncan was the purest evocation of a morning in *Paradise. Carnaval* is a delectable Italian carnival thought out afresh by Barbarians. Likewise, in the old days, when the booth had been set up on our village square, out from between the curtains would peer the pure white face of a tall Pierrot. With tragic little cries, he'd stuff a rag doll full of bran and then throw it at the audience. Unique characters, all of them, their psychology is a disappointment, but they're unique. They're all actors, but all unique.[11]

To do full justice to the relationship, between Fournier and Jeanne, it ought to be established that it brought both partners pleasure as well as pain, that there was tenderness as well as lust, that there were heartfelt endearments as well as bitter recriminations, and this can most effectively be conveyed by quoting liberally from one of Fournier's several lengthy letters to her.[12] This one merely bears the date '1910':

I'm planning to hand this letter to you at your place this evening at the end of this Sunday which, I tell myself, is going to be so beautiful.

There is something which I cannot talk to you about but which I want you to know.

In case we're fated not to see each other any more, I would like you to know how I love you. If, one evening, after we've quarrelled and hurt each other and finally made the break, then at least you'll know all that you've been for me.

On the first day we met, I noticed in your face one or two places where the skin looked slightly rougher. Those are the places I now prefer : now I can't see them without feeling deep tenderness, without a great desire to find sweeter and sweeter words to say to you.

There are gestures, words, movements of yours I've preciously noted without your knowing : I can remember, the first day, your way of suddenly looking me straight in the face, the way you look at someone who's telling a lie.

I'll always remember the sound of your voice, so simple, so serious, so funny.

I can still remember when we went to the theatre that evening, the way your delicate breasts nestled against your chemise.

I also remember those kisses which my grown-up friend gave me on the brow as she said : 'That is the only way you should be kissed, you're still too small !'

I'll never forget that feeling which overwhelmed me that first Friday evening when I felt my elbows were grazed and I suddenly realised 'That's because I've been leaning on my elbows on top of her for several hours.'

And there's also this : Tuesday evening, walking along behind your sister coming back from rue Béranger. I smiled at some childish thing you said, and you suddenly pressed yourself right up close to me.

I can still recall many other things more beautiful still, such as those great shudders of pleasure which go right through you as though you're in great pain and which are so lovely to behold.

This is why you cause me such suffering and why I love you in spite of it.

But there's one thought which tortures me more than anything else. I just can't accept the notion that you were ready to give yourself to the first comer. I could just about accept the thought of your being lost to me – but being lost, eternally lost to everybody ! All that rare and precious gracefulness going out on the streets ! All that you possess, repudiated and ruined. Just think about it : can you really turn yourself into someone with neither heart nor soul nor body, someone to whom nobody could ever again pronounce the word 'love' without feeling shame ?

If you could bring yourself to believe in what I've written, just the tiniest part of it, then I could remain your little boy and you, my big girl.

But if all this serves merely to widen the gulf between us, if it really is the case that only our bodies have sported together and there's nothing else to it, then, I implore you, reject me now, send me away, don't let someone who so deludes himself continue to stay beside you, tear me away from you while there's still time.

While I've been writing this, I've frequently had to steel myself against the temptation of calling you by too sweet a name in case it should make you smile. But now, at the end of the letter, I can no longer resist the temptation of nestling my cheek against yours – my grown-up girl, my little one, my little madonna with the piled-up hair, my angel with the big eyes, my angel with the quiet smile, my little girl who lowers her head to laugh when she makes fun of me, my woman pressing against me who sometimes loves me and sometimes doesn't, my little mother who ties my napkin round my neck, my woman whom I comfort when she's afraid, my housewife, my wife with the burning body, my wife with a body all pure, my wife so chaste, my wife so simple, my darling wife, my wife.[13]

The litany of endearments with which this letter ends, was almost certainly designed not only to melt the heart of the recipient but to reassure the writer. Fournier's conscience never ceased to trouble him over Jeanne, not simply because of the suffering their quarrels inflicted on her, but because he took quite literally her threat to resort to prostitution if he finally deserted her. It was not, however, this threat alone which made him come back repeatedly to her side, after each violent argument had ended with his brusque departure and his announcement that he would never return. His motives for prolonging the relationship were rather more complex, and some insight into their nature is provided in a passage he drafted for his still evolving novel. He provided for his hero a mistress indistinguishable from Jeanne, and it seems safe to assume, given his mode of composition, that the thoughts ascribed to his hero were, in their raw state, very close to his own :

Her beauty, her gracefulness, her youth – if she could only have waited, had known how to plan her life, the love she would have been able to offer any man would have been like Paradise . . . But when she was seventeen she had wrecked everything. Out of all that grace of hers she had made fourteen chapters of a piece of pulp-fiction.

And I've always thought that Meaulnes was attracted by the utter thoroughness of all this waste. He loved – indeed he truly loved – that soul searching desperately amongst the ruins to salvage something from its wrecked youth. I don't accept – what other people often say – that carnal passion was the be-all and end-all of their love. Because of your own lost love, you loved that woman for destroying your chance to love. You did not believe, *grand Meaulnes*, that Paradise could exist on earth and you loved that woman for destroying yours. But what regrets they felt, what a mixture of bitter desire and remorse, when the pair of them reached out for that past which could never again be theirs . . .[14]

If these reflections were Fournier's own as well as those of his hero, then it would surely not be fanciful to infer that the relationship with Jeanne endured because it provided not only substantial if sporadic consolation, but also no less necessary self-punishment. Whenever the affair grew stormy or – rather more revealingly – whenever it became so attractively calm that he was tempted into thoughts of marriage, he seems forcibly to have reminded himself that the one crucial quality she lacked was that she was not Yvonne. In late August 1910, he suddenly interrupted a newsletter to Rivière with the succinct and pregnant comment: 'It's still the same sickness I've been suffering from for five years now. Don't fool yourselves over this. Ever.'[15]

And three weeks later, he wrote to Bichet:

Lhote says he's sorry for me and, as he puts it, 'poor' Jeanne. 'How sad it is,' he tells me, 'not to be able to squander one's love and one's youth.' But how *can* I squander my love, when somewhere out there, my wife is waiting for me, so anxiously, so ardently?[16]

The relationship was useful to Fournier for another vital reason: it provided him with invaluable new material for enlarging the scope of his book. While it would be unfair to suggest that he actively *prolonged* the affair as though he were a scientist collecting data from a series of experiments, he had all the literary man's opportunism when rich 'copy' had been actually presented to him, and he was quick to exploit it. There can be little doubt that he used Jeanne and part of her past history as the model for the key character in his short story, *Le Miracle des trois dames de village* (*Miracle of the three village ladies*), which was completed in the early summer of 1910 and was published that same year in *La Grande Revue* on 10 August. Like all his fiction, it is based on facts observed within his own experience, and is a blend of personal memories and preoccupations ancient and

179

modern. The three ladies of the title are all young, married and poor; when the story opens they are sitting in a closed drawing-room on a cold February afternoon, while the snow-laden wind howls outside. One of the ladies, Madame Henry, begins to play the piano, and for a moment, all three are able to forget their present poverty and relive their happiest memories. When their tea-party is over, and they emerge into the world outside, the magic spell seems to have retained its potency, and 'the world seems to have been transformed into the Paradise which the poor ladies out on a visit have invented for themselves:'[17] the fierce cold wind has dropped, February seems like April, and when each of the ladies meets her husband in turn, as they slowly walk home, she finds him as tenderly solicitous and gallant as in their courting days. But the happiness will not last long for Madame Henry, because her younger sister is waiting at home, stripped naked and beaten by the villagers at the instigation of her fiancé, who has only just discovered that 'he was not the first'.

Fournier has provided here a further variation on one of his favourite themes, the transient and illusory quality of human happiness, only this time without the oppressive feverishness which so marked earlier variants like *La Partie de plaisir* or *Dialogue aux approches de Noël.* The fact that the village ladies' 'miracle' is merely a trick of the light, is not laboured, and the story is all the more effective for its delicate understatement. It is Madame Henry's happiness which is evoked and the story ends with her on the very threshold of disillusionment:

> She reached the last house in the village which was deserted, and there, behind the window, looking down the lane, she saw a girl standing. In the air and against the window-pane, that impalpable blue mist was hovering over everything, as it always seems to in the evening, after rain. All that could be seen was the girl's face and hands pressed against the glass. The rest of her body disappeared into the darkness and the green shadowiness of the room as if she were wearing some lovely robe. And when the men arrived at the start of the village, as worn out by life itself as by a hard day's toil, they said to themselves:
> 'There's the lovely château I once saw in a dream . . . Ah! and there at the window is the girl for whom I've been searching everywhere on earth.'
> They did not know that this girl's name was Marie and that she was naked because her lover had torn up her clothes.[18]

Marie was based on Jeanne, but though she plays a key part in

180

the story, she herself remains a shadowy figure. When next Fournier employed Jeanne as a model, he not only announced to her that he was using her, he assured her that she was now to play a central role.

In June 1910, he and Jeanne spent a few days with André Lhote and his wife in a farmhouse near Orgeville, a lonely hamlet in the heart of Normandy. It was planned as a sort of honeymoon, Jeanne even wearing a borrowed ring for the occasion, but it ended with bitter recriminations and tears on both sides. Three months later, after a further reconciliation and yet another 'final' break, Fournier wrote to Jeanne to announce :

> I'm working without a break several hours each day, at my book. Today I expect to finish the chapter I'm devoting to our trip to Orgeville. You're going to be called Annette.[19]

This chapter was indeed completed in September 1910. The sixteen pages of it still survive within their white folder which bears on the outside a draft epigraph from Leviticus on the alleged side-effects of menstruation : 'And if any man lie with her at all, and her flowers be upon him, he shall be unclean seven days; and all the bed whereon he lieth shall be unclean.' (xv. 24) This would in part explain why the great expectations invested in the Orgeville outing were so pain-fully dashed, and why, when Fournier read the chapter in question to his mother, she should comment :

> There's some merit in that. It's certainly effective. But it's not for young girls just out of convent school! Nobody anywhere has ever dared to write about that sort of thing![20]

Though Fournier's response was promptly to scrap the chapter,[21] the affair with Jeanne nevertheless had profound and far-reaching repercussions on the plans for his novel. On 19 September 1910, he wrote to Rivière to say he had discovered that the plot of his novel now resembled that of Dostoevsky's *Notes from Underground* :

> But this is pure coincidence. Nobody will ever give it a thought because in this book, I'm putting the whole of myself : my theories about everything and something other than my theories; what I would like to have done and – oh the pity of it ! – what I actually did.
>
> And now there's going to be a third part, in which the character from the first (childhood) section will come back, and

at the end there will be a soaring-up higher than purity, higher than sacrifice, above all the desolation, into Joy.[22]

On 28 September 1910, he wrote again about 'Annette' – the counterpart of the heroine 'Anne'; just as 'Frantz' was to be the romanticised version of 'François':

> In my book, I've scrapped more or less three chapters only. They're all to do with 'Annette' but the hidden emotion they conceal derives from *the presence of Another*. You understand, my book is like the story of Keats:[23] *'Some of us have in a prior existence been in love with Antigone, and that makes us find no full content in any mortal tie.'* The only difference is that in this case, it was in this very existence that Antigone was encountered . . .
> In the last part, the hero finds his Antigone again. And at that point, there will be an act of renouncement which I want to make more beautiful than the one in *La Porte etroite*. Because it won't be pointless. Because behind that act of human renouncement you will *sense* the whole Kingdom of joy that's been won.[24]

It is fairly clear that at this stage, Fournier planned for Meaulnes to fall in love with 'Annette' after giving up all hope of ever rediscovering 'Anne', and that he was then to have been confronted with a particularly painful dilemma when, contrary to all his pessimistic assumptions, his first love reappeared, still faithful and still available. What is not so clear is how this dilemma was to have been resolved. Was Meaulnes to have sacrificed his reawakened hopes of supreme earthly happiness with Anne because he was by then committed to Annette? Was he to prefer Moral Duty to Love? Or, in order to enter 'the Kingdom of Joy', was he to have renounced both women? Fournier's letters are silent on this point, but as his affair with Jeanne continued on its painful course, with each partner miserable both apart and together – for all the world like the long-suffering lovers in Constant's classic *Adolphe* – his promise to evoke the mysterious kingdom of joy carried less and less conviction. The effect, in the end, was the progressive elimination of the original theme of sacred and profane love, and the emergence of quite different polarities: innocence and experience, as well as wrong-doing and retribution. No longer was Meaulnes himself to give up his lost Anne because of his love for God; she was now to be denied him because he was no longer worthy.

II

'Man's love is of a man's life a thing apart'; while Fournier was undoubtedly much exercised in 1910 over his protracted affair with Jeanne Bruneau, he continued throughout this whole time to lead what was outwardly a well-ordered and well-integrated existence. He returned home to eat and sleep at his parents' home in rue Cassini each evening, he continued to meet old friends and experienced little difficulty in making new ones. The Fournier who has become known to posterity through his intimate letters was not the Fournier normally on view to most of his friends and acquaintances, and this fact is clearly borne out when one finds him having to *remind* a friend as comparatively close as René Bichet that he was not all he seemed:

> Don't think that I find everything more simple than you do. On the contrary. I find everything terribly complex and there's possibly nobody else in the world as tormented as I am. It's only in my words and actions that I give the appearance of being *determined*, as we say in the country. But my inner thoughts are a hell where I sit and brood.[25]

Fortunately for his peace of mind in the second half of 1910, he was not given an excessive amount of leisure in which to indulge in brooding. From May 1910, he was in regular employment as a literary columnist for the newspaper *Paris-Journal*, serving up a regular diet of gossip about the private lives and future plans of other writers of the day, books forthcoming, literary prizes and banquets, or the results of questionnaires on tastes and trends which, in those days, French crypto-sociologists seemed continuously to be charting. In the period between 9 May 1910, when his first *Courrier Littéraire* appeared in *Paris-Journal*, and the end of December that same year, Fournier published no less than 156 short articles on such diverse subjects as 'Jules Romains at work on *Les Copains*', 'Giraudoux at Harvard', 'Forty Tolstoy translations', 'Valéry Larbaud and R. L. Stevenson' or 'Flaubert's first *Education Sentimentale*'.[26] He regularly complained to his friends about the debasing of his gifts in an unworthy cause, but it provided him with a regular though far from lavish income, and taught him the inestimable lesson of writing tersely to order for a fixed deadline. This discipline could not fail to have salutory effects on his novel-writing and must have been one of the contributory factors which enabled him to announce to his sister on 20 September 1910:

I'm working terribly hard at my book. Each day. I've been having to battle against my anguish and my state of nerves. Now that peace has finally descended, I'm able to get on with my writing again.

For a fortnight I strove to construct the book in the artificial way in which I started it. This wasn't specially productive. In the end, I gave up those methods completely and one fine evening – to quote Mother's words in which I now readily believe – I found my 'road to Damascus'.

I began to write simply and directly, as in one of my letters, using small, terse little paragraphs full of feeling, and I'm telling a fairly simple story which could be my own. I've got rid of all that philosophy and abstraction I was stuffed with. And the marvellous thing is that in spite of it all, the *whole* of me is in what I'm writing. I'm there *entirely*, not just the abstract quint-essence of merely one of my ideas.[27]

In the course of 1910, Fournier supplemented his income from journalism by giving private lessons in French language and literature. As far as is known, he only ever had two pupils: one was a young Frenchman called Dubois who was killed in the 1914–18 war; the other was a young American from Harvard who did not for long remain as obscure as he was then. His name was T. S. Eliot. Fournier set him to learn, and made him declaim, passages from the established French classics. He also communicated his enthusiasm for some of his contemporary favourites, Gide's *Paludes* and *La Porte etroite*, the early plays of Claudel in the collection *L'Arbre*, the prose-poems of *Connaissance de l'Est* and his religious treatise *Connaissance de Dieu et de soi-même*. He also persuaded Eliot to read Dostoevsky in the fairly recent series of French translations. Looking back in 1951,[28] over a gulf of forty years, Eliot could still recall Fournier as a quiet-spoken, witty, elegant young man, who spoke with real conviction of his ambition to write a great novel in the tradition of the great French masters which would replace the *récits* and 'entertainments' which were then *à la mode*. Fournier also introduced Eliot to Rivière and so helped found a friendship which, after the 1914–18 war, was to enrich each of their lives and many pages of *La Nouvelle Revue Française*.

However, the most important of all the new contacts Fournier established in 1910 was that with Charles Péguy. Rivière and Fournier first 'discovered' Péguy during the winter of 1909–10 and they saw him first as the quirky and remarkably pugnacious founder and editor of *Les Cahiers de la Quinzaine*, each issue of which was always given over to a single long article on some burning public issue of the day. They admired his prose style, which seems to have more in common with basic manual skills rather than the literary art, bludgeoning away insistently at an argument until his point is made, or tirelessly aligning almost identical sentences, one after the other, like a peasant ploughing up the reader's mind. Even more, however, they admired his integrity and his avowed determination to serve the causes of Truth and Justice at all costs, spelled out in his policy statement *A nos lecteurs, à nos abonnés* :

> A review only continues to have life in it so long as each issue annoys at least a fifth of its subscribers. Justice lies in seeing that this fifth is not always the same one . . . Because they have observed these rules, our *Cahiers* have slowly formed a link between all those who don't cheat. That is why there are among us so few Catholics, so few Protestants, so few Jews and so few free-thinkers.

Fournier first met Péguy in the early summer of 1910 when he had occasion to interview him for his literary column in his little bookshop at 8 rue de la Sorbonne. His instinctive enthusiasm for him was enhanced by that meeting and very considerably increased in August 1910 when he had occasion to read *Notre Jeunesse*, Péguy's elegiac account of the heroic early days of the Dreyfus Case when it first emerged that there had been a monstrous miscarriage of justice and that a man had been sent to Devil's Island for a crime of which he was entirely innocent.

In September 1910, Fournier wrote the longest letter he ever sent to Péguy, describing and seeking to explain why he admired *Notre Jeunesse* so much :

> I want to use the last hour of my summer holidays to tell you simply how much I love your books . . . Often, over these last months, when I've been enmeshed in innumerable subtleties, I've taken up your books, or rather your chronicles, or should I say your speeches? And they were like heady draughts of sheer enthusiasm.
>
> In a short portrait I've been tracing of you recently, which will doubtless be published, I depict you drunk with ideas, intoxicated with intelligence as Rabelais was drunk with words.
>
> But what I like about you most of all is that you're not a teacher who takes great delight simply in explaining things : you display them, make us see them, and when you do that you become a poet and a visionary.

The other day, I was going with my father through the village where he was born – the little village of Nançay, near Salbris, in the Sologne. And he showed me the old schoolhouse, one which used to have three narrow windows looking over the main street. He said : 'It was a morning like this when the Uhlans arrived after the Army crossed the Loire. Old Gérault, our teacher, went as white as a corpse. He sent us all home, locked the door, and kept on saying : "They've really come, this time! They really have come!" '

I could see it and I could feel it. *It was a morning like this.* It wasn't History any longer. And that's precisely the feeling I get from every one of your books.

Naturally, as far as we're concerned, the Dreyfus Affair is already history. For people of twenty or twenty-five, the Dreyfus Affair doubtless means, as it does to me, that number of the newspaper *L'Aurore* in which the 'J'accuse' letter was published, and which was sent out to every schoolteacher in France. My parents were so distressed they could scarcely bring themselves to read it. I covered one of my exercise books with it and for ages, I had it there under my eyes not understanding what it was all about.

But now I understand. I can see it all. The whole passage in which you show what an unlikeable hero Dreyfus was strikes me as extraordinarily tragic. I can remember how, in the old days, the anti-Dreyfus people used to say, 'Even his supporters don't like him!' I can see now, through reading your book, how much you Dreyfus supporters must have suffered because of that.[29]

He went on to praise Péguy for the same qualities of making everything clear and accessible in matters of religion too, in this particular instance, through his long poem *Le Mystère de la Charité de Jeanne d'Arc* :

What I like more than anything else is the way you love the New Testament. The way in which you bring it down to earth, evoke it in a tangible, living, human fashion – at a time when in the churches it's always read with such a doleful, sepulchral voice.

Once Fournier had established contact with Péguy, it did not take him long to discover that the pair of them had more than a little in common. Like Fournier, he came from the centre of France, from Orléans, but he had had a much tougher childhood, being obliged

186

to help his widowed mother and grandmother earn their living by making rush-bottoms for chairs. Like Fournier, he felt a special sense of kinship with his maternal grandmother and established, through her, his living contact with the poetry of the past. He dedicated one of his early poems 'to the memory of my grandmother, a country-woman who couldn't read, and who first taught me the French language'. It was Péguy's vital contact with his grandmother which prevented him from becoming bitter; through her he felt himself in touch with a way of life which was already old in France 'when the cathedrals were white'; this ancient mode of life, materially poor but with an essential decency about it and its own very real dignity was, in Péguy's view, wholly different in *quality* from the real destitution he felt was being spread ever more widely around him at the turn of the century. His bitterness was reserved for those forces in the modern world which he held responsible for the erosion of the old order – industrialisation, the fetish of universal education and parliamentary intrigue – and these were the enemies against which he regularly fulminated in his *Cahiers*. Like Fournier, he remained incurably nostalgic for a rural way of life which was intimately bound up with his own childhood, but whereas Fournier's response was always poetic, Péguy's was essentially social and political; while Fournier's gaze was fixed on the Arcadian past of The Land without a Name, Péguy was prepared to do battle for the Utopian future of his *Cité de la vie harmonieuse* (*The City of Harmonious Life*), the title of his first major manifesto.

Like Fournier, Péguy had gone to Lakanal at the cost of considerable financial privation for his relatives but, unlike Fournier, he had been able to reward them and himself by winning a coveted place at l'Ecole Normale Supérieure. Like many a *normalien*, he had emerged as a teacher but instead of a blackboard, he used his *Cahiers* for his demonstrations, and for his classroom, he used the Parisian literary world. He remained an unfashionable figure, something of a joke to frequenters of high society *salons* and the pretentious *avant-garde*, and a welcome gift to newspaper cartoonists with his small stature, his large beard, his myopic eyes peering fixedly through thick pebble lenses, his rough serge suit and his heavy hobnailed boots. It did not take Fournier long to discover that this unprepossessing outward appearance and his belligerent public utterances served only to disguise the fact that he was acutely sensitive, extremely vulnerable, and very often in considerable emotional and spiritual anguish.

This anguish was partly caused by the painful situations into which he was regularly driven by his own conflicting convictions over major public issues : like Fournier, he was a 'believer' who refused to attend confession or partake of Mass; he was a confirmed Socialist who planned for the New Jerusalem but who found his most abiding inspiration in the lost heroic age of Joan of Arc; he was one of the most fervent patriots of his day and a fanatical Army man, yet he was ready to weaken both the State and the Army in order to right the wrong done to Dreyfus. His anguish was also due to insoluble problems within his own intimate human relationships : his marriage broke down irreparably, but though his estranged wife was an unbeliever and he was no longer technically a Catholic, he remained convinced that he should stay loyal to her until death; he fell deeply in love with Blanche Raphaël, a Jewish girl whom he had first met as a student, to whom he would always refer simply as *L'Innominata* (*'The Unnamed One'*), but such was his spirit of integrity – like the readers he liked to think he wrote for, he 'did not cheat' – he actively encouraged her to marry Marcel Bernard, a younger man, in July 1910 so as to put her beyond the reach of temptation; it was a decision far from lightly taken and very painfully borne; the sufferings he underwent because of it thereafter was poured out in secret into his poignant *Quatrains*, which remained unpublished till long after his death.

All these still hidden aspects of Péguy's life and character could not fail to strike a sympathetic chord in the heart of Fournier as he gradually came to know him, and because he found so much in Péguy's life to parallel his own, so much that was similar and more admirable, he never ceased to look up to him as an older and better version of himself. For once, Fournier had found a literary master who was neither plainly inadequate, like Paul Fort, nor excessively intimidating, like Claudel, and his gratitude took the tangible form of no less than forty-two separate paragraphs in the course of his two years' stay at *Paris-Journal* and, much more important, a friendship which, for both men, grew progressively deeper and stronger over the few years that were left to them both on earth.

Fournier's obligation to provide regular gossip for his literary column, which first prompted him to interview Péguy, was also instrumental in bringing him into contact with another author whom he and Péguy very much admired : this was Marguerite Audox and she too became a special friend. She was born in Saincoins, in the far south of the Cher *département*, on 7 July 1863, and when her mother died three years later, she and her sister were packed off by the father to the care of the main orphanage in Bourges. There she was brought up by nuns and later became a shepherdess on a lonely farm at Sainte Montaine in the midst of the Berry countryside, where she fell in love with a farmer's son. This love was apparently reciprocated, but marriage was ruled out by the young man's parents as socially impossible, whereupon she travelled to Paris and worked as a seamstress in a minute garret until she was all but blind. To people her solitude, she adopted the habit of writing down all that she could remember about her girlhood and her lost love, and it was this excursion into autobiography which, only slightly transposed, became her most famous and successful novel, *Marie-Claire*.

While in Paris, Marguerite Audox was befriended by Charles Louis-Philippe, Léon-Paul Fargue and Michel Yell, a group of talented minor writers who were particularly interested in both working-class and regionalist fiction of high literary quality. They detected unmistakable signs of this quality in Marguerite Audox's handwritten exercise books, and persuaded her to revise them for publication; this she did, with a powerful magnifying glass and her nose pressed against the page. At first, there was difficulty in finding a publisher, but a champion was forthcoming in the formidable shape of Octave Mirbeau, one of the literary pundits of the day who had himself earlier achieved notoriety with his populist and semi-pornographic novel *Mémoirs d'une femme de chambre*. Through his intervention, *Marie-Claire* was published in 1910, firstly in the May and June numbers of *La Grande Revue*, which had earlier published two of Fournier's pieces, and later, in book form, in October. It won for its author belated recognition and the Prix de la Vie Heureuse for the year, then worth a not inconsiderable 5000 francs.

Fournier found a great deal to admire in *Marie-Claire*, the artful clarity and simplicity of the prose style, the gentle, trusting character of Marie-Claire who does not indulge in self-pity, either when her innocent idyll is abruptly ended or when she makes a sentimental journey back to her orphanage and is present at the death of her favourite Sister, Désirée-des-Anges. What he appreciated most of all, however, was the author's great skill in presenting all the events and characters through the innocent consciousness of a child, and it was because of what he rightly took to be Marguerite Audox's kinship with childhood, just as much as her lack of affectation and her profound attachment to the Berry he also loved, which proved the basis of another friendship which, for each of them, was to endure until death.

III

In spite of continual quarrels with Jeanne Bruneau, the most violent and apparently definitive one of which was in October when Fournier discovered she was still (innocently) corresponding with a former

lover, and stormed out, leaving her with no money to pay the rent,
they were still together at the end of 1910. The letters to her which
have survived from this period still occasionally reproach her for not
having the courage to think and act heroically – the criticism that
runs like a refrain through his letters to Bichet – but rather more
frequent is the tone of marital comradeship, as he reports on his
encounters of the day at work, or genuine solicitude, as he advises
her to safeguard her health. In successive letters, written while she
was away in Bourges, in December 1910, he recalled for her memories
of his sense of loneliness while he was a schoolboy at Brest,[30] and his
sense of sheer entrancement when he used to accompany his mother
out to tea at Epineuil.[31] In each case, he appended a comment which
indicated why he would not take the final step of marrying her.
Having described how he used to long so desperately for companion-
ship at Brest, he added 'Your great fault was that you didn't come
to me then. And that is quite unpardonable. Because it's a fault no
human could possibly rectify';[32] and after evoking the 'other world'
of Epineuil, he declared :

> Part of my life is lived in that other world. A world full of fancy
> and childhood dreams of Paradise. People who are very close
> to me know this well. I used to think that the various women
> I've known would be able to travel there with me. But not one
> of them ever could.[33]

One of the women he encountered had, in fact, transported him
back into the imagined world of childhood, and that was Yvonne de
Quiévrecourt, but that was before they had actually spoken and
before she asked that chilling question 'A quoi bon?' Only Yvonne,
he persisted in believing, could solve all his problems for him, and
fortunately for the peace of mind of them both, she continued to
remain remote. In the meantime, he comforted himself as best he
could by pouring out his sorrows to the loyal and long-suffering
Jeanne :

> I've spent a very bad day. I've been in a state of appalling
> depression. All day long it's been as it sometimes is at night,
> when I suddenly wake up and ask myself questions with a
> feeling of indescribable remorse.
> The feeling that life will have passed by and that nothing
> will have been done, that you're going to present yourself at
> your life's end with your hands as empty as they are at the end
> of the day, and – ah ! this above all ! the feeling that your youth

is over and you haven't done what you ought to have done –
that's the fearful, bitter taste I had all through yesterday, in a
great grey downpour which soaked me to the skin.

Today, that's all behind me, and here I am once again, young,
and arrogant and violent and full of laughter; the rain's dried
up and a fierce great wind is sweeping everything before it under
the cold sun.

If I'd written to you yesterday, what could I have found to
say that wouldn't have hurt you?

As always, when I feel like that, I stayed on late at the
newspaper office, all alone, lingering over this gossip-column with
unspeakable disgust . . .

I stayed awake for part of the night. For a while, I dreamed
I was in a field in front of my parents' house. It was dark and
I no longer recognised the house. It was an admirable night, in
which there were occasional great flashes of blue and people
calling. But I was stuck in that field, sick and afraid, I kept
calling out but nobody answered from the sleeping house.

Don't imagine that I enjoy this despair. I've an indescribable
loathing of it. When this mood of despair used to come over me
in the night at Mirande, I would get up and walk up and down
in the little house where I lived alone. Or else I would read the
Bible like an old Englishman about to die.

Why have I become like this, I who was once so gay and
innocent and good? What can it be that's giving me so much
pain?[34]

It would be tempting to answer that Fournier's pain was compounded
of remorse for his occasional cruelty to Jeanne and unrequited love
for Yvonne de Quiévrecourt, but this might well be to confuse symptoms with some more deeply rooted cause. This same wave of black
despair, coming up to engulf him from some inner depths, was
described in similar terms in the one letter that has survived from his
schoolboy affair with the first Yvonne, which is to say weeks
before he ever saw the second Yvonne, and years before he met
Jeanne. A host of subsequent experiences intensified his sense of
anguish, but the root-cause would seem to be as essentially unaccountable in his case as it was in Flaubert's, an indelible streak of melan-
cholia which was as much part of him as the colour of his hair or his
eyes, and which no human or divine agency was ever able to
eradicate.

Fournier did not fill up the whole of his letters to Jeanne with complaints about all she could never be, or with expressions of self-pity or self-disgust : he also confided in her details of his literary plans and it was in the letter that he wrote to her on 7 December 1910, that he announced he was in the process of concluding another short story, *Le Miracle de la fermière* :

> It's the story of a little peasant boy whom the village school-teacher has sent to boarding-school at the request of the father. The mother isn't willing and neither is the little boy. Once he gets to boarding-school, the little boy is unhappy, the other boys beat him. The town where he is is a whole day's railway journey away. The mother can't read or write, and she's never been away from home. During the night, a dark October night full of rain, she takes a horse and cart, is away for two days and comes back on the third day with the child.
>
> In this story there will be some beautiful country childhood scenery which you'll love.
>
> This story actually happened, it goes without saying. I know the people. It happened because country people are straight and simple folk, and nobody has the right to interfere with their lives, nor to enter their kingdom which nobody really knows.
>
> In addition, this story is true because all stories are true – even the story of Christ's Resurrection. You must believe everything.[35]

Le Miracle de la fermière was eventually published in *La Grande Revue* on 25 March 1911. Although in describing the homesickness the little country boy feels at boarding-school, Fournier is clearly drawing on his own memories, the story is remarkably free of self-pity or indeed, any trace of sentimentality : the boy's nostalgia is conveyed not through adjectives or adverbs, but through the notation of visual details, once taken for granted, now cherished because they form part of a scene that is beyond reach or recall. It was undoubtedly Fournier's most accomplished performance up till that point, and like any other aspiring young author, he at once distributed copies of his latest published work to the writers whose praise he especially valued. Claudel's response was a curt and formal postcard expressing his 'remerciements bien sincères',[36] while Rivière was as loyal and perspicacious as ever : 'Your first great step forward. Go on in that direction.'[37] What he particularly savoured, however, was Péguy's reaction when he called to see him at his *Cahiers* office on 10 April :

> Péguy said to me : 'It's quite straightforward, I'm now going to say something to you I don't often say, because I'm more in

the habit of rejecting copy than commissioning it. But, here goes. When you've got seven pieces like your "Miracle", bring them to me and I'll publish them here. Have you got many in that strain? Ah, *mon vieux*, it's finer than Audoux. There it is, it's solid, it's *real* . . . When you got seven of them, we'll bring them out in a *Cahier*. It's got to be *seven*, you understand, because that's a sacred number.'[38]

Encouraged though he was by Péguy's offer, he could not readily respond to it. He was anxious not to be diverted for too long from his unfinished novel and it was still essential for him to devote much time and energy to his journalism. He still had to concoct a short article almost every other day for *Paris-Journal*, and though he consistently bemoaned the fact that he was dissipating his talents, he was enough of a realist, and a peasant, to protest when his means of livelihood was really threatened. When, in February 1911, he found that his articles were regularly being whittled down to seventy or eighty lines, with a corresponding reduction in his salary, he wasted no time in counter-attacking. He dictated a letter for his friend Bichet to copy out and send to the editor :

The literary column is, with your own editorial on the front page, regularly one of the most interesting things in your admirable newspaper. It would be regrettable to see it disappear altogether . . . [39]

And to make the appeal more persuasive, he asked Bichet to pretend he was a school-teacher from Rouen (he was in fact at that time on Army service), and to make as much as possible of the fact that, confirming his brilliant academic promise, he had passed out top of all France in the *agrégation* examinations of 1910. Bichet balked briefly, which drew from Fournier a tart rebuke, scribbled on a visiting-card, complaining of 'the usual hesitation and timidity', but finally complied, and a week later came Fournier's jubilant message that the plot had succeeded, that he had been restored to editorial favour and his column to its pristine proportions.

When he was not engaged in seeking out copy for his column and working it up into polished articles, Fournier devoted much of his time to his friendships. The absence of letters might perhaps suggest some cooling in his relationship with Rivière, but, in fact, they continued to see each other daily in 1911, even after the Rivières moved out of the family home into a flat of their own at 15 rue Froideveaux; they continued their frequent visits to the theatre and to the Russian Ballet. The Rivières were now expecting their first child, and between irksome bouts of teaching at the Collège Stanislas, Jacques was actively preparing a collection of his major critical essays for the press.[40] Fournier was now on dining terms with Jacques Copeau, a co-director of *La Nouvelle Revue Française* and dynamic founder of the Vieux-Colombier Theatre, and he more often than not attended the weekly banquet organised by the leading journalists of the newspaper, *L'Intransigeant* to which he occasionally contributed.

In the middle of February 1911, Fournier announced to Bichet that he had once again ended his affair with Jeanne Bruneau :

> I left Jeanne a week ago, without unpleasantness, on the best of terms, because of an upsurge of youthfulness that was possibly an upsurge of purity. Since then, I've gone striding through the town like a young god. For how long, I wonder?[41]

When the habitual reconciliation took place on this occasion cannot be known for sure, but he was certainly keeping company with her once more by April, because he wrote a further letter to her then, while she was convalescent in Bourges, in terms that are calm, solicitous and warmly affectionate :

> I'm most annoyed with you, my darling, because the letter I got from you this morning was too short and had been written too quickly. We have so many things to say to each other, to explain and to get finally settled. Do you really think that thirty scribbled lines are enough?
>
> I would guess from what you say that you haven't yet started to go out of doors again. I insist that once your throat is completely better that you go for a long walk with your sister each day down the Lazenay road, that road which follows the curve of a long wall like the wall of a park.
>
> You're possibly wrong not to want to follow, at least for a little while, the doctor's instructions you've been given. The main thing is that you've got to come back to me strong and happy and gay again, like the lovely young woman that you are, and whom I love.[42]

He then went on to describe a recent visit to Marguerite Audoux :

> I meant to stay five minutes and I stayed for two long hours.

We talked for the whole time about . . . love. I've always admired how, in spite of so much distress and so many disasters, this Marie-Claire has always stayed straight and solid and sincere . . . This elderly Marie-Claire paid me some compliments which I want to pass on without false modesty . . . She told me : 'Yes, one of the things I like about you is your sense of certainty, your calmness, your air of confidence . . . And here's something else I won't hide from you : I love it when you visit me because for me, you recall Henri Deslois and Eugene [Marie-Claire's admirers], those young men from the old days, far from here, out in the Berry. It's in the tone of your voice too. You don't notice it straightaway.'

And then I told her that you had also discovered the peasant in me – but, in your case, the peasant who's bad and mad.

The general atmosphere of the letter is so relaxed and amiable that one might well be justified in inferring that the 'things to get finally settled' were some sort of more stable union rather than yet another 'final' break, but the prospect – or threat – of marriage to Jeanne was once again averted by evoking the lost Yvonne. That same month, Fournier wrote to Rivière :

At the present moment, I know an old countrywoman here in Paris whose daughter has run off with a young man. She won't leave town until she's found her again and her other children won't let her out of the house. She says : 'Just let me go out all on my own, just the once, and by the evening I'll have her back again.'

That's the way I could find my love again if only my faith was as great as that.

You mustn't believe that I love anyone else. I'm most unhappy. It's six years now ![43]

It was in only slightly less despairing a mood that a few weeks later, while on a few days' holiday at his grandmother's at La Chapelle, he cycled off on a literary pilgrimage to discover the lonely farmhouse on which Marguerite Audoux based the central idyll of *Marie-Claire*. As soon as he got back to La Chapelle, he recorded his impressions and sent them off to Marguerite Audoux in Paris : it is, for the most part, a lyrical description, carefully registering the precise sights and sounds which struck him : the sandy soil and bracken of the Sologne, the buzzing of flies in the summer heat, the cooing of doves from tall oak-trees, the thatched roofs of old cottages overhanging so low they almost touched the ground, the little shepherd girl, thinly clad, with her flock of sheep, a young cowherd watching him suspiciously out of the corner of his eye – the whole, accompanied by a little sketch-map to let his correspondent see the exact lay-out of the buildings which had been added since she was there. And then, inevitably, the characteristic Fournier conclusion :

> That morning will remain precious in my memory. It's as though everything has been preserved there for you to come back one day. And in that old farmstead surrounded by its great oaks, I'm not surprised that a little girl should have been entranced.
> It was only on my way back and riding down the lane, that I was suddenly overcome with a sense of desolation. To think that everything should be over, my God, that everything should be so hopelessly over. To think that on such a summer's day, not a trace should be left of that love of long ago.[44]

This same note of vain regret for what has been irretrievably lost is the dominant mood of the last short story Fournier ever completed, *Portrait*, written in June and July 1911, and published in the September 1911 number of *La Nouvelle Revue Française*. Like so much of Fournier's fiction, it was solidly based on fact, in this case on a newspaper cutting dated 11 May 1911 which described how a former class-mate of his at the lycée of Brest, one Yves Pony, had gone on to become a naval ensign and then shot himself through the mouth in a fit of despair, at the age of twenty-four, after being refused permission to marry the girl he loved by his prospective father-in-law. Fournier's short story is an imaginary reconstruction of the events leading up to the suicide and the mood in which it is to be related is indicated by the quotation from Péguy which stands at its head :

> We know what it is to feel regret and remorse . . . to feel contrition without having done anything for which to reproach ourselves. And we know that remorse of this kind is the deepest and most indelible of all.

What is most striking about this beautifully written little story is not so much the successful rendering of the singularly unprepossessing central character, or the utterly dreary atmosphere of the provincial boarding-school, but rather the narrator's ineradicable sense of complicity in the final tragedy. He it was who first read to ugly little Davy the account from his favourite book of Dominique's vain love for the lovely but inaccessible Madeleine, and he it was also who later

âteau de Loroy, near La Chapelle-d'Angillon. The principal model for the 'Lost Domain'
Le Grand Meaulnes

Right: Fournier at La Chapelle, September 1905

Below: Corporal Fournier (centre of back row) with his squad at Mailly Camp, 15 June 1908

Bottom: Second Lieutenant Fournier (centre of third row) and men of the 88th Infantry Regiment on manoeuvres at Lacapelle-Livron, 29 April 1913

took Davy to see Barnum's Circus and to stare, unseen, at a beautiful young girl, sitting quietly reading, close enough for them to see her every feature but as remote as if she were in another world. Davy's tragic end, the narrator feels, came about because he tried to move out of his humdrum ordinary world into the romantic world in which he had no real place, and for having tempted him to better himself when he should have left well alone, the narrator implies that he can never forgive himself :

> Suddenly, he found he was appallingly clumsy and stupid and ugly. He remembered *Dominique*; he remembered that morning when we came across the American girl in the garden of the circus. This time, though, he was all on his own, lost on that difficult road in that land of the imagination where I'd so inconsiderately led him. I wasn't at his side to encourage him, to extend a hand to help him make the painful transition. He must have gone home and thought of writing to me, and then he recalled the postcards of his I never bothered to answer. So he decided to say nothing to anybody . . .[45]

The moral of it all would therefore seem to be the same as that of *Le Miracle de la fermière* and also, interestingly enough, that of the heroine of *Le Grand Meaulnes* : it is succinctly stated in Maeterlinck's *Sagesse et Destinée*, one of the books Fournier especially admired in 1904 : 'The desire for the *extraordinary* can often bring great harm to ordinary souls.' It is an axiom that he himself must more than once have deeply pondered as he flogged himself in such futile fashion around the academic race-course in his youth.

When *Portrait* appeared at the beginning of September, the everfaithful Péguy hastened to congratulate the author with one of his charactertistically terse letters :

> I've just read your *Portrait*. You will go far, Fournier, and you'll remember that it was I who told you so. Your affectionately devoted, Péguy.[46]

When he received this message, Fournier had already gone far, though not quite in the sense Péguy intended : he was 430 miles from Paris, on a month's military service with his regiment at Mirande. He was more than normally resentful at having to spend so long, so far from Paris at this particular period in time, because on 23 August, two days before he had had to report for duty, his god-daughter Jacqueline Rivière was born, after a complicated Caesarian section.

In the circumstances, expending all his time and energies on Army drill and autumn manœuvres seemed to him utterly pointless. On 1 September, he wrote to Rivière :

> I'm utterly exiled, utterly miserable, utterly worn out.
> The physical exhaustion I was hoping for has been provided. It's chased away my depression. In fact, it's merely taken its place, that's the long and short of it. Sometimes, I try to bring Jacqueline to mind, I try to picture what she's like and I'm filled with a wild desire to hold her for just a little while. That's all . . .
> From time to time, I say to myself : 'Good grief! Is this really still going on? Can I still be here? Will there ever be an end to it?' Two years ago, I was leading this same detachment of men, at this same hour, along the same road, on the same exercise, and I was saying to myself, 'The captain will doubtless be along in a moment, better take precautions.' When in God's name will they let me have a bit of peace? For five years it's been dragging on like this![47]

Just over a week later, in spite of much vigorous marching and counter-marching around Gascony, he was still not reconciled to the loss of Yvonne. Again he wrote to Rivière :

> I'm filled with torment and black depression. Something's being denied me without which I just can't live. At each bend in the road, and in every billet, I find the same despair faithfully waiting for me. It's the same now as it was two years ago and six years ago. But now it's complicated by an obsession with carnality which wasn't there before.[48]

Four days later while still on manœuvres, he sent a general news-letter to the Rivières to be read by all the family, inside which was an additional short note for Jacques and Isabelle alone :

> It's now the afternoon. The heat is terrible. A light wind occasionally lifts a corner of the tent flap. Great white clouds are massing on the horizon, just as they were three years ago at Mailly Camp, or like that time when I sat in the hay in the barn, twenty miles from Fère-Champenoise, that Ascension Day afternoon with the wind so strongly blowing.
> Pigeons flutter up on to the roof of the farm. Somewhere over there is another building, I can hear a hen clucking. And further

away still, right in the distance, I can see hills baked by the sun . . . Sense of infinite desolation . . . Somewhere, on a little beach close to Quiberon, a young woman sits lost in thought, looking out to sea . . . My grief, still the same as it always was, must now be boring to everybody just as it's sterile for me.

So much for my love.

Now please tear that up and don't give it another thought. Think instead only of the deep and uncomplicated affection I feel for you.

But I was reflecting just now that nobody in all the world can be as exiled as I am. I insist that I do not belong here.[49] A little while ago, I went into the stable. Above the lower door-flap, and between the bars, I could make out a vast, elongated head, a pair of huge eyes and two pricked-up ears. I stroked the horse's muzzle and he seemed pleased. And I thought to myself it's as difficult for me as it is for him to make myself understood in this world.

And that's why it's so difficult to find a really clear style to write in.

I send you kisses,

Henri.[50]

September always tended to inspire Fournier with melancholy thoughts, wherever he spent it, and the chief consolations he found in September 1911 were the visits he paid to the homes of other writers in a break between manœuvres while away on Army service in the far south-west, he took the opportunity to travel to Bordeaux to meet the young poet Alexis Saint-Leger Leger, who was later to adopt the pseudonym of Saint-John Perse and win the Nobel Prize for Literature, and the regional novelist, Michel Yell, who was a close friend of Marguerite Audoux and a magistrate in Fronton, near Toulouse.[51] At the end of the month, after resuming his civilian status in Paris, Fournier spent four days with Rivière at Cuverville, the Normandy country home of another future Nobel Prize-winner, André Gide. In a letter to his sister Fournier described the visit as a complete success:

Now I can understand why you have so much regret for Cuverville.

For the past three days I've been leading the calmest and most restful life you can possibly imagine – and also the laziest. Yet you feel that you could really work here if you wanted to.

There's a great wind blowing and it's raining, which makes life in this house that much more delectable.[52]

Much though Fournier benefited from the stay with the Gides, it was to stand Rivière in even better stead.

IV

Since October 1909, Rivière had been working at the Collège Stanislas, trying to teach philosophy to students who were hoping to pass on to the Military Academy of Saint-Cyr. He hated the work, not only because he had great difficulty in disciplining pupils who were almost as old as he was, but also because his subject, not being on the examination syllabus, was inevitably held in contempt by the class. He was the victim of repeated practical jokes, and that studied insolence which French schoolboys seem always to have been past-masters in serving up, and since he was always particularly highly-strung, life became more and more wretched for him. The breaking-point came on 6 October 1911 when he had occasion to order a loutish pupil to leave the room. The whole class got up and made as if to follow, but in the general stampede towards the door, Rivière won by several lengths. He went straight home and at once dispatched his letter of resignation. The satisfaction of having escaped from an intolerable situation was somewhat mitigated, however, by the reflection that he now had a child as well as a wife to support, and that his occasional reviewing was unlikely to provide a living wage. Fortunately for him and for French literature, Gide was soon at hand with a solution.

The secretary of the *Nouvelle Revue Française* at this time was a young man called Pierre de Lanux, grandson of Gide's old piano teacher (who was the model for the pathetic character of La Pérouse in *Les Faux-Monnayeurs*). Whatever may have been the secretarial merits of Pierre de Lanux, they manifestly did not include accurate proof-reading, and nobody's heart was uplifted in June 1911 when the review appeared with the following gnomic line ascribed to Alexis Leger Leger :

> et du pouce et du doigt essayant une lame (*testing a blade between thumb and finger*).

This contributed little to the elegiac effect to which Leger Leger had been aspiring in his original manuscript on which he had written

> et du pouce et du doigt essuyant une larme (*wiping away a tear with finger and thumb*).

It was first suggested that the obvious need for a replacement should be filled by one Francis de Miomandre, but he magnanimously stepped aside when he learned of Rivière's difficulties, and at the beginning of December 1911, Rivière took up the post he was to fill with such distinction. It meant for him deliverance from emotional and financial bondage, and a triumphal entry into the Promised Land which had virtually been designated as his rightful heritage from the very beginning of his impassioned literary debates with Fournier. Now he could duel to his heart's content with virtually every leading writer in France, and could play a major role in shaping the policy of what was then, and for years remained, the most distinguished literary review in the Western World.

Fournier, for his part, had ruefully to pursue his more modest way as a gossip-writer, and in between the manifold activities demanded of him by the need to produce what had now become a daily column, he laboured intermittently to complete his sadly neglected novel. On 11 October 1911, he wrote to Michel Yell reporting that of the forty chapters he planned to write, only twelve had actually been completed.[53] On 31 October, he wrote to him again, saying:

> I'm still very young but I'm not very happy. I console myself with my book. I want it to sweep everybody off their feet. I want the whole country to read it and I want women to love it . . . But I'm continually being distracted. And when I do find the time, I run away from my work.[54]

Rivière continued to play the role of Fournier's chief confidant and principal technical adviser until *Le Grand Meaulnes* was finally completed, but since nearly all the later amendments in the plans were discussed in conversation rather than through letters, it is impossible to say with much precision when such amendments were made. One cannot, therefore, say when 'Anne-Marie Deschamps' was renamed 'Yvonne de Galais' or when 'Annette' became 'Valentine Blondeau'. One cannot pinpoint the moment in time when Yvonne de Galais was provided with a brother, Frantz, although one can recognise, with his emergence, the logical next step in a sequence which began earlier when he decided not to confine himself to a single hero, fashioned in his own image, but to divide his personality between Meaulnes and Seurel. With the creation of Frantz, Fournier could now give expression to three distinct yet related aspects of his personality and experience: Meaulnes could enact the role he occasionally affected in his letters to 'little' Bichet, dominating, dynamic, riding rough-shod over doubts and difficulties to make his dreams come true; Seurel could reflect that part of himself he had to live with for most of the time, dutiful, diffident and forever yearning because of an incurable sense of deprivation; Frantz could re-enact aspects of his past life shared only with those very close to him, the parents who so readily indulged his ambitious whims, the sister who surrounded him with hero-worship, and the brother-in-law whose honeymoon peace was disturbed by querulous demonstrations of self-pity.

Fournier does not seem to have encountered undue difficulty in constructing the two separate worlds of his novel, the country world where most of the characters spend all their lives, and the Land Without a Name into which the hero wanders, which he seeks ever after in vain. As early as 20 August 1910, he was confidently able to announce :

> I've been working for two days now at my book, working simul-
> taneously on the part which is pure imagination and fantastic
> in construction, and on the human part which is very simple
> and made out of memories. In the end, it could well be that
> my first book will be reduced entirely to the former, because I've
> already made a lot of progress on it.[55]

The confidence voiced in this letter to Bichet was either misplaced or carelessly expressed, because only two days later he reported to Rivière that the 'human' world of his novel was shaping more promisingly than the 'imaginary' world and that it was likely that he would scrap the latter.[56] In point of fact, *both* letters were very soon to be outmoded because he discovered his so-called 'road to Damascus' a month later, and the direct consequence of this was not merely a change in his prose-style, but also a change in his working-methods. From this point on, he set about constructing both his 'real' world and his 'fantasy' world from his own authentic memories, and he did this quite consciously.

The plot that he finally evolved is intricate and almost wholly compounded of details derived and ingeniously re-adapted from Fournier's own experience. The story, narrated by François Seurel, whose parents are teachers in the little village of Sainte-Agathe, opens with the arrival at their school of one Augustin Meaulnes, a charismatic yet secretive youth of seventeen who readily establishes himself as *le grand Meaulnes*, overlord of all the schoolboys' activities. One day, near the end of the autumn term, Monsieur Seurel asks for a volunteer to drive with the fifteen-year-old François to meet the grandparents who are shortly to arrive at the nearest railway station, several miles distant, for their annual Christmas visit. To the surprise of the whole class, Meaulnes, the obvious choice, is not selected, but true to character, he chooses to flout this decision, borrows a horse and cart, and drives off alone for the station.

He never makes his rendez-vous with the grandparents. He takes a wrong turning, dozes off and wakes up to find he is hopelessly lost and that night is falling. He parts company with the horse and cart, sleeps in a deserted barn and spends the following day wandering alone across the desolate Sologne countryside. At last, he comes upon a tumbledown manor-house beside a lake in the middle of the fir-woods, hung with brightly-coloured lanterns and full of children in fancy dress who have all been invited to celebrate the impending marriage of the young and chimerical son of the house, Frantz de Galais.

Nobody sees anything untowards in the arrival of Meaulnes who exchanges his everyday peasant's garb for old-fashioned aristocratic costume and joins in the celebrations. He sits listening to a lovely fair-headed girl playing the piano, and, while little children perch themselves on his knees, he imagines that she is his wife. He meets her again the following morning when the guests take a boat-trip across the lake. He reveals his identity to her and learns that she is Frantz's sister Yvonne. On his grandiose plans for the future, she repeatedly comments *a quoi bon?* but she nonetheless promises him that she will wait faithfully for him to return.

Soon after the party breaks up in confusion. Frantz returns without his fiancée, announces that the wedding is off and departs abruptly into the night. The guests begin to depart in their carts and carriages and Meaulnes finds a place in a coach going in the direction of Sainte-Agathe. As he is being driven away in the darkness, a shot rings out and his final memory of the party is the glimpsed vision of a figure in a white Pierrot costume moving between the trees of the park with an inert body in his arms. Soon after this, he falls asleep and when he is woken up, in the early light of a new day, the coach is back near Sainte-Agathe.

After his return to the village school Meaulnes makes a number of vain and despairing attempts to find his way back to the scene of the party. He confides his secret only to Seurel, and then, only after a prolonged period of reticence which brings the pair of them much unpopularity. He loses his place as leader of the schoolboys to a young stranger with a heavily bandaged head, one of two strolling players who arrive in a caravan and are waiting for the fine weather before presenting their show on the village square. This stranger organises the boys into a military squad which ambushes Meaulnes one evening and steals the map on which he has been attempting to locate his Land Without a Name. The stranger is then faced with dissension in the ranks of his 'troops' so he forms an alliance with Meaulnes and Seurel. He returns the map, with a few details added, and reveals that he too had been a guest at the strange party. All three make a solemn pledge to come to the immediate aid of any one of them, should he ever be in dire need : the alarm signal is to be the call of an owl.

Not long afterwards, with the arrival of the finer weather, the players present their entertainment to the assembled populace on the village square. The star performer is Ganache, the tall, lugubrious Pierrot figure, who keeps vainly trying to climb a small mountain of chairs and who ends his act by throwing a rag doll at the spectators. As the performance draws to its close, the younger performer removes his bandage and stands revealed to Meaulnes as Frantz de Galais. Meaulnes is prevented from speaking to him there and then but confidently expects to do so first thing next day. His hopes are dashed, however, because Ganache has been denounced to the local gendarmes as a poultry-thief, and to avoid arrest, he and Frantz drive away in the middle of the night. Thereafter, Meaulnes makes a further series of unavailing attempts to rediscover the Lost Domain, and finally, in despair, decides that his only chance of seeing Yvonne again is to go to the house in Paris where, Frantz has revealed, she sometimes spends Easter and Whitsun. He leaves Sainte-Agathe and subsequently writes back to report that the house in Paris proved to be deserted, that he had met a girl beside the house who revealed that Yvonne was by now married and that, therefore, the adventure must be considered at an end.

Months afterwards, in high summer, Seurel learns that this news is false. He discovers that the de Galais family has, all this time, been very well known to his favourite uncle Florentin who keeps a large general store in the village of Vieux-Nançay. He makes a hurried visit to his uncle's and is introduced to Yvonne de Galais, who turns out not only to be unmarried but still to be waiting for Meaulnes to return. Uncle Florentin arranges a party on the banks of the Cher where Meaulnes and Yvonne may be reunited.

In great excitement, Seurel cycles to bring the glad tidings to Meaulnes who lives with his widowed mother in another village many miles distant. Seurel spends the night with his elderly aunt Moinel who tells him that she also knows the de Galais family, that she too was present at the famous wedding party at Les Sablonnières, the old manor house which has had to be sold to meet Frantz's heavy debts. Aunt Moinel further reveals that on her way back from the party, she gave a lift to a girl who turned out to be Frantz's ex-fiancée, Valentine; at the last moment, she had felt herself obliged to call off the wedding because she was too disconcerted by Frantz's extravagant tales and attitudes. Seurel's aunt provided Valentine with a home for some weeks but finally, seeing that the girl was continuing to grieve over her broken romance, she announced that Yvonne was married, that Frantz had gone away forever, and that the de Galais family was therefore best forgotten.

Seurel decides that this episode is of secondary importance only, and, consequently, of no interest to Meaulnes. When he calls on him the following morning, his only concern is to deliver the momentous news that, against all the odds, Yvonne de Galais has been found and is still unmarried. Meaulnes is unaccountably disconcerted, hints darkly at certain wrongs he must put right but, nonetheless, allows himself to be persuaded to attend the garden party where he and Yvonne are to be reunited. The party proves something of a disaster: Meaulnes is embittered and moody throughout, loses his temper with Yvonne's aged father, but finally proposes to Yvonne and is accepted.

The wedding takes place five months later but that same evening, Frantz returns and gives his owl call-signal, summoning Meaulnes and Seurel to come to his aid. He is intercepted by Seurel before Meaulnes emerges from the house and demands that they set off in search of Valentine, his lost fiancée. Seurel asks him to leave Meaulnes in peace and undertakes himself to rediscover Valentine and bring about the reunion. Frantz departs without having spoken with Meaulnes who, on hearing Seurel's account of the meeting, insists that it is his duty to find Valentine and speaks once more of the wrongs he must redress. The very next morning, he sets off in quest of the lost girl.

Nothing is heard of Meaulnes for a year. Seurel becomes Yvonne's faithful companion and when she dies soon after giving birth to a daughter, it falls on him to carry her out to the waiting hearse. While putting in order her family papers, he comes across a secret journal in which Meaulnes recorded the chief events in his life after he moved on from Sainte-Agathe to Paris. The girl he met outside Yvonne's Paris home was Valentine who was waiting there in the hope of seeing Frantz, but Meaulnes did not discover her true identity until he himself became engaged to her. As soon as he discovered what he had done, Meaulnes broke off his engagement after a bitter argument, and left Valentine to her fate, even although she assured him that he was abandoning her to a life of prostitution. Overcome with remorse, he had been on the point of setting out to rediscover and rescue her on the very morning when Seurel arrived with the news that Yvonne was waiting for him, after all.

Finally, when Seurel has assumed that he has disappeared forever, Meaulnes comes back to announce that Frantz and Valentine have been reunited, and to claim the baby daughter whom Seurel has effectively adopted. The narrative ends with him taking his baby daughter in his arms and smiling at her through his tears while Seurel imagines the two of them setting out together for further adventures.

Just how consistently Fournier constructed his fiction from his store of real-life facts can be seen if one compares some crucial passages from the Lost Domain sections of the novel with almost identical passages from his notes and letters – the first meeting of Meaulnes and Yvonne de Galais, for example, with the notes of Fournier's first sight of Yvonne de Quiévrecourt, or the spectacle of Yvonne de Galais playing her piano with the description of the little painting by Georges Decote – and by referring to certain of Fournier's working-notes. One such note is especially revealing: it is headed 'Characters' and is followed by a column of suggestions:

> the old folk
> Aunt Morenne
> Grandmother Barthe
> a magic lantern show
> dining-room, child beneath table
> dances – *true* theatre[57]

These references are to Grandmother Barthe who was, of course, his own maternal grandmother, to her sister, Honorine Morenne-Blondeau: in the novel, these were transposed into Adèle and Moinelle, respectively, the two old ladies at the mysterious party who first tell Meaulnes about Frantz's courtship of his fiancée. The 'magic lantern show' could well be that briefly mentioned in a letter to his sister in January 1905,[58] and to judge by certain scenes in the finished novel, the *true* (underlined in Fournier's own notes) theatre must refer to the Russian Ballet production he saw with Jeanne in June 1910: the fussy little Pantalon who struts rapidly among the dancers, the girls who pirouette as they swirl from one room to the other, the grotesque figure of the long-sleeved Pierrot clumsily loping after the fleeing company – all these feature not only in Fournier's *fête étrange* but also in the ballet *Carnaval* which so impressed him in the Diaghilev Paris summer season of 1910. For the conversation between Meaulnes and Yvonne de Galais, he utilised snippets of his own conversation with Yvonne de Quiévrecourt on Whit Sunday 1905: his opening gambit 'You are beautiful', his unexplained comment 'the name I thought of for you was more beautiful', together with her rejoinders, 'we've behaved like children, we've been foolish' and the fateful *A quoi bon?*, *What's the point of all this?* For Yvonne de Galais, however, he invented the one vital additional remark he had listened for in vain in reality : 'I will wait for you.'

The setting for all these festivities in the novel – the thin spire of the ruined abbey rising above the trees, the general atmosphere of decay pervading the dilapidated main building, the lake with its fringe of reeds – all these are reminiscences of Loroy, though, as seen through the wondering eyes of Meaulnes, a house and lake infinitely vaguer and vaster than the Loroy as it is now represented in La Chapelle amongst the merchandise of enterprising postcard-manufacturers.

Characters, scenes and incidences in the 'real' world of the novel were likewise gradually built up from Fournier's own memories, very often after reference to rough notes or prose-poems written very much earlier, or to copies of letters which he had sent to friends. Thus, the description in the novel of Ganache's performance in the circus tent on the village square, is a compound of his impressions of the 'Falling man' seen and admired at a Paris music hall in 1908[59] and of his memories of another clown's rag-filled doll,[60] while his description of Ganache's unforgettable face, 'like that of a drowned man on some mortuary slab', is the replica of his description of a certain Cousin, one of his fellow-soldiers while he was still serving in the ranks. And to demonstrate just one further example of this process, one can refer to the death of Yvonne de Galais. In August 1910, Fournier arrived at the house of one Gustave Tronche (brother-in-law of André Lhote) to congratulate his wife on giving birth to a son, only to find that she and the baby were dying. He wrote soon afterwards to console the widower :

Often I try to recall the power and yet the sweetness with which I saw her battling against death, two hours, one hour before the end.

I remember the burning hot hand she stretched out to me expressing so much friendship. And all the while, you were saying : 'There, you see, for an invalid she doesn't look too poorly, does she?' And I didn't know what to reply to you, I just went on holding her horribly feverish hand in mine.

. . . I'm all alone, heartbroken, quite lost. But I know that I'm less alone, less heartbroken, less lost than you.[61]

This letter, imaginatively adapted, was used for the conversation by Yvonne's death-bed between her father and Seurel. The passage which follows soon after, recording Seurel's grief at the news of

Yvonne's death, is based, with very little alteration, on the letter Fournier wrote to Rivière in July 1907, expressing his anguish immediately after hearing the news of Yvonne de Quiévrecourt's marriage. According to Madame Rivière, the scene in the novel where it is discovered that Yvonne's coffin is too cumbersome to be manoeuvred down the narrow staircase was based on an incident which happened in La Chapelle, following the death of one of their acquaintances called Maria Bureau; and Seurel's farewell gesture in kissing the dead Yvonne's golden hair parallels the surviving lover's final kiss at the end of *La Femme empoisonnée*.[62]

What seems to have most exercised Fournier till very late on in the genesis of his novel was not so much how to build up his two different worlds, but how most plausibly to transport his hero from one to the other and back again. He was no longer content, as he had been in *La Partie de plaisir* merely to deposit his central character into some dream-kingdom without benefit of explanation, neither was he satisfied with the idea, merely mentioned in an early schema, of letting the hero fall asleep in one world and then waking him up in another. He was almost certainly not thinking exclusively of H. G. Wells when in September 1911 he wrote to Rivière of *The Well of the Giants*:

> The 'monster' aspect of this book offends me. I like the marvellous only when it's firmly *anchored in reality*. Not when it overwhelms or surpasses it.[63]

He was still preoccupied with the problem of transporting Meaulnes from one world to the next when he wrote to Yell in October 1911:

> I've spent the morning – or rather those few anguished hours which come before daybreak – sitting on a milestone with *le grand Meaulnes* waiting for daylight to come so that we can see where we are. I want these adventures to be really exciting.[64]

Two months later, he was still preoccupied with the same section of the narrative, Meaulnes mid-way between one world and the other:

> My work isn't going well at all. All the same, I must get back to it. On the road there are three village merchants coming back from a Twelfth Night party. They've broken a shaft of their carriage. And they invite my schoolboy friend, *le grand Meaulnes* to ride beside them. I've got to make a start on repairing that shaft, then we'll be off on fresh adventures.[65]

208

The complete letter from which this quotation was extracted, together with an explanation of how it came to be written, were revealed for the first time in 1963 with the publication of Madame Rivière's *Vie et Passion d'Alain-Fournier*. It was addressed to a woman Madame Rivière named as 'Henriette', a young music-hall singer whom he saw approaching one night at midnight as he was walking home alone from the theatre. 'Henriette' looked at him, promptly detached herself from the group of young people in evening-dress with whom she was walking, and strolled home with him as far as the front door of the Fournier home in rue Cassini. Further confirmation of 'Henriette's' impulsive character is provided in a letter Fournier wrote to André Lhote in November 1911, when, after describing the 'wilful but tragic character' of Frantz de Galais, he went on to say:

> At the moment, I go out occasionally with a girl I'm not in love with but whom I quite like because she's so slim and so amusing. Some of her actions are so funny that people turn round and smile. She'll rush straight out across the street between the vehicles with her head down. She'll grab horses by the bridle . . . But none of this is an expression of joy.[66]

This would seem to have been a fairly uncomplicated case of free adults fairly freely consenting, though it is characteristic of Fournier that he should have preferred to see them both as a pair of naughty children:

> My mother still seems well satisfied with me, but I'm not particularly satisfied either with myself or with you. I can picture all too clearly what you're up to away from me! All the time, giving the whole of yourself to whatever company you happen to be in, just as you'd let yourself go completely with that group of characters I found you singing to the other day.
>
> What on earth are a pair like us doing together? With your little body, as slim and straight as a flute, straight from your heel right to the top of your head, you were made to dance and to make sweet crooning sounds with your voice and to have fun. What does this affair between us signify? I would have broken it off ages ago if I weren't so wicked. We were going in opposite directions and we've held out a hand to each other in passing. And like two schoolchildren at play, each of us has enjoyed the game of holding on to the other's hand for a moment to stop him from moving on. But it's high time we went our different ways.

In any case there are so many things more important than love in this wicked life we're leading.

I'd like our love to be nothing more than the story of two naughty schoolchildren who've been playing truant together and gone stealing nuts. Nothing more than a rapid picnic. So rapid and so consuming that it doesn't even leave any remorse.

And the other day, as we were walking along the Seine embankment, when I was feeling cold and sensed that you were full of nervous tension and depression, I thought to myself; 'It's not even that! It's not even the furtive picnic I wanted it to be.'

All the same, I like you a lot. But what's all wrong about this whole thing is that your happiness wouldn't be mine. We're not looking for the same Paradise.

Let's amuse ourselves a moment longer along the road, before we each go our different ways. What do you say?

I give you a kiss of friendship.

Henri.[67]

According to Madame Rivière, the affair went on for a few weeks after this, with letters being occasionally exchanged by a *poste restante* arrangement. It ended, with no recriminations on either side, when Fournier picked up some letters in 'Henriette's' hand which should have been addressed to another man. After this, he returned for a time to Jeanne Bruneau, if indeed he ever 'left' her throughout this episode, and he was still keeping company with her on what seems to have been at least an affectionate basis in April 1912 when he wrote to the Rivières:

Jeanne was profoundly touched by the words Jacques wrote to her. I see her for a few minutes each day only, because of her Easter work and mine. Now my copy has to be in by quarter past seven.

Never has solitude seemed to me as dangerous as it is at the moment. I feel quite desperately lost.

I'm continuing with *Wuthering Heights*. What a great book.[68]

Apart from a further brief reference in a card to a friend in December 1912,[69] that is the last recorded reference Fournier made to Jeanne Bruneau. When they finally ceased to see each other, and what eventually became of her, is not made clear in the biographies by Madame Rivière or by Jean Loize, though it is implied by each that she married and found some sort of contentment, if not happiness. One would like to think that this is not merely wishful thinking.

210

Though he may not have known it at the time, Fournier's letter to
'Henriette' contained one item which was to prove of much greater
consequence to him than their next lovers' assignation : this was the
news that the day before the letter was written, he had attended the
funeral of Gérault-Richard 'in the mud and the rain and the wind'.
Gérault-Richard, once an extreme Left-Wing *député* for the Paris
Gobelins district, was the director of *Paris-Journal*, and it did not take
long after his death for major changes to be made in the organisation
of the paper. Fournier felt – rightly, as it turned out – that his position
was under threat, and he rightly recognised that this time, not even a
whole sackful of letters from Bichet would have any effect, even
though his friend was now a lecturer in the University of Budapest.

He enlisted the help of Péguy with whom he almost literally signed
the seal of friendship at the beginning of 1912. On New Year's Day,
his message to Péguy was :

> A conversation with you at the *Cahiers* office is like a glass of
> wine at the corner of the table. One re-emerges with warmth in
> one's heart, full of deep certainty and full of joy . . .
> Your *Cahiers* have the same effect. They're good French wine.
> Wine which makes you joyous, grave, compassionate. Holy wine
> too.[70]

In his letters, Péguy was always as parsimonious with words as he
was prodigal of them in his poetry, but his reply was no less friendly
than Fournier's :

> Fournier, call me quite simply 'Péguy' when you write to me.
> I assure you I've well deserved it. Péguy.[71]

Over the weeks which followed, as their surviving correspondence
establishes, Péguy made a number of attempts to find alternative
employment for Fournier either for *Le Figaro* or as secretary to the
politician Emile Ollivier. There was, however, another aspiring
politician who was anxious to engage a secretary – Claude Casimir-
Perier, a close friend of Péguy's since they had first met as lieutenants
in the same 276th Regiment of Infantry. And so it came about that
on 5 May 1912, with Péguy in attendance, Fournier first arrived for
dinner at the Casimir-Periers' imposing Paris residence in the highly
fashionable quai Debilly,[72] beside the Seine and close by the Eiffel
Tower.

7

The Land of Dreams Come True

May 1912–June 1914

> The things you most desire either never
> come at all or, if they do come, never do so
> at the time or in the circumstances when
> they would have given the greatest pleasure.
>
> La Bruyère

The world into which Fournier entered when he joined the Casimir-Periers was, with the possible exception of Gide's estate at Cuverville, quite the wealthiest he had ever known. Claude Casimir-Perier, just a few years older than himself, was son of a former President of the French Republic,[1] and in addition to the luxuriously appointed flat in the quai Debilly, had inherited stately homes at Trie-la-Ville, near Gisors in Normandy, and at Souberbielle, near Cambo, at the foot of the Pyrenees, in the far south-west of France. It was a world which glittered not only with material possessions, but also with bright and highly sophisticated conversation in which the stress was not only on political advancement, which was Claude Casimir-Perier's particular preoccupation, but on the Paris boulevard theatre-world in which his wife, Simone, was one of the most dazzling stars in the last years of *la belle époque*.

Simone Casimir-Perier was born in 1877 and her maiden name was Pauline Benda. Her father was a Jewish banker, while her mother had formerly been a dancer, and it was doubtless because of this latter fact that she entered the world of the theatre at the earliest possible opportunity. Her first stage-name was Pauline Prima. Her first husband had been Charles Le Bargy, a prominent actor-producer at the turn of the century who, she afterwards claimed, brought her much unhappiness and relieved her a great deal of money. He did not, it would seem, relieve her of much else because, according to Madame Simone[2] herself, the marriage was never consummated. In 1906, she left him for Casimir-Perier, and over the following years established a

Jacques Rivière in 1908

Isabelle Rivière in 1908

Paris studio portrait of Fournier by Dornac, 1913   Simone Casimir-Perier in 1913

Charles Péguy in the office of *Les Cahiers de la Quinzaine*, 1913

redoubtable reputation as a powerfully talented actress, specialising particularly in the portrayal of jealousy and passion. Off the stage, she was a vivacious and accomplished hostess, bringing considerable beauty and no mean intelligence to her husband's many dinner-parties.

One of the star-performers at these gatherings was her brilliant first cousin, Julien Benda, one of the most uncompromising of French critics in the first half of the twentieth century, whose most famous publication was to be *La Trahison des Clercs* (1927). Another regular performer was Péguy whose visits were surprisingly frequent, given the ostentatiousness of the surroundings, and his own genuine preference for the homespun. He was always made particularly welcome by Claude Casimir-Perier, to whom he was quite literally a comrade-in-arms, and with whom he shared a passionate concern for Army affairs; he was no less welcome to Simone, in spite of his fondness for lurid infantryman's expletives and his insistence at all times on addressing her husband as 'mon lieutenant'. The attractions of the Casimir-Perier household to Péguy were later explained by very close friends of all the parties concerned :

> Claude had introduced his wife, Simone, to his friend. With her quick intuition, Simone at once saw his exceptional quality and what sort of man he was. Péguy, for his part, was seduced by her wit, her talent, her worldly success, her dazzling conversation, her good nature, her high vitality, her loyalty to her friends, and also by an elegant mode of life to which he wasn't accustomed and which he was far from disdaining, in contradiction to the views of those who've made a point of drawing a picture of him which is far too rustic and plebeian. In the Casimir-Perier household he could enjoy the feeling of being understood, loved, admired and valued at his true worth.[3]

Fournier's early impressions of the Casimir-Periers, as he first got to know them in May 1912, are not on record, but it seems reasonable to surmise, given his social and emotional kinship with Péguy, that his reactions were not dissimilar. On one point, at all events, there can be no dispute; compared with the loyal but docile Jeanne, the spirited and flighty 'Henriette', the shadowy figures of the first Yvonne and 'Laurence', and the lovely but impossibly remote vision of Yvonne de Quiévrecourt, Simone was quite the most impressively equipped woman he had ever met. Though if Fournier's first impressions of Simone are not on record, the same is not true of her first impressions of him. Looking back over a gulf of forty-five years, she recalled how

Péguy had travelled all the way from Paris to meet her on the quayside at Dieppe on her return from an American tour, and how he
announced that in Fournier he had found just the secretary her
husband had been looking for: this was on 4 May:

> Next day, 5 May, I left Trie. That day marked the anniversary
> of my beloved father's death and I wanted to put flowers in the
> chapel where his remains lie at rest. After my visit to the
> cemetery, I went back to quai Debilly and got dressed for dinner.
>
> At seven o'clock, I received René Bizet.[4] He came to gather
> for his paper *L'Intransigeant* the impressions I'd brought back
> from my long stay in America. While we were talking in the
> library, I heard someone opening and shutting the doors of the
> drawing-room, then the sounds of different voices. I recognised
> the gay tones of Péguy, the impatient accents of Claude, and an
> unknown voice which sounded full of calm and discretion.
>
> After a little while, René Bizet went away and I went into the
> next room. There I saw, close beside Péguy, a tall slim young
> man, with a very reserved appearance. He had chestnut brown
> hair, light brown eyes fringed with long curling eyelashes, and it
> was the eyes which gave his face a distinctly melancholy expres-
> sion, as though he was asking Fate and his fellow-men not to
> treat him harshly. He had a straight nose, a beautiful soft mouth,
> brightly shining teeth, a pale complexion, the chin of a child and
> the bearing of a prince.
>
> 'This is the man for you,' said Péguy, 'I've brought him as I
> promised I would.'[5]

It would doubtless be otiose to add that after creating such an
impression of youthful and regal melancholy, Fournier was appointed.

For Claude Casimir-Perier, Fournier was not so much a secretary
as a literary collaborator. To further his political career, he was hoping
to publish a large-scale study of Brest as a Transatlantic port, and
Fournier's task was to help with the report and, from his knowledge
of journalism, advise him on the typographical problems of setting out
a considerable number of train- and steamship-timetables and a
plethora of other statistics. By all accounts, Fournier found it interesting though not very demanding work, and he was allowed ample
opportunity to continue with his own writing and to frequent his old
friends. He would occasionally participate at one of the Casimir-
Periers' *soirées* but all this time, he returned each evening to his
parents' flat in rue Cassini.

According to Madame Rivière, while he was returning home from the Casimir-Periers' one afternoon in the spring of 1912, a piece of paper suddenly dropped at his feet from a balcony in the rue Cassini within sight of the Fourniers' own front door. When unfolded, it turned out to be an invitation from a young female admirer who answered to the name of 'Loulette', had an infant son and a thoroughly unsatisfactory husband. She became Fournier's mistress that very afternoon, and for some time he took great pleasure in wheeling the baby son out in his pram alongside Isabelle and Jacqueline Rivière. The affair came to an end when the husband's suspicions were aroused and he let it be known that he would have no compunction in shooting 'Loulette's' unknown lover if ever he came across him. Madame Rivière's comment at this point should cause readers to look at each other with something like wild surmise :

> Assignations became difficult from this point on but Henri had little regret. But he decided thereafter to leave his own revolver at home for fear of being tempted to shoot back in the case of a collision.[6]

What causes one's mind slightly to boggle, if not one's credulity to waver, at this juncture is not so much the Feydeau atmosphere of it all, as the throwaway suggestion that it was Fournier's normal practice to walk through the streets of Paris in civilian clothes with a revolver about his person.[7]

Of rather more consequence were the relations he continued to maintain with Péguy, and the seventeen short notes and cards they exchanged in June and July 1912[8] are eloquent enough evidence of the way their friendship was prospering. Fournier more than once visited Péguy in his family home at Lozère on the outskirts of Paris and he accompanied him on the first stage of his annual pilgrimage on foot to Chartres Cathedral. On 28 June 1912, he sent word to Péguy to report that one of his dreams had come true and that he had just had his first trip in a biplane; the postcard on which he sent the message pictured both the plane and the pilot. Fournier also took some time and trouble in commenting on some of Péguy's sonnets, as is witnessed by a letter he received on 1 August 1912, accompanied by a poem entitled *L'Aveugle*, with the typically curt comment :

> O creature hard to please, here is a *third* version for you. You'll see from it how submissive I am. Your affectionately devoted Péguy.[9]

Fournier promptly sent back a picture postcard from La Chapelle, where he had departed for the summer holidays while the Casimir-Periers were away in Cambo; on the view, he commented:

> Here you see, my dear Péguy, the loveliest countryside in this world.[10]

He spent the greater part of August 1912 on holiday with his family at La Chapelle and writing again to Péguy, to commiserate with him because his second son, Pierre, was ill with diphtheria, he reported that he and Rivière had just completed a three-day cycling tour which took them on a round trip of nearly two hundred miles along the banks of the Loire. He added:

> The Loire country where there's everything you've ever loved in France. The Loire country! I thought of you, Péguy, while I whispered those marvellous words over and over to myself.
>
> On a postcard I've just sent to Claude Casimir-Perier, I wrote down these two exquisite lines which I remember having read in a letter La Fontaine once sent to his wife while he was on his travels:
>
> > Savez-vous que c'est une gloire
> > D'être pont sur la Loire . . .[11]

He was still full of love for his native countryside in the middle of September when on the eve of his return to work in Paris, he wrote to his sister in Bordeaux:

> In the course of these holidays, I find I'm completely attached to this countryside, to the sort of life I lead here and to the lovely weather which has been going on now for a week. At the entrance to Government Wood I've found a little property and also another one which I'll tell you about. Right now, I'm consumed with the desire to spend the rest of my days there. I don't know where such a desire will lead me. At all events, as soon as I've got six thousand francs, that's what I'll buy. You just can't imagine what a dream it is.[12]

The dream of living in his own little house in the woods had haunted Fournier's imagination since childhood and is a recurrent *motif* throughout his writing. It is both piquant and poignant to see him resolving to translate it into reality now, as he approaches his rendezvous with death.

Back in Paris in the autumn of 1912, Fournier resumed his laborious if desultory preparation of *Brest: port transatlantique*. He continued, at irregular intervals, to produce a 'profile' on some public figure for *L'Intransigeant*,[13] and in October he went so far as to write to Jacques Copeau to ask whether he might occasionally take over his monthly section in *La Nouvelle Revue Française* in which he presented a round-up of news of all the other reviews; he ended this letter, 'Believe me, dear Sir, that if I make this small request, it's mainly because I want to have an official connection with all of you.'[14] For relaxation, in addition to the regular activities of conversation or going to theatres, concerts and art-galleries, there was now the rugby club, *Le Club Sportif de la Jeunesse Littéraire*. Other players included Rivière, Giraudoux, Péguy, Gaston Gallimard and Pierre MacOrlan; Fournier was secretary and there is more than one passage in his letters to Rivière over this period exhorting him to keep in training or, when he is temporarily out of Paris, complaining that nobody will pass on news of their team's results. In the Fournier exhibition mounted in Bourges in 1964, Item 169 was a letter from the secretary, dated 10 February 1913, calling a general meeting: it was counter-signed 'Seen and approved, Frantz de Galais. Augustin Meaulnes.'

On 10 October 1912, Simone Casimir-Perier left for a season on the New York stage. The event was adjudged important enough to call for headlines in the newspaper *Comœdia* – 'Madame Simone leaves Paris' – and the staff reporter, one J. Delini, described the scene at Gare Saint-Lazare when she departed in her reserved compartment, filled with bouquets of flowers and leather suitcases, seen off by a host of friends and her husband 'accompanied by his secretary'.[15] She left Fournier with a delicate – and as events were to prove, an impossible – task to accomplish. Well-founded rumour had it that Henry Bataille, famous for his psychological melodramas, was planning a re-run of his play *L'Enchantement* and Simone was anxious to secure the star part. The difficulty was that the female lead in the original 1901 production had been played by Bataille's good friend Berthe Bady and she was still so much interested, that an overt approach to the author by Simone herself would have lost her the part at once. Fournier commented in a letter to Bichet, who was still at the University of Budapest:

> At the present moment, I have the complete confidence of Simone who's away in America and who's entrusted me with a very serious mission. This is bringing me into contact with illustrious characters for whom I feel supreme indifference, if not pity.[16]

As was his wont when writing to Bichet, Fournier could not resist the temptation once again to chide him for his timidity:

The only serious criticism I have to make of you is the same as it's always been, and over the last year I'll admit you've made great progress in this area. It is – how can I put it? – a certain avarice of the heart, a certain weakness in the arm, which means that you're not sufficiently like *le grand Meaulnes* of the first part of my novel, a chap in whose company anything is possible, who's got faith in himself, so that when you're going with him down a lane or along a street, you sense that everything has become possible, and that at any moment, when you turn the next corner, he's going to smile at you and point out the Lovely Lost Domain which you've only ever seen in your dreams.

Everything is possible, young sir, and you must not draw back or put on a strained smile when I tell you so.

All the same, I have to level this same charge against myself, and I must admit that if I were still a chap like that, I wouldn't be needing another to be him for me. I'm also to blame and the reproaches I'm addressing to you ought really to be directed against that awkward couple we used to make in years gone by, as we went down the boulevard Saint-Michel at eleven o'clock at night.[17]

Fournier's insistence in this letter on the paramount need for faith and resolution had nothing at all to do with the difficult exercise in diplomacy for which Simone had enlisted his services. He went on to declare to Bichet :

In conclusion, and by way of reward, here is the truth which today I convey within the whole of my body and in my every gesture. We're inhibited by too many things. We lavish too many petty regrets and petty desires on petty love affairs which simply aren't worthy of us. One thing alone is really necessary. And since it's so necessary, then it's possible.

It took me seven months for me to make up my mind to write the letter which I now carry with me in the right hand pocket of my jacket, *and it's going to be delivered before the end of this year.* We're dying because of our weakness, we're dying because we don't dare to dare !

The letter he spoke of had indeed been written, towards the end of September 1912, at his parents' home in the rue Cassini, and it was addressed to Yvonne Brochet (née Quiévrecourt). It needs no other introduction and can speak eloquently and elegiacally for itself :

It's seven years now since I lost you. It's more than seven years since you left me on the Invalides Bridge, one Whit Sunday

morning. You said 'We're two children, we've acted foolishly . . .'
And I've never known what I should have replied. Thoroughly
despairing and thoroughly obedient, I stood leaning against a
pilaster of the bridge. I watched you walk out of my life forever.
Once you'd crossed the bridge and before disappearing into the
crowd, you stopped and turned to look back at me – for a long
while. Was it to say a final good-bye, or to stress that I wasn't
to follow you, or did you perhaps have something else to say to
me? I've often asked myself why. And doubtless I shall never
know the answer.

I didn't realise at first that you were lost to me.

From that time on, I've never ceased searching for you. I've
known for five years that you're married. I've known for six
months where you're living. I'm telling you all this briefly and
coldly, and you just can't know what it all amounts to in feverish
nights and in doleful days, days of hope, despair and yearning,
lovely days now lost and gone. I haven't let a week go by without
going down the boulevard Saint-Germain past those very windows where, several times during those fleeting days in that
summer of 1905, you briefly came into view. Among various of
those days one stands out, a Saturday evening when there was
a teeming downpour : you were dressed in black, you had a book
in your hand, you lifted the curtain and you smiled to see me
still out there . . . Since then, nobody has ever lifted that curtain
again.

I've never since failed to go to the Salon de la Nationale on
each anniversary of our first meeting. It was – do you remember?
– the first day of June 1905, Ascension Day, between four and
five in the afternoon. Each time I go back down that great stone
stairway where I looked at you for the very first time, then the
Cours-la-Reine . . . And despairingly, I go again for a boat-trip
across the river which in my memory is so marvellous.

I have forgotten nothing. I've stored up every precious minute
of the little time you'll ever have spent in my life, and every one
of the few words you ever said to me. And every detail too :
your white sunshade in the avenue, and your great brown cloak,
and even the tiny tear you made in your skirt when you boarded
the tram that Whit Sunday morning.

All I have of you are these memories. I've hoarded them all,
the humblest as well as the grandest. I can remember, for
example, the pavement of the boulevard Saint-Germain, where
some children had been writing with chalk. You turned round
to read the writing and you looked at me. But most vividly of all,

I recall with terrible clarity, the moment late on that same Thursday afternoon when on the landing-stage for the Paris river-bus, I had so close to mine the lovely face of a young girl now lost to me. That face was so pure that I was all eyes, and those eyes were brimming with tears.

And as for our long conversation, our one and only conversation on the morning of Whit Sunday, do you think I've been able to forget a single word of it? Ah! why did you keep on repeating *A quoi bon?* with such a gentle, such a despairing expression?

I had only one way, you left me just one way to rejoin you and communicate with you and that was to win literary fame. Well, since you went away, I've published just a few pages only. Did you ever get them? They had some success. Did you know that?

A long novel which I'm concluding, a novel which is centred all around you – you whom I hardly knew – will be coming out this winter. But today just as it was previously, I come towards you with my hands empty.

It seems that Fate has resolved to withhold from me the only thing I've really ever wanted – and that is the way to be with you again.

What else can I say in this letter which perhaps may never reach you?

The loveliest days of my life have been those when I've ardently thought of you, so ardently, and so purely, that I half expected to meet you suddenly, by a miracle.

Most of all, I remember a splendid summer's afternoon, in the French countryside, when I was going down along a sunken lane, between two fields of corn, towards an unknown farm. I could picture you so clearly, suddenly coming towards me, dressed in a light costume, with the white sunshade you carried before, that for a long moment, I was sure you were there by the gateway to one of the fields.

I can also remember another afternoon, on an Ascension Thursday when I hadn't been able to get back to Paris as on each of our other anniversaries. I was on summer manœuvres, lying in the hay in a deserted barn in the vast Champagne plain. And the great burning winds of summer never ceased to blow, talking and singing of my memories, my desolation, my lost love . . .

Now that I've found you again, I approach you with the same great respect and all the purity as on the first occasion. Don't

220

reject me harshly as you did before at first, in front of the Church of Saint-Germain-des-Prés. Remember that afterwards you recognised who I was. You let me speak to you. Because there's more at stake here than love. What's involved is purer and even more mysterious than love. Indeed, though my heart breaks as I say it, I can still say this to you: now it's of no consequence that you're married. Today, that particular sorrow is buried. But what I shan't resign myself to is the thought of not being able to find you again, or never seeing you again, of living the rest of my life without knowing where you are. The thought of having to wait for death as the only way of somewhere joining you again. I beg you to deliver me from this hell. 'Don't damn me by denying me the sight of your face.'

I beseech you to take quite seriously these dreadful words which come from the bottom of my heart: I have no desire to live far from wherever you may be.

All I ask is one simple thing and nothing more. I'm now twenty-six, we're not children any longer, and I know full well what I'm asking. Merely this: not to be any longer completely cut off from you.

You can give me any commands you wish: to get married, to travel far away. I will do whatever you say. But if I'm to be far away from you, let me write to you. And if I'm close to you, let me see you. You can surely grant me that since you've taken everything from me.

Several of my old friends are naval officers and no doubt you know them. I'll easily be able to find them again. They can introduce me to you. I don't want anything furtive. I don't want anything which isn't absolutely innocent. All I want is that, at the very least, you don't simply abandon me, as you did that time on the bridge in Paris, leaving me all alone without the hope of ever seeing you again.

I implore you not to cast me back into hell without first thinking for a long time about the consequences.[18]

By the autumn of 1912, Fournier had come to know that Yvonne Brochet was living in Rochefort north of Bordeaux, one of the three French naval towns which, because of their associations with her, became charged for him with very particular significance. It was for this reason that he added in his letter to Bichet of 2 November 1912:

When you come to the choice of your French transfer, bear this well in mind: you could possibly save my life if you had a teaching post in Brest, Toulon or Rochefort.[19]

221

In the event, Fournier did not find it necessary to rely on the vagaries of Bichet's posting, and for reasons that any self-respecting novelist would have to reject as too implausible for use in a work of fiction. On 5 December 1912, he received a letter from Marc, younger brother of Jacques Rivière. Marc Rivière, who was then twenty years old, recalled the games they had enjoyed together on the occasion of Fournier's solitary visit to the Fermauds' home at Cenon in August 1907. He was now hoping to become a naval doctor, like Yvonne Brochet's husband, and was studying for the entrance examinations to l'Ecole Navale in Rochefort. He had got to know Yvonne's younger brother, who was a naval cadet on the *Borda*, the training ship Fournier himself had once aspired to join, he had met Yvonne's sister, Jeanne, and there seemed a very real prospect of his being able to meet Yvonne herself. Fournier's problem henceforth was the simple but agonising one of choosing the opportune moment.

Throughout 1912, Fournier worked intermittently at his novel, although he does not seem to have made a really concerted effort to complete it until he was at La Chapelle, on vacation, in August. On 24 August, he told Péguy that he was making some progress but felt he was being lured down a sidetrack the far end of which he could not see.[20] On 2 September, he reported to Rivière:

> This time my book *will be finished by 1 October*. I decided the other day to leave everything until I had completed the plan of the final chapters down to the smallest detail. Now that's done. If I can carry out this plan with all the fervour I want, it will be extremely beautiful. I've got the equivalent of about ten chapters to do, but when things are going well, I manage to do a chapter per day.[21]

This confidence was not wholly justified, because on 2 November 1912 he wrote to Bichet:

> This afternoon, at the house of *le grand Meaulnes*, it's the day of the wedding. *It is a lovely icy-cold Thursday afternoon with a great wind blowing* . . . The great imbecile runs away for the first time at nightfall and they bring him back. He runs away a second time before daybreak, and this time he gets clean away. I still have three chapters to write, one in the middle, and two at the end.[22]

Without more precise information, it is difficult to identify exactly which areas of the novel were continuing to pose problems for Fournier, but he would seem to have found the solution to them without much further delay. On 22 November, while looking forward to Bichet's return from Budapest for the Christmas holidays, he was able confidently to announce :

> When you get back here, I shall present you with a salver bearing a typed copy of *Le Grand Meaulnes*.[23]

All the indications are that the outstanding technical problems were indeed solved to Fournier's satisfaction before Bichet's return from Budapest, and that by this date, the novel was in the form in which it was eventually published.

The presentation to Bichet never took place. On 20 December, shortly after his return to Budapest, Bichet attended the annual banquet for former pupils of the Ecole Normale Supérieure. After dinner, he retired to his hotel with two friends who had more than once previously experimented with drugs. On this occasion, they wished to see the effects of taking morphine and invited Bichet to participate. For once 'daring to dare', he allowed them to give him an injection, soon after which the friends departed. At five o'clock in the morning, a hotel employee heard groans coming from Bichet's room. He died in hospital almost immediately on arrival. Fournier, who was entrusted with the task of going through the dead man's papers and effects, discovered, all too late, that the reserved 'little' Bichet and he had a great deal more in common than he would ever have credited. It was only after Bichet's death, apparently, that he discovered he came from a poor country home and from the Loiret region, not far distant from his own native Berry. 'What a link that could have been between us,' he said to his sister afterwards. 'How we would have loved to roam with him through the gorse of his Loiret or the heather of our Sologne, and what fun it would have been to compare our native dialects.'[24] He wrote to Rivière a few days after the funeral :

> I'm reading through his papers with an emotion which is far from purely literary. He was haunted by the fear of dying without confession. He dreamed only of Paradise.
> The very last lines he ever wrote were :
> Pourquoi bouger? Ne sens-tu pas là-haut quelque chose
> Qui ne cesse de rire de notre travail?[25]

Fournier went on to tell Rivière, who was away for the New Year in Bordeaux, that he had found much consolation as well as inspiration in the company of Péguy:

> Long conversations with Péguy have been the great events of my last few days. I wish I had time to write of him at length. I would say, after carefully weighing my words, that there hasn't been since Dostoevsky a man who's so manifestly *a man of God*.
>
> He came this afternoon to read me *La Présentation de la Beauce à Notre-Dame de Chartres*. A vast poem about his pilgrimage. It's greater and more moving than anything he's done. The lines are so exact! Quite perfect! This time there are no concessions to the reader, and no cheating either. It's like Hugo at the age of forty, and that's what he says himself.
>
> Without any warning, we got to a passage about Bichet which reduced me to tears:

> I come also to pray for this poor boy . . .[26]

> A comment from him that afternoon on the subject of morphine ought to become the epigraph for my novel. (That man knows everything and has thought of everything; and his kindness is as infinite as his severity.) Here is his severe maxim:

> > 'Even if God has left a Paradise somewhere here on earth, we wouldn't have the right to enter it before the Day of Judgment.'

At the turn of the year, however, Fournier's mind was occupied with thoughts of profane as well as of sacred love. In that same letter to Rivière, he reported:

> Simone has sent me a magnificent edition of Keats, containing all his poems and all his letters (including those to Fanny Brawne), with two portraits of him, the smaller of which she says looks like me: an old-fashioned portrait in which it seems that every detail of the way I look in a tail-coat has been mischievously noted . . .
>
> For my New Year's present to myself, I've bought *Doctor Jekyll and Mr Hyde*, Benjamin Constant's *Cahier rouge*, *Les chants de Maldoror* (the opening pages of which are desperately childish) and *Le Roman de Tristan et Yseut*, probably one of the loveliest books I've ever read; at any rate, the opening chapters find an answering chord in the very depths of my being: 'possibly one of the holy books', says Péguy.

The version of the Tristan legend which Fournier read was the recently published reconstruction by the great scholar Joseph Bédier, who discovered that all the many Tristan poems in existence can be traced back to a single lost archetype. That Fournier should have been so moved by this particular book at this particular time is as significant as it was to prove portentous. His earliest preferences in the literature of human love had been for inordinately chaste heroines, like Clara d'Ellébeuse in Jammes' novel of that name, or for heroes who loved nobly but, all their lives, in vain, like Cyrano de Bergerac or Dominique; at Lakanal and Louis-le-Grand, he was positively captivated by the vision of Claudel's heroines, Lâla (*La Ville*), Léchy Elbernon (*L'Echange*) and Ysé (*Partage de Midi*), impossibly beautiful and, to their men, essentially remote, even in the act of love; at Mirande, he very strongly identified himself with Myshkin, 'the sick prince', more sinned against than sinning, always quick to detect his partners' inadequacies, and ever ready to dismiss them more in sorrow than in anger. Whatever else the Tristan legend may be, it is none of these things; like *Wuthering Heights*, which overwhelmed Fournier in the autumn of 1912,[27] its theme is human passion, passion so consuming that it must be requited in defiance of all the laws of God or man or Time.

Fournier's responses to the arts were always intensely personal : in the first instance, his strongest preferences would always be for works which helped him establish contact with the spirit of his own lost past, but they could also affect his future in the sense that, seemingly by design rather than by accident, he so often modelled his attitudes as well as his actions on the literary characters he most admired. Bédier's Tristan was to prove no exception.

In the middle of January 1913, Simone Casimir-Perier sailed back across the Atlantic after her New York season. She was no longer interested in securing the female lead in Bataille's play *L'Enchantement*, having been offered the principal part in *Le Secret*, a new play by Henry Bernstein who was immensely successful in *la belle époque* with a series of dramas depicting grand passions in high society. In her memoirs of that period, written almost half a century later, she recalled that homeward trip :

> All I can remember is that while the great waves of the wide ocean pounded against the sides of the *Mauretania*, I discovered, to the rhythm of their monotonous music, that returning to France had come to mean for me seeing Alain-Fournier again.[28]

However, as she later explained, she did not appreciate the full

225

significance of her feelings at this time and was unwilling to contemplate their implications; once back in Paris, on 28 January, she got down to the serious business of learning her part for *Le Secret*.

In an interview from Frédéric Lefèvre, published in *Les Nouvelles Littéraires* on 6 December 1930, Simone revealed that she was first permitted to read *Le Grand Meaulnes* on 10 February 1913. The Casimir-Periers had withdrawn to their country home at Trie for a few days to allow Simone to learn her part in peace, and Fournier accompanied them. He took the typescript of his novel with him and asked his hostess to read it. In her memoirs, she recalled:

> I read through the novel between evening and dawn, and I was so entranced that I slipped a brief note under the author's door so that, as soon as he woke up, he would know the admiration I felt for his work. Its quality didn't surprise me; all the same, I felt a certain pride in having so unerringly identified the rare species to which this young man belonged, who, for me, was able to transform the monotony of existence into such subtle pleasure.
>
> Next morning, we had a long talk about his book. I praised its freshness, the magical unfolding of the plot, the language, all the touches of a born novelist, and I observed that there was a family likeness between his techniques and certain English novels. The faithful friend of Stevenson and Daniel Defoe was delighted to have created such an impression and we returned to Paris well content with each other.[29]

Once back in Paris, they each went about their different business, she to the Bouffes-Parisiens Theatre where the première of *Le Secret* was scheduled for 20 March 1913 while Fournier, for his part, continued to work on the Brest memorandum and to contribute occasional articles for *L'Intransigeant*. On 13 February, he wrote to congratulate Péguy on his latest Cahier, *L'Argent*, which contains his famous long and lyrical defence of the French provincial school-teacher, and declared:

> That's how *le grand Meaulnes* was brought up, for all his faults, between 1891 and 1898. I'll devote a paragraph to it tomorrow for *L'Intran*. I've got to go on being a critic in spite of everything. I've got four different 'notes' to produce this evening![30]

Inevitably, however, diverse though their occupations were, Simone and Fournier were bound to meet daily in the luxurious Casimir-Perier home. Simone later recalled:

> The love which was about to be revealed to us didn't suddenly

226

blaze out like a late summer as soon as we got back from Trie. It continued gradually to wear its slow secret path in two separate hearts, each of which, for absurd social considerations, was reluctant to seduce the other.

Yet there were all sorts of unmistakable signs, visible every day, which would at once have convinced a woman more sure of herself, or a young man more blasé. More than anything else, the desire constantly to see and talk to each other.

Whenever I used to get back to the quai Debilly at about six o'clock, after rehearsing *Le Secret*, there Henri would be.

Perhaps he'd have a book to hand to me, or a piece of information I was curious to have, or some sheet of paper necessary to Claude which would have been mysteriously overlooked that same morning.[31]

Fournier's views on these proceedings are not on record for this particular period. Even assuming that he had already admitted his feelings to himself, he was unlikely to confide them to Péguy, the severity of whose views on marital fidelity in general were abundantly clear to him, and who counted himself a particular friend, if not companion knight-at-arms, of Claude Casimir-Perier. And there is no hint of anything untoward in the few letters that were written over this period to Rivière. However, one such letter is, on more than one count, worthy of comment, though for reasons that have little to do with love, whether for Fournier this was already in bloom or still quietly germinating.

He engaged in a little sport at Rivière's expense, adopting his pose of being a plain man of the people unable to comprehend why anyone should allow himself to be swept away by enthusiasm for mere art :

Why do you have this need to have a literary craze every moment of your life? And why does it now turn out to be Rimbaud? Books are nothing but paper.[32]

And, in much the same extrovert vein, he passed on their rugby captain's orders to jog-trot several hundred yards each day to improve his breathing. He also revealed that the melancholy streak had not been eradicated, first with the news that he had had to live through his regular 'Easter crisis', and then with his comment on the death in childbirth of his favourite cousin, Marie-Rose Raimbault, the eldest of the eight daughters of his favourite Uncle Florent of Nançay :

I won't write about Marie-Rose. Mother will certainly have told you about her death and the terrible grief of Aunt Augustine. Another one of our age-group dead, for whom we have now to say the daily prayers he forgot to say during his lifetime. – I had imagined that after Bichet, the next one to go would be me.

The others in his age-group now amounted to a remarkable total: in addition to Marie-Rose, they included his childhood playmate Alfred Benoist, his school-friends Chesneau and Bichet, and the wives of fairly close acquaintances, like Madame Tronche and Maria Bureau, each of whom also died in childbirth; giving birth to her daughter Jacqueline had all but killed Isabelle Rivière. His pessimistic prognosis was not purely morbid: it was related, in considerable measure, to facts within his own immediate experience.

For the greatest part of April 1913, Fournier was back in Army uniform, carrying out a statutory period of Reserve duty with his regiment which was still based at Mirande. During this period, he was engaged on three distinct sets of manœuvres – participating in an Army exercise in the Tarn-et-Garonne region, negotiating with publishers over a contract for *Le Grand Meaulnes*, and scheming to meet the sister of Yvonne Brochet. Of these three, the military operations were, from every point of view, the least productive, but Fournier did not dismiss them as completely sterile. He wrote to Rivière on 22 April:

> I've been more than five days now in this wretched sort of mediaeval village. For the first couple of days I was monumentally bored. I was like a dog who finds he's suddenly to be shut up in a cupboard. I have to admit that it's only the *present* which matters to me. I recognise that I've often made a complete fool of myself to get something today which was, anyway, promised me for tomorrow. I just can't resign myself. I'll never make a *good* Christian.
>
> All the same, I've felt the occasional upsurge of real joy to feel myself adapting to this chaste, rough, wretched, dreamy monastic style of life under the rain . . . And setting off in the darkness, or just before the break of day, fills me with a most mysterious feeling. At such moments, it's as though some nameless and mystical world almost becomes accessible.[33]

He went on to describe some of his companion officers, including a dipsomaniac captain, and his comment revealed that he still retained his novelist's eye for a likely character:

> All these tales about (the captain) establish him as such a colourful individual that I can't quite see whether there's now room for him in my tragic novel.

This comment does more than provide a clear indication of the extent to which Fournier's fiction was nourished by the facts of real-life experiences: it also indicates a curious lack both of business acumen and of artistic conviction. His novel was now on offer to a number of review-editors and he was still prepared to contemplate dramatic amendments to key areas of the narrative. As late as 3 May 1913, he announced to Rivière that he was strongly tempted to insert into the novel the long letter he had so carefully composed for Yvonne the previous autumn:

> It's absolutely essential that the Journal of Meaulnes should end on a note of very high emotion. This will be the despairing letter he carries everywhere with him and which, in the end, he finally tears up. I shouldn't have to tell you that this letter is already written. I'll arrange it and adapt it, that's all.[34]

In the event, he did not pay this last dramatic tribute of life to art, and the manuscript which was going the round of various publishers was not recalled by Fournier for last-minute revision. However it was not to take long for him to utilise his unposted letter to Yvonne with rather more satisfying effect.

For some weeks before this, the serialisation rights of *Le Grand Meaulnes* had been on offer to a number of the leading French literary reviews including *La Grande Revue*, which had earlier published *Le Corps de la femme* and *Madeleine* for him, and *L'Opinion*, which was at that time being edited by a friend of his, Henri Massis. On 5 April, he had written to Jacques Copeau, a co-director of *La Nouvelle Revue Française*:

> I've reason to believe that *L'Opinion* isn't going to take *Le Grand Meaulnes* . . . I'll know definitely within a week. I'd agreed to let *L'Opinion* have an option because Massis had been asking for it for ages and they were promising irresistible terms, but if they haven't made up their minds by the time the week's out, it goes without saying that I'll then be bringing *Le Grand Meaulnes* to you.[35]

It was at this juncture that occurred the only major quarrel on record between Fournier and Rivière, a quarrel directly attributable to the new alliances he had formed when he joined the Casimir-Perier household. Rivière, who was still secretary of *La Nouvelle Revue Française*, assumed, not unreasonably, that when his review was offered the serial rights of *Le Grand Meaulnes*, it was at the same time being offered the rights to bring out the novel in book form through its own publishing house run by Gallimard. Fournier's other friends had different ideas. Simone Casimir-Perier, in consultation with Péguy and her cousin Julien Benda, believed Fournier's cause would be better served if the book were entrusted to the firm of Emile-Paul. Emile-Paul was at that time the publisher of both Benda and Péguy, and there seemed every chance that he would make *Le Grand Meaulnes* his front-runner for the coveted Prix Goncourt.

Fournier, who was still away in Mirande, explained the background to this imbroglio in a letter to his mother on 28 April and, at the same time, offered her useful advice on how to handle the Casimir-Periers:

> The Periers have, as always, behaved exquisitely towards me throughout this period. Simone has written to me three times, one being an enormous letter written, in my own fashion, with lots of little paragraphs. On the question of my book, she's shown extraordinary dedication. And in behaving in this way, she's so like the character she's playing in *Le Secret*: she wants the people she loves to get their happiness from her and from her alone. She finds all that Péguy's done so far quite absurd. When I got that telegram of hers expressing that bizarre wish to go to rue Cassini, I sensed that she wanted to see you again. I felt real reluctance in having to telegram back to her that she was on no account to utilise any of the texts I've left behind in rue Cassini. So I was very pleased that she'd actually gone ahead and visited you. She must have been delighted with her visit and with your letter. But there's one thing you have to bear in mind, and that is that people of that class have expressions of gratitude and respect showered upon them. You should limit yourself just to what's strictly necessary. People *will* overdo that sort of thing, and it always creates a gulf between them and other folk, in much the same way as their wealth and their over-plush châteaux prevent them from touching and tasting nature and the country-side. A personal comment that's really fair and intimate, coming from someone they respect, touches them a hundred times more than all those formulae from the etiquette manuals which they're tired of hearing. That's why my 'gruff ways' go down so well.[36]

Rivière reacted badly to all these machinations: he was, at this time, suffering the acute torment of a situation he was later to transpose into his autobiographical novel, *Aimée*,[37] the central situation of which is the hero's unrequited love for the wife of one of his close friends: by ironic coincidence, the real-life model of Rivière's fictitious 'Aimée' was also called Yvonne. His response to the negotiations over the publishing rights of *Le Grand Meaulnes* was to send off a letter that Fournier described as a 'ballocking' more violent than anything he'd ever had to endure in the Army. This particular letter is, unfortunately and possibly significantly, the only one of the vast correspondence which was never afterwards found, but Fournier quite clearly gave as good as he got. He recalled that the *Nouvelle Revue Française* set had never gone out of their way to shower favours on him, and then proceeded to acquaint Rivière with some home-truths about his deficiencies:

> In this matter of reproaches, you might look nearer home: perhaps it's your timidity, and undoubtedly it's your indecisiveness, both on their account and on mine, the age you took in *introducing* me, in every sense, to the rest of the set, this perpetual dithering on your part, that's the cause of the woolliness, the general messiness I'm now aware of in my connections with the N.R.F. Aunt Michelle and I were in complete agreement the other day on this very point: as long as you're on the verge of passing out at the mere prospect of taking an *apéritif* at a pavement table outside some café, you're going to go on spreading petty unhappiness like this all around you.[38]

The friendship was strong enough to survive the fury of this spring squall, but the Casimir-Perier group won the day: *La Nouvelle Revue Française* was accorded only the serial-rights and the publication of the book version was entrusted to Emile-Paul.

In the midst of all this haggling which took up the greater part of April, Fournier was more preoccupied with a matter he adjudged of very much greater concern, and it is clear that his irascibility, like Rivière's, was due, in no small measure to amorous frustration. On 11 April, he received a further letter from Marc Rivière announcing that there would be no difficulty in introducing him to Yvonne's sister, Jeanne de Quiévrecourt, if he could travel to Rochefort. Fournier arranged to do this by making a détour on his way back from Mirande to Paris on 1 May. He did not at this stage, communicate either the real purpose, or his great expectations of this journey, to his closest friends, but his mixed feelings of despair and elation may be readily deduced from a letter he wrote to his mother on the eve of his departure for Rochefort:

Yesterday, on a Sunday morning, I cycled out to see an exquisite
little fifteenth-century chapel which looks out right over a huge
ravine and a vast blue valley. It was a lovely day. The wretched
peasants were getting ready for Mass. There was a gentle wind
and I spread out my fingers and let it blow through them.
There was a plum tree in blossom in the sloping garden. Summer
was about to begin . . . And a dreadful sense of desolation swept
over me which I had to struggle against all day long and which
engulfed me till the evening . . .

My little mother, who is so good to me and who is forty-nine
years old today, I wish you a lovely year full of happiness. And
I hope that this year you will lead me to the sacred altar with
a trembling bride you approve of. And I kiss you tenderly, as I
love you.[39]

Four days later, he was recording for Rivière his reactions to the
conversation with Jeanne de Quiévrecourt:

Yesterday I had a conversation with the sister of Yvonne de
Galais. I know now that the young woman has two children.
I sobbed all evening in my room, and I'm crying still even as
I write to you.

The pain is abominable. Beneath my window is a provincial
courtyard bathed in sunshine. A young woman is sewing in
front of the door, beneath the wistaria, in the frightening calm.
With the passing of each new hour on the dial of the church
clock close by, I ask myself whether I can possibly go on
living . . .

I don't want people to feel sorry for me. My love has not been,
has never been unhappy. I can still marvel – after eight years,
and in spite of the pain – at all Yvonne de Galais has given me.
Fate was against us, that's all. All that I had imagined about
her purity and her culture, all the picture I'd built up of her,
whom I knew so little – it's all true! I met her at the time of
my great enthusiasm for Francis Jammes. Well, yesterday, the
first thing her sister talked about was L'Angélus.[40]

– Yesterday was the eighth anniversary of the day when I first
met Yvonne de Galais. And yesterday, at the very moment when
she emerged from the Grand Palais all that time ago, I spoke to
her sister.

It's terrible to have to admit that even now I haven't completely lost hope. I cannot believe that God could have shown
me so much and have promised me so much and will end up

by giving me nothing – in this world, or the *next*, if it comes to that.[41]

Before he posted this letter to Rivière, he had a further conversation with Jeanne de Quiévrecourt, and this did much to console him. He learned that when they were children, the de Quiévrecourt girls used to live in the boulevard Tour-Maubourg, and that they had been boarders at the highly fashionable Sacré Coeur convent in the rue de Varenne.[42] He extracted from Jeanne de Quiévrecourt her sister's address in Toulon, at 2 rue Castel Le Mourillon, and he could prepare to set off back to Paris with the exhilarating thought:

> Before four days are out Yvonne de Galais will know that I've spoken to her sister about her and that I'm proposing to send her a copy of my book.

The news of Fournier's conflicting feelings was enough to bring a sympathetic reply from Rivière which promptly reconciled them after the publishing rights explosion. He could refer only in the most oblique of terms to his own emotional entanglements but these enabled him to deal empathetically with the sufferings of his friend:

> Your letter, which has reached me at a time of terrible weakness, hurts me too much for me to form the slightest view on what you have to say about those matters. All I'm conscious of is your unhappiness. The rest, in effect, is of no significance. And if what I wrote to you was too harsh, then please forgive me.
> I feel for you with all of my being. If I could, I'd so much like to do something to ease your suffering.
> But I've never been able to do anything for you. I can't fathom the reason. Perhaps we got off on the wrong foot from the very start. But, more than anything else, it's because I haven't an open nature; I've never been open with anyone; something is lacking in some corner of my heart. And I suffer greatly because of it.
> Don't worry, this isn't going to be a letter about *me*, or a psychology lesson. All I'm concerned about is what's breaking your heart . . . Yet everything has suddenly become so complicated for me, in a way that's totally crazy. Ah! living is no easy business! And the worst thing is we're never done with it.[43]

The tone of Rivière's letter was more than enough to soften Fournier's heart, though it could do nothing to raise his hopes:

That really is the way to understand me. And what you say about my love is just what needed saying: 'Your unhappiness is beyond the control of any of us. It's God's doing, not ours, and only God, if he so desires, can deliver us from it.'

All day, I've been running away from thoughts of her and now, this evening, here she is beside me like a great cruel angel . . .When I wrote to you, the other day, that 'my nerves are beginning to dance', I was about to add, 'and the ignoble flesh is all a-tremble'. I was afraid you'd think I was exaggerating. But that's how it is. It's there before me like something great and mystical confronting a sinner, which stifles him and defies his comprehension.[44]

However, towards the middle of May,[45] Fournier's hopes were suddenly and dramatically raised once more: a note arrived from Marc Rivière announcing that Yvonne Brochet herself was now in Rochefort and suggesting that he should at once return. On the pretext of visiting a friend, Fournier promptly left Paris. He spent four days in Rochefort and when the moment came for him to return to Paris, he bought himself a small black exercise book at Rochefort railway station. On the train journey back to Paris, he tried to capture his impressions of his second encounter with Yvonne just as he had done immediately after – or even *during* – the encounter of 1905.

After eight years, they finally met again in a stately park, the Jardin de la Préfecture maritime,[46] overlooking the river Charente. The first notebook entry reads:

Friday evening. She shakes my hand wearing her white gloves. Doesn't say anything – but friendly. On the very first evening, I found again the tall, chaste, despairing girl.[47]

While Marc Rivière played tennis with Jeanne de Quiévrecourt, Fournier and her sister walked slowly up and down. The only exchange recorded from their opening conversation is the discovery that they both had a passion for fast car-driving. The following day, Fournier returned to the park to play a tennis singles with Marc Rivière:

I play a gloomy match with Marc which I abandon. While I'm getting changed, Marc comes in and warns me, 'Madame Brochet's here'. I salute her in my jacket – no collar, sandals – then she goes off to the ladies' changing cubicle where she pauses for a moment, turning the key but unable to open the door. I

234

rush over. 'Oh!' she says, 'I'll soon manage it'. While she's getting changed inside, I'm dreadfully on edge. I walk up and down.

There follow further snatches of conversation, discreet at first, then slightly more daring:

'So you've come for a rest to Rochefort?'
    'Just for a few days.'
    'Did you tell your husband everything?' To which, she admitted that she had.
    'We haven't changed. You still have the same expression.'
    'What was it you were writing? That time on the tram? I've often wondered. I saw you scribbling away, scribbling away.'
    'I'll show you one day . . .'

At some point, they were joined by Yvonne's mother who laughed gaily at Fournier's jokes and who, he was informed next day by Yvonne herself, found him 'very nice'. On Sunday, after morning Mass, they again met, in company, in the park, when conversation turned to Fournier's writings.

'I got your reviews,' she says. I express reservations. I say, 'I'm sorry I sent them to you. All very juvenile.' She shakes her head and says, 'I found them interesting'. *'Le Miracle de la fermière* is the best of all the ones I sent you.' 'Oh! you haven't sent all that many . . . I did think of sending you a card, but I didn't know how you'd take it.' 'I beg you not to hesitate another time, out of timidity.'
    'When you come to Brest, my husband will take you out into the country.' She tells me of the long walks she goes for there, how much she loves that countryside. They used to set out on foot in the morning with their lunch and come back in the evening after covering fifteen miles.

But she did not paint a uniformly harmonious picture of marital bliss. One notebook entry reads:

If you'd come three years ago, everything might have been possible. I was unhappy. I thought a great deal about you. I would have written had I could. I didn't get on with my husband at all. We didn't have a single thing in common. Since then we've each made concessions, forgiven each other. Now

I'm the happiest of women. I was to blame too – my stupidity.

It was possibly at this juncture – the Rochefort notebook is unclear on this point – that he decided the moment was at last opportune to hand her the long letter he had composed for her in September 1912 and had been carrying with him ever since. Apparently, she read it through and handed it back with no immediate comment, leaving Fournier to speculate whether or not he had been monumentally tactless. He would seem to have brooded particularly over this in the course of the days that followed, as is demonstrated by the surviving notes of the letter he prepared for her soon after leaving Rochefort, on the first stage of his homeward journey :

First of all I want to repeat what I half whispered when we were shaking hands when I departed :

'I'm leaving in despair because I've not put over my point of view properly.'

Now, once again, I'm far away from you, in a little Norman village. It's the end of a sad summer's morning. I'm thinking of you now that I've seen you again at last. I'm thinking sometimes with joy, and sometimes with bitterness, of the friendship you've offered me, with which I'm going to have to content myself.

I approached our meeting so despairingly, so persuaded in advance of my ill-fortune, that at first this friendship filled me with joy. I had found you again. You had not repulsed me. You'd said : 'Yes, you can come again . . . My husband will go walking with you out into the countryside I love.' I knew that at least I wouldn't lose you all over again. And I, who had for so long given you up for lost, I was almost happy.

I was near to you. I could look at you. Sometimes your gaze rested on me. I was happy.

I discovered again your slow and graceful movements, the way you have of gently lowering your head when you talk, the purity of your face.

I loved your silence. I loved you speaking. Your words were, as they've always been, mysterious, wise and good, unlike the words of all other women.

Having to wait for you filled me with dread, but to hear your footsteps coming down the path, to feel that it was you coming towards me under the shade of the trees and that it was you who was pushing open the gate, was all that was needed to fill me with a profound sense of happiness.

236

I now knew that all those things had been given to me for ever and that you would not take them away. I knew that if, one day, I should feel very unhappy, I come come and ask you for all those things and that you would give them all over again, since we're now friends.

This is why I've been so afraid that I offended you by letting you see that love-letter on Monday morning; and why I've been so quick to declare that I wouldn't dare to write such a thing now, so nervous am I of losing what little I have.

And when you asked me, 'So, you were ill when you came and you're going back cured?', I replied that I was, thinking you were alluding to that dreadful journey, to the suffering it caused and to the headache.

At the time when you asked that question, it's true that I was reassured, at peace, well content once more and I told you so.

That's all I could have said to you then, all, in fact, I did say. But if you could see the letter I wrote to my mother yesterday evening, you would know that there's only one person in all the world with whom I would like to have spent my life. I've seen once more the face of Beauty, Purity and Grace . . .[48]

The margins of the three pages of the rough draft for this letter are festooned with additional sentences : 'I said it's something other than love', 'I'm the happiest of women – and she weeps throughout the night', 'I'd be easier in my mind if you got your husband's permission', 'Promise me you'll never again say *à quoi bon?*'

Whatever the letter that was finally composed from this draft and these notes, it was not sent direct to Yvonne : it was dispatched, probably in the third week of May, to Marc Rivière in Rochefort, with the request to retain it pending further instructions. Although, as will subsequently emerge, Fournier wrote and posted further letters to Yvonne on various occasions in the months that followed, he never saw her again nor does he seem to have made any significant attempts to do so.

Without corroborative testimony from Fournier himself, one can only conjecture over the reasons for his apparent loss of interest in Yvonne. Amongst these, the second meeting with her was surely crucial. While it established that Yvonne was still as beautiful in Fournier's sight as she had ever been, it at the same time destroyed all his lingering illusions. Throughout the long years of separation, Yvonne's most alluring quality for Fournier had been her utter remoteness. Until he met her again face to face, he could still dream occasionally, in the absence of conclusive evidence to the contrary, that his adoration might be reciprocated. He could still cherish hopes that Yvonne might share the view of love which he had so lyrically formulated in the autumn of 1910 :

> Love is what I'm looking for. The sort of love that means swooning away and total surrender. Love as the last word on everything, after which nothing else exists. Riding away after setting the countryside ablaze from one end to the other.[49]

His pretext for rejecting Jeanne Bruneau in 1910 was that she was unable or unwilling to love him on these terms and he clearly believed at that time that, if only circumstances had been otherwise, Yvonne would have been a more sympathetic and compliant partner. Ironically, when Fournier laid down his absolutist terms in 1910, it is just conceivable that Yvonne would have left her home to join him as Frieda Weekley did for D. H. Lawrence, because for reasons that must doubtless now remain a mystery, that was the year when the Brochet marriage seems to have been in particular jeopardy. But by 1913, the family was once again secure. Yvonne was a devoted mother, and when she introduced Fournier to her two children, it was unwittingly, but no less poignantly, to remind him of all that might have been. She was also so loyal a wife that she was simply not prepared to countenance even an exchange of letters, however innocuously they might be worded. Fournier was thus denied the one course of action that might have brought him some consolation, the ambiguous pleasure of demonstrating to her how well he could turn his feelings into words, and the role of faithful but inarticulate friend of the family proved, in the end, to have a strictly limited appeal for him.

To add to Fournier's sense of acute discomfiture when he returned from Rochefort to Paris, there was the challenging proximity of Simone, and the extent to which the two relationships influenced each other in the summer of 1913 is, quite literally, incalculable.

Shortly after Fournier got back to Paris, there was a crucial break in the emotional tension which had been building up between him and Simone Casimir-Perier since her return from New York in January. On the evening of 29 May, Fournier accompanied Rivière to the Champs-Elysées Theatre to see the first performance of Stravinsky's *Rite of Spring*. It turned out to be a historic occasion in the theatrical life of Paris, as tumultuous and frenetic as the first nights of *Hernani* and *Pelléas et Mélisande*. Rivière, who was well established by now as a critic not only of literature but also of painting, music and the ballet, was so shattered by the near riot that broke out in the audience that he went back home alone to his flat and was not able to produce an orderly review until August.[50] Fournier went to the Casimir-Periers' flat in the quai Debilly to give a first-hand account of the performance to Simone who had been acting the lead-role that same evening in *Le Secret*. They talked long through the night, and Fournier left at daybreak for his parents' home. Almost immediately afterwards, Simone sent him a *pneumatique* express-message: 'Mon ami, thanks to you, I've known the beauty of the day breaking. But why did you leave at dawn?'[51] Fournier acknowledged this with a two line *pneu* saying that a letter would follow. It promptly did so and it turned out to be his first declaration of love for her:

> It's hard to speak the truth. It's hard to renounce charades and riddles. Please believe that I'm doing this in dreadful anguish. And now you must learn that I love you, my beautiful girl, with those lovely fine features, my tennis player. You must learn that I love you, lovely lady. You must accept that I love those tender glances you bestow on me.
>
> To be absolutely truthful, for ages now I've been hiding this fact from myself. And on the first night of *The Rite of Spring* I didn't want to speak about it. And as long as you were there, I was afraid I'd suddenly have to admit it. That's the reason for all my obscure resistance.
>
> After that, what regrets, and what distress I've had to suffer. My heavy sleep. One solitary dream. One single thought. I wanted to write to you when I was in the coach, and to leave the letter in your pocket, but that would have been impractical. Next day I thought of sending you that letter from my mother in which she ecstatically sings your praises. In the end, I scrapped all such ideas: I went wandering around, I slept, I waited.[52]

For a further nine paragraphs, he continued to describe his prevarications and then he repeated his declaration of the outset:

> I love you. As I went home after the night of *The Rite of Spring*, I saw that in my life, one thing had ended and that another was beginning – admirable, lovelier than anything, but terrible certainly, and probably fatal. And from that fever, I'm not yet cured ...
>
> I stayed out of doors for the whole of yesterday afternoon. All the time, I thought a word from you might be waiting for me when I got home. When I got back at seven o'clock, there was nothing on the table or on the mantelpiece.

But when it came to dinner-time, there it was beside my plate. Ah! I knew at once what it was. Straightaway I understood. How my heart contracted! How my fingers trembled! My mother and I were dining alone. I thought, affectionately, of what she was saying to me and I did my best to reply, but I just couldn't. No matter how often I held my head in my hands, you never ceased being there, talking to me. I could hear nobody else but you and there were moments when what you were saying was so delightful that I simply had to smile a little.

And now, please, reply. Tell me everything isn't lost. Answer me so that I can write endless letters to you, because this time, I've not really been able to tell you anything.

I can see various solutions.

Either you will reject me completely, and I shall make a complete and immediate break with you. Claude's book is nearly finished and that's the pretext I shall give.

Or else we shall never speak of this letter again, you'll burn it, and you'll retain the lovely friendship you've always had for me. As for me, what will I do? What promise can I make? I'll try to go back to being the well-behaved, silent child you used to know.

Or else you'll respond, my gentle love, my beautiful beloved, my love, my tender love, and I, who have never so much as kissed your hand, will take in my hands that head I love, that head with its soft hair frizzed out or plastered down after all you've put into your acting, that head so lovely – and I shall kiss it.

H. Alain F.

Simone was readily responsive, but never for long on the terms Fournier wished to impose. The pattern of their relationship from the beginning of June 1913 until his final disappearance fifteen months later, is of short periods of rapturous euphoria interspersed with bitter recriminations on his part and moods of black despair. His conditions for the permanent relationship to which he aspired were fairly quickly established : marriage, domesticity, children, these to be brought up as good Catholics. For possibly valid reasons, none of these conditions was met : Simone did not seek a divorce from Claude Casimir-Perier, she was reluctant to sacrifice her acting career when she was at the height of her fame, and the fact that Fournier, nearly ten years her junior, would have been her third husband, precluded any possibility of a church wedding, even were she herself to embrace the Catholic faith. There was also the severely practical consideration that compared to Claude Casimir-Perier, Fournier was relatively impoverished, was ill-equipped to provide financially for Simone and much too independent to permit her to provide for him. It would be idle to pretend that, over the remaining months of Fournier's life, there were not periods of sometimes delirious delight for both of them, but given the intractable demands and obdurate personalities of each partner, it would be more than usually rash to prognosticate on the future of their relationship had he survived the war.

Inevitably, Fournier's newly declared love for Simone affected his relationship with the Rivières. He began to see them rather less frequently and this time, the gap was not filled to anything like the extent it had been in the past, with voluminous letters. In one of the rare letters he wrote to Rivière from this point on, he described his mood and his hopes at Trie-la-Ville where he was holidaying with both the Casimir-Periers :

> I just want to tell you this : happiness is a terrible thing to bear. Especially when it isn't the happiness one had built one's life around. This is all I want to say on that subject.[53]

To which Rivière frankly and perspicaciously replied :

> What sort of reaction do you expect me to make to all you've told me? I see you undecided and torn between two areas of sentiment. I don't feel any more decisive than you do in the face of such complex events. All I can say is that I don't see happiness in this for you . . . Are you looking to me for advice? What advice can I give you when I don't really know the nature of the problem?
>
> In the affair you're now involved in, it seems to me that there are only two possible alternatives : either you'll remain tied to the past, and if that should be so, nothing but sterility will result; or else the present will replace the past and will make you forget it, but you can expect only bitter joys from a love that's come so late.
>
> I'm not being very consoling. Perhaps I don't rightly understand. My over-riding impression is of something impossible. But perhaps impossibility is the very food of love, and perhaps to love makes for certain difficulty in living. I just don't know.[54]

Rivière's prognosis turned out to be rather less accurate than his diagnosis. In the event, Fournier solved the problem by adopting a third alternative unspecified by Rivière : he opted for neither the old

241

order nor the new but allowed each to co-exist within his consciousness. It was an uneasy relationship because each exerted a powerful
claim upon his loyalties, just as each satisfied a different need of his
personality. When his relationship with Simone left him with a
particular sense of grievance, he would turn regularly for consolation
to old friends or to more recent friends who were prized for their
associations with his distant past. So, at the end of June 1913, less
than a month after declaring his love for Simone, he could write to
Marguerite Audoux:

> I wanted to call on you this evening. But I gather they're taking
> me flying and possibly going to smash me up. I would so much
> like to have spent an hour or two in that dear little flat of yours
> where I always find all the calm, all the peace and all the
> kindness I so much need.[55]

Sometimes his loyalties to old friends and new came into open
conflict, such as in July 1913, when he finally opted to go to Trie
with the Casimir-Periers instead of on the annual pilgrimage to
Chartres with Péguy, a decision which caused him such heart-search-
ing later that Péguy was obliged to comment a month afterwards:

> *Mon enfant*, you're beginning to disconcert me a bit with this
> persistent regret of yours at not having come to Chartres with
> me. I went there on your account just as much as for my own,
> you know.[56]

Painful though Fournier's conflict of loyalties sometimes was on
the level of friendship, it was even more acute in matters of love.
On 20 August 1913, for example, he could write from La Chapelle,
where he was on holiday with the Rivières and his parents, a declaration of undying adoration to Simone, who was with her husband
in Cambo. He addressed her, as he always did, by her real Christian
name.

> My best beloved, yesterday evening, I got both your letters
> together, the Saturday one and the Monday one. I can't tell you
> what pleasure, what happiness and what welcome peace they've
> brought me. I read them with indescribable emotion, my heart
> full of tenderness, my eyes filling with the tears of an adoring,
> blissfully happy child when I came to certain phrases, so that,
> for a moment, I couldn't see to read further. My dearest, all
> the tenderness I possess, all the passion, all the desire, all the

ardent friendship and all the love, love, love – it's all for you, my darling . . .

I've never ceased to be with you. I go up hill, down dale, wonder aimlessly hither and yon; a stranger to everything else around me. I walk in the land of our love. I think without respite of all I want to say to you, all I want to tell you. I no longer see events and landscapes in the way I used to do : now they're perceived by you and me at the same time together. And things are all the lovelier for my being able to make you admire them or to describe their beauty to you . . .

My beloved Pauline, my lovely child, I'm thinking that all the time I was feeling so happy on Monday or yesterday, you'd got that wretched letter from me which must have made you sad. My love, just tell yourself this : that whatever may have happened before our love, from now on, it's our love alone which counts, and the happiness you give me, and your heart against mine now that we've found each other. Heart of mine, there's no pain now other than what you can inflict on me, and I know we're not going to hurt each other any more.[57]

Just three days later he was composing a letter for Yvonne Brochet to accompany the copy of Marguerite Audoux's *Marie-Claire* which he had decided to send her. He discreetly singled out for special commendation those sections in the novel where the chief love-interest lay :

I'm allowing myself the pleasure of sending you this book which I've got for you from my old friend Marguerite Audoux. I think you'll like it. I think you'll like the second part, which is so simple and yet so mysterious, which takes place amongst country-folk in Sologne.

It's a book I've greatly admired. And I've just re-read in your copy, still with the same deep emotion, that particularly lovely episode of Sister Désirée-des-Anges.

Since I left Rochefort, I've made a number of journeys and now, for a few weeks, I'm in the village where I always spend part of my vacation. Sometimes it's difficult for me to bear the particular calm and the perfect peace of this Berry countryside. So much calm is meant for people who are happy.

I wonder if I dare ask you, *chère Madame*, to send me occasional news of yourself, your family and your children? Perhaps that's too much to ask? The one excuse I would make for being so forward is the perfect friendship I've for so long felt for you and for those you love.

How is that dear little boy I kissed? And that charming and turbulent little girl who came and sat on my lap? I would like you to tell me about them. I would like to think that the conversation we began at Rochefort hasn't ended for ever. There are a thousand things about my life and work I should like to tell you about. Perhaps you'd not be too bored to listen? And I'm certain your replies couldn't fail to contain valuable advice for me. In all you say, I find a wisdom and a gravity I never find in other young women.

Chère madame, please convey my most sincere and respectful regards to Monsieur Brochet, whom I hope very much one day to meet, and rest assured of my most faithful friendship.

Henri Alain-Fournier.[58]

So concerned was Fournier over the wording of this covering letter, that he consulted both the Rivières and Péguy. Péguy turned out to be so sensitive himself to the etiquette of friendship that he refrained from giving any advice:

What can I say? I'm much less informed about the details of your life than you seem to think. Forgive me, but I'm a little set in my ways because of my own misfortunes, and I now have a horror of anything that might look like issuing directives. But I'm well and truly in touch with your spirit and your work.

When I see the incredible lengths I've gone to in order not to lose friends, and have lost them just the same, I have a panic terror lest I commit some indiscretion with you or seem to exercise an atom of control.[59]

This was a face of Péguy never seen by the readers of the *Cahiers*, to whom he was essentially a pugnacious warrior, permanently embattled against the iniquities of the modern world.

Yvonne Brochet replied promptly to Fournier's letter but not in encouraging terms. He reported to Rivière at the beginning of September:

Yes, I've had a reply from Rochefort. But all that has now taken on an unmistakably desolate taste of something too far in the past. Truly she was – truly she is – the only person in the world who could have given me peace and rest. I'll probably not now know peace in this world.[60]

Fournier's emotional dilemma might seem to have been resolved a fortnight later when he arrived in La Chapelle with the Casimir-Periers from Cambo, after a detour to visit Rivière and his family in Cenon. There, the past and present once more came temporarily and embarrassingly into conflict when the *bien-pensant* Fermauds firmly declined to entertain a party which included a notorious *divorcée*. Fortunately for Fournier, no such problems of etiquette had to be solved in La Chapelle, and when once Claude Casimir-Perier had departed on business to Paris, Fournier and Simone were, for the first time of any real consequence, able to spend several days on end, virtually unrestrictedly, in each other's company; this was conceivably the happiest time they ever spent together in the whole of their relationship, and they each later looked back on it as a sort of honeymoon. No sooner had Simone departed to rejoin her husband and her acting company in Paris, than Fournier was writing lyrically of the happiness they had just shared and was already apprehensive that it could never be repeated :

> My dearest love, my beloved wife, my Pauline, my beauty, it's dreadful to have to start trying to live again here without you. Ah, how heavy my heart was when I came back into the house. I was rash enough to take a few steps into your room when evening came. My love, your perfume lingered still; there was a pin and a blonde hair on the little table. For five days, I wasn't able to creep in, furtively like that, without hearing a low voice saying to me : 'Shut the door. Come and kiss me . . .' and I swear that I seemed to hear you saying it still. How difficult it was not to burst into tears. How hard, hard it is, my wife, to do without you. This morning, the rain came endlessly down over all the countryside, as it always does at the end of the holidays. The house, down below, had once again taken on the appearance of a country house that's been left cold and derelict. And we're all sad without you, and we daren't start to talk, and we're dying by degrees because you're here no longer.
>
> Ah, how sad it is no longer to be able to hear my darling preparing for a night of love. Ah! how hard it is no longer to be able to wake up in the first light of morning and no longer hear the footsteps of the men going down the passage on their way off to work, whilst our room has been mysteriously lit up the whole night through . . .
>
> It's hard that you are not my wife. It's frightful not to be able to fall asleep against you this coming evening.[61]

The following afternoon, he sang again the praises of his beloved and, had she but known it, paid her the supreme compliment of attributing to her the power of replacing his beloved countryside in his hierarchy of affections:

> My wife, I think of your beauty and your grace which have quite won over everyone here who loves me. I think of your red night-dress which you'd put on each evening to wait for me, of our whispered conversations, of our kisses, of our stifled laughter. I think of those five days of our secret honeymoon in which it seems as though we've used up all the happiness that's due to us on earth. Love, love, say it isn't over, that I'll know again your caresses, your hair, your sweet woman's mouth, our tender jokes, my hands enclosing the whole of your secret body, our faces pressed close together, each helplessly searching the other's face for signs of that tense beauty inscribed there by the pleasure and the joy of giving ourselves to one another with nothing held back.
>
> My adored wife, my angel, my darling, I am now yours utterly. No longer for me is there countryside, season of the year, or vacation. The countryside here around me, where I was born, is as dead as a cemetery now that you've gone. My only wish is to depart and to fly to wherever you may be. Wait for me, my love, I'm coming, give oh! give me your mouth, give me your body, give me your pleasure. Say to me again: 'I want you.' How I like you, how I love you, and other tender and mysterious words which are the words of our love and my pleasure, and my torment, and my joy, and my pain . . .[62]

And he looked forward to the joys they would soon be sharing back in Paris, in the furnished flat they had secretly begun to rent for their rendez-vous in the boulevard Arago.

The ecstasy had been as real as ecstasy ever can be, but the euphoria did not last for long. Just a week later, immediately on his return to Paris, he was once again writing to Yvonne Brochet in Rochefort:

> *Chère Madame,*
> I've just got back to Paris. Since you expressly forbade me to do so, I am not sending you a long letter I wrote to you in answer to your letter of 15 September.
> I am dreadfully sad and disconsolate.
> Will you please tenderly kiss for me your two charming babies.

And please accept my respectful friendship.

Henri Alain-Fournier.[63]

All that is known of his mood in the weeks thereafter must be deduced from the three pages of a diary he began to keep on 26 October 1913 and promptly abandoned a week later: it briefly expresses Fournier's sense of frustration over Simone's reiterated reluctance to meet him at their love-nest in the boulevard Arago because of her exhaustion resulting from playing each night in the new production of *Le Secret*.[64] The flat in boulevard Arago was normally used in the daytime only and one has, on occasions, almost forcibly to remind oneself that after he himself had enacted a tolerably passable imitation of Julian Sorel or the third side of a triangle in a well-made Second Empire play, Fournier would invariably repair each evening to his parents' flat in rue Cassini.

In view of what must have been an excruciating conflict of amorous loyalties at this particular moment in time, it must have come as a more than usually welcome occasion for relief and rejoicing when, at the end of October 1913,[65] *Le Grand Meaulnes* appeared in book form for the very first time, and Fournier could, at long last, claim that he was a fully fledged author.

Le Grand Meaulnes had first begun to appear, in serial form, in *La Nouvelle Revue Française*, the opening instalment being published in the July issue and others following successively each month until November. As it appeared, it brought in a number of appreciative letters for Fournier, the most interesting of which to have survived being those from Péguy.

After receiving his July copy of *La Nouvelle Revue Française*, Péguy wrote one of his characteristic one-sentence notes to Fournier:

I'm opening *Le Grand Meaulnes* and already I'm afraid of what I'm going to find there.[66]

Fournier at once assumed that Péguy did not approve of the more ethereal qualities of the first part of his novel and wrote at once to explain and defend himself. He was, at this time, with the Casimir-Periers at Trie-la-Ville, and the letter must be read in the context of his newest friendships competing against the old.

Your letter doesn't surprise me. But it makes me deeply sad. I knew that you weren't going to like *Le Grand Meaulnes*. And yet, as I've already told you, what little romance there is in the book, and the little touches of magic lantern, fantasy, Russian ballet and English adventure story, have to be paid for by so much regret, by such painful yearning![67]

In his business-like way, Péguy wrote across the head of this letter, as he always did on incoming mail, *vu* ('letter seen') and added *erreur profonde* ('profoundly wrong'). Just how mistaken Fournier had been in doubting him, he established with each successive issue which drew from him such characteristically pithy comments as 'As I thought. Still good stuff'.[68] and '*Mon petit*, you must send me a set of proofs of the end of *Le Grand Meaulnes* whatever the state they're in. I'm anxious about it. How could you have believed for an instant that the big brother would be a stranger to me. Alas, he's all too much my guest and my master,'[69] and finally, 'How beautiful it is, Fournier. Would you reserve a copy forthwith for the *Cahiers* plus a copy of the preceding number?'[70]

The jury to award the Goncourt Prize was due to meet on 3 December 1913, and the critical notices which *Le Grand Meaulnes* attracted when it first appeared in book form at the beginning of November have to be seen in this context. Almost without exception, the newspaper critics chose to vent their aggressiveness by scoring political points, or to demonstrate their erudition by knowing references to the author's real or imaginary literary masters: on 7 November the nameless reviewer of *Le Courier Européen* found 'one is reminded of the bizarre characters of Italian theatre. This is sometimes disconcerting and disturbing, in spite of the real beauties of the book'; on 22 November, in *L'Homme Libre*, the poet Jean Pellerin announced, 'Yesterday appeared this tale made up of childhood impressions, this remarkable thesis on the modern peasant'; on 22 November, drawing up a list of runners and prices for the Goncourt Prize the *Bonnet Rouge* commented darkly 'The silhouette of *Le Grand Meaulnes* appears in profile behind Alain-Fournier, secretary of Casimir-Perier *fils*; he has a protector, but he has talent'; on 26 November, in *Le Temps*, one of the pundits of the day, Paul Souday, identified Fournier as a candidate of the Right Wing, found *Le Grand Meaulnes* an uneasy blend of nineteenth-century Romanticism and eighteenth-century melodrama, described the author as short-winded and the last part of the novel as 'an obscure imbroglio fit only for pulp-fiction'; on 30 November, from Rheims, the critic of *L'Indépendant rémois* admired the mystery, charm and realism of the book, resolved to turn a blind eye to Fournier's technical immaturity and to try not to notice the ghost of Dickens; on 2 December

1913, in *Le Temps Présent* Henri Clouard detected in the novel 'a sort of halo around a living reality', identified Fournier as 'a pupil of Gide who has read a great deal of Dickens and some Barrès' and singled out for special mention 'a certain background of moral scruples with just a touch of Christian Protestantism'.[71]

Only one of these very early critics of *Le Grand Meaulnes* was unstinting in his praise, André Billy in *Paris-Midi* who hailed it as a masterpiece on 18 November, and declared, 'Ah! how close one must still have to be to one's eighteenth birthday to have so light and tender a pen.' Any other laudatory comments that were scattered through other reviews was almost invariably directed at the 'romantic' or 'fantastic', or 'charming' qualities of the book, at precisely those ethereal aspects which, as Fournier made plain in his explanatory note to Péguy, have to be set against the dark dénouement. A few critics mentioned the obvious tension in the novel between 'reality' and 'dream'; not a single one discerned the no less obvious contrast between 'innocence' and 'experience'. It was in this atmosphere compounded of incomprehension, malice and pretentiousness, spiced with that regard for the profit-motive which must always be in attendance when literary prizes are awarded, that on 3 December, the battle for the 1913 Goncourt Prize was joined.

The Académie Goncourt was a literary society which had been set up by the last will and testament of Edmond de Goncourt. The will directed that the ten members who constituted the Académie should meet once per month for dinner in a restaurant, and after the November meeting each year, award a cash prize to the novel which, by clear majority vote, had been the best imaginative prose work published in the twelve months preceding. After 1912, the members met for lunch instead of dinner and in December instead of November. The 1913 deliberations were amongst the longest and most complicated in the history of the award and the jury-panel had to vote on no fewer than eleven occasions before a clear, though by no means unanimous, decision was arrived at. Fournier's highest total of votes was five, on the ninth count, but he received none at all in the eleventh and final round, when the decisive figure of six votes was finally achieved by a previously unfancied outsider, Marc Elder, for his novel of Breton fishing folk, *Le Peuple de la mer*.

Newspaper comment on *Le Grand Meaulnes* after the Goncourt result was announced was no more elevated or perceptive than it had been in the weeks preceding; once again, the settling of old scores or the spotting of literary influences became the cardinal rules of the game: on 4 December, having graced *Le Grand Meaulnes* with the ambivalent epithet 'remarkable', *L'Action française* concentrated its attention on *La Maison blanche*, 'the book of Jewboy Werth, the case-history of a suppurating otitis'; on the same day, Fournier's friend Henri Massis, writing in *L'Eclair*, mourned the passing of Symbolism, and sought to praise *Le Grand Meaulnes* by describing it as being like plays of 'Shakespeare acted by characters from Madame de Ségur', a well-known authoress of rather sugary caution- ary tales; on 5 December, the Left Wing *Humanité* inveighed against the 'lack of dignity of these annual comedies' and observed that *Le Grand Meaulnes* was 'curious'; on 8 December, in *L'Aurore*, Robert Kemp declared that the *fête étrange* was 'a blend of Edgar Poe [sic] enlivened by a touch of Verlaine' and added 'the mystery drags on too long. The novel ends sadly, in a *cas de conscience* artificially fabricated by the author'; on 13 December, in *La Revue Bleue*, Lucien Maury spotted two sources hitherto unsuspected, Shakespeare's *Midsummer Night's Dream* and Selma Lagerlöf's *Wonderful Voyage of Nils Holgersson*, a book Fournier had not in fact ever read up to this point but which, doubtless on account of this allusion, he acquired very shortly afterwards and which became a particular favourite of his.

For the critic of the *Gazette de Lausanne*, Meaulnes was 'vague and elusive', Yvonne de Galais 'thoroughly conventional' and Frantz de Galais 'non-existent, yet unaccountably, for all that, they were all very much alive and very lovable'; he linked the grounds of Fournier's Lost Domain with Verlaine's *'vieux parc solitaire et glacé'*,[72] and the green curtain and four armchairs of the *fête étrange* with Schumann's *Carnaval*. The year ended with a display of withering contempt and the faintest of praise from the mighty Gustave Lanson, soon to be director of the Ecole Normale Supérieure, who announced in *Le Matin* on 24 December that 'There is in this work of Fournier's, a fantasy which very little affects me : the lack of credibility about everything is all the more shocking because this fairy tale, which ought to take place in some land of dreams, is all supposed to happen in the real world of the present day.'[73]

Only one critic of real contemporary standing saw fit to praise *Le Grand Meaulnes* for its elegiac qualities : this was Rachilde, who on 16 December in *Le Mercure de France*, detected unmistakable traces of Symbolism in the novel but went on at once to declare : 'Rest assured, everything is real, yet a strange wind blowing from some mysterious beyond readily familiar to children and adolescents, rustles the pages in your hands. Poor *grand Meaulnes*, everything happens as he wants it to, but always too late. What matter though : you've opened for us the gates of your youthful Paradise.'

All in all, then, Fournier could not be wholly satisfied with the immediate critical reaction to his first book. The reviewers had missed the vital point of it all, had, almost without exception, praised it or blamed it for the wrong reasons, and it did not seem that he had achieved his minimal objectives of learning that his book was being widely read and his face widely known. He could rejoice in the acclaim of his close friends, Rivière, Péguy and Marguerite Audoux, but they were so loyal that their support could virtually be taken for granted. He was denied the praise he most dearly wanted: he sent an inscribed copy of *Le Grand Meaulnes* both to Yvonne Brochet and her husband; Yvonne's father, who had arranged her marriage in the first place, chose once more to intervene in her life. Fournier's faithful intermediary, Marc Riviére, reported from Rochefort on 25 January 1914:

> Madame Brochet has asked me to let you know that she wrote a letter to thank you, but that her father positively forbade her to send it.[74]

His only consolation was to hope that his second novel might win the acclaim which seemed to have been denied the first, and he returned accordingly to *Colombe Blanchet*.

The first reference to *Colombe Blanchet* recorded in Fournier's published correspondence, is in a letter to Rivière dated 22 April 1913 and further references are scattered intermittently throughout his letters until the outbreak of the First World War. The novel was far from finished when Fournier left to rejoin his regiment just before the outbreak of war, but enough notes and fragments have survived for one to be able fairly confidently to pronounce upon his working methods and his intentions.[75]

The original plot of *Colombe Blanchet* was as follows: most of the action was to take place in a small French country town riven by bitter local political rivalry, and the chief male character was to have been Jean-Gilles Autissier, a young teacher at the local school who arrives on the scene at the opening of the novel. At the outset, he is at once seen to be idealistic, romantic and in love with love. He has a brief affair with a girl called Laurence which ends abruptly when he discovers that she has had other lovers before him. He continues his search for the virginal girl of his dreams and eventually finds her in the person of Colombe Blanchet, youngest daughter of old Blanchet, the mayor of the little town and the sworn enemy of the school-teachers. She shares his high-souled view of love, and at the beginning of the school holidays, they decide to flee together from the troubles of the town in the hope of starting a life of their own elsewhere. They depart on bicycles and spend three innocent days and nights in the countryside, sleeping in a barn on one night and in an old abandoned house on the next. But an embittered former lover of Laurence has set off in pursuit after them, and to settle his score with Autissier, when he at last overtakes the pair, he tells Colombe of the earlier affair between Autissier and Laurence. At this point, Colombe is so distressed at the shattering of her ideals, she first forgives Autissier and then drowns herself. The novel was, from the start, to have been preceded by the quotation from *The Imitation of Christ* which so struck Fournier towards the end of his two years of Army service in September 1909 :

I seek a pure heart and there will I dwell.

In the course of the months Fournier spent working in what was clearly spasmodic fashion at this novel, he made important emendations to the dénouement. He averted the tragic conclusion by allowing Colombe to enter a convent instead of drowning herself, but more radical still, he invented an entirely new character, Emilie Blanchet, Colombe's elder, more experienced and more practical sister, who finally consoles him for his previous disappointments. He was also planning to interweave with the main romantic plot, all the complications of the petty political manœuvring, and to build up a number of minor characters such as Voyle, another of the young schoolteachers, with a formidable collection of female conquests, and Autissier's landlord Marazano, a smuggler and petty thief, whose great exploit in the novel was going to have been the furtive disposal, piece by piece around the countryside, of a lady's bicycle he had stolen, about which the local police were growing anxious to question him. Fournier announced, with great enthusiasm, that he had resumed work on much of this new material in a letter to his sister dated 26 June 1914 :[76] events did not permit him to work on it much longer.

As in the case of *Le Grand Meaulnes* or, indeed, of all Fournier's imaginative writings, *Colombe Blanchet* was to have been a transmutation of his own memories, both ancient and modern : the petty political intriguing in the novel would have drawn heavily on his childhood recollections of similar rivalries in Epineuil; the small-town setting in the novel would have been Mirande transfigured, and the household of the fictitious Marazano solidly based on the real-life counterpart of Monsieur Hidalgo of Mirande. As for the characters,

Autissier's preoccupations and certain of his experiences would clearly have been modelled on Fournier's own, while the imaginary biography of Laurence would have been a compound of the life-stories of the 'Laurence' of Mirande and of Jeanne Bruneau. The discovery of the derelict house in the forest would have been yet another variation on one of Fournier's favourite themes, but the role of the belatedly created Emilie, persuading the hero to renounce his unattainable ideals and settle for a less romantic reality, is surely not so much a memory translated as an example of latter-day wish-fulfilment.

How Fournier planned to reconcile his now 'happy' ending with the theme of the quest for purity is hard to imagine; the epigraph from *The Imitation of Christ* was, till the last, retained at the head of his draft, and a Fournier anything less than serious, or even heart-broken, over the prospect of lost innocence would have been a Fournier utterly transformed. All the indications are that this trans-formation was not effectively achieved in the remainder of his life-time.

In the late summer and early autumn of 1913, he helped Péguy complete his latest poem, 'Eve', by listening to and commenting on the work as it was evolved:[77] this is a vast poem on the theme of the expulsion from Eden, beginning with a long and detailed evocation of the beauties of Paradise then giving way to an even longer cata-logue of the evil ways into which Man has fallen. The affinity between 'Eve' and *Le Grand Meaulnes* has subsequently not gone unnoticed,[78] and Fournier's own abiding preoccupation with the theme of lost innocence and its consequences could not but have been intensified through his renewed contact with Péguy's mind and work. It is clearly apparent in the work-notes that have survived for Fournier's unfinished play, *La Maison dans la forêt*.

It was inevitable, given Simone's commitment to the theatre and to Fournier, that sooner or later, he should have been persuaded to write a play. In July 1913, he wrote to Rivière with details of Simone's first recipe for winning him theatrical fame:

> Simone has just been working out with me a plan for drama-tising one of Stevenson's novels and staging it in America on the scale that successful productions are mounted there. 3,000 performances – my fortune's made![79]

Nothing has survived of the plans for this project, assuming any were ever committed to paper, and it was not until January 1914 that he actively returned to the idea of writing a play and, in fact, began work on the first scene of *La Maison dans la forêt*.[80]

The original plot was as follows: Harold, a young man whose mistress has been unfaithful to him, renounces Paris and women and all their works, and comes to live in a lonely house in the very heart of a dense forest. His only companion is Philippe, his faithful game-keeper and a widower, and the pair of them contentedly while away the hours and chase away their regrets shooting game in the sur-rounding woods. One day, when they are preparing breakfast, their dogs begin to bark furiously, and they snatch up their guns and rush out into the early morning leaving the door ajar in their haste. A few moments later, two ladies enter, one young and beautiful, the other middle-aged, not so beautiful, and absolutely furious. The young lady's name is Eléonore, and it quickly transpires that she has run away from a school excursion party, eager to see for herself the legendary Harold, whose amorous misfortunes and vows of everlasting misogyny have been recounted to her at school by a fellow-pupil, Harold's sister. The middle-aged lady is Mademoiselle Saint-Pourçain, who has seen Eléonore's illicit departure from the school party and is resolved to lead her back to the academic fold without delay. What happens thereafter is best indicated by a brief note in Fournier's papers:

16 January 1914. 4 a.m. Av. de l'Observatoire. The little girl and the three bears.

The men are heard returning, the ladies hasten to hide, they leave behind one or two traces of their presence, each of the men in turn detects these and each keeps silent because he believes the other is secretly harbouring a lady friend somewhere on the large and com-modious premises. After a deal of misunderstanding and near disaster, the truth is finally revealed, and the play ends with the promise of Harold's marrying Eléonore and Philippe's marrying Mademoiselle Saint-Pourçain.

This scenario seems to have been very rapidly conceived in January 1914 but very little of it was translated into dialogue. By 7 February, the setting had already been changed from the 'heart of a vast forest' to 'the suburbs of London', Philippe transformed from a gamekeeper into a footballer, and the plot much complicated with the addition of a brawl off-stage, various characters physically assaulted by a berserk Harold, and the police anxious to locate him to assist them in their inquiries. There is no further mention of *La*

Maison dans la forêt in his notes after an entry dated 19 April, and it is, therefore, more than likely that it was finally abandoned because of his failure to bring the plot tightly under his control. The notes and fragments which have survived, however, clearly suggest that had the original scenario been adhered to, the result might well have been quite enchanting, a light but not entirely frivolous trifle in the mode of Musset. The notion of setting the house in the woods or in the suburbs of London indicate that Fournier was continuing to found his imagined worlds on a basis of fact and on lived experience, and this emerges alas from the mere five pages which have survived of a tentative bid to dramatise one of his own short stories, *Le Miracle des trois dames de village*, under the title of *La Jeune Dame de village* : his brief stage-directions for the setting of the play state : 'a lost village. drawing-room piano. at Madame Benoist's', the house he most loved to visit in the Epineuil of his childhood and where, on a sunny Ascension Thursday afternoon in June 1905, he imagined that a blonde girl was leading him.

While, in his attempts at imaginative writing in 1914, Fournier was forever being lured back towards the past, in his other day-to-day activities he was very much caught up in the present. Although he had completed his work on *Brest: port transatlantique*[81] which had reached proof-stage by January 1914, he continued to serve as Casimir-Perier's secretary. In March, he accompanied his employer to Béziers in Provence, where he had decided to stand in the national election as a candidate of the 'Fédération des Gauches', a label which deceived neither the mainly Left-Wing electorate nor the local press which described him as a 'multimillionaire'. Fournier had cultivated an interest in politics from his childhood on, listening attentively to his father's analyses of the programmes and personalities of the Epineuil local politicians, and regularly attending debates in the Chamber of Deputies while attending his lycées in Paris. Once, he had even gone so far as to declare in a letter to Rivière :

> Sometimes, I would like to be a *député*, to make dangerous campaign speeches to the peasants, shout into their deaf ears, make them love me or hate me. Sometimes I find myself planning practical new schemes, wondering how I could set up a secondary education system that would be free, compulsory and de-centralised, and to see in that the future of the world.[82]

Now in Provence, in the spring of 1914, he could make this dream at last partly true. He could place his political preoccupations and his literary flair in joint harness by composing the manifesto for his employer, singing the praises of Casimir-Perier's character and rather nebulous economic programme while castigating his opponents: Albert Milhaud, a Radical schoolmaster from Fournier's former lycée, Louis-le-Grand, and Edouard Barthe, the Socialist candidate and existing *député*, up for re-election. It is unlikely that Fournier ever had the chance to harangue the voters in person, because he returned to Paris after a few days to leave Casimir-Perier to deliver his own speeches around the large though thinly-populated constituency, made up of seventy-one separate *communes*. In the event, Fournier's prose did as little to charm the hard-headed electors of Béziers as it had done to sway the jury of the Académie Goncourt a few months earlier; when the result of the poll was declared on 26 April 1914, Barthe was resoundingly re-elected with 11,000 votes, Milhaud was second with 7,000 and Casimir-Perier, who had been fatally branded in the vine-growing constituency as a sugar-beet grower, came last with a mere 1,098.[83]

Fournier's brief visit to Provence was not wholly wasted. He was able to see a part of France which was completely new to him, such as the enchanted city of Carcassonne which, he told Rivière, he saw at daybreak and promptly decided was the home of Puss-in-Boots and the Prince.[84] He was also able, for the first time, to see the Mediterranean which had occupied a privileged place in his private mythology ever since it became associated with Yvonne de Quiévrecourt. He alluded to this as discreetly as possible in the postcard he sent to her on 14 March 1914:

> From the shore of the Mediterranean, which I've loved for a long time before actually seeing it, I now send you, *chère Madame*, my most respectful and friendly regards, and kisses for your two charming babies.[85]

In the meantime, his affair with Simone Casimir-Perier was passing through the blackest and stormiest of its various phases. Fournier had a compulsive urge to set down in words the most vivid of his emotional experiences, unhappy as well as happy. This was most strikingly demonstrated on the occasion of his two meetings with Yvonne when he tried to record his impressions in all their immediacy while actually sitting near her on the tram in 1905, and, in his black notebook, when the train was driving him away from Rochefort in 1913. He had been quick to set down a frank account of his feelings in the letters he dispatched to Jeanne Bruneau and to 'Henriette', and now, between

13 January and 20 April 1914, he recorded, in a secret notebook, the varied thoughts and sentiments inspired in him from day to day by his latest mistress, Simone.[86]

Many of the notebook entries express how much she had now come to mean to him. He wrote on 13 January, 'She is as necessary to me as a glass of water or a piece of bread', and his anguished letters to his parents from London in 1905 revealed just how necessary bread was to him. On 23 January, he recorded a waking dream of being able to live beside her:

> My beautiful beloved, somewhere there is a frozen lake where we could skate together, a garden all in white where I could take you by the arm, a road where we could go for a long walk before nightfall and a room where we could now be sitting together beside the fire. The lovely winter is passing us by, and that happiness I speak of is passing too far away from where we are. At least, today, there will have been the desire I've felt for you almost as lovely as happiness, and I'll think of this as I'm falling asleep and it will be next to my heart right through the night. My love, with your face so small, so beautiful, so dear to me, just a word from you can give me so much courage and confidence and joy.[87]

On 28 January, he noted:

> Since we loved, I haven't any love or desire or needs or hopes which are not for her

and added the following day:

> To say I thirsted for her is to understate it: I needed her to come in order to live – She did come but I was out.[88]

On 31 January, he roughed out a note to her:

> The true reason for my writing to you is that doubtless you're not happy. I'm not happy either. I don't know which of us is in the wrong. But I think that you're the one who's more unhappy, more tired, more angry, more all alone and I really must come and kiss you, even if I've resisted for a moment because of a thousand good reasons.
> How I love you. And how I too am lonely.[89]

He occasionally fretted over the ways in which she interfered or refused to cooperate with his work, in particular with *La Maison dans la forêt*; thus, on 9 March, he commented:

> Our collaboration will have to be effective – or scrapped altogether.

But the root cause of the unhappiness he continued to experience in his affair with Simone remained what it had always been: her reluctance to leave her husband and devote herself exclusively to him. His misery was made all the worse because she was a professional actress acting every evening in a series of successful plays and engaged, all too readily for his taste, in the extravagant endearments and displays of affection for even the comparative stranger which are part of the traditional life-style of any theatrical community. He compiled a list of his grievances in the particularly bitter and despairing letter he composed in draft on 22 March:

> The long evening is passing without you. I keep hoping for some sign of you which I know isn't going to come. At every creak of the stair, I listen and I wait, but I know all too well it won't be for me. People talk to me but I don't listen. All I can think of is how to stop the tears which so painfully and bitterly keep coming into my eyes. What will I have meant to you, when you think back to me later in your life? I wonder. And what will there be left of me when you no longer love what you've already taken from me?
>
> There is nothing but regret, nothing but heartbreak, nothing but disillusionment in my love. A moment ago, when I came round the corner of the avenue, the icy wind swirled round and went right through me . . . But nothing could hurt me as much as seeing you in your home and hearing you talk the way you do.
>
> What have I ever held in my arms, what have I loved, what have I believed in that is really and truly mine? Everywhere I see you on display, everywhere showering compliments, receiving everybody's confidences, dishing out advice to all and sundry.

He then proceeded to enumerate the occasions, over the two days preceding, when she had listened to the playwright Bernstein's account of his love-life, showered passionate kisses on Curel, another fashionable dramatist of the day, and displayed far more of her bosom than, in his view, decency or theatrical dictates strictly demanded. He asked, in the spirit of *Le Corps de la femme*:

> Doesn't love begin to teach you about modesty, even to those for

whom it's not meant anything at all? It isn't your fault. You've adopted the practice of displaying and giving all you possess, even if it means there's nothing left for love to discover. I'm different, I live in a solitary secret world where you find your greatest pleasure in anticipating love, and where you hoard everything for love like a miser.

Doubtless I'm the one who ought to change my way of life. It would be a thousand times better if I resigned myself to being the person you want me to be when you manage to find the time to visit me. And when all is said, I really do want to pledge myself to stop reproaching you in this way. But then, no doubt, we wouldn't be loving in the same way.

It may seem as if I'm delivering a cold lecture to you but I'm in the most terrible pain. What is it inside me that's so unsatisfied, so desperately demanding relief? You who ought to be able to do so much for me, my love, *you* are the one who is filling me with this odious desire to run away from it all, to stop living altogether, to stop drinking down this hateful poison drop by drop.

And yet, if I turn away from letter-writing just for a moment, if I sit down by the fire in this dining-room where I'm all alone, if I try to read and reflect, I see again the expression you wore in the early days of our love, the face I've so deeply loved. At the beginning of that afternoon when we went to L'Oeuvre theatre together, you had a special way of looking at me in front of all those people, silently, with quiet and gentle pride. It made me want to come so close to you, to nestle my head against your knees. That silence, that love so vast and so still, that chastity, that tenderness, oh how I've longed for them, how often I've thought they were going to be given back to me, and how far they are away from me, my love, this evening.[90]

In the event, Fournier would seem finally to have decided not to post this letter, but he continued to record his causes for grievance over the weeks that followed. Thus on 5 April 1914, he noted:

As soon as we move on to serious ground, we're no longer united.[91]

While on 10 April 1914, he wrote:

I wish to tell her about the feelings I've had during the day: *Nils Holgersson*, the first time I propose to read her an extract from it, she sends me packing; the second time I try to speak to her about it, she doesn't even reply. The kingdom of our feelings and our researches just isn't the same. She is the World.[92]

The last entry in Fournier's secret notebook for 1914 is dated 20 April, at which point something like a reconciliation would seem to have taken place because on the following day, Fournier could enumerate once more for her his reasons for and memories of loving. He dated the letter '21 April, 3 a.m.':

There are a thousand little tendernesses which I couldn't say or do to you yesterday, my little child, my wife.

I'm coming to join you right away. But before I do so, I want to tell you how the mere thought of you and of your love sometimes seizes hold of me, stops me in my tracks and intoxicates me.

I see again that dear sweet face of yours which yesterday expressed such pain. And with a feverishness and in a religious spirit you just can't imagine, I repeat, over and over, those poor frightened words you spoke to me, and I melt with the desire to fold you in my arms and hold you close to me, my wife who has suffered so much, my little child who has been so ill.

There is a certain tenderness now in my feelings for you, a certain tremor in my passion, a certain depth in my attachment to you, which these months of your illness have revealed in me and the existence of which I didn't suspect.

And now I'm more deeply inside you, much more a part of you, more interfused with the heat of you, the breath of you, the very blood of you, than at the profoundest moments of our physical passion.

My darling, I walked about your room yesterday; I couldn't give you my hand to support you, to ease your suffering, because the door was open. I could say nothing to you nor do anything for you. But I'd have shed my own blood to stop your pain . . .

My beloved, my adoration here on earth, my little god, all that I admire most in this world, all that I love, all that is lovely and true and sure and good, all that is charming and delicate and sweet and tender . . .

Last night, I thought back to those first days when I was close to you; and in my memory I rediscovered one by one all the wishes I then expressed for our future friendship: that I should spend more time with you, that you would tell me everything, that I should advise you and help you, that I could devote myself to you, that the time might come when you could no longer live without me. But already, these were the wishes of a lover. These were wishes which could only come true in a great love – and, at the time, I didn't know it.

I am yours. I love you.[93]

Because Simone's unspecified illness meant that she was no longer devoting her afternoons to rehearsing and her evenings to public stage-performances, she was able to spend much more time in Fournier's company than she had done in the frustrating weeks previously, but the basic situation was still unaltered : she remained the wife of Claude Casimir-Perier while Fournier was still, nominally, his secretary. This was still the position two months later when Fournier wrote an unusually euphoric letter to his sister, describing the joys of living with Simone on the Perier estate at Trie-la-Ville :

She is either reading or asleep close beside me, in a landscape which really is 'The Happy Valley', a landscape which is either all blue or all golden, depending on whether it's in shade or sunshine, or landscape with geraniums, lawns, a river, a little wood and two park benches which have been given different names like those you come across beyond Newfoundland. There's the seat of Felicity and the seat of Ill Fortune. For some time past we've not been sitting on the latter.[94]

On the same day, he wrote no less euphorically to André Lhote :

Here, my very simple life is divided between literary and rustic labours. Five hours on *Colombe Blanchet* regularly each day. Every so often, we spend our time swarming bees for the hives. Yesterday, they were raking up the hay on the lawn. This afternoon, there's a great heap of hay in front of the chestnut trees.[95]

But if Fournier and Simone were by now master and mistress of their situation, they were no longer in control of their destiny. Fournier's letters to his sister and Lhote were both dated 26 June 1914 : on 28 June, Francis Ferdinand, Archduke of Austria, was assassinated in Sarajevo.

8

The Land at the World's End

July–September 1914

> The paths are rough. The hillocks are
> covered with broom. The air is still. How
> far away are the birds and the springs. If
> we advance any further, it can only be the
> end of the world.
>
> Rimbaud[1]

Throughout July 1914, while the members of the Triple Entente and
the Triple Alliance were being reminded of their treaty-obligations to
each other, and all were making their covenant with death, Fournier
and Simone were enjoying the second of their 'honeymoons'. Fournier's
mood of high euphoria almost comes up off the page of the last letter
he ever wrote to Rivière, arranging a rendezvous with him in Bordeaux
while *en route* for the Casimir-Periers' country estate down in Cambo:

> Colombe (*Blanchet*) is in excellent health. She's already had
> three offers of marriage : the first from a big Swiss periodical;
> the second from old Hébrard; the third from a rich Parisian who
> wishes to remain anonymous . . .
> The book which has amazed and amused me most for months,
> quite bowled me over in fact, is *Moll Flanders* which I've just
> bought . . .
> Fine weather here – which is to say that since mid-day, there's
> been a tremendous storm which makes some of us pass out with
> fear, fills others with delight and devastates the garden.
> I've got a thousand things to tell you which I can't bring to
> mind right now because I'm being distracted. I kiss all three of
> you *en bloc*.[2]

What was to prove their final meeting with Fournier proved to be
a social catastrophe for the Rivières, and they both brooded over it

262

inordinately for years afterwards. In her major biography of her brother, Madame Rivière has left a vivid, though possibly distorted, picture of Simone in the Hotel de France at Bordeaux on 20 July, commenting on every mouthful of food consumed by Fournier during the luncheon reunion, and bestowing a hundred sou piece on every employee in the hotel who have been lined up to salute her regal departure: the seal was set on a disastrous encounter when, after promising to give the Rivières a lift to the outskirts of Bordeaux, Simone and Fournier swept away in their open Delaunay tourer leaving them open-mouthed at the hotel entrance.[3]

Fournier wrote next from Cambo to excuse the oversight with all the cavalier insouciance of Frantz de Galais:

> *Mes chers enfants,*
> We were furious with you!
> Why on earth didn't you remind us that you wanted a lift to Uncle Feur's? We only remembered about it when we got to the outskirts of Bordeaux. You really are too stupid!
> That apart, we departed saying all the best things possible about you.
> We drove through the Landes, five towns and a hundred villages all illuminated with festive lights in our honour, we hadn't the slightest doubt.
> Now we're here, very relaxed, very content, very happy.
> We both send kisses.[4]

When general mobilisation was decreed in France on 1 August 1914, Fournier and Simone were in Bayonne, just over a hundred miles from his regimental headquarters in Mirande. He at once sent a reassuring postcard to his sister:

> How is it with you? I'm rejoining Mirande tomorrow. I'm pleased that Jacques will be in the same Army Corps as me. We were sure war was coming. I depart content. I expect to see you again soon. Meanwhile, a long hug for you and Jacqueline and all those left with you at Cenon. Your brother, Henri.[5]

Three days later, he wrote to his sister again with news as momentous to him as the outbreak of war:

> I've been here in Mirande since midnight on Sunday. Simone managed to have me driven from Cambo by car. She spent the night in a hotel in the middle of the upheaval caused by the arrival of 10,000 men. The following night, all on her own, she

drove through the storm to Pau to fetch me some indispensable things I need, all the rail-links having been cut. She's been admirable. I'd like you to become very fond of her. We've promised to marry each other after the war. For days and days now, Claude was in Vittel with God knows who, saying he'd be arriving at any minute. Finally, the war came and cut off his road home. What a lesson and what an augury! All this while, Providence arranged it so that she and I weren't separated for a single hour. She would like to be at your side throughout the war. We've been trying to get Father and Mother to Cambo, but I'm not sure where exactly they are right now. I'm writing to them. I'm so glad you're beside all Jacques' aunts who love you. How's Jacqueline? I dreamed of her all through the night. Fancy the darling girl being born in time to see these tremendous happenings. The atmosphere here is the same as it is on the eve of summer manœuvres with the difference that there's now great enthusiasm, that the reservists are all singing as their trains arrive, and that if you speak to a reservist about his family, he turns away his head for a moment and stares elsewhere – then it's back to normal again and we know it's war. I don't know why I feel so strongly we're going to win. We've got every vestige of luck on our side. And all the signs are favourable.

How's Jacques? Where is he? He must be writing to you about it. What times we're living in!

My little Isabelle, you must write to me. There's a letter from each of us to which the other has each to reply. In your letter to me there was a short passage in which you said that you'd been worried for a while but that now it was over, and this gave me something to think about. That's all over now, isn't it?

My dear Isabelle, forgive me for writing so little and so badly. I'm in the officers' mess where everyone is talking and gossiping and smoking. My dear girl, what an extraordinary thing – and yet so simple too – to think that it's come at last, and that Jacques and I are far away. I wish so much I could have held you tight before going away : I think that would have been very sweet, very lovely, very comforting.

Down on the square, I can hear the crowd of reservists cheering. The town-crier has just announced that following the violation of Belgian neutrality, England has, from midnight, mobilised her fleet and her army.

Many of my former soldiers are still under my command. They kept saying this morning: '*Mon lieutenant*, how good it is to be back with you again.'

THE LAND AT THE WORLD'S END

My sister, my darling sister, I know that you're going to bear this separation from Jacques as you have to do. I know that you're brave as you're kind and sweet. I know I'll see you again soon.[6]

To Simone, he described the same scenes of enthusiasm at Mirande, and expressed his love and gratitude to her for having at long last agreed to marry him:

I'm surrounded by people who insist on talking to me, so I no longer quite know what I'm writing. This letter must take the place of kissing you and holding you in my arms. My love, that departure on the road to Tarbes! Your little head, looking back at me from the distance. The tears one doesn't feel flowing. I didn't dare look at you again when you came back because I was afraid it would start all over again. It was so hard, so heavy to bear. My Pauline, it was as though you were the one who was being sent off to war and I was the one being kept behind. My wife, I read your letter on the road as soon as there was light enough to see. I knew in advance what I was going to read. Nothing in all the world could have affected me more. Now when I hear them saying, 'I'm leaving my wife behind, I'm leaving my daughter', I feel the urge to say 'And I have a fiancée who will wait for me. My young Jewish wife with whom I'll present myself before God.' 'O God, please make Pauline and me a married couple pleasing in your sight': that's been my prayer for a long time now, each evening and each morning . . .

And now, my little darling, I think that at this moment you must be driving alone through the night back towards Cambo. My beloved girl, I take your soft hair in my hand, I place your head against my cheek. I went to get my cases from the hotel bedroom and I opened the door of the bedroom where we slept amidst the bed-bugs! They'd put the little cradle back inside. My dear wife. With each passing minute, I seem to hear you calling: Henri. My darling . . .

I would be in tears now if my comrades weren't all around me, elbow to elbow and right in front of me. My life, I shall live only to come back to my fiancée. My love, my blood, my flesh, I carry you inside me, I hold you all warm and adorable against me. My lovely love. All around me, there are extraordinary, charming, courteous, excited people, as well as some old fogeys. And there, right before my eyes, the wonderful way you look at me . . .[7]

In the middle of all this enthusiasm both for public and private causes, and with the public transport services extended and congested to the utmost limits, Fournier's parents undertook a journey as hazardous and as remarkable as anything in his fiction. They spent four days travelling by train from La Chapelle to bid farewell to their children. On 6 August, they arrived in Bordeaux to console their daughter; on 7 August, they travelled to Marmande to see Rivière, and on 8 August they journeyed south to Mirande to see Fournier before he set off for the Western Front. On 9 August, he and his regiment moved fifteen miles north to Auch, and Simone took the Fournier parents by car to see the regiment's final ceremonial parade before it left to join the developing battle. In the course of these proceedings, Simone first broke the news to Madame Fournier that she and her son were planning to marry when the war was over. Simone reported this to Isabelle Rivière on 18 August:

> Just imagine, your mother arrived unexpectedly at Mirande to find us installed in more or less the same room! I explained everything to her on the eve of Henri's departure. She was very moved but happy.[8]

On 12 August, Fournier bade farewell to his parents and the troop trains began to lumber towards the battlefields of the Marne. Rivière, whose regiment formed part of the same Army division as Fournier's, later described their trains' slow progress from the south to the north of France, passing through the Berry close to Bourges, where the trains used to come and go for the family holidays in the morning of Fournier's world:

> Over the course of three days, trains, following one another along the same tracks with just a few hours between them, transport us, at the pace of a man walking, right across France. We pass through the same stations where women come to pin holy medals on to our chests and across the same fields, where the peasants take off their hats as we pass, as if the train were already our funeral procession. We hear the same *Marseillaise* bawled by almost the same voices flavoured with garlic because each of us is on the march with men from Gascony.
>
> Did Fournier get out at Bourges station, did he see Sancerre up on its hill, where I spent the night? Did he receive, as I did, at Saint-Florentin, a hard-boiled egg, sent flying through the air towards the crowds of soldiers by a Red Cross lady on top of a wagon? We were absolutely famished.

At all events, he must have seen, as I did, that aeroplane shattered to bits amidst the wreckage of those railway wagons near the station of Brienne-le-Château : merely a collision, the first accident of the war, which made us laugh because we hoped for so much better to follow.

He must have come into Suippes just as I was pulling out, limping along and already quite exhausted.

And perhaps on the same day as I did, out there in the heart of the Argonne, in the great dale of Les Islettes which reverberated like a cathedral under that dark sky, between those black trees, he may first have heard the guns . . .[9]

By 17 August, Fournier was well into Lorraine, and on 20 August, taking advantage of the first protracted period of calm since setting out from the south, he wrote quite the longest of all his letters to Simone. He placed at the head a declaration of fidelity set out like an epigraph :

> My beloved,
> I love you.   I am yours
> For all eternity.   Your Henri.

Then, he at once proceeded to express his sense of thankfulness at having the thought of her love to console and inspire him :

Today, our second rest-day in a remote village near the border, I want to write this letter to you which can only arrive late if indeed it ever arrives at all. As soon as we come to a halt, as soon as we begin to take a rest, the life begins to drain out of me at the thought of being separated from you. Yesterday and today, thinking of you and wanting you made me delirious. My comrade-in-arms, that stout young lieutenant, has been married for seven months. He talks about his wife in an ardent, chaste, religious and passionate manner which I find infinitely pleasing. In the evening, once we're bivouacked, if we're not too tired to talk, what he says makes me think of the past and the future with a longing which makes me feel quite faint. I know now, my love, where to find happiness, the free and joyful life, the Fortunate Island, but the whole war stands between it and me.

Then he warned her not to be too free with her advice or her solicitude, and he expressed strong disapproval of her suggestion that she might join the Ambulance Corps :

You know that I have little respect for the medical profession.

You know that I despise their myopic materialistic view which sees no further than tendons, veins, bones and grey matter . . . I would not like to think, Pauline, that you're going to be on that side of life while we're on the other. All the same, if, after reading that, you still reckon it's your duty to go with such people, I'll not oppose your decision to go.

He assured her that his concern was wholly to protect her against herself :

There can be no doubt now that we're absolutely sure of one another. I thought it very childish of you, the other day in Mirande, to imagine that anything could ever have happened in my life which was not for you or hadn't come from you.

Then he recounted a recent dream which suggests that he was not wholly convinced by his own protestations of new-found confidence :

The other evening, when I was worn out and upset by a bowl of hot milk I drank after dinner, I had a very painful dream. I'm going to tell you all about it because it was complicated yet very clear and very real. I'm going to tell you about it because I promised to tell you everything, even at the risk of disturbing you. You were wearing mourning for Claude's parents. It was in your interest not to concern yourself with me any longer. This was something incomprehensible and hateful. I struggled against it. My parents kept trying to console me. I was quarrelling with them. I was sure that you were incapable of acting out of self-interest. I was sure you'd come back of your own free will. There were several acts which were played out in very vivid, life-like settings. Finally you decided to write to me. It was a letter with a black border round it and it was brought to me by Alfred Benoist, that boy who's now dead and who had a bit of *le grand Meaulnes* about him. On the envelope were the words 'for Alban' (which is one of my names nobody ever uses, and I found myself wondering whether you'd called me by that name out of tenderness or irony). I was convinced that this letter was going to summon me back to you and that our love would have proved stronger than your resolutions. But I was a bit disappointed : the letter dealt only with newspapers, with some position or other on *Paris-Journal* which you'd found for me. As I read it, I clearly saw that it was just a pretext for renewing contact. I sensed that it was not out of self-interest but out of consideration that you'd taken on some duty, still unrevealed, which was threatening our love – and that you were already in the process of weakening. But then I woke up . . .

It's quite crazy, while I'm so far away from you, to be recounting a dream to you in this fashion. But this one has been haunting me right through the morning. It's the first time I've had a dream in which you've been trying to break away from me. And if I describe it to you, it's partly to exorcise its power . . .

He went on to describe a visit to the regimental chaplain, who blessed a medallion for him which had the reputation of being able to deflect any bullets fired at the wearer, then, like many another soldier, he begged his beloved to let him have a picture of her and a daily letter to cheer his loneliness :

My darling, my girl, my lovely one, my fiancée, my love, when I'm quite overcome with yearning and with the sadness of no longer having you with me, I re-read your letters. In those blue pages, I rediscover all the confidence and all the ardour I require. I'm afraid that what you saw at Auch (the bungled speeches, the feebly-organised colour ceremony, the giggling troops, the whole barracks atmosphere) might have led you to doubt in the holy flame, our spirit of sacrifice, our sacred desire for victory. My love, you must not stop ardently believing in what we're doing. Just remember that we're on the march before the dawn, that we march for days on end without knowing the reason why, and consider all the patience, all the religious spirit we require to overcome the heart-break we feel at having lost all we love. Remember that perhaps we'll soon be lying in the trenches in water and cold and mud, under fire. You must say nothing to us, or think no thoughts which in any way threatens our faith or diminishes our strength. I look to you to supply all my strength, all my courage, all my daring, all my scorn for death . . .

Looking back over this letter, I seem to have spent the whole time lecturing you. Probably I've taken the advantage of having a sealed letter to say all the things I can't write on open cards. Ah! my love, if you know with what perfect faith, and what infinite abandon I've surrendered myself to you, you'll already have pardoned me.

Your child,
Henri.[10]

Four days after Fournier wrote this letter, and only three weeks after general mobilisation, Rivière was out of the war. On 24 August, his 220th Infantry Regiment was in action near Etain, in the forests of Lorraine. There was a violent skirmish in the darkness, Sergeant Rivière lost all contact with his section and after a terrifying night on his own in the forest, he was captured by the Germans and marched off across the border, herded into a railway truck with other captured French soldiers and, after a nightmare journey lasting four days, incarcerated in a prisoner-of-war camp at Koenigsbrük, in Saxony. Fournier naturally had no knowledge of these events when he wrote to his sister on 28 August to report that the sounds of battle were not too far distant :

> We've travelled a long way and done a great deal of marching. We're getting close. We're beginning to hear the cannons firing in the distance. 'Happy the ripe ears of corn', as Péguy says.[11] If anything should happen to me, you are the one I'm entrusting with the mission of going to rue Cassini, opening my box and my book-case, burning all that doesn't have to do with Simone and giving her the rest. I'm absolutely counting on you to do this for me. I'll write to you again on this subject because I think it'll be a little while yet before we go into action.
>
> I've passed through a village within 200 yards from the precise spot where Jacques was without being able to see him or even stop![12]

At about this same time, aware that he would soon be in action and concerned about the possible outcome, Fournier wrote in similar spirit to Marguerite Audoux on the subject of two letters he had written to her in 1913 about his meeting with Yvonne Brochet at Rochefort :

> I'm in the battle in the East of France. Anything might happen to me any day now.
>
> I hope very much to see you again in November. But, having thought it over, just as a precaution, I've decided that I ought now to send my kisses to you and to my sister.
>
> I also want you to carry out a small act of sacrifice for me : you'll give me great peace of mind if you destroy the letters I sent you last August about my journey to Rochefort. There must be no more talk of that now.
>
> There is now someone else I love more than anything else in the world. There must be no chance of these letters ever coming into her hands one day and making her think that there could ever have been any division or any restrictions in the immense

love I feel for her. I'm absolutely relying on you to get those letters burnt. All the rest are yours to keep. With great tenderness and in perfect friendship, I hold you now in a long, firm embrace, my kind, dear friend.[13]

By 3 September, Fournier had discovered that Rivière was missing. On that date, he wrote to Simone to report that he had at last managed to visit 'Rivière's' regiment, the 220th, but that he had hunted through the lines and billets for him in vain. Survivors of the disastrous action of the night of 24 August could only report that Rivière had not got out of the woods with them near Etain. Fournier could not conceal his profound concern :

He must have been wounded at Etain. Was he picked up by our side? Is he now in a military hospital somewhere? Have the Uhlans taken him prisoner? No-one knows . . .

I think there are grounds for hoping and believing he isn't dead, according to what I've discovered about the way that battle was fought and the way that many managed to get away. Perhaps he's linked up with some other unit, although I think they ought to have got him back to his own section by now. Ah! I shouldn't like to have died on a night like that. I pray that God didn't make him die that night . . .[14]

He could never have known the fate of his other great friend, Péguy, who was in the 276th Infantry Regiment which was fighting on a different sector of the by now thoroughly disorganised front : on 5 September, he was shot through the head and killed instantly while leading his men in an infantry charge. He was forty-one and had already written his own magnificent epitaph :

> Heureux ceux qui sont morts dans les grandes batailles
> Couchés dessus le sol à la face de Dieu.
> Heureux ceux qui sont morts sur un dernier haut lieu,
> Parmi tout l'appareil des grandes funérailles.

The death may have been heroic, but the setting was rather less so : Péguy's body was found face down in a field of beetroot.

The Fifth Prussian Army had managed to cross the Meuse on 30 August, and Fournier's regiment was regularly in action thereafter in an attempt to halt or turn the Germans' advance. On 6 September, when his unit was pulling back after an all-night action, Fournier was seen by Pierre Maury, who later became a Protestant pastor, and who recalled the encounter long after the war had ended :

It was about five in the morning, in a little wood to the west of Souilly. A hail of shrapnel had just spattered down near the group I was with. Some men were killed, others wounded. A captain who knew me well came across with a smile which he contrived to make sadly reproachful: 'Well, then, Maury, where's that God of yours in all this?' The question left me disconcerted and almost afraid. At that moment, a young lieutenant whose serious expression had previously struck me, came quietly over. He'd just got back from a night patrol, bullets had ripped his uniform, and you could feel he was in the grip of acute nervous tension. Yet he spoke very calmly and his words have remained for me the truest and most evangelical you can pronounce on the problem of suffering: 'I don't know exactly *where* God is in this war because none of us can solve the riddle of existence, but I know that I'll be shot down only when He wants, how He wants and where He wants.' It was Alain-Fournier.[15]

With the German armies threatening to break through at any moment and to sweep on into Paris, the French Government withdrew to Bordeaux where, as luck would have it, Isabelle Rivière and Simone Casimir-Perier had also decided to seek temporary refuge. Simone at once sought to exercise her not inconsiderable charisma by securing a personal interview with the notoriously susceptible Minister of Justice, Aristide Briand, and asking him to have Fournier transferred from the front-line infantry to some non-combatant unit away from immediate danger. She was immediately successful because although Fournier's final postcard to his sister, posted on 11 September, eventually arrived spattered with mud from the trenches, it announced that he had recently been transferred:

I'm getting your letters all right, my dear little Isabelle. Some of them reach me in the very thick of the fighting. I'm in excellent health. I hope to get closer to Jacques soon. I'm now attached to cavalry headquarters. I'm supremely confident in the outcome of this war. Pray to God for us all. And have faith. Long and tenderly, I enfold you and Jacqueline in my arms. Your brother

Henri.[16]

By 20 September 1914, however, apparently after chafing at having been detached from his men, Fournier was back with his infantry unit and now commanding the 23rd company as the battle raged on for the control of the Heights of the Meuse. He and his men were not in continuously violent action, but spent most of their time patrolling the dense plantations of beech trees on the steep slopes to the south-west of Etain, where Rivière had been captured a month previously. After spending the night of 22 September in the tiny hamlet of Vaux-les-Palameix, they received orders to take up a position along a track running through Saint-Rémy wood along the crest of the hill. A preliminary reconnaissance had established that the area was un-occupied and Fournier's company pressed slowly forward through thick early morning mist and steady rain. Fournier's immediate superior, the choleric Captain Grammont, apparently had one straightforward military objective which he pursued with fanatical insistence : it was to locate the Germans and then attack and kill as many as possible. The first part of this objective was all too readily achieved, though not quite in the circumstances even Grammont would have considered desirable. The French reconnaissance patrol had not probed deeply enough on its earlier sortie : Fournier's company had moved forward through a gap between two German positions and was proceeding to operate not in no-man's land, but behind the enemy lines. When a fusillade of shots rang out *behind* them, Grammont's instinctive response was to order his men to fix bayonets and charge – but to charge where? Shots were by now coming from all directions, bodies beginning to fall, and the whole action ended in the half-light between the trees in panic and total confusion. A handful of survivors somehow managed to thread their way back to the French lines but Fournier was not amongst them.

The battle for the Meuse Heights raged on till 26 September at which date, trenches were dug by both sides, and the opposing lines of barbed wire strung out from the North Sea to Switzerland, where they remained more or less fixed for a further four years. The position where Fournier presumably fell, and was conceivably promptly buried, was intermittently blasted by shot and shell throughout this period and no trace of him was ever afterwards found.

During the war and immediately afterwards, his relatives, who would not readily accept that further hope was futile, cross-examined the handful of survivors who escaped from the wood; some were later taken prisoner by the Germans and could not be closely questioned until the war was over. The accounts were tantalisingly conflicting : a stretcher-bearer reported that he returned to the scene of the ambush next day, and came across the corpses of five or six soldiers, but that there was no French officer's body amongst them; another witness swore he saw a wounded French officer being carried away on a stretcher and that he glimpsed an ambulance waiting behind the trees (like Ganache's gipsy caravan in the grounds of the Lost Domain waiting to receive the wounded Frantz); one survivor testified that Fournier ran forward waving his pistol, shouting 'Vive la France!' and was shot in the chest, while another reported no less confidently that he died instantly and silently, shot through the head.[17]

The final official verdict was that Lieutenant Fournier was killed in action on 22 September 1914.

He was not, of course, by any means the only soldier to vanish without trace in the First World War, but it is singularly appropriate that the creator of *Le Grand Meaulnes* should have no known grave, disappearing, like his hero, at the end of his story, leaving no trace and leaving so many questions unanswered about his ultimate destiny. It is no less appropriate that he should have vanished at the time that he did because one of the principal themes of *Le Grand Meaulnes* is the elusiveness and the fickleness of happiness, never accessible when it is most desperately needed. It would be vain to speculate how durable Fournier's happiness would eventually have proved had he survived the war, but one can be certain that after searching so long and so unavailingly for happiness throughout his life, he finally went to his death convinced that at last he had found it.

9

Aftermath

1914 and after

What thou lovest well remains, the rest is dross
What thou lov'st well shall not be reft from thee
What thou lov'st well is thy true heritage
Whose world, or mine or theirs or is it of none?
First came the seen, then thus the palpable
    Elysium, though it were in the halls of hell,
What thou lovest well is thy true heritage.

Ezra Pound : *Homage to Sextus Propertius*
From Canto LXXXI

I

Though the passage of Time has left its inevitable mark upon them, the rural settings where Fournier spent his most formative years have not been wholly transformed : flowers no longer adorn the school-house or the front-doorways of Epineuil but the village and the banks of the Cher are essentially still unspoilt; the peace of La Chapelle-d'Angillon has been irretrievably shattered by the motor-car, but away from the thunderous *route nationale* which bisects the village, quiet lanes lead away into the Berry countryside which is as secretive and peaceful as ever; the château of Loroy has long since been re-occupied and restored, and its grounds and pool domesticated, but the slim spire of the ruined abbey beside it still rises above the fir woods like a finger up-raised for silence; a vast radio telescope now tilts its great bowl towards the sky beside Nançay yet all around lie the brooding heathlands of Sologne, its mood of desolation still as dominant today as when it mirrored Fournier's melancholy at the end of his summer holidays. Changes there have been in each of these scenes but Fournier could recognise them still.

All but one of the supporting actors in the drama of Fournier's life are now dead. The conclusion of their life-stories is worth recounting because each of them is not lacking in its own drama or pathos; indeed one is tempted to say of the survivors what Seurel said of Meaulnes after his last departure:

> everything, for ever afterwards, in (their) memory was troubled and transformed by the presence of the one who had such an effect on all (their) lives and who left no peace behind him even after he had taken flight.

Rivière died on 14 February 1925, struck down suddenly by typhoid fever which his prisoner-of-war experiences had left him too enfeebled to resist for long. He had felt a sense of acute personal humiliation at being captured so soon in the war and became obsessed by the desire to escape back to France. His first real chance to do so came when he was transferred from the Koenigsbrück Camp in Saxony to Hülsberg Camp in Hanover, and he managed to get away with a companion. He was recaptured forty miles from the Dutch border and savagely beaten up. Two days after being taken back to the prison camp, he and his companion were awakened in their solitary cells at midnight by the commandant, marched to the perimeter fence, and placed against it while four guards took up their positions in front of them with rifles at the ready. It turned out eventually not to be the preliminaries to their execution but a technique for persuading them to divulge their escape-route.

In July 1916, Rivière was found guilty of helping a Russian prisoner to escape and sentenced to twenty-five days' solitary confinement, with a small allowance of soup only every four days. He had never been the most robust of men and now began to suffer chronically from insomnia, anaemia, fevers and general debility. He was finally examined by a panel of Swiss doctors set up by the Red Cross to examine prisoners seeking to be interned in Switzerland on medical grounds, and though he was recognised as being in this category, he was not finally transferred to Engleberg until June 1917. There he was joined by his wife and daughter, who stayed with him for the duration of the war, and there he was visited by André Gide and Jacques Copeau, who offered him the editorship of the *Nouvelle Revue Française* which he took over in 1919 when he was finally repatriated.

Throughout the period of his captivity and his convalescence, Rivière continued to brood and to write. He composed an apologia for Christianity (*A la trace de Dieu*), the first version of the novel based on his platonic love-affair in the months before the war (*Aimée*), a remarkably magnanimous and acutely perceptive study of the German character (*L'Allemand*), and a journal in which he recorded his changing moods and persistent preoccupations. He became convinced that he had somehow betrayed Fournier in his hour of greatest need and wrote on 7 November 1914:

> The bitterness he displayed, the insistent demands he sometimes used to make, were due to the fact that he had a much deeper need of me than had any of my other friends. There was always a sense of urgency when he sought me out. He wouldn't countenance any delay: his whole life was at stake. And the jealousy he felt for others was rooted in the belief that they were stealing from him something *they didn't need in the way he did*. That's the complete justification and explanation of his mode of conduct. The fault is mine completely.
>
> I believe very firmly that there's such a thing as mystical responsibility. In Henri's destiny, as in everyone else's, there was a single crucial moment, a point when it could have turned to good if he'd been given the help, the little bit of support he needed. And I was the one who could have given it to him. And I didn't know how to. I literally withdrew. I took away what he needed most to draw on: myself.
>
> And yet, no, I'm not completely guilty. Something else entered into our friendship, something defective, a certain ill-fortune, something which made all our plans miscarry, something for which neither of us was to blame, which bore a closer resemblance to his destiny than to mine. This is what weighed down on me and bound my arms and made me invent all sorts of grounds for complaint. Something quite extraordinary, something beyond my own power to control impelled me to deny the help I could have given him. I made myself twenty times more available to twenty other people who weren't worthy of him, and who were much less dear to me than he was. I made myself much more unjust to him that I was naturally capable of being. Something sterner and crueller than me was reacting through me against him.[1]

And just as Fournier was obsessed for years by Yvonne de Quiévrecourt's chilling reminder of reality, *à quoi bon*, so Rivière was haunted by the vision of his final sight of Fournier in July 1914, driving away from the Bordeaux hotel with Simone after that disastrous lunch. He wrote in his war-time diary on 9 November 1914:

Dreadful despair at the memory of our last encounter, so false, so forced, so broken-up with interruptions. None of the things around us, none of the things we said belonged to us. And that departure, with that bit of absent-mindedness at the last minute! That woman![2]

He returned to this theme on 3 January 1915 :

I keep on seeing Place Richelieu in Bordeaux with Isabelle and I going across it, heading towards the Hotel de France where Simone had invited us. It's in this form that Henri's memory keeps coming back to torture me.

How typical that that horrible meeting should have turned out to be the final one! How characteristic of our whole story, our story in which bad luck decided to take such a hand! How well it summed up all our irritation and all our misunderstandings! These all seemed to be embodied in that woman who was there between us.[3]

From 1919 on, Rivière worked ceaselessly and selflessly as editor of *La Nouvelle Revue Française* over what is generally conceded as the golden age of its life, and he devoted himself with characteristic fervour and *finesse* to championing the cause of his last great literary idol, the still misunderstood and unappreciated Marcel Proust.

When death came for Rivière, it came so suddenly and so brutally, that one is tempted once more to subscribe to Fournier's view that theirs was a generation doomed to be short-lived. Madame Rivière afterwards softened the picture of her husband on his death-bed by touches suggesting that his end was somehow welcomed as a merciful release, and at different times, she ascribed to him two distinct death-bed utterances which contributed to this effect : 'Now I'm miraculously saved!' or, alternatively, 'Henri, I'm coming!' That these words were actually spoken was not denied by another witness of his dying moments, but he recalled later utterances and a grimmer reality; this witness was Jacques Copeau, a very close friend of the Rivières and, by now, himself a fervent Catholic. The last words Copeau heard Rivière speak came when he was desperately fighting for breath, and they were 'It's too terrible what's happening to me, understand? The end of my life . . . Oh! the end of my life . . . my life . . . my life . . . my life.'[4] Three times his breathing stopped altogether and three times he was revived. Another friend who saw him after he had finally died said 'He looked as though he had been assassinated.' He was buried on the hill beside his beloved aunts' garden at Cenon looking out to Bordeaux and the sea. He was thirty-eight.

Fournier's mother died peacefully on 12 June 1928, unreconciled to the death of her son, and still persuaded that Fate had all along meant her to be singled out for exemplary misfortune. In January 1916, she sent a New Year's card to Péguy's widow, thanking her for a greetings-card she had recently received; it was, she said, 'a precious and painful reminder of the happy time when her son set off, at the side of his great friend Péguy, on their pilgrimage to that beautiful cathedral, and came back radiant with faith and hope. Ah! why wasn't Notre Dame de Chartres able to protect them?'[5] In August 1919, in the midst of the painfully protracted law-suit mounted by Simone Casimir-Perier to retrieve Fournier's papers from Isabelle Rivière, she concluded a farewell letter to Simone with the words:

> I'm in great distress because I know that from this time on, we shall never see one another again. But there have been a great many times latterly when I've realised you were lost to me . . .
> Au revoir, my dear Simone. Since I've lost Henri, I'm resigned to everything. I know that whatever I do, ill fortune will always make a point of conspiring against me and that I shall always be crushed.[6]

A major source of Madame Fournier's unhappiness in her declining years was the erratic behaviour of her husband and this, in turn, can be attributed in no small measure to concern for their missing son. It was to preserve a united family that Monsieur Fournier transported himself, his wife and his belongings from La Chapelle to Paris in February 1908. The price he paid turned out, in emotional terms, to be rather more than he could afford. Till that time, he had lived all his life in the countryside, he had adored his flower-garden and his fishing, and he never found an adequate substitute in the suburbs of Paris: the long daily journey to school by crowded bus and *métro* became a daily torment to him. The disappearance in action of his son finally brought matters to a head, and he himself disappeared from the family circle for years afterwards, to live an obscure and lonely life in a succession of boarding-houses. He returned, repentant, to the family home in 1928, threatened to leave again in an upsurge of his ingrained school-teacher's anti-clerical antagonism when his grand-daughter became a nun in 1929, but he stayed on in his daughter's home where he died peacefully in his sleep on 22 January 1933. He was seventy-two.

Marguerite Audoux, Fournier's devoted friend and gentle confidante, died on 1 February 1937, and, according to her biographer, Georges Reyer, Fournier's was the last name she uttered before her death.[7] Jacqueline Rivière, Fournier's god-daughter, thoughts of whom regularly cheered him in his blacker moments before the war, died in her Benedictine convent in Dourgne, in the south of France, on 17 December 1944. She had suffered from a long-standing heart condition and was just thirty-three.

Yvonne Brochet (née Quiévrecourt) died on 29 December 1964. In the course of the half-century by which she survived Fournier, she dutifully accompanied her naval officer husband on his various postings to Brest, Lorient, Bordeaux and the Ile d'Indret, near Nantes, and she kept up her two flats in Versailles and in central Paris. She and her close relatives made a very deliberate point of shunning all publicity, and all Fournier's biographers respected her wish for seclusion by not divulging her real name until after her death. In most studies of Fournier which were published before that date, she was regularly given the same name as the fictitious heroine whose portrait she inspired, 'Yvonne de Galais'. On the subject of names, one curious fact has come to light about her which may or may not be of particular significance: she came to dislike her husband's surname – 'Brochet' simply means 'pike' – and she preferred instead to be called 'Madame de Vaugrigneuse' which, as well as being the name of one of Maupassant's heroines, was also the name of her husband's maternal grandmother. In 1939, while thanking Isabelle Rivière for a presentation copy of *Images d'Alain-Fournier*, she revealed that Fournier had not been forgotten:

I know that your *Images* will bring me much emotion. I already greatly love the first few pages which I cut yesterday evening. Nobody has been closer than you and your dear husband to the exceptionally delicate nature of your brother.

How can I thank you for the gift of this book with so precious a dedication? I cannot find the words to express it, but you will be able to find words to complete them from your heart which is so close to the heart of *Le Grand Meaulnes*!

I've several times thought of coming to see you but I haven't dared to do so and then . . . you would have been disappointed. Far better for me to remain within the aura within which your brother enclosed me, and which was fashioned by him and his dreaming.

Perhaps you may meet my daughter one day: she would interest you, I think, and you would like her. Alain-Fournier is a god for her. My son shares his sister's admiration.'[8]

Yvonne Brochet's husband, Captain Brochet died in the military hospital of Val-de-Grâce on 25 March 1953 : he had known from the outset the identity of the real-life heroine of Yvonne de Galais, and he himself made a point of recounting the background to his daughter on her fourteenth birthday. Like Jacqueline Rivière and Alain Rivière, she entered Holy Orders, and for many years now, she has lived in a convent in Rome. The son, who became a Lieutenant-Colonel in the French infantry, was killed in Algeria on 15 April 1957. Yvonne Brochet herself went into a decline shortly after this, and for the last years of her life, lost the use of her memory and her faculties. She died peacefully, indifferent to everybody and everything around her, in the hospital of Notre-Dame-du-Perpétual-Secours at Levallois, and was buried beside her husband and her son in the Père-Lachaise cemetery, close by Fournier's first Paris home. She was seventy-nine.

Isabelle Rivière died on 18 June 1971. After the death of her husband, she became a novelist in her own right, her auto- biographical *Bouquet de roses rouges* being awarded a special prize by the Académie Française, but she devoted by far the greatest part of her time and energy to defending the reputation of her brother. She did this principally by editing his letters to herself and her parents, his letters to René Bichet and the correspondence between him and her husband. She kept careful care of all Fournier's other papers in her house in Dourgne, where she was as open-hearted and open-handed to admirers of her brother as she was bitter and im- placable towards those she considered to be his enemies and detractors. She produced two invaluable volumes of reminiscences about her brother, *Images d'Alain-Fournier*, which was first published in 1938, and *Vie et Passion d'Alain-Fournier*, which came out a quarter of a century later. It is a much vaster worker than the *Images*, quite different in tone and character. The chief reason for this was not unconnected with the publication, in 1957, of Simone's volume of memoirs, *Sous de nouveaux soleils*, in which, for the first time, she made public her liaison with Fournier in the last fifteen months of his life.

The Rivières were resentful towards Simone Casimir-Perier almost from the outset, and this resentment was considerably increased when *La Nouvelle Revue Française* was denied the book-publishing rights of *Le Grand Meaulnes*; it was intensified still further as a result of that unfortunate final luncheon party in July 1914 : the quotations from Rivière's war-time journals give some indication of how deeply the iron had gone into his soul. Open hostility was made manifest in 1919 when Simone brought her action to secure possession of all Fournier's manuscripts, judgment eventually going to Isabelle Rivière, and for more than sixty years afterwards, peace was never once

declared between the parties. All references to Simone were meticulously excised from the volumes of Fournier's letters edited by
Madame Rivière and for decades, the last love of his life was referred
to only by a Kafkaesque initial.

When hostilities were actively resumed in the middle of the 1950s,
each party employed a stalking-horse before engaging in open war-
fare. The first shots were fired for Simone by the critic Clément
Borgal, in a series of review-articles and a monograph:[9] the theme
he adumbrated, which Simone herself later filled out in her memoirs,
was that she was the one true love of his life who would have brought
him enduring happiness. Ever since, French gossip-columnists have
tended to adopt the practice of referring to her as 'la fiancée d'Alain-
Fournier' or even as 'la fiancée du Grand Meaulnes'.

The first riposte from the opposing faction came not from Madame
Rivière herself but from another of Fournier's biographers, Jean-
Marie Delettrez, who promptly produced a pamphlet entitled
Quelques rectifications aux souvenirs de Simone,[10] in which he demonstrated that virtually every statement of fact in the memoirs which
could be independently verified was patently inaccurate. Madame
Rivière's much more massive counter-attack came in 1963, and
largely consisted of substituting for the picture of Fournier as a
chevalier sans peur et sans reproche, as represented in her earlier
Images, the portrait of an idealistic but compulsive womaniser, able
to resist everything except sexual temptation. The strategy, presumably, was to demonstrate that Simone was not the first 'real' and
fully consummated love of his life, but merely the latest in a series
of conquests, and the tactics took the form of copious quotations from
letters and journals previously kept well hidden. Simone's reaction to
this was the publication, in the following year, in Le Figaro Littéraire,
of seven of Fournier's letters to her, coupled with the announcement
that the remainder of his letters to her had been deposited in the
Bibliothèque Nationale. At the time of writing, in the autumn of 1973,
there the matter rests, with Madame Simone, by now a widow twice
over,[11] and an established novelist in her own right, still formidably
active in her mid-nineties.

To do full justice to the spectacle of mutual antipathy sustained
at such a pitch, over such a period of time, would require the pen
of a Balzac or a Mauriac, and hubristic would be the mere biographer
who attempted to do so. Rash too would be the biographer who
tried to adjudicate definitively between Guelphs and Ghibellines,
although it must appear evident to any fair-minded independent
observer that each party to the dispute is open to the charge of
misrepresentation, distortion and omission: Fournier's earlier love for

Yvonne de Quiévrecourt cannot be explained away as literary calf-love, and though the course of his love for Simone exhibits disturbing similarities to his love for Jeanne Bruneau, it cannot be dismissed as a mere *passade*. On the vexed question of whether the last love of his short life would ultimately have matured into a relationship as permanent as human relationships ever can be, the only feasible verdict must surely be 'not proven' : there are just too many imponderables. All that one can usefully conclude is that Fournier must have had some truly exceptional qualities of character to have inspired such exemplary devotion in two such formidable, and formidably opposed, champions.

It was not, however, because of his own divided loyalties, or because of the single-minded loyalty he could inspire in others, that Fournier's name was inscribed in the Pantheon, or the lycée of Bourges retitled in his honour in 1937 :[12] it was because he was the author of *Le Grand Meaulnes* and, in conclusion, the posthumous fortune of his one completed novel is what we must now briefly consider.

II

It was only after Fournier's death that *Le Grand Meaulnes* started to win the vast public following that he had hoped for in his lifetime. The beginnings were modest enough, with the award of a small literary prize, the Prix Académique Davaine, in 1917, but in the 1920s and 1930s its fame spread widely and spectacularly both in France and abroad. Edition after edition has since been sold, often in the most lavish of formats. It has been translated into thirty-three different languages; it has been the subject of theses for higher degrees in such diverse universities as Montpellier, Neuchâtel, Brussels, Hamburg, Paris, London, Cambridge, Indiana and Melbourne; it has been turned into a ballet, now in the repertoire of the Royal Ballet Company of Sadler's Wells;[13] it has been adapted as a radio play for the BBC and several times rebroadcast;[14] it has been made into a commercially successful film;[15] it has received the ultimate apotheosis of being made a prescribed text on a wide range of 'A' level and University syllabuses. It is, in other words, a 'classic' and its reputation would now seem thoroughly secure amongst that group of novels the French seem to have made peculiarly their own, the *roman personnel*, each deeply rooted in the author's own experience and each named after the central character : *René, Adolphe, Sylvie* and, Fournier's own personal favourite, *Dominique*.

Quite how much the reputation of *Le Grand Meaulnes* owes to extra-literary considerations would be difficult to establish with accuracy. Undoubtedly, part of the success it achieved in the France of the 1920s must have been due to the by then mythical figure of Fournier himself, the French equivalent of Rupert Brooke – or, in a later age, of Sidney Keyes, Richard Hillary, Keith Douglas or Alun Lewis – the young writer of genius struck down in his prime with most of his promise unfulfilled. The atmosphere of the 1920s in France, as elsewhere in war-ravaged Europe, put escapism at a premium, as a French observer perceptively noted in 1931 :

I believe the men of our time have clung to their adolescence for much longer than those of previous generations. I blame the war for this. It meant a violent break in the normal evolution of our generation. It imposed an abrupt and violent maturity on us which left us nostalgic for our adolescence and, once we'd escaped from the nightmare, we felt the need to find our youth again, to link up with our past, to complete our inner development. We grew up too soon, before our adolescence was really over, and the whole of our post-war literature bears the mark of this disruption . . . The whole of our post-war literary output is marked by a two-fold preoccupation with adolescence : on the one hand, the cult of adolescence, of one's own personal adolescence, and on the other, the need to be rid of it in order to obtain a more thorough knowledge of the world and a philosophy of life which will be less disturbed and less opaque.[16]

For the many readers of this persuasion, *Le Grand Meaulnes* could not have been more welcome because it was – and remains still – the most delicate rendering so far achieved in literature of the romantic adolescent consciousness : with the enchanted Lost Domain to escape to in the opening part of the novel, and a highly idealistic set of moral values propounded throughout, it could not fail to win over a vast reading public appalled or bemused by the restlessness of their shell-shocked era. The 'escapist' element and the noble moral values have since combined to make it an irresistibly 'safe' and at the same time, thoroughly enjoyable set-book for senior schoolchildren right to the present.

To concede all this, however, is not the whole explanation of the success *Le Grand Meaulnes* has achieved : for a variety of further reasons, it has won the lasting affection of a considerable number of more sophisticated readers too, and for every hostile critic like the American Donald Schier, who found in it 'only one half-pennyworth of tawdry adventure to an intolerable deal of saccharine',[17] there have been innumerably more, like Havelock Ellis, who would reply, pityingly, 'there are people to whom it seems a simple and insignificant story, just as there are people who inhale in vain the most exquisite fragrance of flowers, or . . . find trivial the music of Mozart'.[18]

There are qualities intrinsic to *Le Grand Meaulnes* itself which account for its abiding success rather more adequately and more plausibly than any sociological analysis of its various readers, and over the years, these have attracted the attention of a wide range of scholars and critics. The work they have produced varies considerably in quality and scope. Some, which seemed worthy and workmanlike in their time, like the studies of Fernand Desonay,[19] Walter Jöhr,[20] and Jean-Marie Delettrez,[21] now seem rather pedestrian. Others are notable for a *parti-pris* which would seem either to have blinded the authors to certain basic facts or to have read words into *Le Grand Meaulnes* which simply are not there: thus, although no novel can ever have been more deliberately composed than *Le Grand Meaulnes*, it was hailed by Christian Dédéyan as a precursor of Surrealism,[22] and although neither God, Christ nor the Virgin Mary is mentioned from the beginning of the novel till its end, *Le Grand Meaulnes* has been represented as an apologia for Catholicism by such critics as Albert Léonard,[23] Aimé Becker[24] and Michel Suffran.[25] Analysis of the claims they advance for annexing *Le Grand Meaulnes* to their particular faith will readily establish that they lean far too heavily on the religious allusions Fournier made in his letters while he was planning *Le Jour des Noces*, the schema he abandoned in 1910; students seeking prime examples of the 'intentionalist fallacy' in literary studies need look no further than the works of these critics.

Although in the fifty years after his death Fournier won the fame which eluded him in life, he was, with only a few exceptions, little better served by his critics throughout this period than he was at the time of the Prix Goncourt campaign: for too often critics singled out the dream-like qualities of the first part of the novel and ignored or wrote off the rest. André Gide, for example, in his Journal,[26] reported a sense of disappointment when he finally got round to reading *Le Grand Meaulnes* in 1931, but praised the 'irrecapturable freshness' of the first part; Denis Saurat declared that 'all who are wistfully inclined should be loyal to *Le Grand Meaulnes*, at least for fifty pages, which may be transmitted down literary anthologies', but while praising its 'grand start' deprecated its 'rather floundering to an unfortunate ending.'[27] This same deplorable inclination to fragment the novel has nowhere been more pointedly illustrated than in Britain where since 1931, a well-known publishing house has been marketing

285

the Part One of *Le Grand Meaulnes* only,[28] as a text for, presumably, junior schoolchildren. One awaits wtih interest and no little impatience, their edition of *Madame Bovary* (reduced to the natural descriptions only) or of *Les Liaisons dangereuses* (confined, of course, to the beginnings and the endings of the letters).

One can readily understand why Part One of *Le Grand Meaulnes* has been singled out for particular praise because it is here that Fournier's narrative technique is most exquisitely effective. The reader's attention is caught and held with the quite masterly opening chapter which sets the scene with admirable economy of means and, with its clear suggestions of the disruptive effects of Meaulnes' arrival, hints powerfully at the momentous events still to come. Suspense is sustained by the deft building up of atmosphere and by the employing of a narrator who is himself involved in the action and is not, therefore, omniscient. Although, from the very outset, Seurel at once establishes that he is recording events years after they have happened and is all along aware of the final outcome, he re-creates events in the order and manner in which he originally perceived them. The reader is, therefore, made to see through Seurel's eyes, Meaulnes' riding off in the farmer's cart, 'standing up, with one foot on the front rim of the wagon, like a Roman charioteer', the return of the empty cart some hours later, 'like a piece of wreckage washed up by the high seas', the return of Meaulnes after three days' absence, with straw on his clothes 'and, above all, the appearance he presented, of a traveller who was exhausted, famished yet lost in wonder', the old-fashioned silk waistcoat with its mother-of-pearl buttons and Meaulnes, restlessly pacing up and down in the small hours, through the shadowy attics above the school house, 'on the borders of that mysterious land where once already he had taken flight'. Only after the reader's expectations have been thoroughly aroused, does Fournier at last condescend to reveal where Meaulnes has been and once again, he recounts events from the most dramatic of viewpoints, though this time, in the third person, through the wondering eyes of Meaulnes. With no conscious straining after effect but instead, by the notation of precise concrete detail appealing either to the visual or the auditory imagination, Fournier involves the reader in Meaulnes' adventure, enables him to share his initial discomfiture at losing his way as night falls over the lonely, wintry countryside, then the two moments of premonition when he savours the foretaste of inexplicable happiness to come, and finally *la fête étrange* itself, into which he literally stumbles, yet where he seems to be a welcome guest.

The dream-like atmosphere of the party is largely created by rapidly juxtaposing scenes which are realistic enough in themselves but seem to have no connection with one another : a fat man bearing a pole hung with festive lanterns declares that Wellington was an American; a fifteen-year-old boy dressed like a pupil from an English public school, struts past on tip-toe; girls skip by and pirouette in a mist of lace; very old men and women sit talking calmly at a long dining-table; a long-sleeved Pierrot gallops down seemingly endless corridors; children watch a magic lantern show; a fair-haired girl quietly plays her piano while little children perch themselves on Meaulnes' knee and the following morning, on a day stolen from Spring, the loveliest girl he has ever seen promises that she will wait for him to return.

It is easy to appreciate why all of this should have captivated so many readers : it is exquisitely fashioned, our world is starved of magic, and this is high romance in the spirit of *Thomas the Rhymer* or *La Belle dame sans merci*, of what Coleridge captured in *Kubla Khan* or in this less well-known passage from his *Anima Poetae* : 'If a man could pass through Paradise in a dream and have a flower presented to him as a pledge that his soul had really been there, and if he found the flower in his hand when he awoke – Ay! and what then?'

'What then?' indeed : mutilators of the text of *Le Grand Meaulnes* would do well to ponder, because Fournier's aura of enchantment is not left undisturbed. Frantz de Galais makes his petulant entrance, in an atmosphere of gloom and storm, and peremptorily decrees that the party must end. From this point on, the party is taken over by tipsy adults and 'in the park, which for two days, had been full of so much grace and so much wonder, this marked the beginning of the disruption and the desolation.' Meaulnes hears snatches of two folk songs on the stormy night air : the first clearly hints of licentiousness

> D'où donc que tu reviens, petite libertine?
> Ton bonnet est déchiré
> Tu es bien mal coiffé

while the refrain of the second is a farewell to love

> Mes souliers sont rouges . . .
> Adieu, mes amours . . .
> Mes souliers sont rouges . . .
> Adieu, sans retour!

That re-iterated message of finality in the second song is, though

Meaulnes does not appreciate it at the time, directly applicable to him : the party is indeed at an end, for him, and the gaily-coloured lanterns will never be lit for him again.

In bestowing the most enthusiastic of their praises upon this first part of *Le Grand Meaulnes*, Fournier's critics are committing the error of which he wrongfully accused Péguy in July 1913 : isolating the magic and ignoring the tragic qualities of the novel. In fact, Fournier created the enchanted world of Part One of *Le Grand Meaulnes* only in order to destroy it utterly in Part Three, and this point is hammered home with an insistence one would have thought should have been obvious when, after years of hopeless searching, Meaulnes at last rediscovers the Lost Domain. A grand picnic is organised, with the express purpose of reuniting him with Yvonne de Galais, and, without mounting bitterness, Meaulnes proceeds to call the roll of all his most cherished memories of the fancy dress party that has never ceased to haunt his dreams. Change and decay is all around : the old manor house has been demolished, the lake has been filled in, the yacht on which he sailed with Yvonne has been sold to pay off family debts, the romantic bric-à-brac of his bedroom has been thrown away; he pretends not to notice that some of the children who once danced so delightfully, now grown older, are viciously ill-treating a donkey; he now knows that the Pierrot, whom those children pursued down the passage-ways, is a vagabond and petty thief. Of the *fête étrange*, only one mocking vestige remains, the least looked for yet the most appropriate :

> Mes souliers sont rouges . . .
> Adieu, mes amours . . .
> Mes souliers sont rouges . . .
> Adieu, sans retour !

Meaulnes lifted his head and listened. It was merely one of the airs sung by the loitering peasants at the Domain without a name on the last night of the party, when everything was already in ruins . . . One last vestige – the most miserable at that – of those lovely days which could never come again . . .'

There is, of course, *one* other vestige, the lovely figure of Yvonne de Galais herself, but Meaulnes is profoundly ill at ease in her presence. He is only too well aware that he has forfeited whatever rights he may ever have had to the lost domain : when he first woke up at the *fête étrange*, it was to find his bedroom 'lit up by green lanterns'; now, he has seen lights of another colour and with another significance in the back streets of Bourges ('here and there, to indicate a bawdy house, a red light was burning') – and it is to this world, frequented by army officers who boast of their extra-marital adventures as they swill their liquor, that he believes he has consigned Valentine – in whose honour the original party was staged. If the theme of Part One of the novel is the Earthly Paradise, the theme of Part Three is no less certainly Paradise Lost, and it is entirely consistent with this theme that Meaulnes should approach his wedding so full of guilt and foreboding and that Yvonne de Galais, like every other vestige of the first enchanted party, should finally be destroyed. In the light of this, it simply passes all credence that critics could ever have labelled *Le Grand Meaulnes* a *conte bleu* to reassure 'the wistfully inclined', or have stated, like Miss Janet Adam Smith, for example, that 'for all Yvonne's death and Seurel's desolation, *Le Grand Meaulnes* is not a tragic book at all'.[29]

The transition between the enchantments of Part One of the novel and the desolation of Part Two is effected by a section in which the dominant note is frustration. Meaulnes tries repeatedly to find his way back to the Lost Domain, all his efforts are thwarted, and when he finally leaves, with heavy heart, for Paris, his defeat is emphatically underlined by images of gloom and depression : rain falls remorselessly out of leaden skies, a funeral procession is held up at the village cross-roads, the coffin rests on the very spot scorched by the last fire of the wandering players, one of whom is Frantz de Galais, and over everything hangs the mingled odours of washing being dried indoors beside the fire, and food spilt and scorching on an over-hot stove. In this section of *Le Grand Meaulnes*, as indeed throughout the whole novel and his earlier stories and poems, Fournier's great artistic strength is in his ability to convey mood through the selection of telling evocative detail. He is rather less impressive in analysing motivation and in working out the mechanics of his plot.

The first point in the novel where most readers begin to experience difficulty in suspending their disbelief is in Part Two, back in the everyday world of the village school of Sainte-Agathe after the discovery and the loss of the Domain without a Name in which they are normally perfectly ready to believe. Why, most readers ask – if not as they read, then certainly as they reflect afterwards – why does Meaulnes take so long to recognise Frantz de Galais once he has become a temporary fellow-pupil? Admittedly, his only previous sight of Frantz was of his candlelit profile in an extremely dark room, and for most of his stay at Sainte-Agathe, Frantz's head and the whole of one side of his face are swathed in heavy bandage, but Meaulnes, who is said to be obsessed with the need to find his way back to the mysterious domain, reacts with unconscionable slowness to the hints Frantz regularly and heavily drops about his true identity. His suspicions do not seem to be aroused when Frantz volunteers the information that he too was a guest at the *fête étrange*, or that he tried to commit suicide three months previously (that is, at the precise time of the *fête* which finally ended with the sound of a revolver shot and the fleeting glimpse of a terrified Pierrot carrying a limp body), even when, for good measure, he commented 'I've abandoned everything. Now for me, there's no more father, no more sister, no more house, no more love . . .' Even at this, Meaulnes does not begin to suspect, neither does he recognise the unbandaged Ganache whose features made such a vivid impression on him in the Wellington Room at the château. It is only some days later, when Frantz finally removes his bandage and stands before him in almost the same lighting conditions as at the first encounter, that Meaulnes cries out 'Look at the gipsy! Look! *At last* I've recognised who he is!' That 'at last' will have been echoed by many a reader.

It is possible to explain away Meaulnes' curious obtuseness by taking into account such contrivances as the thick bandage which so effectively conceals most of Frantz's features or Frantz's remarkable elusiveness which, for various not implausible reasons, keeps him for most of the time out of Meaulnes' company, but for the author to have to rely so heavily on accidents and external trappings to advance his plot would be a major technical weakness. In fact, there is a perfectly plausible explanation for Meaulnes' slow reactions, and this is that in spite of all his protestations, he does not, even at this early stage, really want to return to the Lost Domain. The readiness with which he more than once allows Seurel to dissuade him from setting out in search of Yvonne, and his barely credible lack of insistence on speaking there and then with Frantz as soon as he has discovered his true identity, strongly suggest that he really prefers his *princesse* to be *lointaine* and the prolongation of desire to its fulfilment. It could well be that like Saint-Exupéry, who in a later context, sadly recognised that he could not recapture his lost childhood Eden, he has realised that 'One can never again re-enter that infinite world, because it is the *party* and not the park that one would have to reconstitute'.[30] The reader's difficulty is that none of this is made explicit in the novel itself: it all has to be inferred, and not every reader is willing or able to take the trouble to do so.

The second major point of difficulty and controversy in the novel concerns the reasons for Meaulnes' reluctance to meet Yvonne again once the lost domain has been found, and his abrupt departure the day after his wedding. His motives for hesitating have now changed : whereas in Part Two, he made ineffectual efforts to rediscover the Domain largely because of his fear of being disappointed, now in Part Three, he is wholly inhibited by his guilty conscience. It is in his handling of this section of the novel that Fournier's technical immaturity is most manifest, and it is hard to resist the conclusion that material which was potentially rich in human and dramatic interest has not been exploited to the maximum advantage.

It is surely a major error in dramatic timing to provide the explanation for Meaulnes' bizarre past behaviour with the time-worn device of a secret journal which, in this instance, is brought to light *after* the tragic dénouement, and here the pernicious example of *La Porte etroité* must very likely be taken into account. Part Three of the novel would have been immeasurably more poignant had the reader known earlier the agonising nature of Meaulnes' predicament, the conflict between his love for the down-to-earth and devoted Valentine and his failing fidelity to the inaccessibly dream-like Yvonne and, later, between the temptation to accept the unhoped-of chance to marry the miraculously rediscovered Yvonne and the need to redeem his pledge to Frantz and retrieve Valentine from a life of shame. The nature of Meaulnes' relationship with Valentine was transformed, by successive revisions in Fournier's drafts, from the frankly carnal to the purely platonic, with the result that, in the version of the novel that was finally published, his transgression is spiritual rather than physical : he no longer feels worthy of Yvonne de Galais not because he has been sexually disloyal, but because he has lost faith in his dream. The reader is asked to accept that merely to have formed a close but innocent relationship with a woman other than Yvonne is sufficient to account for his bitterness and his sense of contamination; as he says despairingly to Seurel :

I'm sure now that when I discovered the Domain without a Name, I was at some peak of perfection and purity which I shall never again attain. Only in death, as I once wrote to you, can I expect to recapture the beauty of that moment . . .

Meaulnes' obsessive regret for his loss of purity might have been more commensurate with his situation in the earlier drafts of the novel, when Valentine was unequivocally his mistress. Fournier's letters and the expurgated versions of the Meaulnes-Annette (Valentine) *liaison* reveal intimate first-hand knowledge of a situation more intense and bitter than any that was allowed to develop in the final version of the novel. What has been gained in 'purity' has been at the cost, if not of plausibility, then certainly of humanity, and it is hard not to fault Fournier here, as at the end of his *Essai de Transposition*, for a certain failure of artistic nerve. If it is objected that, on the contrary, Fournier is here demonstrating commendable tact by avoiding the excessively tasteless situation of making Meaulnes the ex-lover or even the ex-fiancé of Frantz de Galais, brother of his own true love, then one must immediately counter by asking how successful a creation is Frantz in himself, and how vital is he within the economy of the novel.

Frantz was the last character of consequence to be introduced into *Le Grand Meaulnes* and he is, on every count, quite the least convincing. It is not difficult to believe in his most striking traits of character – the way he oscillates between self-glorification and self-abasement, his gift for organising and for disorganising other people, his lordly airs and graces and his childish fits of the sulks – because these are all too human and all too frequently encountered in the world of everyday. What is most incredible about him is not that he is in any way inconsistent but that, on the contrary, he is so consistently, indeed so obsessively, theatrical. Having brought the *fête étrange* into being, he decrees that it should come to an end, dismisses Meaulnes with an imperious 'I am not to be disturbed!', writes what amounts to a suicide note, and tries to blow his brains out. He next appears at Sainte-Agathe disguised as a gipsy and promptly organises a commando-style raid at dead of night on the Seurels' schoolhouse; he lures Meaulnes into an ambush, steals the sketch map showing a section of the way back to his own home and returns it, with a grand gesture, only partly completed; he exacts from Meaulnes a solemn promise that he will at once come to his aid in response to his call and rewards him by passing on Yvonne's Paris address when he could, just as conveniently, have revealed the way back to the Domain; he tantalises Meaulnes by divulging his true identity at the end of his circus performance and then steals away like a thief in the night to elude the attentions of the local *gendarmerie*; nothing more is heard of him until Meaulnes' wedding night when he arrives quite unaccountably, having, for reasons which are never made clear, left his caravan far away and marched non-stop for thirty hours to remind Meaulnes of his schoolboy promise to respond to his call at his hour of greatest need; he departs again, as abruptly as he arrived, announcing mysteriously, 'In three days' time we'll be on the road to Germany!' The cumulative effect of all this extravagant behaviour is to make him not so much a credible human being as a mythical and vaguely symbolic figure from some other dimension, for the most part a lord of misrule or an imp of the perverse. On his appearance just after Meaulnes' marriage, when the notes of his owl-call signal ring out like the horn on the wedding-night of Hernani, he is transformed into something like the Romantic voice of conscience.

What is no less remarkable is that his compulsive theatricality brings out the theatrical in the characters with whom he comes into contact; not only do they readily condone his deplorable behaviour, they extravagantly admire him : Yvonne, who is quite the most level-headed character in the whole novel, is heart-broken 'to have lost a brother so endearing and so much admired in spite of all his follies'; for Meaulnes, he is 'the most wonderful chap in all the world', and his parents are happy to indulge him like a medieval princeling, giving him his own little house in the woods when he is just a few years old, and permitting him to become engaged at the age of fifteen; Valentine reveals that had she attended her engagement party at the nameless manor 'in the lanes and in the court-yard, from their hiding-places in the shrubbery, unknown childen would have been there to fête us with cries of 'Long live the bride! How fantastic he was.' Seurel remains, for the most part, lukewarm about Frantz's activities finding 'this childishness hard to tolerate in a youth already showing signs of age' and he reproves him 'for his obstinately continuing to act out this absurd role of Romantic hero', but he, in turn, is inspired by Frantz's presence to fix a further rendez-vous with him in conventionally Romantic terms, 'at exactly this hour, in a year and a day', and even he, unsympathetic though he is to all that Frantz stands for, concedes that 'there was a time when he had been so alive with the arrogance of youth that he could have got away with absolutely anything'. The reader's problem is that so much of Frantz's attractiveness is never sufficiently realised within the novel itself : it has all to be taken on trust, on the testimony of the other characters, and when this is contrasted with what Frantz actually says and does in the novel, the credibility gap is, more often than not, just too wide to cross. When critics hostile to *Le Grand Meaulnes* attack it as being 'an unbearable melodrama in which the characters are wildly improbable, none of the situations is plausible and none of the feelings true to life',[31] they are nearly always thinking of Frantz de Galais and of him alone.

It might be possible to argue a case for the plausibility of Frantz on the grounds that he takes sadistic pleasure in venting his spite on Meaulnes because he does not relish the prospect of his friends being happy while he is sad, or that he simply happens to see life as melodrama and so, quite consistently, behaves melodramatically himself, but the very need to marshal arguments to justify a character's behaviour is a sure sign that he has not been fully realised. Like many other last-minute *trouvailles*, he seems to have misled his creator by his spurious attractiveness and in the end, he has created as many technical problems as he promised to solve. It is hard to resist the conclusion that the chief justification for Frantz's behaviour, indeed for his very existence, in *Le Grand Meaulnes*, is that he is an absolutely vital cog in the machinery of the plot: reflection will readily show that without him, the wheels of the plot could scarcely even begin to turn.

What is very much open to question is whether the plot which Fournier finally fabricated was the only one conceivable for his artistic purpose. Could not the theme of innocence and experience have been equally well illustrated without Frantz? To portray the punishment for loss of purity, was it absolutely necessary to involve Meaulnes so ambivalently with the ex-fiancée of the brother of his first beloved? To have dispensed with Frantz altogether would have deprived the novel of the (in any case doubtful) benefits of a certain formal symmetry but this would, at the same time, have eliminated the melodramatic elements and occasional coincidences which hostile critics have always been quick to seize upon.

To concede that such hostile critics here have something of a point is not, however, necessarily to admit that *Le Grand Meaulnes* is irremediably flawed: it could well be that they are approaching the book in the wrong spirit and applying to it inappropriate criteria. Though the characters are developed consistently from what is 'given' about them, it seems somehow beside the point to evaluate them by naturalistic standards: the realistic elements of the novel are intermittently enlivened by fantasy, and what are sometimes taken for dream-like features are firmly tethered to the world of everyday; it seems at one level to be merely a tale of adventurous schoolboys and the ecstasy of first love, yet there is another level, clearly discernible, which demands to be accorded symbolic value. It has been well observed that the 'logic of the novel is emotional not rational'.[32]

How, then, should *Le Grand Meaulnes* be approached? To try to see it through the eyes of childhood as some of its greatest admirers have recommended,[33] is to imply, quite erroneously, that it is a children's book and is, in any event, to demand what, for most readers, is simply impossible. While it may not be fruitful to pursue too far the analogy between *Le Grand Meaulnes* and the Grail legend, the ideal way to view the novel might nevertheless be, as several critics have suggested, as a modern-dress version of the medieval tale of chivalry: in the best of these, there are to be found the same blend of love, dream, adventure and high endeavour, and the evoking of both character and scene by quick deft touches.

A critic who attacked *Sir Gawain and the Green Knight* because 'none of its situations is plausible' or rejected *The Romance of Tristan* because the characters' behaviour is extravagant, would clearly not have understood the rules of the particular game those authors were playing. Might not the same be true of the critics who find *Le Grand Meaulnes* too melodramatic to be palatable and the characters not true enough to be good? As one of Fournier's defenders once suggested, 'Why shouldn't *Le Grand Meaulnes* be the novel of chivalry of which each century provides its own particular version? Every age gets the Grail it deserves and it matters little if, at his Round Table, Alain-Fournier has seated two or three rather prosaic knights.'[34]

Perhaps the surest sign that *Le Grand Meaulnes* is now safely established as a classic is less the fact of its consistently impressive sales figures, and its being translated into such a wide range of other languages and other art forms, than the fact that it has continued to receive the attentions of newly evolved critical techniques. Amongst the more perceptive and stimulating of recent analyses several are particularly noteworthy, though the price the critic has had to pay for the freshness and ingenuity of his approach has, in almost every instance, been a case which is regularly over-stated and a view of *Le Grand Meaulnes* which is invariably partial.

In 1954, the American scholar Robert Champigny provided a number of perceptive new insights into the character of Fournier and his work, for example, when likening his love for Yvonne de Quiévrecourt to Kierkagaard's love for his Regina, or when suggesting 'if Meaulnes was so doggedly incapable of finding the road back to Yvonne, was it not because he did not really want to find it?'[35] Unfortunately, Champigny's study is vitiated by his reluctance to distinguish between Fournier himself and the fictitious world he created, an approach typified in such gnomic pronouncements as the following:

Neither Seurel nor Frantz had the power to transform death into life, aesthetically speaking. In Fournier's death, not his life, aesthetic logic became actual: it was Seurel and Frantz who died in September 1914, not Meaulnes.[36]

In 1963, following the leads provided earlier by such critics as Marcel Abraham and René Vincent,[37] Léon Cellier sensitively analysed *Le Grand Meaulnes* as a modern variant of the mediaeval tale of chivalry, only to arrive at the needlessly strident conclusion that the final picture of Meaulnes departing with his baby daughter was alternatively like some sneak-thief making off with the swag or like Cain doomed to be forever obsessed by thoughts of fratricide; Fournier began by writing a novel of 'knightly initiation' and this ended with humiliation rather than apotheosis because the author was, in spite of outward appearances, not a Romantic but a radical sceptic.[38]

In the following year, Michel Guiomar produced one of the most stimulating of all studies in the now well-stocked field of Fournier criticism, by applying to *Le Grand Meaulnes* the 'depth-analysis' techniques pioneered by Gaston Bachelard: he produced a fascinating account of Fournier's consistent use of 'Doubles' – for example, not only the obvious analogies between the names François and Frantz, but also unsuspected parallels between Meaulnes and Frantz and between Yvonne and Valentine – and a range of themes hitherto undetected, such as Fournier's obsessive preoccupation with 'Death', 'the House' and 'Motherhood'. All of this is much more convincing than his own central thesis which is that the chief interest of *Le Grand Meaulnes* is the light it sheds on the psyche of the author, and his 'discovery' that the most traumatic event in the whole of Fournier's life was when his parents moved from Marçais to Epineuil when he was five years old. This single event, Guiomar maintains, reverberates through *Le Grand Meaulnes* and even pre-determined the pattern of his love-life:

> Alain-Fournier's inspiration as a novelist did not come from the woman he called Yvonne de Galais. On the contrary, it was a novel, still deeply hidden and still unknown to him but planned in advance in every detail which provoked the Encounter in the Cours-la-Reine, ensuring that the first exchange of glances would be enriched with a significance already pre-determined by profound tendencies within Alain-Fournier himself.[39]

The most recent in date of these advanced modern analyses was that produced in 1973 by Marie Maclean[40] who, unlike Guiomar, has concentrated on the book itself for its own intrinsic qualities and not as the major item of evidence in the investigation into Fournier's subconscious. It could be said to be a triumph of inter-disciplinary and cosmopolitan disciplines because Marie Maclean, an Australian, has enlisted in her cause the terminology of the French critic Roland Barthes, the techniques of the Russian formalists Tzvetan Todorov and Vladimir Propp, and the insights into the phenomenon of *homo ludens* provided by the Dutch historian Jan Huizinga. The result is an engrossing and thoroughly convincing demonstration of the extremely intricate structure of *Le Grand Meaulnes*, whether it be viewed as a pattern of concentric or inter-locking circles or as a pyramid with the circus-scene, in the centre of Part Two, as the apex. She also makes a number of persuasive suggestions, *pace* Propp, about the 'magical' or 'fairy-tale' elements of the novel, such as the blacksmith's forge, the implications of crossing water, of staring at one's reflection, the necessity for Meaulnes to find his way back to his Lost Domain unaided, or the obsessive recurrence of the number three both in structure and situation : all of these details bring out much more clearly than heretofore the inner coherence of the novel and, at the same time, provide further reasons for its enduring appeal.

Marie Maclean's close study of the structure of *Le Grand Meaulnes*, together with the minute analysis of its language and imagery by such expert linguists as G. Timmermans,[41] Professor Stephen Ullmann[42] and Claude Vincenot,[43] all triumphantly reveal how far Fournier studies have advanced in sophistication and in rigour since 1920, when the critic Edmond Pilon could naïvely comment :

> There are some works as delicate as a pastel drawing, so diaphanous, so fine spun, of such a special subtlety and sweetness that one cannot touch them without removing their bloom. The adventure of Meaulnes belongs to this category.[44]

Stimulating though the most recent contributions to Fournier studies have been, they have all, no doubt because of their particular terms of reference, missed one point about *Le Grand Meaulnes* which is of paramount importance and since, in my view, it has never received adequate attention,[45] I propose to examine this now by way of conclusion. What is at issue is the extent to which the dominant mood and distinctive 'flavour' of *Le Grand Meaulnes* is determined by the *persona* of the story-teller, François Seurel.

Seurel's attitude towards the narrative is quite remarkably possessive, and the other characters in the novel are allowed very few opportunities indeed to address themselves directly to the reader : the account of Meaulnes' first discovery of the mysterious domain is provided not by Meaulnes himself but by Seurel and, at the end of the novel, after transcribing only a few pages of Meaulnes' secret notebook, Seurel states that because the handwriting is barely legible, 'it's necessary for me to take over at this point and reconstruct the whole of this part of his story'. In Part Three of the novel, Meaulnes is replaced or, at the very least, seriously rivalled as the character of central interest by Seurel himself. It is Seurel who discovers the whereabouts of the Lost Domain and after this discovery, it is Seurel who is the first to meet Yvonne de Galais; it is Seurel who bears the glad tidings to Meaulnes and who, in the face of Meaulnes' inexplicable reluctance, insists on reuniting him with Yvonne; it is Seurel's conversations with Yvonne which the reader is privileged to overhear at far greater length than those of Meaulnes; it is Seurel who sits beside Yvonne on her death-bed and Seurel who has to carry out her corpse towards the waiting grave. All this time, Meaulnes is far away looking for Valentine, and his year-long search for her and final rediscovery of her are dismissed in a single line. Seurel, then, is almost omnipresent throughout the novel, his voice is the first and last that the reader hears, and he is obliged to listen to it almost throughout.

All of this might be beside the point if Seurel were a thoroughly colourless personality, or a mere lens through which the reader is allowed to view events, but is he? Many critics have assumed that he has indeed no character of his own, and of these, Mr Alan Pryce-Jones is thoroughly typical :

> One might have expected the narrator himself to have possessed some special quality. Not at all : he is the foil for Meaulnes, the passive agent upon whom Meaulnes works his vast activity. We know his name is François; we know he has a damaged knee; but we never get to know very much more about him, so absorbed is he in the personage of Meaulnes.[46]

These comments seem to me the very opposite of the truth. Seurel does indeed have 'some special quality' and it determines the idiosyncratic atmosphere of the whole novel : the aura of mysteriousness with which he surrounds everyday scenes reveals both his powers of keen observation and his capacity for wonderment; the belief that the countryside around him stretches out to infinity expresses his childlike sense of space; his sense that Nature is brooding, resentful and vaguely menacing is the corollary of his great love of domestic calm and cosiness, and with the recurrent evocations of the cold and wind-swept landscape can be contrasted a striking number of references to secure and enclosed havens – the schoolhouse kitchen and the black-smith's shop at Sainte-Agathe, the farm and the barn where Meaulnes takes shelter on his way to the Lost Domain, the old manor-house itself, Frantz's little house in the woods – which, cold and draughty though some of them may be, hold out the promise of peace and seclusion amidst the surrounding desolation. To Seurel, they are all places of particular delectation and this is made manifest in the language he employs to describe them : it is never flat and prosaic, it is consistently warm and evocative.

The key traits of his personality are in fact insinuated into the reader's consciousness in the very first chapter of the novel before Meaulnes has even made his appearance, let alone begun to 'work his vast activity', and they are also, in part, subtly explained. Thus his basic timidity and acute uneasiness can be accounted for by the legacy of his crippled knee, and by the effect of his mother's seemingly permanent anxiety : the opening paragraphs are fairly riddled with words like 'despair', 'anxiously', 'fearfully' and 'disquiet'. Seurel is to express the *malaise* of the opening throughout the novel, in his fear of happiness, and the premonitions of impending disaster he feels when cycling to tell Meaulnes that he has found Yvonne, or in the course of the picnic staged in their honour or as he lurks outside the newly-weds' cottage on the very evening after the marriage.

It is in the opening chapter also that Seurel's capacity for hero-worship and romantic exaggeration is demonstrated. Because he himself is so timorous and over-protected, he immediately falls under Meaulnes' spell. He is intrigued by the 'mysterious and superior air' Madame Meaulnes adopts when speaking of her son, and positively astonished at the freedom with which Meaulnes is allowed to roam the countryside in search of wild birds' eggs. The extent of Seurel's astonishment is both significant and instructive : Meaulnes is seventeen years old at this point, and the activities described by his mother are surely, even in the less permissive world of the 1890s, those that a youth of his age and station might reasonably be expected to pursue as a matter of course. To the inordinately sheltered Seurel, they appear exceptionally remarkable, and he readily casts Meaulnes in the role of a vigorous and free-ranging hero; indeed, he never ceases, thereafter, to see him through a highly-coloured romantic haze, in the 'magic glow' of the Catherine wheel which Meaulnes ignites to mark his arrival.

Meaulnes is certainly involved in some highly dramatic situations, but part of the heroic aura which continuously surrounds him is just as certainly fashioned by Seurel. Meaulnes is clearly accorded some of the credit for the healing of Seurel's knee which is unaccountably made better at the very time of his arrival. When Meaulnes leans in characteristic silence against the door of the blacksmith's shop, it is Seurel who touches up the picture by comparing him, in his own mind's eye, to the youthful Robinson Crusoe. And with the very last sentence of the novel, Seurel reveals that in spite of every conceivable sort of personal disappointment, his private view of Meaulnes remains as incurably romantic as ever :

And already I could picture him, in the night, enfolding his daughter in his cloak and bearing her off on some new adventure.

If it seems laboriously pedantic to stress that it is not night, but early morning, when Seurel makes this pronouncement, and that when he makes it, Meaulnes is not stealing away but standing in front of him, holding his gurgling infant high in the air, it is only to make the crucial point that so much that the casual reader and not so casual critic assume actually happens, in fact takes place only in Seurel's highly colourful imagination.

What is also established in the opening chapter is that Seurel's feelings for Meaulnes are very mixed indeed. If he hero-worships Meaulnes for the glamour and excitement he brings to Sainte-Agathe, he also profoundly resents the dramatic break that Meaulnes obliges him to make with his established way of life. After evoking his childhood before the advent of Meaulnes, a childhood that seems full of loneliness, coldness, poverty and gloom, Seurel goes on to reveal his inveterate tendency to romanticise and his distinctly ambivalent attitude towards Meaulnes:

> Someone has come to rob me of all these peaceful childhood pleasures. Someone has blown out the candle which used to light up for me the sweet maternal face bent over the evening meal. Someone has extinguished the lamp around which we used to be a happy family group, after the darkness had come down and father had fixed the wooden shutters across the French windows. And that someone was Augustin Meaulnes whom the other boys quickly christened *le grand Meaulnes*.

Seurel's mixed feelings for his hero are perhaps most tellingly expressed just after Meaulnes has left the village forever in order to pursue his quest of Yvonne in Paris:

> Now here was the strange bit about it. Though I was overcome with a sense of desolation, I also felt a sense of release. With Meaulnes gone, and that adventure story of his brought to its inconclusive end, I seemed at least to have been freed from that strange anxiety, that mysterious obsession which prevented me from behaving like the rest of the crowd. With Meaulnes gone, I was no longer his brother-in-arms, his fellow trail-finder. Once more I could be an ordinary village lad again, and to achieve that status, it was merely a matter of following my own most natural inclinations.

Seurel is in error here, as are the readers and critics who take his words on trust. He is no 'ordinary village lad' : he is more sensitive and more imaginative than any of them, no less so, indeed, than Meaulnes himself, and he is haunted, even more than Meaulnes, by his memories of the past. His most distinctive tone is elegiac and his most characteristic mood is melancholy, gently wistful in the opening section of the novel when Meaulnes dominates the action, increasingly despairing as events move to their tragic climax and he takes the centre of the stage himself.

As the narrative unfolds, Seurel's sense of deprivation is remorselessly intensified. When Meaulnes rides out of his life for the first time, he is left 'with the feeling that in that old-fashioned carriage, it was (his) own youth which was being borne away forever.' Thereafter, he is involved in a whole series of poignant situations. He rediscovers the long lost beloved of his best friend and himself falls in love with her at their very first meeting. She has already been invested with an aura of high romance by Seurel long before their encounter, and when they meet, he reports quite simply that she is the most beautiful girl in all the world. He claims that 'when she held out her hand to me before leaving, there was between us, more clearly than if it had been expressed in many words, a secret understanding that only death was to bring to an end, and a friendship more moving than a great love', but his subsequent reactions belie this.

His demeanour before Yvonne is at all times punctilious and his loyalty to Meaulnes is unfaltering, but certain of his secret actions and certain of his tricks of narrative style reveal the true extent of his involvement. In spite of the fact that marriage to Meaulnes has changed her name, Seurel persists to the end in calling her 'Mademoiselle de Galais'. On the afternoon of Yvonne's wedding, Seurel states that Meaulnes has at last made friends with their former arch-enemy, Jasmin Delouche, and adds disingenuously :

And this explains how he and I both happen still to be prowling about the place, at four o'clock, after the other wedding guests have all departed.

On the next evening, Seurel returns alone, and uninvited, in the dusk to take up his mysterious vigil outside the cottage of the newly-married couple :

I didn't like to intrude at such a late hour on the day after a wedding, and till quite late on, I prowled about [that significant verb again] the edge of the garden and through the adjoining grounds.

On the next evening, he returns yet again, hoping to speak to Meaulnes or Yvonne but not daring to knock. When Yvonne dies, Seurel reflects, with a matter of fact recourse to the first person plural that is all too revealing:

> We had at last found the lovely girl and we had won her. She was my comrade's wife and I loved her with that deep and secret devotion for which there can be no words. I simply had to look at her and I was content, just like a little child. One day, perhaps, I should have married another girl and Yvonne would have been the very first to learn my great new secret . . .

A suppressed variant of this passage would have been even more explicit:

> Yvonne, I too loved you, although I never told you so. I didn't want to tell you and you didn't guess. Now you will never know. I would have loved other girls, I'd have told you about them, and you would have consoled me. Yvonne, this is how I would have loved you . . . I would not have been brusque and impulsive like Meaulnes. But what am I saying? You would never have ceased to be that wonderful girl one always seeks in vain.

Deprived of love though he may be, Seurel is not deprived of Yvonne's company and, in the course of the action, he in fact spends very much more time in the company of Yvonne than Meaulnes himself is allowed to do, and this enables him to savour to the full the acrid taste of all that can never be his. When Meaulnes is far away, Yvonne takes Seurel to Frantz's little secluded house, and he is, just for a moment, able to indulge in bitter-sweet rêverie:

> From Yvonne's manner, one would have thought the house belonged to the pair of us and that we had left it unattended while we were away on a long journey.

There follows the strange but suggestive episode of the dead chicks, a tone-poem in the most melancholy mode,[47] and Seurel becomes 'her most faithful companion during the whole of a spring and summer the like of which will never come again'. Autumn returns, Seurel reflects that 'our youth is over and our hopes of happiness are lost'; he yearns for the more distant past; 'tenderly and longingly, I thought of the muddy lanes of Sainte-Agathe'; he talks with Yvonne in the September drizzle about the ruin of their dreams and shortly afterwards, she dies a lingering death after a particularly agonising labour. Seurel's grief is as sincere as it is unrestrained, but he mourns for more than Yvonne :

> All is pain, all is bitterness now that she's dead. The world is empty, the holidays are over. Ended are the long drives through the remote countryside, and over too is the mysterious fête . . . Now there's nothing but sadness, just as it used to be.

And now for the first and only time, he can take Yvonne in his arms, and like the bridegroom he would like to have been, he can carry her over the threshold :

> Holding close the inert body, I bend over the head of the woman I'm carrying, I take a deep breath and draw into my mouth some strands of her golden hair : dead hair with a taste of earth. This taste of earth and death, this weight on my heart, is all that is left to me of the great adventure, and all that is left of you, Yvonne de Galais, the girl who was so ardently sought – and so deeply loved . . .

All this while, Meaulnes is out of sight and virtually out of mind, 'working his vast activity' elsewhere. But even this is not the end of Seurel's sorrows. For a year after Yvonne's death, he acts as a parent to the baby daughter who survives her; then Meaulnes returns from the unknown, and Seurel, ambivalent towards his friend to the last, is forced to realise that 'the child had at last found the companion she had unconsciously been waiting for and I realised all too clearly that *le grand Meaulnes* had come back to claim the one joy that he had left to me . . .'.

In the course of the action, therefore, Seurel has lost everything he holds most dear – his childhood peace, his youthful dreams, Yvonne de Galais, Yvonne's nameless daughter and Meaulnes himself – and in the fifteen years which have elapsed since all these momentous events occurred, he seems to have found no adequate consolation. Much of the intervening time seems to have been spent in brooding and, not surprisingly, when the time comes for his tale to be told, it is anything but colourless or matter-of-fact; it is, on the contrary, positively shot through with nostalgia, Seurel's own distinctive mood. He feels eternally disinherited, feels it compulsively to such an extent that his imprint on the whole book is quite indelible; indeed, his personality is so stamped across the narrative that the whole book could, perfectly appropriately, be re-entitled *Le Petit Seurel.*

Of all the characters in *Le Grand Meaulnes*, Seurel has by far the most in common with Fournier himself : they both consistently glorify the past to the detriment of the present, they are both hypersensitively attuned to the beauty, the mystery and, occasionally, the menace, of natural landscape, and they are both inconsolable for lost childhood, lost love and lost innocence; they are both, in a word, thorough-going nostalgicians. But they have something else in common more important than any of these : they are both *artists*. Each has to learn the artist's bitter lesson that before he can begin to re-create his Paradise, he must first lose it utterly; for each, it is the feeling of total loss which inspires the urge to restore, the need for revenge over circumstance and for victory over Time.[48]

In life, Fournier's hopes of earthly happiness withered beneath that glacial and insistent question of Yvonne de Quiévrecourt : *A quoi bon? A quoi bon?* What's the point of persisting like this when it's quite impossible? *Le Grand Meaulnes* provides the triumphant answer : the point is the creation of an imperishable masterpiece. In life, Fournier's love for Yvonne, 'begotten by Despair upon Impossibility', could never be realised; in his only novel, it will survive as long as men have eyes to see, as resistant to change and decay as the figures frozen forever on the side of their Grecian urn :

> Bold Lover, never, never canst thou kiss,
> Though winning near the goal – yet, do not grieve;
> She cannot fade, though thou hast not thy bliss,
> For ever wilt thou love, and she be fair !

ENVOI

Be not so desolate
Because thy dreams have flown
And the hall of the heart is empty
And silent as stone,
As age left by children
Sad and alone.

Those delicate children,
Thy dreams, still endure:
All pure and lovely things
Wend to the pure.
Sigh not: unto the fold
Their way was sure.

Thy gentlest dreams, thy frailest,
Even those that were
Born and lost in a heart-beat,
Shall meet thee there,
They are become immortal
In shining air.

The unattainable beauty
The thought of which was pain,
That flickered in eyes and on lips
And vanished again:
That fugitive beauty
Thou shalt attain.

The lights innumerable
That led thee on and on,
The Masque of Time ended,
Shall flow into one.
It shall be with thee for ever
Thy travel done.

AE

Notes

The following is a key to the abbreviations used in the notes throughout this book:

B : *Lettres au Petit Bichet* : Emile Paul, 1930.

F : *Lettres d'Alain-Fournier à sa famille* : Emile Paul, 1949.

Im : Isabelle Rivière : *Images d'Alain-Fournier par sa sœur Isabelle*, Emile Paul, 1938.

M : *Miracles*, Gallimard, 1924.

P : *Péguy–Alain-Fournier Correspondance*, L'Amitié Charles Péguy, 1972.

R : *Correspondance Alain-Fournier–Jacques Rivière*, Gallimard, 4 volume edition, 1926.

Vie : *Isabelle Rivière: Vie et Passion d'Alain-Fournier*, Jaspard, Polus, Monaco, 1963.

Except where otherwise stated, the place of publication is London for all sources in English, and Paris for all sources in French.

1 AN ATLAS OF NOSTALGIA

1. Schiller: 'On Simple and Sentimental Poetry' in *Essays Aesthetical and Philosophical*, G. Bell, 1875, p. 314.
2. Arnold: Preface to *Essays in Criticism*, 1st series.
3. Yeats: *The Land of Heart's Desire.*
4. For much fuller accounts of the treatment of this theme, consult Elizabeth Armstrong: *Ronsard and the Age of Gold*, Cambridge University Press, 1968, and Harry Levin: *The Myth of the Golden Age in the Renaissance*, Indiana University Press, 1969.
5. Rousseau: letter to Malesherbes, 26 January 1762.
6. Levin, op. cit., p. 4.
7. Blake: 'The Echoing Green' from *Songs of Innocence.*
8. Baudelaire: *Mœsta et errabunda.*
9. Charles Kingsley: 'Young and Old', song from *The Water Babies.*
10. Dylan Thomas: *Fern Hill.*

11. John Earle: *Microcosmographie*, 1628. For this reference, I am indebted to Professor George Boas who has made a succinct but thorough study of evolving attitudes to children in *The Cult of Childhood*, The Warburg Institute, 1966.
12. Henry Vaughan: *The Return*.
13. For a particularly perceptive study of this development, consult Peter Coveney: *The Image of Childhood*, Penguin Books, 1967.
14. Cyril Connolly: *Enemies of Promise*, Penguin Books, 1961, pp. 271–2.
15. This phenomenon is closely examined in Justin O'Brien: *The Novel of Adolescence in France*, Oxford, 1939.
16. George Sand: *Histoire de ma Vie*, 1854.
17. Gabriel Compayré in *L'Adolescence*, Alcan, 1909.
18. Edmond Jaloux in *Les Nouvelles Littéraires*, 4 January 1930.
19. Léon Cury in *Les Jeunes Gens dans le roman d'avant guerre*, 1918.
20. Henri Massis: *Le Romantisme de l'Adolescence*, 1924.
21. The only really complete portraits of adolescence in French literature are, in my view, Romain Rolland's young Jean Christophe in the novel of that name and Roger Martin du Gard's Jacques Thibault in the Thibault chronicle: significantly, each of these is a saga which extends over several volumes.
22. Henry de Montherlant: *La Relève du Matin*, Gallimard, 1920, pp. 149–50.
23. François Mauriac: *Le Désert de l'Amour*, Livres de Poche, 1967, p. 215.
24. Montherlant: Preface to Luce Arny's novel, *Anna, premier visage*, 1938.
25. R. II. 385, 26 December 1906.
26. R. II. 205–6, 22 August 1906.
27. R. III. 325, 15 April 1908.
28. R. IV. 191, 3 March 1910.
29. Pavese: *Il mestiere di vivere*, Turin, 1952, p. 249; quoted in Levin, op. cit., pp. 161–2.
30. R. II. 13, 21 March 1906.
31. R. IV. 156, 1 August 1909.

2 THE LAND OF LOST CONTENT

1. Charles Péguy, 'L'Argent', in *Oeuvres en Prose 1909–1914*, Gallimard, 'Bibliothèque de la Pléiade', 1961, p. 1099.
2. Paul Valéry, 'Au Sujet d'Adonis', in *Oeuvres*, Gallimard, 'Bibliothèque de la Pléiade', 1957, p. 483.
3. Full details of the Fournier family background will be found in the appendices to Jean Loize's monumental biography, *Alain-Fournier, sa vie et 'Le Grand Meaulnes'*, Hachette, 1968 (hereafter cited as 'Vie').
4. This story and a fuller portrait will be found in the chapter 'Maman-Barthe' in Im, pp. 115–26.
5. The following text of the petition was provided in the Catalogue to the exhibition devoted to 'Alain-Fournier et son pays' organised in 1964 by the Maison de la Culture of Bourges:

> Les soussignés ont l'honneur de vous donner l'avis que, à Epineuil, l'on vient de confié [sic] l'emploi d'instituteur-adjoint à la femme de l'instituteur. Nous protestons contre ce changement, car nous préférons que l'instruction soit donner [sic] a [sic] nos enfants par un homme . . .

6. Bourges Exhibition Catalogue, Item Number 79.
7. Im, pp. 27–30.
8. In particular, Guy Dupré in an article entitled 'Alain-Fournier n'était pas un enfant de chœur', *Arts*, 16 September 1959.

9. Vie, p. 505.
10. Unpublished letter to André Lhote, 7 July 1910.
11. R. I. 145, 4 October 1905.
12. Im, pp. 206–9.
13. ibid., pp. 49–52.
14. Letter to Louis Pergaud, 25 October 1912.
15. Letter to the 'first Yvonne', 11 April 1905, quoted in Loize, op. cit., p. 62.
16. 'Conte du soleil et de la route', M, pp. 95–6.
17. From Les Fêtes Publiques, an unpublished essay written in 1908.
18. Letter to Jeanne Bruneau, 11 December 1910, Vie, pp. 147–8.
19. Letter to Simone, 20 August 1914, published in Le Figaro Littéraire, pp. 24–30, September 1964. See also p. 268.
20. R. III. 241, 21 August 1907.
21. R. I. 59, 13 August 1905.
22. R. I. 61–2.
23. ibid.
24. Unpublished letter to André Lhote, 3 July 1910. An edition of the complete correspondence between Fournier, Rivière and Lhote is now being prepared by M. J. G. Morgenthaler to be published by Fayard.
25. R. III. 256–7, 29 August 1907.
26. R. IV. 54–5, 27 September 1908.

3 THE LAND OF EXILE

1. Proust: Conclusion of Le Temps Retrouvé.
2. In Hommage à Alain-Fournier, Le Mail, 1929, pp. 8–12.
3. A selection of the most successful of these photographs was displayed in the Alain-Fournier Exhibition staged in Bourges in 1964. The most regularly reproduced photograph of the collection is that taken by Henri himself, depicting his parents, grandparents, sister and Théodule Bijard in front of the Barthes' house at La Chapelle-d'Angillon.
4. R. I. 260–1, 11 October 1906.
5. F. 29, 27 October 1901.
6. R. IV. 294–5, 1 September 1911.
7. F. 31, 17 December 1901.
8. R. IV. 53, 27 September 1908.
9. Letter to Jeanne Bruneau, 7 December 1910, Vie, p. 142.
10. 'Portrait', M., p. 204.
11. R. I. 164, 30 October 1905.
12. Bourges Alain-Fournier Exhibition Catalogue, Item 122.
13. F. 23, 5 October 1901.

4 THE LAND OF PROMISE

1. Claudel, letter to Jacques Rivière, 3 March 1907; Jacques Rivière à Paul Claudel: Correspondance, 1907–1914, Plon, 1926, p. 23.
2. F. 42, November 1903.
3. R. II. 188, 7 August 1906.
4. Jeanne-Rivière Leproust, 'Sur mon frère', Nouvelle Revue Française, October 1931, p. 514.
5. R. III. 247, 25 August 1907.
6. A la Trace de Dieu, Gallimard, p. 231.
7. Letter to André Waltz, quoted in Hommage à Jacques Rivière, N.R.F., p. 402.

8. Introduction to *Miracles*, pp. 13–14.
9. ibid., pp. 14–15.
10. Francisque Vial, in *Hommage à Alain-Fournier*, p. 16.
11. M., p. 18.
12. R. II. 22, 21 March 1906.
13. R. I. 49, 13 August 1905.
14. Letter to Jacques Rivière, 28 September 1904, first published in Jean Loize: *Alain-Fournier, sa vie et 'Le Grand Meaulnes'*, Hachette 1968, p. 51.
15. F. 49, 50, 20 March 1905.
16. F. 53–5, 20 March 1905.
17. Details from Isabelle Rivière, Im, pp. 190–6 and 199–206.
18. Loize, op. cit., p. 56.
19. Letter to Rivière, 17 August 1904. First published in Loize, op. cit., p. 56.
20. First published in Loize, op. cit., pp. 60–3.
21. See Chapter 1, p. 26.
22. The details first appeared in Loize, op. cit., p. 61, Note 1.
23. First published in the Bourges Alain-Fournier Exhibition Catalogue, Item 140.
24. First published in Vie, p. 329.
25. Rivière archives.
26. B. 139–40, 6 September 1908.
27. F. 57, 3 July 1905.
28. R. I. 13, 9 July 1905.
29. F. 77, 25 July 1905.
30. F. 73, 18 July 1905.
31. R. I. 15–16, 9 July 1905.
32. F. 77, 25 July 1905.
33. R. I. 20, 9 July 1905.
34. R. I. 17, 9 July 1905.
35. R. I. 118, 23 September 1905.
36. R. I. 17, 9 July 1905.
37. R. I. 54, 13 August 1905.
38. R. I. 82, 27 August 1905.
39. Quoted in letter from Fournier to his sister, F. 167, 17 March 1906.
40. R. I. 58, 13 August 1905.
41. F. 106–7, 28 August 1905.
42. R. I. 119, 23 September 1905.
43. F. 120, 9 September 1905.
44. R. I. 119, 23 September 1905.
45. R. I. 141, 4 October 1905.
46. F. 122, 16 October 1905.
47. R. I. 142–6 passim, 4 October 1905.
48. Waltz, art. cit., p. 405.
49. R. I. 159–61, 27 October 1905.
50. R. I. 154, 12 October 1905.
51. R. I. 239, 22 January 1906.
52. R. I. 294 and 306, 9 November 1906.
53. F. 296, 12 September 1908.
54. 11 October 1911, *Rivière–Claudel Correspondance*, ed. cit., p. 240.
55. R. III. 182, 5 July 1907.
56. R. I. 187, 16 November 1905.
57. R. I. 170, 2 November 1905.
58. F. 132, 30 November 1905.
59. R. I. 253–4, 22 January 1906. This letter-extract was found after his death among the notes and rough drafts for *Le Grand Meaulnes*.
60. R. I. 219, 10 January 1906. cf. Yeats: 'I am very religious, and deprived by Huxley and Tindall, whom I detested, of the simple-minded religion of

my childhood, I had made a new religion, an almost infallible church of poetic tradition, a fardel of stories, and of personages, and of emotions, inseparable from their first expression, passed on from generation to generation by poets and painters with some help from philosophers and theologians. I wished for a world where I could discover this tradition perpetually, and not in pictures and in poems only, but in tiles round the chimney-piece and in the hangings that kept out the draught. I had even created a dogma: "Because those imaginary people are created out of the deepest instinct of man, to be his measure and his norm, whatever I can imagine those mouths speaking may be the nearest I can go to truth" ', *Autobiographies*, Macmillan, 1955, pp. 115–16.

61. F. 68, 13 July 1905.
62. F. 133–5, 30 November 1905.
63. F. 141, 26 December 1905.
64. R. II. 14, 21 March 1906.
65. R. I. 259, 29 January 1906.
66. F. 146, 7 February 1906.
67. R. I. 259–60, 29 January 1906.
68. R. I. 281, 17 February 1906.
69. F. 166, 17 March 1906. Fournier's father was a school-teacher in Marçais from 1888 to 1891. See page 17.
70. R. I. 282–3, 17 February 1906.
71. R. I. 292–3, 17 February 1906.
72. R. II. 29, 3 April 1906.
73. R. II. 83, 30 April 1906.
74. F. 173, 30 May 1906.
75. R. II. 112–14, 27 May 1906.
76. R. II. 127, 7 June 1906.
77. R. II. 140–1, 24 June 1906.
78. B. 61–2, 31 July 1906.
79. Fournier to Rivière, 22 August 1906, 1948 two-volume edition of correspondence, Vol. I, p. 305.
80. R. I. 250, 22 January 1906.
81. B. 63, 31 July 1906.
82. R. II. 178, 5 August 1906.
83. R. II. 226–9, 3 September 1906.
84. R. II. 200, 22 August 1906.
85. R. II. 259, 11 October 1906.
86. R. II. 305, 9 November 1906.
87. R. II. 258, 11 October 1906.
88. R. II. 301, 9 November 1906.
89. R. II. 317–18, 14 November 1906.
90. These have now been published: v. *Paul Claudel, Francis Jammes, Gabriel Frizeau: Correspondance 1897–1938*, Gallimard, 1952.
91. B. 119, 5 January 1907.
92. R. III. 32, 26 January 1907.
93. B. 103, 30 November 1906.
94. R. II. 384–5, 26 December 1906.
95. R. III. 22, 26 January 1907.
96. R. III. 26, 26 January 1907.
97. *Rivière–Claudel Correspondance*, ed. cit., pp. 1–5 *passim*.
98. A detail suppressed by Madame Rivière and published for the first time in Loize, op. cit., p. 78.
99. Letter of 26 January 1907. Excised from 1926 edition of correspondence. In Volume II of 1948 edition.
100. R. III. 28–33 passim, 26 January 1907.
101. R. II. 205–6, 22 August 1906.

102. This same mood is beautifully caught in Kipling's wistful poem, *The Way through the Woods*.
103. R. II. 358–9, 15 December 1906.
104. R. I. 360, ibid. Rimbaud was by no means the first to express the view that the world we see about us is only a theatrical backcloth and that behind it are forces beyond our comprehension. To go no further back in time than the early nineteenth century, one can cite that much-anthologised passage from the First Book of Wordsworth's *Prelude* in which he describes the doubtful pleasures of bird-nesting or rowing a skiff through the darkness over Patterdale, and, even more appositely, one can cite Leopardi: 'To the sensitive and imaginative man, who lives as I have lived, feeling continuously and imagining, the world and its objects are in a sense double. He may see with his eyes a tower, a landscape, hear with his ears the sound of a bell, and at the same time, he will see another tower, another landscape, he will hear another sound – in this second kind of object is situated all the beauty and pleasure of things.'

Neither was Rimbaud the last to try to register such feelings: at much the same time as Fournier embarked in search of the Other Landscape, or shortly afterwards, Proust wrote that superb passage in *Combray* in which the young Marcel, out for a country drive, is haunted and taunted by the sight of the spires of Martinville against the sky.

105. The quotation is from Mallarmé's most popular – and most accessible – poem, 'Brise Marine', the *cri de cœur* of all academic examinees:

> La chair est triste, hélas! et j'ai lu tous les livres.
> Fuir! là-bas fuir! Je sens que des oiseaux sont ivres
> D'être parmi l'écume inconnue et les cieux!

cf. Yeats's 'I would that we were, my beloved, white birds on the foam of the sea.'

106. This solitary letter, dated 27 May 1907, was published in 1946, in a special edition by Emile-Paul in the series 'Les Introuvables'.
107. R. III. 168, 29 June 1907.
108. R. III. 198–9, 17 July 1907.
109. R. III. 208, 24 July 1907.
110. R. III. 223, 27 July 1910. See also Isabelle Rivière, 'Les donneurs de sérénades' in Im, pp. 274–8.
111. She was married in Toulon on 17 October 1906 to a naval doctor called Brochet, a graduate of the medical school in the University of Bordeaux. While in Versailles, she used to stay at 5 rue Montbauron.
112. R. III. 223, 27 July 1910.
113. ibid.
114. F. 217, 15 August 1907.
115. R. III. 232, 19 August 1907.
116. Letter of 29 August 1907. Excised from 1926 edition. Vol. II of 1948 edition, pp. 154–5.
117. R. II. 256–7, 29 August 1907.
118. First published in three successive numbers of the review, *L'Occident*, October–December 1907.
119. M., pp. 128–9.
120. Fournier's original description of the mother and children on the Seine is in a letter sent to Rivière on 24 June 1906, R. 138–9. All the other allusions will be found *passim* in the earlier chapters of this study.
121. R. II. 114, 27 May 1906.
122. R. III. 289, 2 October 1907.
123. F. 218, 2 October 1907.

5 THE LAND OF LOST ILLUSIONS

1. Fournier: letter to André Lhote, September 1909, quoted in *Vie*, p. 119.
2. R. II. 363, 15 December 1906.
3. Letter to Bichet, 27 May 1907, published separately by Emile-Paul in 1946.
4. R. III. 270, 27 September 1907.
5. F. 233, 12 December 1907.
6. F. 228, 8 December 1907.
7. F. 240, 12 December 1907.
8. F. 231, 8 December 1907.
9. R. III. 310, 24 December 1907.
10. R. III. 327, 20 April 1908.
11. Im, p. 307.
12. R. III. 321–2, 1 January 1908.
13. F. 261, 30 May 1908.
14. R. III. 363, 4 June 1908.
15. B. 124–5, 10 August 1908.
16. Rivière first outlined his plan for this novel in a letter to Fournier dated 25 June 1907: 'The subject of my book is going to be *everything*, everything there is within me – the contradictory positions I adopt over everything, my feelings, my ideas, my passions, my ideologies, my prejudices, *everything*', R. III. 152.
17. R. IV. 16, 26 August 1908.
18. F. 283–4, 1 September 1908.
19. R. IV. 23–4, 5 September 1908.
20. Given Rivière's resolve to include the whole of himself in his novel, one can readily understand why he decided to abandon it after his engagement and marriage. Only one chapter survives, the ironically entitled, *Les Beaux Jours* (*Happy Days*), in which the hero and his new bride climb a hill, and find melancholy serenity in their reflection that death is inevitable and that all is vanity. Cf. Rupert Brook's sonnet, written in 1910, *The Hill*.
21. F. 285, 1 September 1908.
22. B. 135–9 passim, 6 September 1908. 'Clitandre' is the name bestowed on the figure of the archetypal unrequited lover in Verlaine's poem 'Mandoline'.
23. See page 67 of this study.
24. F. 290–1, 12 September 1908.
25. F. 301–2, 16 September 1908.
26. R. IV. 49, 20 September 1908.
27. F. 307–8, 23 September 1908.
28. Tennyson: 'Ulysses'.
29. R. IV. 53, 27 September 1908.
30. F. 316–18, 20 October 1908.
31. F. 319, 24 November 1908.
32. F. 312, 15 October 1908.
33. R. III. 215, 26 July 1907. To reinforce his warning, Rivière referred Fournier to Claudel's *Pensée en mer*, one of the most personal and moving prose-poems in his collection, *Connaissance de l'Est*. It expresses the sentiments of the expatriate who returns home on leave and discovers that he is, in fact, homeless:

> This is what makes returning sadder than departing. The traveller comes back into his own home like a mere guest: he is a stranger to everything and everything is strange to him. Servant, just leave that coat hanging there: don't put it away! Once more, he must depart. At the family table see how he sits down, a suspect and precarious guest. He's no relative! This passer-by you've welcomed in, his ears still full of the clatter of trains and the roar of the sea, swaying, like a man in a dream,

with that powerful motion he still feels beneath his feet and which will soon bear him away again – he's not the man you saw off at that fatal quayside. Separation has taken place, and the exile into which he went now follows him everywhere.

34. It was published in monthly instalments in the *Annales de philosophie chrétienne* between November 1908 and March 1909.

35. The first number of this illustrious review appeared, in fact, on 15 November 1908, under the direction of Eugène Montfort. One of the articles it contained was an attack on Mallarmé and another was supercilious towards d'Annunzio. The founders were so affronted that the director was dismissed and fresh plans drawn up to ensure that the review would be particularly receptive to contemporary work, especially that which was spontaneous and exciting and, above all, well written. The new 'first' number appeared on 1 February 1909.

36. B. 148, 19 December 1908.

37. First published in 1944 in Holland in a clandestine review, *Poésie 44*.

38. This covering letter appeared for the first time in Loize, op. cit., p. 181.

39. R. IV. 70, 31 December 1908.

40. R. IV. 129, 20 May 1909.

41. R. IV. 81–3, 3 March 1909.

42. Published in *Hommage à Jacques Rivière*, special number of *La Nouvelle Revue Française*, 1 April 1925, p. 764. *La Partie de Plaisir* was first published in the review *Schéhérazade*, Paris, 15 September 1910.

43. Published in *Hommage à Alain-Fournier*, special number of *Le Mail*, Winter 1929, pp. 22–5.

44. First published in Loize, op. cit., p. 189.

45. R. IV. 93–4, 18 April 1909.

46. F. 327–8, 2 May 1909.

47. B. 155–6, 7 May 1909.

48. This same quotation occurs in a letter from Fournier to Rivière dated 22 August 1906, R. II. 200. In Fournier's letters and prose-poems of 1908–9, the word 'fever' appears as insistently as the adjectives 'distant' and 'mysterious' appear in his writings in 1907.

49. F. 339, 17 May 1909.

50. F. 335–7, 17 May 1939.

51. R. IV. 125–9 passim, 20 May 1909.

52. See page 43 of this study.

53. R. IV. 132–6 passim, 2 June 1909.

54. F. 343, 10 June 1909. The quotation is from the opening poem in Claudel's *Vers d'Exil* which first appeared in the review *L'Ermitage* on 15 July 1905. It begins:

> Paul, il nous faut partir pour un départ plus beau !
> Pour la dernière fois, acceptant leur étreinte,
> J'ai des parents pleurants baisé la face sainte
> Maintenant je suis seul sous un soleil nouveau.

The penultimate stanza reads:

> Voici l'heure brûlante et la nuit ennuyeuse !
> Voici le Pas, voici l'arrêt et le suspens.
> Saisi d'horreur, voici que de nouveau j'entends
> L'inéxorable appel de la voix merveilleuse.

55. This quotation is again Claudel's, from a letter he wrote to Rivière on 28 April 1909, *Rivière–Claudel Correspondance*, ed. cit., p. 187. At this

point in his letter, Claudel is praising G. K. Chesterton's book *Orthodoxy* which develops the theme of the polarities which should create for the Christian a fruitful tension – joy and penitence, pride and humility, gratification and renunciation.

56. F. 337, 17 May 1909.
57. *Dans le tout petit jardin* was first published in *Miracles*, pp. 137–40. *La Maison verte* and *Ce fut une soirée d'avril* were modified and subsequently incorporated in *Le Grand Meaulnes*.
58. R. IV. 140, 18 June 1909.
59. R. IV. 153, 27 July 1909.
60. R. IV. 140, 18 June 1909.
61. First published in *La Grande Revue* in June 1915, and reprinted in *Miracles*.
62. M., pp. 150–1.
63. R. IV. 165–6, 5 September 1909.
64. M., pp. 142–3.
65. R. IV. 146, 7 July 1909.
66. F. 350, 14 July 1909.
67. Cf. 'Judge not according to the appearance', *St John*, VII. 24, and 'He that is without sin among you, let him first cast a stone at her', ibid, VIII. 7.
68. R. IV. 145–6, 7 July 1909. Wagram is a village near Vienna where Napoleon defeated the Archduke Charles on 6 July 1809.
69. R. IV. 156, 1 August 1909.
70. F. 360, 5 September 1909.
71. R. IV. 164, 5 September 1909.
72. Vie, pp. 100–2. For Fournier's account of the last meeting with 'Laurence', see pp. 165–6 of this study.
73. R. IV. 166, 5 September 1909.
74. R. IV. 174–6 passim, 21 September 1909.
75. F. 357–8, 14 August 1909. The first words are a quotation from the opening scene of Claudel's play *L'Echange*.

6 SWEET LAND OF LIBERTY

1. Michel in *L'Immoraliste*.
2. Im, p. 315. Marthe and Thomas Pollock are characters in Claudel's play *L'Echange*.
3. *Le Bouquet de roses rouges*, p. 216. In this 'novel', Paul Claudel is renamed Matthieu Champel. Jacques Rivière features as Michel Clairfont and Fournier as Sylvain Deslaurents, 'Laurents' being the name of the farm where Grandmother Barthe was brought up. The book deals with the early years of the Clairfonts' marriage and, in particular, their difficulties in producing their first child.
4. M, p. 160.
5. ibid, pp. 169–70.
6. Letter to André Lhote, 16 January 1910; first published in *Revue des Jeunes*, 15 March 1936.
7. R. IV. 196–7, 4 April 1910.
8. R. IV. 245–6, 20 September 1910.
9. Quoted in Vie, p. 121.
10. These were the principal singers in the first Paris production of *Pelléas et Mélisande*.
11. Unpublished letter to André Lhote, 3 July 1910.
12. These have all been published *in extenso* in Vie, pp. 120–53 and 176–7.
13. Op. cit., pp. 125–6. The crucial endearment in the final paragraph is the word *femme* which can, of course, mean 'woman' or wife'. The crescendo

towards which Fournier's litany seems to me to rise justifies, I would argue, the use of the second term in my translation.

14. ibid., pp. 122–3.
15. R. IV. 232, 24 August 1910.
16. B. 170, 11 September 1910.
17. M, p. 177.
18. ibid., pp. 179–80.
19. Letter to Jeanne, September 1910, Vie, p. 136.
20. R. IV. 244, 20 September 1910.
21. A substantial section of it, minus the epigraph, appeared in M, pp. 211–17, under the title *La Dispute et la nuit dans la cellule*.
22. R. IV. 244, 19 September 1910.
23. Fournier is in error here: it was in fact Shelley who wrote these words in a letter to John Gisborne on 22 October 1821. v *Letters of P. B. Shelley*, Vol. II, ed. F. L. Jones, Oxford University Press, 1964, p. 668.
24. R. IV. 255–6, 20 September 1910.
25. B. 166, 11 September 1910.
26. Two collections of extracts from Fournier's gossip articles have so far been published: in the review *La Chronique de Paris*, pp. 1–13, in December 1943, and in a limited edition, *Mon courrier littéraire*, published in Liège, by Editions Dynamo, in 1958. Forty-two extracts from the articles Fournier devoted to Péguy are included in Auguste Martin's study *Péguy et Alain-Fournier, Cahiers de l'Amitié Charles Péguy*, 1954. A complete edition of Fournier's newspaper articles has now been prepared by M. André Guyon: there are more than 900 pages of typescript.
27. R. IV. 251–2, 20 September 1910.
28. In a conversation with R. Gibson in 1951.
29. P, pp. 4–5. The profile of Péguy was not published in the lifetime of either writer: it appears in this same volume of correspondence, pp. 6–7.
30. See pp. 42–3 of this study.
31. See p. 28 of this study.
32. Letter to Jeanne, 7 December 1910, Vie, p. 142.
33. Letter to Jeanne, 11 December 1910, ibid., p. 148.
34. Letter to Jeanne, 9 December 1910, ibid., pp. 144–5.
35. Letter to Jeanne, 7 December 1910, ibid., p. 143. The real-life incident which inspired this story is recounted in a letter to Rivière dated 27 September 1907, R. III. 271.
36. R. IV. 276, 21 April 1911.
37. R. IV. 268, 13 April 1911.
38. R. IV. 267, 11 April 1911.
39. Details and this letter to Bichet, dated 16 February 1911, were first published in Loize, op. cit., pp. 280–1.
40. *Etudes*, published by Gallimard in 1911.
41. Letter to Bichet, 11 February 1911, first quoted in Loize, op. cit., p. 281.
42. Letter to Jeanne, April 1911, Vie, p. 152–3.
43. R. IV. 274, 21 April 1911.
44. Letter to Marguerite Audoux, first published in Georges Reyer: *Un cœur pur: Marguerite Audoux*, Grasset, 1942, p. 166.
45. M, p. 210.
46. P, p. 10, 8 September 1911.
47. R. IV. 290–1, 1 September 1911.
48. R. IV. 297, 9 September 1911.
49. 'Je ne suis pas d'ici' is a reference to an aria from *Pelléas et Mélisande* which was a particular favourite of Fournier's: *Je ne suis pas d'ici, je ne suis pas née là*. It is sung by Mélisande and the implication is that she comes from a world other than this.
50. F. 369–70, 13 September 1911.

51. Fournier met Saint Léger-Léger through the agency of Rivière who had, in turn, been first introduced to him in 1906 through their mutual friend Gabriel Frizeau, the Bordelais bookseller. Michel Yell's real name was Jules Iehl and his best though little-known novel, *Caüet*, was first published in 1912.

52. F. 371, 29 September 1911.

53. First published in Aimé Becker, *Itinéraire spirituel d'Alain-Fournier*, Corrêa, 1946, p. 141.

54. Becker, op. cit., p. 142.

55. B. 162, 22 August 1910.

56. R. IV. 231, 24 August 1910.

57. From the archives of M. Alain Rivière.

58. 'Yesterday evening we had a (not very) magic lantern show.' v. F. 52.

59. See p. 136 of this study.

60. See p. 176 of this study.

61. Unpublished letter to Gustave Tronche, August 1910; from the archives of M. Alain Rivière.

62. See pp. 139–40 of this study.

63. R. IV. 293, 1 September 1911.

64. Letter to Michel Yell, 11 October 1911. Becker, op. cit., p. 141.

65. Letter to 'Henriette', 11 December 1911. Quoted in Vie, p. 172. This episode, which was to have been called 'The Three Merchants of Urçay', was not used in the novel, though three pages of it survive amongst Fournier's papers. Urçay is a village near Epineuil-le-Fleuriel.

66. Unpublished letter from Fournier to Lhote, 1 November 1911.

67. Vie, pp. 172–3.

68. R. IV. 322–3, 5 April 1912.

69. The letter-card was sent to Gustave Tronche on 3 December 1912 and said somewhat enigmatically: 'Jeanne Bruneau is in the country. But it would be a simple matter – overnight if need be – for me to make her come back'. First published in Loize, op. cit., p. 326.

70. P, p. 11.

71. Letter of 3 January 1912, ibid., p. 12.

72. Quai Debilly has since been renamed 'Avenue de New York'.

7 THE LAND OF DREAMS COME TRUE

1. Claude Casimir-Perier's father, Jean-Paul-Pierre (1847–1907), was President between 27 June 1894 and 15 January 1895. His grandfather, Auguste-Casimir-Victor-Laurent (1811–1876), was also a prominent politician, while his great-grandfather, Casimir-Pierre (1777–1832), a wealthy banker, was an even more famous politician, one of the leaders of the Liberal opposition and under the Bourbon Restoration, and a very tough Minister of the Interior who forcibly put down several civil insurrections in 1831.

2. This mode of address is not as discourteous as it might sound. Madame Casimir-Perier, who married the poet and critic François Porché in 1923, preferred to be called plainly 'Simone' in her rôles both as actress and writer.

3. Jean and Jérôme Tharaud, *Pour les fidèles de Péguy*, Dumas, p. 8.

4. René Bizet, not to be confused with René Bichet, was a friend of Fournier's whom he first met at the Lycée Voltaire. He was a journalist on the paper *L'Intransigeant* to which Fournier contributed occasional 'profiles'.

5. Simone: *Sous de nouveaux soleils*, Gallimard, 1957, p. 234.

6. Vie, p. 192. Fournier was still on terms with 'Loulette' in May 1913 when he reported to Rivière that she had had an accident and would not be able to 'distract' him for some time to come; R. II. 431.

7. cf. Monsieur Seurel's endearing habit of taking an ancient pistol with him when accompanying his schoolboys on their ramble through the Spring woods in *Le Grand Meaulnes*.
8. See P, pp. 16–27.
9. ibid., p. 28.
10. ibid., p. 30.
11. Letter to Péguy, 24 August 1912, ibid., p. 33.
12. F. 373–4, 18 September 1912.
13. Among the figures he profiled for *L'Intransigeant* in 1912 were Julien Benda, Léon-Paul Fargue and Bernard Combette. For details, see Loize op. cit., p. 314 and p. 326. See also Jean Bastaire: 'Péguy par Alain-Fournier dans *L'Intransigeant*', in *Cahiers de l'Amitié Charles Péguy*, March 1972.
14. Letter to Jacques Copeau, 20 October 1912. Vie, p. 206, n. 1.
15. Loize, op. cit., p. 322.
16. B. 184, 2 November 1912.
17. B. 180–1, 2 November 1912.
18. Letter to Yvonne Brochet, September 1912, Vie, pp. 186–9.
19. Sentence excised from the letter of 2 November as first published in *Lettres au Petit B*, but restored in Loize, op. cit., p. 325.
20. P, p. 34.
21. R. IV. 325–6, 2 September 1912.
22. B. 182, 2 November 1912.
23. B. 193, 22 November 1912.
24. From an obituary notice on Bichet by Isabelle Rivière, B. 49.
25. R. IV. 331–2, 3 January 1913.
26. Like Péguy himself, Bichet came from the Beauce, and it was therefore appropriate that a place for him should be found in a poem of homage to the saint who had spiritual care of the region. The full reference to Bichet reads:

> Nous venons prier pour ce pauvre garçon
> Qui mourut comme un sot au cours de cette année,
> Presque dans la semaine et devers la journée
> Ou votre fils naquît dans la paille et le son.
>
> O Vierge, il n'était pas le pire du troupeau.
> Il n'avait qu'un défaut dans sa jeune cuirasse.
> Mais la mort qui nous piste et nous suit à la trace
> A passé par ce trou qu'il s'est fait dans la peau.
>
> Le voici maintenant dans votre régence.
> Vous êtes reine et mère et saurez le montrer.
> C'était un être pur. Vous le ferez rentrer
> Dans votre patronage et dans votre indulgence.

27. cf. letter from Fournier to Bichet, B. 185, 2 November 1912. 'I've now read *Wuthering Heights* by Emily Brontë. I can't remember whether you've read it yet. What a terrifying book!'
28. *Sous de nouveaux soleils*, p. 240.
29. ibid., p. 241.
30. P, 17 February 1913, p. 37.
31. *Sous de nouveaux soleils*, p. 243.
32. R. IV. 336, 25 March 1913. Rivière's 'craze' for Rimbaud resulted in what still remains one of the most perceptive and stimulating of the vast number of books and articles devoted to the enigma of Rimbaud's personality and poetry. It was first published in successive issues of *La Nouvelle Revue*

Française in July and August 1914 when, because of other events, it failed to make the impact it deserved.

33. R. IV. 344, 22 April 1913.
34. R. IV. 357, 3 May 1913.
35. Quoted in Vie, p. 211.
36. ibid., pp. 213–14.
37. First published by Gallimard in 1922. The considerable anguish which this affair caused Rivière is expressed not only in *Aimée* but also, *passim*, throughout his prisoner-of-war *Carnets*, ed. I. and A. Rivière, Fayard, 1974.
38. R. IV. 351, 2 May 1913.
39. F. 381–2, 28 April 1913.
40. *Dès l'Angélus de l'aube au l'angélus du Soir*, a collection of poems by Francis Jammes, first published in 1898.
41. R. IV. 352–3, 2 May 1913.
42. Now the Rodin Museum.
43. R. IV. 357–8, 4 May 1913.
44. R. IV. 359, 5 May 1913.
45. The time of Fournier's second meeting with Yvonne has been contested, Madame Rivière insisting that it was mid-May 1913 and Simone that it was August 1913. Unfortunately, no dated documents have yet come to light from this period to end the controversy one way or the other. Fournier seems to have written in August 1913 to Marguerite Audoux to describe his visit to Rochefort. On the other hand, when interviewed by Jean Loize, Marc Rivière was convinced that the Rochefort encounter must have taken place before June 1913 when he sat his entrance examinations for l'Ecole Navale, op. cit., p. 351. One might also add that, on the evidence of her memoirs, Simone's attitude to dates could, at least on occasions, be cavalier: she stated that Fournier's first meeting with Yvonne de Quiévrecourt took place in 1909.
46. Since renamed 'Jardin de la Marine'.
47. Vie, p. 229. All the subsequent quotations from the Rochefort notebook are from this work, pp. 229–37 passim.
48. ibid., pp. 234–5.
49. R. IV. 256, 20 September 1910.
50. *'Le Sacre du Printemps*. Ballet par Igor Stravinsky.' N.R.F., August 1913.
51. Vie, p. 244.
52. Letter to Simone, 31 May 1913, *Le Figaro Littéraire*, 24/30 September 1964.
53. R. IV. 360, 12 July 1913.
54. R. IV. 366, 8 August 1913.
55. Letter to Marguerite Audoux, 28 June 1913. Quoted in Vie, p. 262, note 1.
56. Letter dated 22 August 1931, P., p. 45.
57. First published in *Le Figaro Littéraire*, art. cit.
58. First published in Vie, pp. 263–4.
59. Letter dated 22 August 1913, P., p. 45.
60. R. IV. 372, 3 September 1913.
61. Letter to Simone, 20 September 1913, *Le Figaro Littéraire*, art. cit.
62. Letter to Simone, 21 September 1913, ibid.
63. Letter to Yvonne Brochet, 29 September 1913. Text printed in catalogue issued by Coulet and Faure bookshop, Paris, September 1964.
64. Vie, pp. 281–2.
65. Copies of the book became available at the end of October 1913. The official date of publication was 14 November 1913.
66. 4 July 1913, P., p. 39.
67. 7 July 1913, ibid., p. 40.
68. 7 August 1913, ibid., p. 43.
69. 6 September 1913, ibid., p. 48.
70. 6 October 1913, ibid., p. 49.

71. With the exception of the full quotation from the Paul Souday review, these and other references will be found in Loize, op. cit., pp. 391–3.
72. c.f.   Dans la vieux parc solitaire et glacé
             Deux ombres ont evoqué le passé . . .
                  Colloque Sentimental.
73. These and a selection of other critical comments from this period will be found in Loize, op. cit., pp. 396–8.
74. Quoted in Vie, p. 280.
75. The only completed chapter of *Colombe Blanchet* was published in the *Nouvelle Revue Française* in December 1922, pp. 669–78. Numbered Chapter IV and entitled 'Le Pari' (The Wager), it shows Autissier and a group of other young teachers agreeing to award a cash prize to the first of their number who succeeds in inviting any local girl to his rooms.
76. F. 384, 26 June 1914.
77. cf. letter from Péguy to Fournier of 23 August 1913. 'If you can give me a full half day when you get back. I shall ask you to read the three thousand lines now written and whatever will have been added between now and then. I'm a little lost to have to work without any kind of reaction.' P., p. 45.
78. 'Eve' was first published on 28 December 1913 as the 14th *Cahier de la Quinzaine* of the 15th Series. The opening stanzas will readily convey the manner and flavour of the whole:
    Jésus parle.

> – O mère ensevelie hors du premier jardin,
> Vous n'avez plus connu ce climat de la grâce,
> Et la vasque et la source et la haute terrasse,
> Et le premier soleil sur le premier matin.
> Et les bondissements de la biche et du daim
> Nouant et dénouant leur course fraternelle
> Et courant et sautant et s'arrêtant soudain
> Pour mieux commémorer leur vigueur éternelle . . .

79. Postscript to letter of 12 July 1913, first published in Vie, p. 256.
80. A full account of Fournier's work on *La Maison dans la forêt* is provided in Vie, pp. 295–307.
81. It was published in April 1914 by Hachette.
82. R. II. 227–8, 3 September 1906.
83. Details from Loize, op. cit., p. 414.
84. R. IV. 377, 14 March 1914.
85. Item in Coulet and Faure Catalogue, September 1964.
86. Extensive quotations from this secret notebook will be found in Vie, pp. 286–94 and 308–36.
87. op. cit., pp. 287–8.
88. op. cit., p. 291.
89. op. cit., p. 292.
90. op. cit., pp. 315–6.
91. op. cit., p. 324.
92. op. cit., p. 322.
93. Letter to 'Simone', 21 April 1914. First published in *Le Figaro Littéraire*, September 1964.
94. This fragment of Fournier to his sister, from a letter dated 26 June 1914, was not included in the *Lettres à sa famille*. It was first published in Vie, p. 357.
95. Unpublished letter from Fournier to Lhote, 26 June 1914.

8 THE LAND AT THE WORLD'S END

1. From 'Enfance', *Les Illuminations*.
2. R. IV. 379–80, 31 July 1914. Hébrard was the editor of the national newspaper *Le Temps*.
3. Vie, pp. 358–62.
4. op. cit., p. 362.
5. F. 304–5, 1 August 1914.
6. F. 385, 4 August 1914. The passage relating to Simone was not published till 1964, in Vie, p. 365.
7. Letter to Simone, 3 August 1914; first published in *Le Figaro Littéraire*, September 1964.
8. Vie, p. 370–1.
9. Introduction to *Miracles*, pp. 81–2.
10. Letter to Simone, 20 August, 1914. First published in *Le Figaro Littéraire*, September 1964.
11. The allusion is to the most anthologised of all Péguy's poems, the eulogy of the soldiers killed in a just war. It serves as the central pivot in the much longer 'Eve', standing between the long evocation of Eden and the catalogue of modern man's iniquities. There are eighteen stanzas on the theme of the Happy Warrior which are all variations on the equation between the soldier's death and the harvesting of ripened seed:

    > Heureux ceux qui sont morts, car ils sont retournés
    > Dans la première argile et la première terre.
    > Heureux ceux qui sont morts dans une juste guerre
    > Heureux les épis mûrs et les blés moissonnées.

12. F. 388–9, 28 August 1914.
13. Quoted in Vie, p. 391.
14. op. cit., p. 396.
15. Pierre Maury, 'Une conversation avec Alain-Fournier', in *Foi et Vie*, Volume XXXIX, 1938, pp. 213–14. It would be misguided to attach too much theological significance to this utterance: just over a month previously, Fournier had expressed the view that Providence had intervened to enable him to spend the last few days of peace exclusively in Simone's company.
16. F. 389–90, 11 September 1914.
17. See Vie, pp. 430–1 and 520–2, and Loize, op. cit., pp. 438–40.

9 AFTERMATH

1. Jacques Rivière, *Carnets*, Fayard, 1974, pp. 86–7.
2. ibid., pp. 88–9.
3. ibid., p. 150.
4. *Hommage à Jacques Rivière*, p. 440.
5. P., p. 52.
6. Quoted in Vie, p. 526.
7. v. *Un Cœur Pur: Marguerite Audoux*, Grasset, 1942.
8. Letter from Yvonne Brochet to Isabelle Rivière, 20 January 1939, published in *Les Nouvelles Littéraires*, 4 March 1965.
9. *Alain-Fournier*, Editions universitaires, 1955.
10. Published in 1957 by Emile-Paul.
11. Claude Casimir-Perier was killed in action in March 1915. In 1923, Madame Simone married the poet and dramatist François Porché who died in 1944. On retiring from the stage, she went on to establish a second reputation as a writer and in addition to her memoirs, has published seven novels. Of

these, the one which attracted most attention has been *Le Paradis Terrestre* (1939), largely because it is said to be a thinly disguised transposition of her relationship with Fournier. v. Vie, pp. 505–6.

12. A memorial plaque was unveiled at the lycée Alain-Fournier on 23 May 1937. Jean Giraudoux, who was invited to the ceremony but was unable to attend, sent a characteristically whimsical letter to be read out in his absence, and it concluded with the often-quoted words, 'I too was a little Meaulnes'.

13. Under the title of *La Fête étrange*, it was first choreographed in 1940 by Miss Andrée Howard to music by Fauré with décor by Sophie Federovich.

14. Under the title of *The Milk of Paradise*, adaptation by Barbara Bray; first production January 1956.

15. Directed by Jean-Gabriel Albicocco, and given its première in Bourges, in October 1967.

16. Marcel Brion, in *Les Nouvelles Littéraires*, 19 December 1931.

17. In an article in the *Modern Language Journal*, March 1952, p. 132.

18. Introduction to the (first) Françoise Delisle translation of *Le Grand Meaulnes* entitled *The Wanderer*, Houghton Mifflin, New York, p. xxvii.

19. Fernand Desonay: '*Le Grand Meaulnes*' *d'Alain-Fournier*, Brussels, 1941 and 1963.

20. Walter Jöhr: *Alain Fournier, Le Paysage d'une âme*, Neuchâbel, 1945.

21. Jean-Marie Delettrez: *Alain-Fournier et 'Le Grand Meaulnes'*, Emile-Paul, 1954.

22. Christian Dédéyan: *Alain-Fournier et la Réalité Secrète*, Julliard, 1948.

23. Albert Léonard: *Alain-Fournier et 'Le Grand Meaulnes'*, Desclée de Brouwer, 1943.

24. Aimé Becker: *Itinéraire spirituel d'Alain-Fournier*, Corrêâ, 1946.

25. Michel Suffran: *Alain-Fournier ou le Mystère Limpide*, in the series significantly entitled 'Conversions célèbres', Wesmael-Charlier, 1969.

26. André Gide: *Journal 1889–1939*, Gallimard, 'Bibliothèque de la Pléiade, 1948, p. 1150.

27. Denis Saurat: *Modern French Literature, 1870–1940*, Dent, 1946, p. 105.

28. *Le Grand Meaulnes, Part I*, edited by G. I. Dunn, Oxford University Press.

29. The *New Statesman*, 27 June 1953.

30. Saint-Exupéry, *Terre des Hommes*, Gallimard, 1939, p. 129.

31. P.-A. Cousteau in *Je suis partout*, 13 August 1945.

32. Robert Champigny, *Portrait of a Symbolist Hero*, Indiana University Press, Bloomington, 1954, p. 48.

33. For example, Joseph Paves: 'To derive the most precious enrichment from Meaulnes, you must surrender yourself to him fully and frankly . . . to penetrate to the heart of his work, you must read it with the total belief that children bring to their reading of any story, no matter how strange it may be'; *Le charme de Meaulnes*, in 'Etudes', 5 February 1938.

34. Jacques Vier: 'Alain-Fournier et *Le Grand Meaulnes*', in *Littérature à l'emporte-pièce*, Editions du Cèdre, 1958, p. 162.

35. Champigny, op. cit., p. 28.

36. ibid., p. 160.

37. Marcel Abraham: 'Promenade avec Alain-Fournier', in *Homage à Alain-Fournier*, p. 83.
René Vincent: '*Le Grand Meaulnes*, roman de chevalerie', article in *Combat*, February 1939, No. 32.

38. Léon Cellier: '*Le Grand Meaulnes*' *ou l'initiation manquée*, Archives des lettres modernes, Minard, 1963.

39. Michel Guiomar, *Inconscient et Imaginaire dans 'Le Grand Meaulnes'*, Corti, 1964.

40. Marie Maclean: *Le Jeu Suprême*, Corti, 1973.

41. G. Timmermans: *Recherches sur le style poétique du 'Grand Meaulnes'*, Annales de la Faculté de Lettres de Toulouse, V, 1956.

42. Stephen Ullmann: 'The Symbol of the Sea in *Le Grand Meaulnes*' in *The Image of the Modern French Novel*, Oxford University Press, 1960.
43. Claude Vincenot: 'Le Rêve dans *Le Grand Meaulnes*' in *Revue des Sciences humaines*, April–September 1966.
44. From *Les Amis d'Edouard*, Champion, 1920, p. 28.
45. These ideas were first developed, and at rather greater length, in the introduction to my critical edition of *Le Grand Meaulnes* published by Harrap in 1968. See in particular pp. xcviii–cvii and p. cxii.
46. Introduction to *The Lost Domain*, Oxford University Press, p. xiv.
47. This passage is, in fact, only a slightly amended version of a passage from *Le Pays sans nom*.
48. This point has also been made in a well-argued article by Martin Sorrell: 'François Seurel's Personal Adventure in *Le Grand Meaulnes*', Modern Language Review, January 1974, pp. 79–87. Sorrell argues, to my mind persuasively, that Seurel's possessive attitude towards the narrative is a form of revenge over Meaulnes for so thoroughly dominating him fifteen years previously.

Index